INTRODUCING ARCHITECTURAL THEORY

This is the most accessible architectural theory book that exists. Korydon Smith presents each common architectural subject—such as tectonics, use, and site—as though it were a conversation across history between theorists by providing you with the original text, a reflective text, and a philosophical text. He also introduces each chapter by highlighting key ideas and asking you a set of reflective questions so that you can hone your own theory, which is essential to both your success in the studio and your adaptability in the profession. These primary source texts, which are central to your understanding of the discipline, were written by such architects as Le Corbusier, Robert Venturi, and Adrian Forty. The appendices also have guides to aid your reading comprehension; to help you write descriptively, analytically, and disputationally; and to show you citation styles and how to do library-based research. More than any other architectural theory book about the great thinkers, *Introducing Architectural Theory* teaches you to think as well.

Korydon Smith is an architecture professor in the U.S. who teaches courses in architectural theory, methods, and design at all year levels.

INTRODUCING ARCHITECTURAL THEORY

DEBATING A DISCIPLINE

EDITED BY KORYDON SMITH

Routledge
Taylor & Francis Group

NEW YORK AND LONDON

First published 2012
by Routledge
711 Third Avenue, New York, NY 10017

Simultaneously published in the UK
by Routledge
2 Park Square, Milton Park, Abingdon, Oxon OX14 4RN

Routledge is an imprint of the Taylor & Francis Group, an informa business

Library of Congress Cataloging in Publication Data
Smith, Korydon H., 1977-
    Introducing architectural theory : debating a discipline / Korydon Smith.
      p. cm.
    Includes index.
    1. Architecture—Philosophy. I. Title. II. Title: Debating a discipline.
    NA2500.S555 2012
    720.1—dc23   2011032850

ISBN: 978-0-415-88837-0 (hbk)
ISBN: 978-0-415-88838-7 (pbk)

Typeset in FS Albert and Amasis
by Keystroke, Station Road, Codsall, Wolverhampton

Printed and bound in the United States of America on acid-free paper by Edwards Brothers, Inc.

Table of Contents

PART 2: DIALECTICAL READINGS IN ARCHITECTURE

TECTONICS

CHAPTER 1: SIMPLICITY AND COMPLEXITY

CHAPTER 2: ORNAMENT AND AUSTERITY

CHAPTER 3: HONESTY AND DECEPTION

CHAPTER 4: MATERIAL AND IMMATERIAL

USE   141

CHAPTER 5: FUNCTION AND FORM   143

CHAPTER 6: FUNCTION AND FORM (PART 2)   180

CHAPTER 7: BODY AND BUILDING   211

Preface

TO EDUCATORS: THE IMPETUS FOR THIS BOOK

The formal study of architectural theory remains absent from many architectural design programs, or, if present, the structure of many academies and curricula place architectural theory as an autonomous, peripheral course. This is especially the case in undergraduate curricula. Undergraduate architectural education is often composed of a triad— architectural history, architectural technologies, and architectural design. Coupled together, these areas promote a comprehensive understanding of the discipline. Though theory is often paired with history, i.e., "history/theory," the impetus for this book stems from the premise that architectural theory underpins all facets of the discipline—history, technologies, and design. Architectural theory is the discipline.

If architectural theory is both broad in scope and synonymous with the discipline, then why has it become merely a side-show at so many institutions? As architectural educators, we might impugn accrediting agencies for ever-expanding requirements; or we might blame the emergence and rise of a variety of iconic issues of our time, e.g., sustainability or digital design media; or we might admonish ourselves for atomizing architectural education into autonomous, specialized knowledge domains. In any case, if the importance and vitality of architectural theory is to be regained in the minds of students—amidst a crowded, evolving, and competing set of courses—creative pedagogies are much needed. What might these pedagogies be? No doubt, design educators throughout the world have been discussing this question for years. As such, this book results from the development and implementation of a pedagogical alternative to architectural theory.

Introducing Architectural Theory: Debating a Discipline stems from curricular and pedagogical conversations I have had with colleagues near and distant. Several colleagues, especially those teaching design or studio courses, voiced several interrelated concerns about students' conceptual and critical thinking abilities. There was frustration about the tendency of students to "compartmentalize" knowledge, a kind of amnesia regarding concepts or principles learned in previous architectural history, technology, or studio courses. There was also anxiety that students lacked skills in both vertical thinking ("intellectual discipline") and lateral thinking ("intellectual agility"). There was concern that students tended, too quickly, to embrace fashionable trends or dogmatic positions, and, commensurately, dismiss historically-based or more subtle architectural theories or propositions. Presumably, these same concerns have been voiced for decades in faculty meetings around the world.

With these discussions, there was speculation regarding the sources of these perceived deficiencies: Were these propensities cultural or generational? Were the problems developmental? Was the curriculum to blame? Was it some combination of these? Or was it simply undue expectations or misperceptions on the part of the faculty? With little control over cultural factors and greater authority over curricular matters, the faculty at a public university in the United States where I was teaching, brainstormed a variety of pedagogical changes. Among them was an architectural theory course, which Dr. Darell W. Fields and I developed. We contended, as does this book, that architectural theory is vital to undergraduate and beginning graduate design education, and that the absence or marginalization of architectural theory exacerbated the problems stated above. The faculty concurred, but vacillated on how to best integrate architectural theory into the curriculum.

We confronted a number of practical issues. The course had to fit within the larger curricular structure, and it had to be developmentally appropriate for undergraduate students. Likewise, we were interested in creating a course that would affect students' long-term thinking about architecture. Though tremendously overused in higher education today (and at risk of oversimplification here), we wanted the course, foremost, to provide students with strategies for critical thinking. Architectural theory would simply be the medium. We aspired for students to not only understand the origins and trajectories of various architectural theories but also to verbalize and re-conceptualize their own predilections of architecture.

As the course took shape, we articulated four major goals and 13 learning objectives. It was in the spirit of these objectives that this book was formed:

1.   Advance each student's ability to understand the various trajectories of architectural thinking today and across history, including the ability to:

      a.   discern the similarities and differences of various theoretical texts, be they contemporaneous or separated by vast amounts of time
      b.   understand the relationship between disparate positions in architectural theory
      c.   understand the difference between *architectural* theory and other forms of theory, e.g., philosophy, art, etc.

2.   Advance each student's ability to be more self-aware about one's architectural predilections and be able to contextualize them relative to other architectural theories, including the ability to:

a. understand the relationship between one's positions in architectural theory/ideology and other similar and disparate views
b. better understand the implications of one's ideas and work
c. incorporate new architectural ideas/theories into one's thinking/work
d. adapt one's own architectural thinking and predilections.

3. Advance each student's critical thinking skills, including the ability to:

a. more critically engage the content of studio courses
b. more critically question the work of one's colleagues and the profession.

4. Advance each student's reading and writing skills, including the ability to:

a. clearly identify the meanings and value of various architectural texts
b. more effectively seek out and identify texts that help to strengthen one's future studio (and future professional) work
c. clearly articulate the ideas of others in written form
d. more clearly articulate one's own ideas in written form.

With these goals and objectives arose three assertions regarding the structure and pedagogy of the course. First, the course would not be comprehensive; it would not be a "survey" of architectural theory, but a narrowly selected set of texts. Second, the course would not be chronologically organized nor would historical context be a primary factor in the course (we had the luxury of three well-taught architectural history courses leading up to our proposed course), rather, the course would put forth a set of architectural issues that cut across architectural history and remain relevant in contemporary practice. Third, the course would not delve into texts by philosophers, social theorists, and literary critics; it would focus predominantly on the writings of architects, from Vitruvius to Venturi, Palladio to Pallasmaa.

All three assertions signalled a paradigmatic shift in architectural education, and a risky one at that. With these premises we were seriously diminishing the number of texts we would cover. We were also forfeiting a deep understanding of the cultural, economic, and technological contexts in which a particular architectural idea arose. We were also sacrificing writings from other disciplines—literary criticism, philosophy, biology, etc.—that have gained momentum in the discipline of architecture over the past five decades.[1] The supreme gain, however, was a highly thematic and episodic course, a course organized around major themes in architecture that have multiple viewpoints and that are highly relevant to the discipline today. This enabled two significant pedagogical shifts to be implemented: (1) using the "dialectic" as the organizing structure for the course and (2) using in-class debates and in-class writings as the modus operandi.

In its colloquial form, the dialectic is a dialogue.[2] It arises as a dichotomy, a debate between two opposing positions, ideas, or theories. But, through the desire to reconcile

1. In recent years, architectural theory has been criticized for borrowing too heavily from peripherally related disciplines (e.g., semiotics), thereby drawing focus away from the historical centers of the discipline. Similarly, popular media (and architects themselves) often rely on metaphorical or analogical language when discussing various architectural works. The reliance on cursory allegories is problematic for undergraduate design education, because it obfuscates the essential, complex, and interwoven components of the discipline: context, space, use, tectonic expression, etc. The architectural theory course discussed here, therefore, focused primarily on texts written by architects, regarding tectonics, etc., rather than on texts written by philosophers or theorists who discuss architecture analogically. These latter texts—e.g., Deleuze's "Postscript on the Societies of Control"—are highly influential to the discipline of architecture, but are more appropriate at the graduate level. Likewise, although texts were the primary medium for the course, it was made clear to the students that architectural theory is evidenced not only in texts but also (and maybe to a greater extent) in constructed works. For example, even without Le Corbusier's *Towards a New Architecture*, Le Corbusier's theories are evident in his constructed works.

2. The dialectic is a Socratic concept, but saw advancement from a number of philosophers, including Johann Fichte in the 18th and 19th centuries. The

the debate, the dialectic transcends the dichotomy. Through negation, aggregation, compromise, or transformation of one or both sides of the debate, a third proposition emerges. The dialectic, as such, possesses three parts: thesis, antithesis, and synthesis. This triumvirate became the structure for the course. Reading assignments, in-class discussions, and writing assignments would all be organized this way. Making decisions about what would be included in (and what would be excluded from) the course readings then became the greatest challenge. Not only was delimiting the texts a significant task in designing the course but it was also a major hurdle in organizing this book.

Despite the relative smallness of the discipline of architecture, there is a large amount of architectural theory, including an array of anthologies and compendia. There are a variety of ways in which architectural theory compilations have been organized. Some books are organized chronologically, some are organized geographically, and some are organized thematically.[3] There are benefits and drawbacks to each organizational strategy.

The organization of the present work is closest to the thematic strategy, but, more precisely, it is organized dialectically. Each chapter contains readings from three different authors, representing three different viewpoints. I have provided a brief introduction for each dialectical set of readings. It needs to be noted, however, that, for pedagogical reasons, introductions to each chapter are kept brief. Introductions outline the thesis, antithesis, and synthesis of each chapter topic. Rather than providing a deep, interpretive history of the topic, the images and questions that precede each chapter are intended to initiate a dialogue within and among students. Educators using this book may wish to have students complete self-reflective writings or group discussions about these questions prior to completing each set of readings. The introduction to each chapter then serves as a transition between students' initial thoughts and the deeper, more critical discussion that arises while reading the dialectical set of texts. Each chapter concludes with a series of analytical, synthetic, self-reflective, and prospective questions.

Having now taught and revised the aforementioned architectural theory course over several years, it is clear to me that the dialectic strategy is useful for two major reasons. First, its structure is readily accessible to students. Students do not need a full understanding of Socrates', Fichte's, Hegel's or other philosophical works to understand it. The structure of the dialectic possesses both a binary construct—*thesis* and *antithesis*—which is developmentally and culturally consistent with a majority of beginning architecture students, and a means by which to transcend the binary—*synthesis*. The structure provides both a normative foundation and an investigative springboard for critical inquiry. Second, the dialectical structure provides a means to analyze architectural theories outside of a historical continuum. This frees the curriculum and pedagogy of the course from the chronological system in which history and theory are often delivered. It allows for a thematic approach, contemporary and prospective in its trajectory, which better resonates with student cognition. Thus, *Introducing Architectural Theory: Debating a Discipline* is an attempt to bring architectural theory back to the center of the architectural education experience.

dialectic is more fully explained in Part 1 of this book.

3. For example, both K. Michael Hays, ed., *Architecture Theory since 1968* (Cambridge, MA: MIT Press, 1998) and Joan Ockman, ed., *Architecture Culture 1943–1968: A Documentary Anthology* (New York: Rizzoli, 1993) are organized chronologically. *Architectural Theory from the Renaissance to the Present* (Los Angeles: Taschen, 2002) is organized geographically. Hanno-Walter Kruft, *A History of Architectural Theory from Vitruvius to the Present* (New York: Princeton Architectural Press, 1994) is a combination of both of these strategies, as is the case for Harry Francis Mallgrave, ed., *Architectural Theory: Volume I: An Anthology from Vitruvius to 1870* (Malden, MA: Blackwell Publishing, 2006) and Harry Francis Mallgrave and Christina Contandriopoulos, eds., *Architectural Theory: Volume II: An Anthology from 1871–2005* (Malden, MA: Blackwell Publishing, 2008). Kate Nesbitt, ed., *Theorizing a New Agenda for Architecture: An Anthology of Architectural Theory, 1965–1995* (New York: Princeton Architectural Press, 1996) and Jay M. Stein and Kent F. Spreckelmeyer, eds., *Classic Readings in Architecture* (New York: McGraw-Hill, 1999) are thematically organized.

Acknowledgments

I want to thank Jeff Shannon, Dean, Fay Jones School of Architecture, and Marlon Blackwell, Head, Department of Architecture, at the University of Arkansas for their support of this project. Thanks also go to Lanny and Becki McIntosh for providing the McIntosh Faculty Research Award, which assisted with obtaining copyright permissions for this book.

Much appreciation goes to Wendy Fuller, Editor, Architecture, Routledge—Taylor & Francis. Her critical feedback and assistance was invaluable from the very beginning of this project. Likewise, Laura Williamson, Editorial Assistant, Architecture, Routledge—Taylor & Francis, was a tremendous asset to the development and production of this work.

Immense gratitude goes to Andrew Arkell and Ginger Traywick, architecture students at the University of Arkansas, for their help in editing and proofing texts, identifying images, and providing a critical and insightful student perspective.

I also want to thank the reviewers of this book for their insights and commentary on how to improve the quality of this book. Additional thanks go to Frederick Courtright of The Permissions Company, Inc. for assistance in securing copyright permissions.

Finally, special thanks go to my two sons, Eston and Khale, for all I learn from them, and to my wife Julie, whose emotional sustenance, friendship, and love is inspirational.

List of Sources

The author and publishers gratefully acknowledge the following permissions to reproduce material in this book. Every effort has been made to identify the owners of copyrights and to obtain permission to reproduce copyrighted material. If any proper acknowledgement has not been made, or permission not received, we invite the copyright holders to inform us of the oversight, and any omissions will be rectified in future editions.

Alberti, Leon Battista. Excerpts from "Book III: Construction," in *The Art of Building in Ten Books*. Joseph Rykwert, Neil Leach, and Robert Tavernor, trans. (Cambridge: MIT Press, 1988), 61–91, first published in 1486. Used with permission from MIT Press.

Banham, P. Reyner. "Ornament and Crime: The Decisive Contribution of Adolf Loos," *Architectural Review* 121 (1957): 85–88. Used with permission from Emap Ltd.

Breuer, Marcel. "Where Do We Stand?," *Architectural Review* 77, April, (1935): 133–136. Used with permission from Emap Ltd.

Burns, Carol. "On Site: Architectural Preoccupations," in *Drawing, Building, Text: Essays in Architectural Theory*, ed. Andrea Kahn (New York: Princeton Architectural, 1991), 147–167. Used with permission from Andrea Kahn.

Eisenman, Peter. "Post-Functionalism," *Oppositions* 6, fall, (1976): unpaginated. Used with permission from Peter Eisenman.

Forty, Adrian. "Context" and "Function," in *Words and Buildings: A Vocabulary of Modern Architecture* (London: Thames & Hudson, 2000), 132–135, 174–195. Used with permission from Thames & Hudson.

Gregotti, Vittorio. "On Simplicity," in *Inside Architecture*. Peter Wong and Francesca Zaccheo, trans. (Cambridge: MIT Press, 1996), 83–87. Used with permission from MIT Press.

Gregotti, Vittorio. "Territory and Architecture," *Architectural Design* 55, no. 5/6 (1985): 28–34. Used with permission from Vittorio Gregotti.

Hearn, M. Fil. "Truth to the Medium: Using Materials," in *Ideas that Shaped Buildings* (Cambridge: MIT, 2003), 255–269. Used with permission from MIT Press.

Hill, Jonathan. Excerpts from *Immaterial Architecture* (New York: Routledge, 2006), 2–3, 72–77. Used with permission from Routledge—Taylor & Francis.

Hill, Richard. "Purpose, Function, Use," in *Designs and Their Consequences: Architecture and Aesthetics* (New Haven: Yale, 1999), 175–210. Used with permission from Yale University Press.

Hosey, Lance. "Hidden Lines: Gender, Race, and the Body," *Journal of Architectural Education*, v.55, n.2 (2001): 101–112. Used with permission from Blackwell Publishing.

Jacobs, Jane. "Introduction," in *The Death and Life of Great American Cities* (New York: Random House, 1961), 3–25. Used with permission from Random House.

Laugier, Marc-Antoine. "General Principles of Architecture," in *An Essay on Architecture.* Wolfgang Herrmann and Anni Hermann, trans. (Los Angeles: Hennessey & Ingalls, 1977), 11–22, first published in 1753. Used with permission from Hennessey & Ingalls.

Le Corbusier. Excerpts from *Le Modulor.* Peter de Francia and Anna Bostock, trans. (Cambridge: Harvard University Press, 1954), 34–35, 37, 45, 50, 55–58, 60–61, 63, first published in 1948. Used with permission from the Foundation Le Corbusier.

Le Corbusier. Excerpts from *The Radiant City: Elements of a Doctrine of Urbanism to Be Used as the Basis of Our Machine-age Civilization.* Pamela Knight, Eleanor Levieux, and Derek Coltman, trans. (New York: Orion, 1967), 90–97, 112–126, first published in 1935. Used with permission from Penguin Group.

Le Corbusier, "The Plan of the Modern House," in *Precisions.* Edith Schreiber Aujame, trans. (Cambridge: MIT Press, 1991), 123–139, first published in 1930. Used with permission from MIT Press.

Loos, Adolf. "Ornament and Crime," in *Ornament and Crime: Selected Essays.* Michael Mitchell, trans. (Riverside, CA: Ariadne, 1998), 167–176, first published in 1908. Used with permission from Ariadne Press.

Moore, Kathryn. "Genius Loci: Hidden Truth or Hidden Agenda?" *Landscape Design* 321, June (2003), 44–52. Used with permission from the Institute of Landscape Architects.

Norburg-Shulz, Christian. Excerpts from *Genius Loci: Towards a Phenomenology of Architecture* (New York: Rizzoli, 1979), 6–23, first published in 1979. Used with permission from Rizzoli.

Palladio, Andrea. Excerpts from *The Four Books on Architecture.* Robert Tavernor and Richard Schofield, trans. (Cambridge, MA: MIT, 2002), 56–58, 60–61, 77–78, 94, first published in 1570. Used with permission from MIT Press.

Pallasmaa, Juhani. Excerpts from *The Eyes of the Skin: Architecture and the Senses* (Chichester: John Wiley & Sons, 2005), 26–37, first published in 1996. Used with permission from John Wiley & Sons.

Relph, E. Excerpts from *Place and Placelessness.* (London: Pion, 1976). Used with permission from Pion Ltd.

Rowe, Colin. "The Mathematics of the Ideal Villa," in *The Mathematics of the Ideal Villa and Other Essays* (Cambridge: MIT, 1982), 1–28, first published in 1976. Used with permission from MIT Press.

Ruskin, John. "The Lamp of Truth," in *The Seven Lamps of Architecture* (New York: Dover Publications, 1980), 29–69, first published in 1849. Public domain.

Rykwert, Joseph. "Ornament Is No Crime," in *The Necessity of Artifice* (New York: Rizzoli, 1982), 92–101, first published in 1975. Used with permission from Rizzoli International Publications, Inc.

Schumacher, Tom. "Contextualism: Urban Ideals and Deformations," *Casabella* 35, no. 359/360 (1971): 78–86. Used with permission from Mondadori.

Sullivan, Louis. "The Tall Office Building Artistically Considered," in *Kindergarten Chats and Other Writings* (New York: Dover, 1979), 202–213, first published in 1896. Public domain.

Tschumi, Bernard. "Violence of Architecture" and "Spaces and Events," in *Architecture and Disjunction*

(Cambridge: MIT, 1996), 121–134, 141–149, first published in 1983. Used with permission from MIT Press.

Venturi, Robert. "Nonstraightforward Architecture: A Gentle Manifesto" and "Complexity and Contradiction vs. Simplification or Picturesqueness," in *Complexity and Contradiction in Architecture* (New York: Museum of Modern Art, 1966), 16–19. Used with permission from the Museum of Modern Art.

Venturi, Robert, Scott Brown, Denise, and Izenour, Steven. Excerpts from *Learning from Las Vegas* (Cambridge: MIT Press, 1972), 18–20, 34. Used with permission from MIT Press.

Viollet-le-Duc, Eugène-Emmanuel. Excerpts from *Discourses on Architecture.* Benjamin Bucknall, trans. (New York: Grove Press, 1959), first published ca. 1863. Used with permission from Grove/Atlantic, Inc.

Vitruvius, Marcus. Excerpts from *The Ten Books on Architecture.* Morris H. Morgan, trans. (New York: Cambridge, 1999), 17–32, 72–75, 84–86, first published ca. 25 B.C.E. Public domain.

Wright, Frank L. "Continuity" and "Interior Space Comes Through," in *An American Architecture* (New York: Horizon, 1955), 205–219. Used with permission from Horizon Press.

ILLUSTRATION CREDITS

Figure 1.1   Photo courtesy of C. Murray Smart

Figure 1.2   Photo courtesy of Joe Mabel, Wikimedia Commons

Figure 2.1   Photo © 2008, Korydon Smith

Figure 2.2   Photo © 2004, Korydon Smith

Figure 3.1   Photo © 2004, Korydon Smith

Figure 3.2   Photo 2007, courtesy of David Liff, Wikimedia Commons

Figure 4.1   Photo © 2004, Korydon Smith

Figure 4.2   Photo courtesy of Charvex, Wikimedia Commons

Figure 5.1   Photo © 2005, Korydon Smith

Figure 5.2   Photo © 2004, Korydon Smith

Figure 6.1   Photo © 2004, Korydon Smith

Figure 6.2   Photo © 2004, Korydon Smith

Figure 7.1   Photo © 2003, Korydon Smith

Figure 7.2   Photo © 2003, Korydon Smith

Figure 7.3   Illustration courtesy of the Foundation Le Corbusier

Figure 8.1   Drawing from Palladio's *Four Books on Architecture*

Figure 8.2   Drawing from Borromini's *Opus Architectonicum*

Figure 9.1   Photo courtesy of Steve Luoni

Figure 9.2   Photo courtesy of Tim de Noble.

Figure 10.1   Photo © 2004, Korydon Smith

Figure 10.2   Photo courtesy of Daniel Schwen, Wikimedia Commons

Figure 11.1   Photo courtesy of Sturmvogel 66, Wikimedia Commons

Figure 11.2   Photo courtesy of Marlon Blackwell

Figure 12.1   Photo © 2004, Korydon Smith

Figure 12.2   Photo© 2003, Korydon Smith

Part 1

DEBATE in ARCHITECTURE

Introduction

TO STUDENTS: WHY ARCHITECTURAL THEORY IS VITAL

THEORY IN ARCHITECTURAL EDUCATION

As a student, architecture reviews and critiques can be both invigorating and stressful. You share the work you have done over the past weeks, months, or year. You present your goals, process, and results. You present various drawings and models, as well as some written text or verbal commentary. Likely, the final review is a requirement given by your professor or program, and, maybe for some of you, you would prefer not to go through with it. Some might truly look forward to this opportunity, to candidly present what you believe are the strengths and weaknesses of your work, and to gain insights from an esteemed group of critics. Maybe some of you are hopeful to receive praise for your hard work and commendations for your successes. Some students simply do not want to miss all the potential drama.

In any case, the excitement and stress of final reviews stems from the unpredictability of it all. As reviews begin, it is a mystery as to what will and won't be said, what students will receive accolades and what students will be derided, and how the flow of the conversation will evolve. Part of the unpredictability is surely caused by the critics, but what appears to be random and unmanageable might well be within the student's control.[1] Many students are unaware of how they can direct their own reviews, rather than standing by as passive observers. This book, *Introducing Architectural Theory: Debating a Discipline*, provides a foundation for gaining authority of your work and your reviews.

When students stand in front of a panel of critics and embark on a discussion of the goals, methods, and outcomes of their work, knowingly or unknowingly, they are launching a theoretical position. This position—and all the aesthetic and pragmatic value judgments it contains—becomes more and more tangible as critics shift uncomfortably in their chairs, lean forward with enthusiasm, or slump with boredom. Named or unnamed, it is then from a similar or distant theoretical stance that the subsequent critique

1. Final reviews—or "juries"—in architectural education have come under criticism. See: Kathryn Anthony, *Design Juries on Trial: The Renaissance of the Design Studio* (New York: Van Nostrand Reinhold, 1991); Helena Webster, "The Analytics of Power: Re-presenting the Design Jury," *Journal of Architectural Education, 60* (2007): 21–27.

2. Quotation from W. B. Walsh, *Theories of Person-Environment Interaction: Implications for the College Student* (Iowa City: American College Testing Program, 1973), 5. For further definitions and purposes of "theory," see: Robert Dubin, *Theory Building, Revised Edition* (New York: The Free Press, 1978); Thomas S. Kuhn, *The Structure of Scientific Revolutions* (Chicago: University of Chicago Press, 1962); Paul D. Reynolds, *A Primer in Theory Construction* (New York: The Bobbs-Merrill Company, 1971); and Walsh, *Theories of Person-Environment Interaction.*

3. Theory stems from three Greek terms: *theoros* (spectator), *theorein* (to look at), and *theoria* (contemplation). For a discussion on the Greek origins of theory, see: Andrea W. Nightingale, *Spectacles of Truth in Classical Greek Philosophy: Theoria in its Cultural Context* (Cambridge: Cambridge University Press, 2004). For other definitions of theory, see: Robert Dubin, *Theory Building, Revised Edition* (New York: The Free Press, 1978); Thomas S. Kuhn, *The Structure of Scientific Revolutions* (Chicago: University of Chicago Press, 1962); Paul D. Reynolds, *A Primer in Theory Construction* (New York: The Bobbs-Merrill Company, 1971); and Walsh, *Theories of Person-Environment Interaction.* The prefix "theo," common to the aforementioned Greek terms, is also worth noting, because it is common to the term "theology," the study or philosophy of religion. In early Eastern Christian theology, *theoria* was the enlightenment

materializes. As such, theory is central to architectural education. Understanding architectural theory is essential.

On the first day of the semester, in the architectural theory course I teach, I always ask students several questions: What is "theory?" How is it useful? What excites you about theory? What scares you about it? Many students are excited about theory and what it connotes—ruminating on the significance of this or that architect or architectural work. To many other students, "theory" is seen as a set of enigmatic texts produced by obscure authors—boring, heady, and impractical. Many students feel alienated by this. Contributing to this feeling, architectural theory is often marginal to the educational experience, often reserved for elective courses, graduate study, or as a supplement to undergraduate history, technology, or design courses. As such, it is difficult to see how theory is useful, much less seeing why studying architectural theory is necessary.

Defined another way, architectural theory is neither formal nor textual, neither cryptic nor pretentious. Theory is the most vital component of the architecture curriculum. Explicit or implicit, architectural theory is the means by which architects and architectural scholars situate themselves in the world. This positioning is not merely based on embracing fashionable discourses, but is part of clarifying one's architectural line of thinking. It is how the discipline of architecture began and has evolved. Theory is what underpins all aspects of architecture—technological, cultural, economic, and aesthetic. Theory is embedded in the everyday aspects of architecture: daily conversations between students and instructors, editorials in popular architectural media, etc. Built forms, themselves, are a manifestation of theory. In essence, architectural theories provide the foundation from which any student or practitioner asserts a particular stance or value structure of architecture. It is through theories that architects align with or dispute other architects or architectural works. This book is about this ongoing debate, *architectural theory*.

DEFINING ARCHITECTURAL THEORY

Humans make theories to explain the world around them. "Theory building develops out of our need to make sense out of life."[2] Philosophy and religion are two examples of this human desire to explore and explain the meaning of life. As such, "theory" and "philosophy" are often synonymous.[3] In fact, many library databases use the term "architecture philosophy" rather than "architecture theory."[4] The term "philosophy," however, may be misleading, as it suggests something ephemeral, hypothetical, or non-concrete. In actuality, architectural theory serves a practical role. Though "practice" is often seen as the complement to "theory," architectural theory fulfills a rational, pragmatic, and concrete purpose.

Architectural theory began with Marcus Vitruvius' *Ten Books on Architecture*, written in the first century B.C.E.[5] The book was a practical guide to the design and construction of towns, infrastructure, and public buildings, and private residences. The book also included discussions of material properties and usage, proportion and geometry, and site orientation, all of which are issues still relevant to architecture today. Published architectural theory remained absent until the Renaissance, when Alberti published the *Art of Building in Ten Books* in the late 15th century, which closely modeled Vitruvius' work.[6] Since that time, architects, architectural critics, and architectural historians have published thousands of articles and books on a range of architectural topics, all with practical implications.

It is important to understand that, unlike the natural sciences or the social sciences, theories in architecture often emerge from less formalized, more individualistic paradigms.[7] Many architectural theories are the writings of individual architects. These writings are frequently the subjective opinions of these architects, not necessarily rooted in objective empirical research. As well, architectural theory is not just found in books, but is part of the ongoing conversations that take place in architecture academies and practices around the world.

In the natural sciences, theory refers to an intellectual construct used to understand a set of phenomena. Scientific theories usually focus on the explanation or prediction of causal relationships. They can be *explanatory*—deductive and verifiable, such as the Pythagorean Theorem in mathematics—or *exploratory*—inductive and speculative, such as the String Theory in physics. This concept possesses both a common ground and a divergence from social science theories, where the focus is on human behavior rather than natural phenomena. Compared to other disciplines, architectural theory is less easily circumscribed.[8] Architectural theory is vast and diverse, and encompasses at least three main areas:

1. *theories of architectural technology:* principles of structure, ventilation, drainage, lighting, etc.
2. *theories of architectural history:* social phenomena and patterns, linguistic analyses, analyses of physical artifacts, etc.
3. *theories of architectural design:* organizational strategies, design methods, spatial concepts, aesthetic judgments, etc.

Likewise, some architectural theories are scientific (e.g., Daniel Bernoulli's principles of fluid dynamics); some are sociological (e.g., Edward Hall's concept of proxemics); and some are ideological (e.g., John Ruskin's *Seven Lamps of Architecture*).

In all cases, the merits of a theory are based on its reliability, validity, repeatability, and application. "To be useful, theories must exhibit certain qualities: comprehensiveness, clarity and explicitness, consistency, parsimony, and heurism."[9] Theories evolve over time in order to better achieve these criteria. Theories also change for two other reasons: (1) empirical substance, and (2) cultural resonance. Empirical substance is the extent to which a theory is accepted by experts in a given discipline; cultural resonance is the extent to which a theory is accepted by society. For example, heliocentrism, the theory that the planets revolve around the sun, was asserted multiple times throughout history, beginning with scholars in Ancient Greece. The concept was scientifically proven by Copernicus and his contemporaries in the 16th century, but it did not gain social acceptance until well

given by God, the highest form of knowledge. This concept is paralleled in other Western and Eastern religions as well. Putting aside any particular religion, it has been said that primitive and advanced religions originated for any number of reasons—social, political, biological, legal, technological, metaphysical, etc. See, for example: Émile Durkheim, *The Elementary Forms of Religious Life* (Oxford: Oxford University Press, 2001), Carol Cosman (trans.), first published 1912; E. E. Evans-Pritchard, *Theories of Primitive Religion* (Oxford: Clarendon Press, 1965); F. Max Müller, *Anthropological Religion: The Gifford Lectures Delivered before the University of Glasgow* (London: Longmans, Green, and Co., 1892); Daniel L. Pals, *Eight Theories of Religion* (New York: Oxford University Press, 2006); and J. Samuel Preus, *Explaining Religion: Criticism and Theory from Bodin to Freud* (New Haven: Yale University Press, 1987).

4. This includes individual libraries, as well as major classification schemas, such as the Universal Decimal Classification (UDC) used throughout Britain and much of Europe.

5. In essence, what we now call architecture emerged from various interpretations of Vitruvius's *Ten Books on Architecture*, as asserted by a number of authors of architectural theory anthologies. This includes: Bernd Evers, "Preface," in *Architectural Theory from the Renaissance to the Present* (Los Angeles: Taschen, 2002), 6; Hanno-Walter Kruft, *A History of Architectural Theory from Vitruvius to the Present* (New

York: Princeton Architectural Press), 21–29; Harry F. Mallgrave and Christina Contandriopoulos, *Architectural Theory, Volume II: An Anthology from 1871-2005* (Maldwell, MA: Blackwell Publishing, 2008), xxix; and Cristof Thoenes, "Introduction," in *Architectural Theory from the Renaissance to the Present* (Los Angeles: Taschen, 2002), 8–19. Vitruvius is essential to an understanding of architectural theory not merely for etymological reasons but also due to ties with a diverse range of concepts that contemporary theory addresses. Many of the themes discussed by Vitruvius—philosophy and ethics, tectonic expression, urban planning, and other issues—cut across architectural history. Marcus Vitruvius, *Ten Books on Architecture*. Morris H. Morgan, trans. (New York: Cambridge, 1999), 72–75, 84–86, first published ca. 25 B.C.E.

6. Leon Battista Alberti, *The Art of Building in Ten Books*. Joseph Rykwert, Neil Leach, and Robert Tavernor, trans. (Cambridge: MIT Press, 1988), first published in 1486.

7. Many architectural theories are less strongly rooted in positivistic inquiry, and more commonly stem from a wide range of constructivist, deconstructivist, critical theory, phenomenological, and other paradigms. A paradigm possesses several facets: (a) the *assumptions* one makes about the world around them, (b) the *questions* one chooses to ask about that world, and (c) the *methods* one uses to pursue answers to those questions. As stated by Hatch: "When you are standing within the circle of

after Copernicus' death in 1543, as the theory conflicted with the dominant religious beliefs of the time.

Bringing this all together, architectural theory is part science, part history, part ideology, part sociology, and part aesthetic judgment. Therefore, I have developed the following definition of architectural theory:

> the evolution of the objective principles and subjective values that guide individual and collective decisions about, and assessments of one's own and others', architectural works.

The definition consists of three dichotomous pairs. The first pair stems from the notion that architectural theory encompasses a wide range of empirical, cultural, and ideological premises. "Objective principles" refers to scientific theories, such as, structural, lighting, or acoustic phenomena and concepts; "subjective values," on the other hand, are belief systems and ideologies, such as, aesthetic predilections and political agendas. The second pair illustrates that architectural design decisions may be "individual" or "collective." "Individuals" include architects, clients, critics, etc.; "collectives" include architectural academies, groups of architects sharing similar beliefs, or groups in society who possess a common cause. The last dichotomous pair points to the tension between self and other, "one's own" and "others'" architectural works. This is especially important for students developing their own identities as architects, seeking to situate themselves in the larger discipline of architecture. Students have often voiced to me the tension they see between asserting their own burgeoning theories of architecture and the more matured, often conflicting, views of their instructors. The final piece of the definition is the introductory phrase "the evolution of." Architectural theories are part of a continuum, an ongoing debate, which guides the structure of this book.

THE STRUCTURE OF THIS BOOK

The book begins with a discussion of the role of debate in architecture: "Debating a Discipline: Architecture, Argument, and the Concept of the Dialectic." This section illustrates how architecture is an ongoing debate about a number of topics: aesthetics, structure, functionality, tectonics, context, politics, economics, culture, etc. Architectural and non-architectural examples illuminate how debate is related to the concept of the "dialectic." Unlike most debates, which contain two opposing sides, dialectical debates involve three parts: thesis, antithesis, and synthesis (described in the next chapter as original, reflective, and philosophical). The thesis is the originating theory or idea, the antithesis is an opposition to the thesis, and the synthesis is an attempt to reconcile or transform the previous two. The dialectical structure forms the organization for the remainder of the book (chapters 1–12).

Chapters 1 through 12 are divided into three categories—tectonics, use, and site—the most central topics in architectural design. Each category possesses four chapters.

Each chapter begins with a pair of contrasting images, a diptych of two architectural works, along with a set of prompting questions. These images and questions are intended to prompt dialogue and debate within and among students. Each chapter is then followed by a brief introduction to the topic and the three dialectical readings that follow. For example, Chapter One, "Simplicity and Complexity," opens with an image of Stonehenge and an image of the Modern Art Museum of Ft. Worth, Texas. The chapter introduction then explores the terms "simplicity" and "complexity" as they apply to architecture. The dialectical set of readings for that chapter begins with Marcel Breuer's discussion of the importance of formal, spatial, and material simplicity; proceeds with Robert Venturi's assertions about the importance of complexity in architecture; and concludes with Vittorio Gregotti's ruminations on the difficulty of achieving simplicity. Like the other chapters, that chapter concludes with a set of questions and a list of further readings.

At the end of the book, you will find several resources. These appendices are intended to provide added advice about (1) reading comprehension and analysis, (2) different genres of writing, (3) different citation styles, and (4) conducting library-based research. You are urged to consult these appendices before, during, and after you have completed the chapters in this book.

THE FUTURE OF ARCHITECTURAL THEORY

It is an exciting time to study architecture. While the primary subjects of architecture two millennia ago—tectonics, use, and site—remain central to the discipline, new materials and technologies are emerging every day and environmental, social, and economic challenges are growing. This makes it a vital time to study architectural theory. Undoubtedly, as architects of the future, you and your peers will question your roles relative to these emerging challenges and opportunities. The debate will likely center on the ways that structure, space, form, material, program, and context are transformed to address these issues. Debates in architectural theory will be transformed. You will participate in that transformation. And, in hindsight, end of semester reviews will seem tranquil by comparison.

logic created by the assumptions of your paradigm, the positions taken by those working in other paradigms simply do not make sense. Paradigms are indeed completing ways of thinking about how the world is or is not ordered, what counts as knowledge, and how and if knowledge can be gained." For discussions of the concept of paradigms and the relationship to theory, see: J. A. Hatch, *Doing Qualitative Research in Education Settings* (Albany, NY: State University of New York Press, 2002), 19; and Thomas S. Kuhn, *The Structure of Scientific Revolutions* (Chicago: University of Chicago Press, 1962). For further discussion of architectural paradigms see: Linda Groat and David Wang, *Architectural Research Methods* (New York: John Wiley & Sons, 2002), 73–98.

8. For further definitions of architectural theory and the diverse range of theories, see: Paul-Alan Johnson, *The Theory of Architecture: Concepts, Themes, and Practices* (New York: Van Nostrand Reinhold, 1994).

9. For information on student identity development, see: Nancy J. Evans, Deanna S. Forney, and Florence Guido-DiBrito, *Student Development in College: Theory, Research, and Practice* (San Francisco: Jossey-Bass, 1998), 17.

Debating a Discipline

ARCHITECTURE, ARGUMENT, AND THE CONCEPT OF THE DIALECTIC

THE ASPIRATIONS OF ARCHITECTS

According to architectural philosopher Karsten Harries, throughout history architects have pursued the "dream of the complete building."[1] For centuries, architects have sought a synthesis and reconciliation of form and function, tradition and innovation, context and building, art and engineering, and other issues. Vitruvius, in the 1st century B.C.E. stated that architecture must be durable, convenient, and beautiful.[2] Wright, in the 20th century, argued for an "organic architecture."[3] In both cases, and in the 2,000 years of architecture between them, the aspiration was a complete, integrated whole, where nothing could be added or taken away. "Despite the efforts of . . . generations of architects the dream of the complete building remains unrealized."[4] Nevertheless, like the residents of Italo Calvino's city of Zobeide, architects keep pursuing this dream.[5]

As each architect pursues her or his aspirations, the discipline of architecture evolves. The course of architectural theory is changed by each generation of architects as they debate the relevance of current and historic principles and ideals. These "debates" take many forms. Some architectural debates were staged in front of an audience, like the 1989 debate in Chicago between Peter Eisenman and Leon Krier titled "My Ideology Is Better than Yours."[6] Other debates were between contemporaries and played out through built works, e.g., Bernini vs. Borromini during the Roman Renaissance, or occurred through written works, e.g., Ruskin vs. Viollet-le-Duc in 19th-century Europe. Yet other debates took place between architects that were separated by centuries, such as Le Corbusier's refuting of the canons of Classical architecture championed by Vitruvius, Alberti, and Palladio.

The case of Le Corbusier is indicative of the morphology of architectural theory. In an era of rapid advances in technology and changes in social structures, Le Corbusier set out to create a new architecture. He sought to dismantle Classical tenets of architecture—symmetry, firm grounding, etc.—and replace them with his own. Systematically, Le Corbusier developed his own "five points"—free plan, piloti, etc.—each a direct

1. Karsten Harries, "The Dream of the Complete Building," *Perspecta* 17 (1980): 36–43.
2. Marcus Vitruvius, *The Ten Books on Architecture*, Morris H. Morgan, trans. (New York: Dover Publications, 1960).
3. Frank L. Wright, *An American Architecture*. Edgar Kaufmann, ed. (New York: Horizon Press, 1955).
4. Harries, 36.
5. Italo Calvino, "Cities and Desire 5." In *Invisible Cities*. William Weaver, trans. (San Diego: Harcourt, Inc., 1974), 45–46.
6. Peter Eisenman and Leon Krier, "Peter Eisenman versus Leon Krier: My Ideology Is Better than Yours," *Architectural Design* 59 (1989): 6–18.

counterpoint to Classical doctrine.[7] Le Corbusier's extensive built and written work, everything from furniture design to urban planning, influenced both his contemporaries and innumerable designers thereafter. Le Corbusier's principles of city planning, however, were later criticized by a variety of scholars who touted the importance of "contextualism."[8] Contextualism, in turn, was met by a "fuck context" mantra at the end of the 20th century.[9] This string of ideas—from Classical tenets, to Le Corbusier's five points, to Jane Jacobs' critique of Le Corbusier's urban ideals, to Rem Koolhaas's interrogative uncertainty—is one example of how architectural theory evolves. This is an exemplary dialectic.

THE CONCEPT OF THE DIALECTIC

Centuries after the rediscovery and republication of Vitruvius's *Ten Books on Architecture* during the Renaissance, non-architectural philosophers, such as Johann Gottlieb Fichte and Georg Wilhelm Friedrich Hegel in the 19th century, fundamentally altered the logic systems of the Western world. As a result, various disciplines, including architecture, were radically transformed by the notion of the dialectic. In essence, dialectical philosophy, which built upon the premises put forth by Socrates and Plato in the 5th and 4th centuries B.C.E., eclipsed Vitruvius's theoretical triad of "firmness, commodity, and delight."[10] The dialectic was a tool of categorization and critical analysis, or what Ficthe regarded as *wissenschaftslehre*, "the science of knowledge."[11] According to Fichte, the dialectic contained three parts: thesis, antithesis, and synthesis.[12] "Thesis" referred to an originating idea, position, or argument; "anthithesis" was the opposite or counter-argument to the thesis; and "synthesis" was the reconciliation or transformation of the thesis and antithesis. Put together, the dialectic provided philosophers with a strategy for writing and evaluating philosophical concepts.[13]

DIALECTICS: A FEW EXAMPLES

The concept of the dialectic is often used as a teaching tool. In a sociology or psychology class, for example, the teacher might ask the students: Which plays the greatest role, "nature" or "nurture"? Students then debate with one another (and in their own minds) what is more significant "nature" (a person's biology and genetic make-up) or "nurture" (a person's life experiences and upbringing). Students typically opt for one or the other and begin formulating arguments to support their opinions. At this phase, they are working either in the thesis, "nature," or the antithesis, "nurture," sides of the debate (the thesis and antithesis, in this case, are interchangeable). As students debate further, however, they begin to realize the roles that both genetics and upbringing play. They integrate the two sides of the debate, discussing how nature and nurture are related and how both nature and nurture affect human psychology and sociology, what would be called "synthesis."

Teachers might ask similar questions regarding race, religion, or gender: For example, who has a more difficult adolescence, boys or girls? The dialectic appears simple on the surface, but the process of the debate reveals the complex and diverse factors

7. Le Corbusier, *Towards a New Architecture*, Frederick Etchells, trans. (New York: Dover Publications, 1986).

8. "Contextualism" was developed at Cornell University in the 1970s by Colin Rowe and others, including Thomas Schumacher. See: Tom Schumacher, "Contextualism: Urban Ideals and Deformations," *Casabella* 35 (1971): 78–86.

9. "Fuck context" is a phrase seen in: Office for Metropolitan Architecture, Rem Koolhaas, and Bruce Mau, *Small, Medium, Large, Extra-Large* (New York: Monacelli Press, 1995), 640. It also appears in Forty's analysis of the term "context" in Adrian Forty, *Words and Buildings: A Vocabulary of Modern Architecture* (New York: Thames & Hudson, 2000), 135.

10. Vitruvius.

11. Johann G. Fichte, *The Science of Knowledge* (Philadelphia: J.B. Lippincott & Co., 1868).

12. Among German philosophers, Kant, Hegel, and Heidegger, arguably, have had the most significant influence on architecture. For discussions on the three aspects of the dialectic—thesis, antithesis, synthesis—see Fichte, *The Science of Knowledge*.

13. It should be noted that both forms of the dialectic —Fichte's and Hegel's— are merely two means of categorization. Other systems of thought and categorization may be equally useful. See, for example, Michel Foucault, *The Order of Things: An Archaeology of the Human Sciences* (New York: Random

involved in answering the question. Often, the question is not about gender, but is a discussion about parenting, schooling, body image, or some other issue.

Similarly, a political science class might engage subjects about federal spending: Where should more money be spent, on education or healthcare? One objective might be for students to understand how federal funds are spent in each of these areas. Another objective might be for students to know the quantitative and qualitative outcomes of these expenditures. A third objective might be for students to verbalize their own views and opinions, to better understand their own political affiliations. This is often a primary goal of dialectical questions, to foster students' consciousness about their own assumptions, values, and ideals. It is a primary reason for the structure of this book.

DIALECTICS IN ARCHITECTURE

Architecture is filled with dialectics: mass and void, light and shade, inside and outside, movement and repose, enclosure and opening, natural and constructed. Although there is a degree of opposition between the terms in each pair—e.g., enclosure and opening or light and shade—it is not about choosing one side of the dialectic over the other; both sides are necessary. Likewise, many dialectics in architecture operate along a continuum or gradient, such as: transparent, semi-transparent, translucent, semi-opaque, and opaque. There are also dialectics that occur across each of these pairs. For example, enclosure and opening have a direct effect on light and shade, which, in turn, influences movement and repose. Architectural design is a process of making incremental, though interrelated, decisions. This is the inherent complexity of architectural design, the cyclical integration of diverse, sometimes conflicting, issues: tectonics, use, and site (the three major topics covered in this book).

In 1982, at the Graduate School of Design at Harvard University, a debate was staged between renowned theorists and architects Peter Eisenman and Christopher Alexander.[14] What emerged was nothing short of entertaining, as Alexander accused Eisenman of "fucking up the world." The entertainment value aside, the debate serves as a clear example of the dialectic. Alexander, building on a mathematics background and a precedent-based approach to architecture, discussed the importance of "harmony" in architecture, the proportional relationships among the spaces and elements of a building or urban design. Eisenman challenged these views and stated that, for "harmony" to be recognized and appreciated, "discord" was essential.

Similarly, in 1999, Harvard hosted another debate, this time between well-known urban theorists Andres Duany and Rem Koolhaas.[15] Although it did not gain the same publicity as the Eisenman–Alexander debate, the dialectic was equally at play. Duany argued for a return to historically well-established processes and principles of urban design, a heightened sensitivity and control over public and private planning, infrastructure, space, and use. Koolhaas, on the other hand, made a case for reduced urban design control and for happenstance.

House, 1970). Nevertheless, it is also worth noting that the tripartite dialectical system directly parallels the works of contemporary architectural scholars. See, for example, Alan Colquhoun, "Three Kinds of Historicism," in *Theorizing a New Agenda for Architecture: An Anthology of Architectural Theory, 1965–1995*, Kate Nesbitt, ed. (New York: Princeton Architectural Press, 1996), 200–210.

14. The debate between Peter Eisenman and Christopher Alexander took place in November 1982, but was later published by Harvard University as: "Discord over Harmony in Architecture: Peter Eisenman and Christopher Alexander in Discussion," *Studio Works* 7, (2000): 48–57.

15. The debate between Andres Duany and Rem Koolhaas, mediated by Alex Krieger, was later published by Harvard as: "Exploring New Urbanism(s)," *Studio Works* 7, (2000): 134–145.

These two events are exemplars of the ongoing debate of architecture.[16] The discipline of architecture, however, is full of debates, and few of them take place in front of a captive audience. Discussions between students and teachers, between clients and architects, and between critics and theorists contribute to these ongoing debates. What is the most significant building in architectural history? What dissatisfies you most about the architecture of the past 20 years? What is the most pressing issue in architecture today? How does the discipline of architecture need to change in the future? These questions prod us and they cause architecture to change. New materials are invented. New spaces and forms are made. New uses are accommodated. Architects form new ideals about what architecture could be and must be. You have the opportunity to participate in this debate, and the chapters ahead will facilitate this.

THE CHAPTERS AHEAD

Each of the 12 chapters explores a particular dialectical topic in architecture, a debate with multiple points of view. Each chapter provides a way of seeing how architectural theories originate, transform, and continue to evolve. The three readings for each chapter generally follow Fichte's dialectical construct of thesis, antithesis, and synthesis. More accurately, they follow a system laid out by Hegel that loosely paralleled Fichte's construct. In *The Philosophy of History*, Hegel stated there were three forms or approaches to history: "original," "reflective," and "philosophical."[17] These are the terms used in the chapters ahead.

"Original" texts are made up mostly of architectural treatises written by significant historical architects, such as, Alberti, Palladio, and Loos, who established foundational theoretical propositions made evident in their built works. "Reflective" texts are represented by author–architects, such as, Banham, Eisenman, Venturi, and Pallasmaa, who placed the ideas and buildings found in the previous category under particular scrutiny, paving the way for more self-conscious, more critical transformations of architectural theory. "Philosophical" texts are more challenging to classify and, in many cases, are the origins of a new "thesis." They represent a synthetic, critical eye toward both the history and the future of architecture. As a dialectic or triptych, the original, reflective, and philosophical texts of each chapter cover both a broad span of architectural history and a wide range of architectural philosophies. The goal is to open up questions that have relevance to you now, as a student, and that will remain significant as we continue debating a discipline.

16. Another good example of an architectural dialectic discussed in Andreas Huyssen, "The Hidden Dialectic: Avantgarde—Technology—Mass Culture," in *After the Great Divide* (Bloomington: Indiana University Press, 1986), 3–15.

17. Fichte's dialectical structure is often attributed, erroneously, to Hegel, i.e., the "Hegelian dialectic." The reader should note that Hegel's tripartite system of "original," "reflective," and "philosophical" was developed for different purposes than Fichte's dialectic. Hegel used these terms to define three different approaches to historical research. The Fichte and Hegel constructs are described here as parallel simply for pedagogical purposes. See: Georg W. F. Hegel, *The Philosophy of History*, J. Sibree, trans. (New York: The Cooperative Publication Society, 1900).

Part 2

DIALECTICAL READINGS in ARCHITECTURE: TECTONICS

Chapter 1

SIMPLICITY and COMPLEXITY

FIGURE 1.1
Photograph of the megaliths at Stonehenge, Wiltshire, England (ca. 3000–2500 B.C.E.).

FIGURE 1.2
Photograph of the pond and gallery pavilions at the Modern Art Museum of Ft. Worth, Texas, United States (1999–2002). Architect: Tadao Ando.

INTRODUCTORY DISCUSSION

1. Of the two images above, which better represents the concept of "simplicity" in architecture? Which better represents "complexity" in architecture? Why?

2. What are the various definitions and connotations of the terms "simplicity" and "complexity" in architecture? What are the characteristics of an architecture of simplicity? What are the characteristics of an architecture of complexity?

3. Which is more appropriate in architecture today, simplicity or complexity?

Introduction

In 1958, Peter Blake—American architect, critic, educator, editor of *Architectural Forum*, and once-director of New York's Museum of Modern Art—wrote that "the only trouble with a simple little word like 'simple' is that so many people think it is synonymous with 'easy.' In real life, of course, 'simple' often means 'difficult.'"[1] Blake wrote about Le Corbusier, Phillip Johnson, Frank Lloyd Wright, Marcel Breuer, Ulrich Franzen, and other proponents of Modernist architecture and minimalism. Most notably, however, it is in "The Difficult Art of Simplicity" that Blake made the aforementioned statement and extensively discussed the work of Ludwig Mies van der Rohe. Regarding Mies's use of the structural steel frame, Blake wrote, "Mies's system of simplicity . . . is one of the most important resources architecture can claim."[2]

Mies, among the most renowned of minimalist architects, did not coin the phrase "Less is more." He did, however, help make it the slogan for a generation of architects. Impressive is the fact that Mies wrote relatively little; it was through his large body of built architectural works that Mies propagated this phrase. Mies's work, according to Blake, was also assisted by its place in history. Mies followed an era of great uncertainty and diverse opinions about aesthetic expression, technological innovation, and style. Mies provided certainty; "Less is more" provided certainty. Nevertheless, as Blake recognized, Mies's architectural and verbal statements conceal "considerable expense," "thought," and "trouble." Architecture is influenced by a wide array of issues: tectonics, use, and site; aesthetic and economic trends; architect–client–public relationships; conventions and innovations; and a variety of other factors. With this diversity of issues, and the conflicts among them, one might say that architecture is inherently "complex."

So, which is it—"simple" or "complex"?

Consider this question as you explore the texts of this first chapter. Marcel Breuer's "Where Do We Stand?" serves as the *original text* for the chapter, as Breuer articulates the theories of what he describes as the "New Architecture." In that essay, Breuer, an architect and furniture designer, used the ironic phrase "maximum simplicity" to describe this "New Architecture" of Modernism. While Breuer's design work clearly demonstrated

1. Peter Blake, "The Difficult Art of Simplicity," *Architectural Forum* (May 1958): 127.

2. Ibid., 131.

affiliation with other Modernists, he recognized, like Blake, that Modernist architecture was "not such a simple matter," that "architecture is an alarmingly many-sided complex." In any case, Breuer plainly stated that he and other protagonists of Modernism sought "clarity" by emphasizing "structural laws and practical functions" and aesthetic "simplicity and a renunciation of all irrational forms."

On the other hand, an excerpt from Robert Venturi's *Complexity and Contradiction in Architecture* serves as the *reflective text* in this chapter. In a radical departure from Modernist ideals, Venturi turned the slogan of "Less is more" into his own "Less is a bore." Rather than arguing for "clarity," as Breuer did, Venturi contended "ambiguity," "complexity," and "contradiction" as essential parts of architecture.

Coming full circle, Vittorio Gregotti's "On Simplicity" serves as the *philosophical text* for this chapter. Gregotti stated, "Designing a simple building has become a very complicated problem." Similar to Venturi, Gregotti identified that the challenge of simplicity exists in developing a synthetic whole: "A building is simple not because its shapes conform to elementary geometry, not because all of it is immediately visible, or because the logic is evident in its connections, but because all its parts voice their necessity . . . reciprocally."

Through Breuer, Venturi, and Gregotti, you will see that the discussion about simplicity and complexity involves nearly all aspects of architecture—history, geography, structure, functionality, tectonics, and, most certainly, aesthetics. There is maybe no more fundamental—and vague—debate in architecture than the debate regarding simplicity vs. complexity. As stated by Adrian Forty, "'Simple' must be one of the most overworked words in the architectural vocabulary."[3] While hundreds of architects, critics, and architectural educators have argued vehemently for "an architecture of simplicity" or "an architecture of complexity," the debate is no more resolved today than it was a century ago.

3. Adrian Forty, "Simple," in *Words and Buildings: A Vocabulary of Modern Architecture* (New York: Thames & Hudson, 2000), 249.

Original Text:

MARCEL BREUER, "WHERE DO WE STAND?"

First Published in 1935

I would ask my readers to be resigned to a purely theoretical handling of this question, since I shall assume that they are already familiar with the tenets of the New Architecture and what it looks like. They will know, for instance, that these buildings are conceived of in severe terms—a maximum simplicity, wide openings for light, air and sunshine; balconies, flat roofs, minutely studied practical floor-plans, a scientific basis, strong emphasis on mechanization; industrial methods of production with a tendency towards standardization; light colours, new materials used for their own sake and a reconception of housing and town-planning in the light of social and economic research. Therefore I want to confine myself to a statement of what is really fundamental in our thought and work.

In the past I have been opposed to over much of this theorizing about the New Architecture, believing that our job was to build, and that our buildings sufficed, since they speak plainly enough for themselves. I was, moreover, not a little alienated to observe that there was often a considerable discrepancy between these theories and the personalities who advanced them. The danger of all theorizing is that, by carrying one's arguments too far, one is apt to leave the world of realities behind one.

Parts of the principles of the Modern Movement have been extensively adopted, but they have been compromised by being used separately without any co-ordinating relation to the aims of that Movement as a whole. A closer examination of the ideology of the New Architecture has therefore become a pressing necessity.

The protagonists of the Modern Movement have been occupied with the classification and development of their intellectual principles and the carrying out of their individual designs This meant that further propaganda was left to chance, industrial advertisements and the technical press. Much has been distorted, much overlooked, as a result. Modern terminology has been put under tribute for snappy slogans; and each of these serves only some isolated detail. A correlation of these heterogeneous parts to their unifying whole is still lacking. Whereas the pioneers of the Modern Movement have now succeeded in establishing a very broad intellectual basis, which is in harmony with their own work, the younger generation still confines itself to rigid formalization.

I should like, therefore, to give a more general survey that will cover a wider field than these catch-phrases. To do so, however, is not such a simple matter. Architecture is an alarmingly many-sided complex, and as soon as one leaves the technical sphere all conceptions tend to become vague and overlapping.

I intentionally renounce historical comparisons, and leave to others the task of contrasting our age with epochs of the past, and showing us from history what leads to progress or decay, what to art or architecture.

What, then, are the basic impulses of the New Architecture? In the first place an absence of prejudice. Secondly, an ability to place oneself in immediate objective contact with a given task, problem or form. Thirdly, being unfettered by tradition and the usual stock-in-trade of the intellectual departmental store. Let those who prefer respectful transition from the principles of one school or style to those of another, adopt them if they will. What we believe is what we have perceived, experienced, thought, proved and calculated for ourselves.

At this point I should like to consider traditionalism for a moment. And by tradition I do not mean the unconscious continuance and growth of a nation's culture generation by generation, but a conscious dependence on the immediate past. That the type of men who are described as modern architects have the sincerest admiration and love for genuine national art, for old peasant houses as for the masterpieces of the great epochs in art, is a point which needs to be stressed. On journeys what interests us most is to find districts where the daily activity of the population has remained untouched. Nothing is such a relief as to discover a creative craftsmanship which has been developed immemorially from father to son, and is free of the pretentious pomp and empty vanity of the architecture of the last century. Here is something from which we can learn, though not with a view to imitation. For us the attempt to build in a national tradition or an old-world style would be inadequate and insincere. To pride oneself on such things is a bad symptom. For the modern world has no tradition for its eight-hour day, its electric light, its central heating, its water supply, its motor roads and filling stations, its bridges and its steel motor-liners, or for any of its technical methods. One can roundly damn the whole of our age; one can commiserate with, or dissociate oneself from, or hope to transform the men and women who have lost their mental equilibrium in the vortex of modern life— but I do not believe that to decorate their homes with traditional gables and dormers helps them in the least. On the contrary, this only widens the gulf between appearance and reality, and removes them still further from that ideal equilibrium which is, or should be, the ultimate object of all thought and action.

It may, perhaps, seem paradoxical to establish a parallel between certain aspects of vernacular architecture, or national art, and the Modern Movement. All the same, it is interesting to see that these two diametrically opposed tendencies have two characteristics in common: the impersonal character of their forms; and a tendency to develop along typical, rational lines that are unaffected by passing fashions.

It is probably these traits that make genuine peasant art so sympathetic to us—though the sympathy it arouses is a purely platonic one. If we ask ourselves what is the source of the solid unselfconscious beauty, the convincing quality and reasonableness of peasant work, we find that the explanation lies in its unconsciously, and therefore genuinely, traditional nature. A given region only has a few traditional crafts and uses a few definite colours. Roughly speaking, the same things, or variants of the same things, have always been made there. And even these variations are obedient to a regular and recurrent rhythm. It is their uninterrupted transmission through local and family associations which conditions their development and ultimately standardizes them as type-forms.

In one direction at least our efforts offer a parallel—we seek what is typical, the norm; not the accidental but the definite *ad hoc* form. These norms are designed to meet the needs, not of a former age, but of our own age; therefore we naturally realize them, not with craftsmen's tools, but with modern industrial machinery.

If one examines a *bona fide* example of industrial standardization, one cannot fail to perceive that it is representative of an "art," and that that art has only reached this point of perfection by a sort of traditional development which is the result of exploring the same problem over and over again. What has changed is our method: instead of family traditions and force of habit we employ scientific principles and logical analysis.

Please do not misunderstand me. I do not for a moment mean that peasant art and the Modern Movement have any connection in fact with one another. All I wanted to do was to bring out the similarity between certain tendencies which have led, or can lead, to relative perfection in each. In any case, we can all admit that there are numbers of old peasant farmsteads that we find far more stimulating than many so-called "modern" houses.

To sum up: it is quite untrue to say that the Modern Movement is contemptuous of traditional or national art. It is simply that the sympathy we feel for each does not take the form of making us want to use either as a medium for the utterly different purposes of the present day.

I should like to divorce the "unbiased" aspect of the New Architecture from association with terms like "new," "original," "individual," "imaginative," and "revolutionary." We are all susceptible to the persuasion of that word "new." Society pays its need of respect to anything new by granting it a patent. It is common knowledge that international patent law is based on two principles: "technical improvement" and "newness." Thus novelty becomes a powerful commercial weapon. But what is the Modern Movement's real attitude to this business of "newness"? Are we for what is new, unexpected and a change at any price, in the same way that we are for an unbiased view at any price? I think we can answer this question with an emphatic negative. We are not out to create something new, but something suitable, intrinsically right and as relatively perfect as maybe. The

21

"new" in the Modern Movement must be considered simply a means to an end, not an end in itself as in women's fashions. What we aim at and believe to be possible is that the solutions embodied in the forms of the New Architecture should endure for 10, 20, or 100 years as circumstances may demand—a thing unthinkable in the world of fashion as long as modes are modes. It follows that, though we have no fear of what is new, novelty is not our aim. We seek what is definite and real, whether old or new.

This perhaps invites the retort, "Be sincere. Look into your motives without trying to make your introspection too moral or positive. Don't all of us get sick of everything after a time? Doesn't everything, even architecture, become tiresome in the end? Isn't our thirst for change greater than we care to admit?"

Here we reach a point where logic ceases to be logical, where consistency loses sense, and anticipation is impossible, because history provides examples for and against. It [is] easy, but futile, to indulge in prophesy. I would rather interrogate that unwritten law of our own convictions, the spirit of our age. It answers that we have tired of everything in architecture which is a matter of fashion; that we find all intentionally new forms wearisome, and all those based on personal predilections or tendencies equally pointless. To which can be added the simple consideration that we cannot hope to change our buildings or furniture as often as we change, for example, our ties.

If by "original," "individual," or "imaginative" artistic caprice, a happy thought or an isolated flash of genius is meant, then I must answer that the New Architecture aims at being neither original, individual, nor imaginative. Here, too, there has been a transformation in the meaning of terms. According to our ideas, modern architecture is "original" when it provides a complete solution of the difficulty concerned. By "individual" we understand the degree of intensity or application with which the most various or directly interconnected problems are disposed of. "Imagination" is no longer expressed in remote intellectual adventures, but in the tenacity with which formal order is imposed upon the world of realities. The ability to face a problem objectively brings us to the so-called "revolutionary" side of the Modern Movement. I have considerable hesitation in using the word at all, since it has recently been annexed by various political parties, and in some countries it is actually inculcated into school-children as an elementary civic virtue. In fact, revolution is now in a fairway towards becoming a permanent institution. I believe that what was originally revolutionary in the Movement was simply the principle of putting its own objective views into practice. It should also be said that our revolutionary attitude was neither self-complacency nor propagandist *bravura*, but the inward, and as far as possible outward, echo of the independence of our work. Although, as I have just pointed out, to be revolutionary has since received the sanction of respectability, this causes us considerable heart-searchings: the word inevitably has a political flavour. In this connection it is necessary to state that our investigations into housing and town-planning problems are based primarily on sociological, rather than on formal or representational, principles. In short, that our ideas of what developments were possible were based on the general needs of the community.

All this has led some people to believe that the Modern Movement either was, or was bound to become, a political one. Our opponents resuscitated this old accusation so as to be able to assail us with political propaganda. Other bodies of opinion tried to force us to define our position by such arguments as: "You make radical proposals for improvement which can only be realized in a radically different form of society. Architecture is the expression of its age, and so, of the circumstances, social structure and political conformation of that age. If your work has no political bias and it is not your main object to realize a political programme, you are simply Utopians who, as things are today, will sooner or later be dragged into impossible compromises."

To which I would reply:

"It is an error to imagine that architecture in its broadest sense is determined by political considerations. Politics, of course, play an immensely important part in architecture, but it is a mistake to identify that part with anyone of its different functions. To come down from the general to the particular:

The technical and economic potentiality of architecture is independent of the political views of its exponents. "

"It follows that the æsthetic potentiality of architecture is also independent of their political views; and likewise the intensity with which particular architects may apply themselves to the solution of particular functional problems."

Politics and architecture overlap, first, in the nature of the problems presented to the latter; and, secondly, in the means that are available for solving them. But even this connection is by no means a definite one. For instance, how does it help us to know that Stalin and the promoters of the Palace of the Soviets competition are Communists; or the reasons why they became Communists? Their arguments are very much the same as those of any primitively-minded capitalistic, or democratic, or Fascist, or merely conservative motor-car manufacturer with a hankering for the cruder forms of symbolism. In spite of the undeniable influence of politics in every sphere of life and thought, no one can deny that each of these spheres has a highly important unpolitical side to it, and that that side determines its nature. As an architect, I am content to confine myself to analysing and solving the various questions of architecture and town-planning which arise from their several pyscho-physical, co-ordinating and technical-economic aspects. And I believe that work of this kind leads to material advances which have nothing to do with politics.

The second dominant impulse of the Modern Movement is a striving after clarity, or, if you prefer it, sincerity. No romantic tendencies are implied in either of these terms. They do not mean that we wear our hearts on our sleeves, or invite all and sundry to pry into our homes and private lives through our long horizontal windows.

This particular exemplification of "clarity" has caused a great deal of harm—in the same way that the desire to show construction openly arrived at has often led to the violation of structural principles or their naïvely childish overemphasis. Clarity interpreted

23

in this spirit has been responsible for a decidedly uncomfortable world full of screw-heads and intellectual exhibitionism. With a little goodwill and a pinch of crass stupidity, the famous principle of inside-out "exteriorization" can be relied upon to conjure up a perfect wilderness.

The principle of clarity, as we understand it, expresses itself in the technical and economic fields of architecture, through emphasis on structural laws and practical functions; and in the æsthetic field by simplicity and a renunciation of all irrational forms. The New Architecture might be compared to a crystalline structure in process of formation. Its forms correspond to human laws and functions, which are other than those of nature or organic bodies. In its more immediate conception this New Architecture of ours is the "container" of men's domiciles, the orbit of their lives.

Are our buildings identifiable with descriptions such as "cold," "hard," "empty-looking," "ultra-logical," "unimaginative and mechanistic in every detail?" Is it our aim to trump the mechanization of offices and factories with the mechanization of home life? Whoever thinks so has either only seen the worst examples of modern architecture, or else has had no opportunity to live in or make a closer inspection of the best. Or possibly there is some confusion in his ideas. Does he perhaps mean pompous when he says "human"; dark-brown wallpapers when he invokes cosiness, empty pretence when he demands "peacefulness," and a brothel when he refers to love? Anyhow, he attributes intentions to us which we have never had and can hardly be accused of embodying in our work.

The origin of the Modern Movement was not technological, for technology had been developed long before it was thought of. What the New Architecture did was to civilize technology. Its real genesis was a growing consciousness of the spirit of our age. However, it proved far harder to formulate the intellectual basis and the æsthetic of the New Architecture intelligibly than to establish its logic in practical use. I have often found that something like a functional kitchen equipment has made hypercritical people far more accessible to our ideas; and that they have not infrequently ended by becoming reconciled to our æsthetic as a result. The ease of this method of approach led certain modern architects to outbid each other in broadcasting technical progress, and to rely on theoretical deductions supported by columns of figures. A deliberately statistical attitude to architecture ensued, which degenerated into a competition as to who could go furthest in denying it any sort of æsthetic moment. The engineer was proclaimed the true designer, and everything was declared beautiful that was technically efficient.

I think we can take it that this tendency has nearly seen its day. Engineering structures are by no means necessarily beautiful *qua* engineering structures, though they may often be beautiful either because their builders had a marked talent for formal design, or as a result of that scientific tradition which in the process of time evolves a satisfactory industrial form for everything—the norm type, the standard. There is, of course, a great deal to be said for the practical objectivity of engineering methods in facing technical problems. The engineer has been responsible for several things which, in contrast to many architectural designs of the last century, were at least useful. But we must call things by their proper names, and not bamboozle ourselves into believing that the achievements of engineering are *ipso facto* beautiful.

To sum up again: clarity to us means the definite expression of the purpose of a building and a sincere expression of its structure. One can regard this sincerity as a sort of moral duty, but I feel that above and beyond this it is a trial of strength for the designer, which sets the seal of success on his achievement. Nor do I see any Puritanism in our cult of simplicity, but rather a zest for obtaining greater effect with less expenditure; and the satisfaction of fashioning something out of nothing with intelligence and arrangement as one's only resources. By which I mean winning colour, plasticity, and animation from a flat white wall. Simplicity in this sense connotes both attainment and quality.

Where does rationalism end and art begin in the New Architecture? Where is the dividing line between them, and how is it fixed? I could not trace that frontier if I tried. Architecture seems worthy of notice to me, only in proportion as it produces an effect on our senses, and our senses are strangers to rationalizing processes. It is the same to me whether this effect, which we can, if you like, call "beauty," has been created by an engineer or an artist; whether it is the result of what is called speculative research, or what is called intuition. I care nothing for any differentiation as between these methods, but I care a great deal whether I feel at ease in the finished building. Besides, I do not wish to invalidate the super-rational basis of the Modern Movement which is its unwritten law, by any passionate assertion of principles. All the same, a few of them can be indicated here.

We have no use for beauty in the form of a foreign body, of ornament, or of a titivating of undesigned structural elements; nor even as an arbitrary magnification of certain dimensions, a purely transient vogue. We have no use for architecture that is labelled symbolist, cubist, neoplastic or "constructivist." We know that the essential and determining elements of a building can be wholly rational without this rationalism in any way affecting the question of whether it is beautiful or ugly.

Everyone who has planned, designed and constructed, knows:

1. That in spite of the most logical volition, the decisive impulse towards co-ordination very often occurs through uncontrollable reflexes.
2. That even in the most objective exploration of a given problem by the logical method of procedure, in nearly every case a final, one might almost say illogical, choice between different combinations has to be made.
3. That the commanding and so to speak convincing impressiveness of really inspired construction is the outcome of an inflexible tenacity which is almost passionate, and that that passion transcends mere logic.

Perhaps the slogan: "Art and technique as a new unity," which Gropius coined some years ago, most nearly expresses the idea that in the New Architecture these concepts are no longer separable.

I now come to the third dominant impulse of the Modern Movement: the relation of unbroken elements to one another—contrast. What is aimed at is *un*schematic design. Whoever supposes that our preference for flat roofs inclines us to adopt flat tops for our coffee-pots; that the cubic forms of our buildings will be echoed in our lighting fixtures; or that our guiding principle of establishing unity and a certain harmonious relation between all these things can be labeled as a "style," has entirely misunderstood our objects. There is no hard and fast formula for doing this or that in the New Architecture. Wherever you find identical forms in different places, you can be sure it was due to the adoption of a similar solution for a similar problem. But when a cupboard begins to look like a house, the house like the pattern of a carpet, and the pattern of a carpet like a bedside lamp, you can be certain that it is not modern work in the sense that modern is used in this article.

We strive to achieve a definite design for all different elements, and we arrange them side by side without dressing them artificially for the purpose. These elements receive different forms as a natural consequence of their different structure. Their complete individuality is intended to establish a kind of balance which seems to me a far more vital one than the purely superficial "harmony" which can be realized by adopting either a formal or a structural common denominator. We reject the traditional conception of "style" first, because it gainsays sincere and appropriate design; and secondly, because the link between quite justifiable differences in appearance produces the sort of contrast we consider is characteristic of modern life. Contrasts like house and garden, a man's working and home life, voids and solids, shining metal and soft materials—or even living organisms like animals and plants—can all be realized against the stark plain surface of a wall; also in the opposition of the discipline of standardization to the freedom of experiment that leads to its development. Such contrasts have become a necessity of life. They are guarantees of the reality of the basis we have chosen to adopt. The power to preserve these extremes without modification (that is to say, the extent of their contrast) is the real gauge of our strength.

But what about the æsthetic of the New Architecture? Its dogmas are the kind that cannot be formulated. The important thing for me is that the New Architecture exists, and that it fulfils a vital need for all of us.

Reflective Text

ROBERT VENTURI, EXCERPTS FROM *COMPLEXITY AND CONTRADICTION IN ARCHITECTURE.*

First Published in 1966

NONSTRAIGHTFORWARD ARCHITECTURE: A GENTLE MANIFESTO

I like complexity and contradiction in architecture. I do not like the incoherence or arbitrariness of incompetent architecture nor the precious intricacies of picturesqueness or expressionism. Instead, I speak of a complex and contradictory architecture based on the richness and ambiguity of modern experience, including that experience which is inherent in art. Everywhere, except in architecture, complexity and contradiction have been acknowledged, from Gödel's proof of ultimate inconsistency in mathematics to T. S. Eliot's analysis of "difficult" poetry and Joseph Albers' definition of the paradoxical quality of painting.

But architecture is necessarily complex and contradictory in its very inclusion of the traditional Vitruvian elements of commodity, firmness, and delight. And today the wants of program, structure, mechanical equipment, and expression, even in single buildings in simple contexts, are diverse and conflicting in ways previously unimaginable. The increasing dimension and scale of architecture in urban and regional planning add to the difficulties. I welcome the problems and exploit the uncertainties. By embracing contradiction as well as complexity, I aim for vitality as well as validity.

Architects can no longer afford to be intimidated by the puritanically moral language of orthodox Modern architecture. I like elements which are hybrid rather than "pure," compromising rather than "clean," distorted rather than "straightforward," ambiguous rather than "articulated," perverse as well as impersonal, boring as well as "interesting," conventional rather than "designed," accommodating rather than excluding, redundant rather than simple, vestigial as well as innovating, inconsistent and equivocal rather than direct and clear. I am for messy vitality over obvious unity. I include the non sequitur and proclaim the duality.

I am for richness of meaning rather than clarity of meaning; for the implicit function as well as the explicit function. I prefer "both-and" to "either-or," black and white, and sometimes gray, to black or white. A valid architecture evokes many levels of meaning and combinations of focus: its space and its elements become readable and workable in several ways at once.

But an architecture of complexity and contradiction has a special obligation toward the whole: its truth must be in its totality or its implications of totality. It must embody the difficult unity of inclusion rather than the easy unity of exclusion. More is not less.

COMPLEXITY AND CONTRADICTION VS. SIMPLIFICATION OR PICTURESQUENESS

Orthodox Modern architects have tended to recognize complexity insufficiently or inconsistently. In their attempt to break with tradition and start all over again, they idealized the primitive and elementary at the expense of the diverse and the sophisticated. As participants in a revolutionary movement, they acclaimed the newness of modern functions, ignoring their complications. In their role as reformers, they puritanically advocated the separation and exclusion of elements, rather than the inclusion of various requirements and their juxtapositions. As a forerunner of the Modern movement, Frank Lloyd Wright, who grew up with the motto "Truth against the World," wrote: "Visions of simplicity so broad and far-reaching would open to me and such building harmonies appear that . . . would change and deepen the thinking and culture of the modern world. So I believed."[4] And Le Corbusier, co-founder of Purism, spoke of the "great primary forms" which, he proclaimed, were "distinct . . . and without ambiguity."[5] Modern architects with few exceptions eschewed ambiguity.

But now our position is different: "At the same time that the problems increase in quantity, complexity, and difficulty they also change faster than before,"[6] and require an attitude more like that described by August Heckscher:

4. Frank Lloyd Wright, *An American Architecture*, ed. Edgar Kaufmann (New York: Horizon Press, 1955), 207.

5. Le Corbusier, *Towards a New Architecture* (London: The Architectural Press, 1927), 31.

6. Christopher Alexander, *Notes on the Synthesis of Form* (Cambridge: Harvard University Press, 1964), 4.

7. August Heckscher, *The Public Happiness* (New York: Atheneum Publishers, 1962), 102.

The movement from a view of life as essentially simple and orderly to a view of life as complex and ironic is what every individual passes through in becoming mature. But certain epochs encourage this development; in them the paradoxical or dramatic outlook colors the whole intellectual scene. . . . Amid simplicity and order rationalism is born, but rationalism proves inadequate in any period of upheaval. Then equilibrium must be created out of opposites. Such inner peace as men gain must represent a tension among contradictions and uncertainties. . . . A feeling for paradox allows seemingly dissimilar things to exist side by side, their very incongruity suggesting a kind of truth.[7]

Rationalizations for simplification are still current, however, though subtler than the early arguments. They are expansions of Mies van der Rohe's magnificent paradox, "less is more." Paul Rudolph has clearly stated the implications of Mies' point of view:

All problems can never be solved. . . . Indeed it is a characteristic of the twentieth century that architects are highly selective in determining which problems they want to solve. Mies, for instance, makes wonderful buildings only because he ignores many aspects of a building. If he solved more problems, his buildings would be far less potent.[8]

The doctrine "less is more" bemoans complexity and justifies exclusion for expressive purposes. It does, indeed, permit the architect to be highly selective in determining which problems he wants to solve. But if the architect must be committed to his particular way of seeing the universe, such a commitment surely means that the architect determines how problems should be solved, not that he can determine which of the problems he will solve. He can exclude important considerations only at the risk of separating architecture from the experience of life and the needs of society. If some problems prove insoluble, he can express this: in an inclusive rather than an exclusive kind of architecture there is room for the fragment, for contradiction, for improvisation, and for the tensions these produce. Mies' exquisite pavilions have had valuable implications for architecture, but their selectiveness of content and language is their limitation as well as their strength.

I question the relevance of analogies between pavilions and houses, especially analogies between Japanese pavilions and recent domestic architecture. They ignore the real complexity and contradiction inherent in the domestic program—the spatial and technological possibilities as well as the need for variety in visual experience. Forced simplicity results in oversimplification. In the Wiley House, for instance, in contrast to his glass house, Philip Johnson attempted to go beyond the simplicities of the elegant pavilion. He explicitly separated and articulated the enclosed "private functions" of living on a ground floor pedestal, thus separating them from the open social functions in the modular pavilion above. But even here the building becomes a diagram of an oversimplified program for living—an abstract theory of either-or. Where simplicity cannot work, simpleness results. Blatant simplification means bland architecture. Less is a bore.

The recognition of complexity in architecture does not negate what Louis Kahn has called "the desire for simplicity." But aesthetic simplicity which is a satisfaction to the mind derives, when valid and profound, from inner complexity. The Doric temple's simplicity to the eye is achieved through the famous subtleties and precision of its distorted geometry and the contradictions and tensions inherent in its order. The Doric temple could achieve apparent simplicity through real complexity. When complexity disappeared, as in the late temples, blandness replaced simplicity.

Nor does complexity deny the valid simplification which is part of the process of analysis, and even a method of achieving complex architecture itself. "We oversimplify a given event when we characterize it from the standpoint of a given interest."[9] But this kind of simplification is a method in the analytical process of achieving a complex art. It should not be mistaken for a goal.

8. Paul Rudolph, *Perspecta: The Yale Architectural Journal,* 7 (1961): 51.

9. Kenneth Burke, *Permanence and Change* (Los Altos: Hermes Publications, 1954), 107.

An architecture of complexity and contradiction, however, does not mean picturesqueness or subjective expressionism. A false complexity has recently countered the false simplicity of an earlier Modern architecture. It promotes an architecture of symmetrical picturesqueness—which Minoru Yamasaki calls "serene"—but it represents a new formalism as unconnected with experience as the former cult of simplicity. Its intricate forms do not reflect genuinely complex programs, and its intricate ornament, though dependent on industrial techniques for execution, is dryly reminiscent of forms originally created by handicraft techniques. Gothic tracery and Rococo rocaille were not only expressively valid in relation to the whole, but came from a valid showing-off of hand skills and expressed a vitality derived from the immediacy and individuality of the method. This kind of complexity through exuberance, perhaps impossible today, is the antithesis of "serene" architecture, despite the superficial resemblance between them. But if exuberance is not characteristic of our art, it is tension, rather than "serenity" that would appear to be so.

The best twentieth-century architects have usually rejected simplification—that is, simplicity through reduction—in order to promote complexity within the whole. The works of Alvar Aalto and Le Corbusier (who often disregards his polemical writings) are examples. But the characteristics of complexity and contradiction in their work are often ignored or misunderstood. Critics of Aalto, for instance, have liked him mostly for his sensitivity to natural materials and his fine detailing, and have considered his whole composition willful picturesqueness. I do not consider Aalto's Imatra church picturesque. By repeating in the massing the genuine complexity of the triple-divided plan and the acoustical ceiling pattern, this church represents a justifiable expressionism different from the willful picturesqueness of the haphazard structure and spaces of Giovanni Michelucci's recent church for the Autostrada.[10] Aalto's complexity is part of the program and structure of the whole rather than a device justified only by the desire for expression. Though we no longer argue over the primacy of form or function (which follows which?), we cannot ignore their interdependence.

The desire for a complex architecture, with its attendant contradictions, is not only a reaction to the banality or prettiness of current architecture. It is an attitude common in the Mannerist periods: the sixteenth century in Italy or the Hellenistic period in Classical art, and is also a continuous strain seen in such diverse architects as Michelangelo, Palladio, Borromini, Vanbrugh, Hawksmoor, Soane, Ledoux, Butterfield, some architects of the Shingle Style, Furness, Sullivan, Lutyens, and recently, Le Corbusier, Aalto, Kahn, and others.

Today this attitude is again relevant to both the medium of architecture and the program in architecture.

First, the medium of architecture must be re-examined if the increased scope of our architecture as well as the complexity of its goals is to be expressed. Simplified or superficially complex forms will not work. Instead, the variety inherent in the ambiguity of visual perception must once more be acknowledged and exploited.

Second, the growing complexities of our functional problems must be acknowledged. I refer, of course, to those programs, unique in our time, which are complex because

10. I have visited Giovanni Michelucci's Church of the Autostrada since writing these words and I now realize it is an extremely beautiful and effective building. I am therefore sorry I made this unsympathetic comparison.

of their scope, such as research laboratories, hospitals, and particularly the enormous projects at the scale of city and regional planning. But even the house, simple in scope, is complex in purpose if the ambiguities of contemporary experience are expressed. This contrast between the means and the goals of a program is significant. Although the means involved in the program of a rocket to get to the moon, for instance, are almost infinitely complex, the goal is simple and contains few contradictions; although the means involved in the program and structure of buildings are far simpler and less sophisticated technologically than almost any engineering project, the purpose is more complex and often inherently ambiguous.

Philosophical Text

VITTORIO GREGOTTI, "ON SIMPLICITY."

First Published in 1996

Simplicity, as a process of adhering to the essence of use, to lack of ornament, and to mimesis of the technical reproducibility and expressive rigor of utensils, has, as we know, been the most prominent and common stylistic banner of modernity in this century.

But if one abandons the idea that a moral, tenacious pride in modesty and an egalitarian, *sachlich* striving can serve as mimeses of collective reason, progress, and liberation, then it certainly seems more difficult to enumerate the values of simplicity in times of highly complex and intense signals. At the very least, the matter of simplicity in architecture becomes subject to different possible interpretations.

Designing a simple building has become a very complicated problem, at least for those who believe that simplicity in architecture is not something natural or spontaneous, does not result from restoring linear deduction, is not tautology, simplification, a retreat from the complexity of reality, or, least of all, a relinquishing of invention.

Simplicity today stands on a dangerous ridge. One slope harbors pure opposition to market coercion, to contrivances that lack an aim or an internal reason for expression. On the other side lie in ambush oversimplification and poverty of invention, aphasia and the mannerism of poetic silence—in brief, the inarticulate superstition of simplicity.

In other words, to me simplicity is not simplification, and above all not simplification as a formal model. Eloquent simplicity can be reached through great effort, but it is never a good starting point, nor, above all, an objective at any cost. Architecture is not simple; it can only become simple.

Nor would I like, in these times of noisy, exhibitionistic redundancy of communication, to be ideologically forced to take the side of simplicity as an *a priori* mimesis of logical and moralistic rigor. That is important, but remains transitory.

The fragmentation in our times certainly calls for some solid points, some secure, well-fastened nails. But I believe that such solidity must be reconstructed not through reduction but rather by pushing project research until it succeeds in breaking through the tangled web of complication in order to rebuild, in view of the specific situation, a hypothesis for a structure that will organize architecture according to the practice of a meticulous, although consciously provisional, clarity.

It is very difficult today to imagine a return to order that could be more than a coat of whitewash over the disorder and conflicts of our times, if it does not confront the unresolvable contradictions placed daily before our eyes by notions such as logic and reason. Simplicity must make contradiction itself clear and comprehensible without denying its existence and its value as a material for establishing difference.

The reasons behind a simple building must reveal, not cover, the fissures of doubt; they must reconnect and not isolate. They must first address their own limits, and must limit the risks of instituting a law that lacks the necessary internal order. That is, they must realize that its balance is precarious, but at the same time pursue it with tenacity.

A simple building must thus compose its own image as the superficial tension of complexity; for there is no level of complexity that cannot be expressed through the clarity of simplicity without simplification.

In that sense, a building is never simple enough. To free oneself from the super-fluous; that is, to identify what is superfluous without confusing it with the richness of curiosity, of a question, of questioning, requires an accurate and difficult effort toward discrimination, even though solely liberating oneself from the superfluous clearly does not guarantee access to the heart of simplicity.

A building is simple not because its shapes conform to elementary geometry, not because all of it is immediately visible, or because the logic is evident in its connections, but because all its parts voice their necessity, both reciprocally and with respect to the meaning of the specific architectural solution. In simplicity there must be nothing pre-established, nothing immobile. Instead, all must be balance, measurement, relation between points, vital organization, mysterious transparency.

It must give the impression that everything contained in the project is absolutely inevitable and certain, but that there is still always something essential beyond what has been organized.

In that sense, oscillation, cancellation, and the suspended tension of parts can also share the rigor of simplicity, and participate in the golden and absolutely general rule of economy of expression.

On the other hand, to propose simplicity in architecture is not, today, to propose a totality, a closure within a benign form of the absolute. Rather, it presents itself as the illumination of a brief fragment of truth, like the laborious deciphering of a small phrase of a text whose overall meaning remains unknown.

A simple building can also have an interior whose functions, spaces, uses, and distributions are complex; an interior rich in interrelations rather than in form, for which simplicity is, above all, a triangulation of the experimental field.

But a simple building is also the opposite of a car body that covers and unifies a complex motor constructed by a different rationality, a body that denies access to the mechanism of function and only reveals the aspect of performance. Rather, the simple building simultaneously guards and reveals its essence.

Moreover, a simple building cannot avoid referring to some attempt at refoundation, a refoundation of sense and representation that is also constructed as a reorganization of the system of functions, a radical rethinking of the reasons behind the organism and its public and contextual role.

Simple is, in that sense, also the opposite of mixed, combined. It refers to the idea of unity and homogeneity, of being devoid of possible additions, in which compositional elements endowed with autonomous life do not figure. It is, in other words, something that has reached a state in which it seems that nothing can be added or taken away, and in which all the reasons in its composition have found their own, provisionally definitive arrangement.

Architecture—great architecture—has always attempted to reduce the problems of construction, use, context, and symbolism to one single reason. The simple building carries firmly with it, even when such reasons become remote, the unitary arrangement of its components as the basis for its own specific identity.

The simplicity of a building, moreover, has to do with silence. It is the creation of a pause in the tumult of language; it identifies the divergence of sense among signs; it appears as the proud fixation of an infinite series of hesitations, tests, erasures, experiences; it is the rewriting of what we have always known. The simple project destroys all neuroses about the future, gives back to the past, to paraphrase Merleau-Ponty, not survival, which is a hypocritical form of oblivion, but a new life that takes the noble form of memory.

The simplicity of a building also represents an aspiration to find one's place near the origin of architecture itself, to look as if one had always been there, firmly fixed to the earth and to the sky, in an open discussion with the surroundings that starts with the recognition and critique of the identities and distances of each.

A simple building, in other words, rests on a principle of settlement as it does on its own physical foundations. It is the ability to clearly identify such foundations, including the connection with the earth and the geography that represents its history, that allows an architecture to achieve simplicity; that is, to become necessary in all its parts and connect itself directly to the principles of its own synthesis.

Writing and Discussion Questions

ANALYSIS

1. What was Breuer arguing for and against? What excerpt/quotation best represents this?
2. What was Venturi arguing for and against? What excerpt/quotation best represents this?
3. What was Gregotti arguing for and against? What excerpt/quotation best represents this?

SYNTHESIS

1. Regarding concepts of simplicity and complexity, discuss one major difference regarding Breuer's, Venturi's, and Gregotti's texts.
2. Regarding concepts of simplicity and complexity, discuss one primary commonality regarding Breuer's, Venturi's, and Gregotti's texts.

SELF-REFLECTION

1. For each of the texts, discuss a major issue with which you most agree and most disagree; reflect upon why you hold these views.
2. Select a recent design project, or a current project on which you are working. Discuss the characteristics of the project in regards to simplicity and complexity, in light of the discussion and texts introduced in this chapter. What attitudes regarding simplicity and complexity does your work illustrate?

PROSPECTION

1. Select one of the texts listed in the bibliography for this chapter; locate and read it. To what degree is that text and the attitudes it represents still relevant to architecture today and in the near future?

2. What will be the role of simplicity and complexity in architecture in the near future? Will simplicity and complexity be predominantly about conceptualization, design process, or the final composition; some combination of these; or something else? In other words, if a fourth text were added to this chapter, what would the argument be?

Other Readings on Simplicity and Complexity

Delbecke, Maarten. "Mannerism and Meaning in *Complexity and Contradiction in Architecture*," *Journal of Architecture*, 15 (2010): 267–282.

Forty, Adrian. "Simple," in *Words and Buildings: A Vocabulary of Modern Architecture* (London: Thames & Hudson, 2000), 249–255.

Kroll, Lucien. *Architecture of Complexity*, trans. Peter B. Jones (Cambridge: MIT Press, 1987).

Le Corbusier. "The Engineer's Aesthetic and Architecture," in *Towards a New Architecture*, trans. Frederick Etchells (New York: Dover Publications, 1986), 9–20. First published 1931.

Manson, Steven, and O'Sullivan, David. "Complexity Theory in the Study of Space and Place," *Environment & Planning A*, 38 (2006): 677–692.

Martin, Reinhold. "Complexities," *Journal of Architecture*, 3 (1998): 187–209.

Schindler, R. M. "Space Architecture," in *Architecture and Design, 1890–1939: An International Anthology of Original Articles*, eds. Tim Benton, Charlotte Benton, and Dennis Sharp (New York: Whitney Library of Design, 1975), 183–85. First published in 1934.

Semper, Gottfried. "The Four Elements of Architecture," in *The Four Elements of Architecture and Other Writings*, trans. Harry Francis Mallgrave and Wolfgang Herrmann (Cambridge: Cambridge University Press, 1989): 74–129. First published in 1851.

Soane, Sir John. *Sir John Soane: The Royal Academy Lectures*. ed. David Watkin (Cambridge: Cambridge University Press, 2001).

van Eyck, Aldo. *Aldo van Eyck: Writings*, eds. Vincent Ligtelijn and Francis Strauven (Amsterdam: Sun Publishers, 2006). First published 1947–1998.

Wagner, Otto. *Modern Architecture: A Guidebook for His Students to this Field of Art*, trans. Harry Francis Mallgrave (Santa Monica: Getty Research Institute, 1988). First published in 1896.

Chapter 2
ORNAMENT and AUSTERITY

INTRODUCTORY DISCUSSION

1. Of the two images above, which better represents the concept of "ornament" in architecture today? Why?
2. What are the various definitions and connotations of the term "ornament" in architecture? For example, how is "ornament" similar or different from terms like "decoration," "application," "integration," "function," etc.?
3. How is or is not "ornament" an appropriate concept or term in architecture today?

FIGURE 2.1
Photograph of the exterior façade of Santi Luca e Martina, Rome (7th century: main church plan; 17th century: reconstruction and façade). Architect: Pietro da Cortona.

FIGURE 2.2
Photograph of the interior marble walls of the German Pavilion at Barcelona, Spain (1929: original Construction and Dedication; 1986: reconstruction). Architect: Ludwig Mies van der Rohe.

Introduction

Prior to the Second Industrial Revolution of the late 19th and early 20th centuries, ornamentation was central to architecture. The study of architecture was the study of ornament. Debates regarding ornament centered on the manner in which ornament was to be deployed. In 1828, for example, German architect Heinrich Hübsch saw style as the "essence" of art and architecture and posed the question, "In what style should we build?"[1] While his contemporaries argued the virtues or shortcomings of various styles—Moorish vs. Romanesque, Greek Corinthian vs. Roman Corinthian—Hübsch sought a new style. He believed that each country or region might develop its own contemporary style, rather than mimic the styles of the past. Vernacular ornament would be derived from: (1) "usual" building materials, e.g. stone and wood, (2) the material and construction methods at the time, (3) responses to regional climate, and (4) human social and environmental needs. The debate over what style was most appropriate grew more impatient as the 19th century came to a close and took a radical turn at the dawn of the 20th century.

With the emergence of the technologic, economic, and scientific mindset of the late 1800s, ornament itself was called into question. The debate switched from Greek vs. Roman vs. *Rundbogenstil* ("round-arch-style," which was closest to Hübsch's preference) to one of ornament vs. non-ornament, "ornament vs. austerity." This marked the beginning of the Modernist movement, exemplified in the works of Le Corbusier, Adolf Loos, and others. This dispute between ornament and austerity was concretized by Loos's essay "Ornament and Crime."

"Ornament and Crime," first written in 1908, and later translated and published in French, English, Japanese, Hebrew, and other languages, provided a wide-reaching manifesto on Modernism. Given its radical departure from prior philosophies of architecture, "Ornament and Crime" exemplifies the materialization of a new paradigm and serves as the *original text* in this chapter. The text condemned ornament: "Ornament *is* Crime," or, as Reyner Banham put it, "Ornament equals Crime." Loos paralleled ornamentation to cultural evolution.[2] Loos argued that primitive cultures utilize elaborate ornament, while modern cultures evolve toward more refined, reserved, and unadorned buildings and

1. Hübsch defined "style" as the "common character" of a set of buildings, evidenced by the "size," "degree of decoration," "and manifold combinations of walls, ceilings, piers or columns, doors, windows, roofs, and cornices." Heinrich Hübsch, *In What Style Should We Build?: The German Debate on Architectural Style*, trans. W. Herrmann (Santa Monica: Getty Center, 1992), 65–67. First published in 1828.

2. In "Ornament and Crime," it needs to be noted that Loos uses the phrase "negro tribesman." Today, this and other remarks made by Loos would be considered highly inflammatory, discriminatory, and unfounded. The reader needs to place Loos's remarks in their geographical and historical context. It was a time when European colonization of Africa, Asia, and other parts of

40

products, toward austerity. The use of ornament in Modern architecture or product design, according to Loos, was immoral, the work of "a criminal or a degenerate."

In 1957, Reyner Banham discussed the significance of Loos's text in "Ornament and Crime: The Decisive Contribution of Adolf Loos," the *reflective text* in this chapter. In that essay, Banham substantiated the resounding impact that Loos's work had on art and architecture of the 20th century, but criticized that Loos's text was "not a reasoned argument but a succession of fast-spieling double-takes and non-sequiturs holding together a precarious" argument.

This chapter culminates with Joseph Rykwert's *philosophical text* "Ornament is No Crime" (first published in 1975). In it, Rykwert outlined various attitudes regarding ornamentation throughout architectural history, including both sociological and technological factors, and the overarching themes therein. Coming full-circle, back to pre-industrial philosophies of ornamentation, Rykwert concluded that ornament may "be seen not as a problem of ornament or not ornament, but as a problem of meaning."

As the most recent of these texts (Rykwert's) is more than three decades old, the question needs to be raised: In what ways is the debate of "ornament vs. austerity" relevant to architecture today? The answers are multiple, and the reader needs to consider this overarching question as she/he reads the subsequent texts. On one hand, it may be that "ornament vs. austerity" has returned to something more akin to Hübsch's question: In what style should we build? For instance, globalization—immigration in particular—has created a reaction whereby a variety of cultures are seeking not a homogenous, international architectural style, but a more diverse, potentially historical, expression of localized cultures. On the other hand, a "Third Industrial Revolution" has emerged. It is marked by new material and production technologies, e.g., "building information modeling" and "mass-customization," which have led to new concepts of "functional ornamentation."[3] Possibly, the debate about ornamentation is as vibrant as it has ever been. As Banham stated, "'Ornament and Crime' is still good fighting talk."

the world was still prevalent. Cultural differences—religious, racial, linguistic, etc.—were used to justify conquest and colonization. At the same time, a pseudo-medical science of physiological and anthropometric differences between racial groups was emerging. This was coupled with the fact that few Europeans had direct contact with rural, indigenous tribes and European museums exhibited African artifacts in austere, non-cultural contexts. Misperceptions of tribal cultures were prevalent. See, for example, Basil Davidson's *The African Genius* (Boston: Little, Brown, 1969), where the Euro-centric view of Africa is described, and Nicholas Thomas's, "Licensed Curiosity: Cook's Pacific Voyages," in John Elsner and Roger Cardinal (eds.) *The Cultures of Collecting* (Cambridge: Harvard University Press, 1994), where the decontextualized display of cultural artifacts is discussed.

3. See, for example: Farshid Moussavi and Michael Kubo, eds, *The Function of Ornament* (New York: Actar, 2006).

Original Text

ADOLF LOOS, "ORNAMENT AND CRIME."

First Published in 1908

In the womb the human embryo goes through all phases of development the animal kingdom has passed through. And when a human being is born, his sense impressions are like a new-born dog's. In childhood he goes through all changes corresponding to the stages in the development of humanity. At two he sees with the eyes of a Papuan, at four with those of a Germanic tribesman, at six of Socrates, at eight of Voltaire. At eight he becomes aware of violet, the color discovered by the eighteenth century; before that, violets were blue and the purple snail was red. Even today physicists can point to colors in the solar spectrum which have been given a name, but which it will be left to future generations to discern.

A child is amoral. A Papuan too, for us. The Papuan slaughters his enemies and devours them. He is not a criminal. But if a modern person slaughters someone and devours him, he is a criminal or a degenerate. The Papuan covers his skin with tattoos, his boat, his oars, in short everything he can lay his hands on. He is no criminal. The modern person who tattoos himself is either a criminal or a degenerate. There are prisons in which eighty percent of the inmates have tattoos. People with tattoos not in prison are either latent criminals or degenerate aristocrats.

The urge to decorate one's face and anything else within reach is the origin of the fine arts. It is the childish babble of painting. But all art is erotic.

A person of our times who gives way to the urge to daub the walls with erotic symbols is a criminal or a degenerate. What is natural in the Papuan or the child is a sign of degeneracy in a modern adult. I made the following discovery, which I passed on to the world: *the evolution of culture is synonymous with the removal of ornamentation from objects of everyday use*. I thought by doing so I would bring joy to the world: it has not thanked me for it. People were sad and downcast. What depressed them was the realization we could no longer create new ornament. What? We alone, the people of the nineteenth century, were not capable of doing something every negro tribesman could do, something every age and nation before us had done!?

The objects mankind created in earlier millennia without ornament have been casually tossed aside and allowed to go to wrack and ruin. We do not possess a single workbench from the Carolingian period, but any piece of trash having even the slightest decoration was collected, cleaned up, and put in an ostentatious palace built specially to house it. And we made our way sadly around the showcases, ashamed of our impotence. Every epoch had its own style, and ours alone should be denied one!? By style people meant ornamentation. But I said, "Do not weep. Do you not see the greatness of our age resides in our very inability to create new ornament? We have gone beyond ornament, we have achieved plain, undecorated simplicity. Behold, the time is at hand, fulfillment awaits us. Soon the streets of the cities will shine like white walls! Like Zion, the Holy City, Heaven's capital. Then fulfillment will be ours."

But there were hobgoblins who refused to accept it. They wanted mankind to continue to strain under the yoke of ornament. Mankind had reached the point where ornament was no longer a source of pleasure, where a tattooed face, instead of increasing people's aesthetic pleasure as it does for the Papuans, diminished pleasure. People had reached the point where they liked a plain cigarette case, while they would not buy a decorated one, even if the price was the same. They were happy with their clothes, and glad they did not have to go around dressed like fairground monkeys in red velvet trousers with gold braid. And I said, "See, the room where Goethe died is more splendid than all your renaissance pomp, and a plain piece of furniture is more beautiful than your museum pieces with all their inlay work and carving. Goethe's language is more beautiful than all the flowery language of the Nuremberg pastoral poets."

That displeased the hobgoblins, and the state, whose task it is to obstruct the people's cultural progress, decided to promote the development and revival of ornamentation. Woe to the state whose revolutions are made by its civil servants! Soon in the Vienna Museum of Applied Art there was a sideboard called "The Miraculous Draught of Fishes," soon there were cupboards with names like "The Bewitched Princess," referring to the decoration with which these unfortunate pieces were covered. The Austrian state takes its task so seriously it ensures the ancient footcloth does not disappear entirely from within the bounds of the Austro-Hungarian monarchy. It forces every cultured twenty-year-old man to spend three years marching in footcloths instead of in knitted hosiery. After all, every state works on the assumption that a primitive population is easier to govern than a cultured one.

The epidemic of ornament enjoys state recognition and state subsidy, then. For my part, however, I see that as a retrograde step. I do not accept the objection that ornament is a source of increased pleasure in life for cultured people, the objection expressed in the exclamation, "But if the ornament is beautiful!" For me, and with me for all people of culture, ornament is not a source of increased pleasure in life. When I want to eat a piece of gingerbread, I choose a piece that is plain, not a piece shaped like a heart, or a baby, or a cavalryman, covered over and over with decoration. A fifteenth-century man would not have understood me, but all modern people will. The supporters of ornament think my hunger for simplicity is some kind of mortification of the flesh. No, my dear Professor of Applied Arts, I am not mortifying the flesh at all. I find the gingerbread tastes better like that.

It is easy to reconcile ourselves to the great damage and depredations the revival of ornament had done to our aesthetic development, since no one and nothing, not even the power of the state, can hold up the evolution of mankind. It can only be slowed down. We can afford to wait. But in economic respects it is a crime, in that it leads to the waste of human labor, money, and materials. That is damage time cannot repair.

The speed of cultural development is hampered by the stragglers. I am living, say, in 1912, my neighbor around 1900, and that man over there in 1880. It is a misfortune for a state if the culture of its inhabitants stretches over too great a time span. The peasant who farms in the shadow of the Großglockner lives in the twelfth century. On the occasion of the festival procession to celebrate the Emperor's jubilee we shuddered to learn that here in Austria we still have tribes from the fourth century. Happy the land that does not have many cultural stragglers and laggards. Happy America! Here in Austria even in the cities there are people who are not modern, people still living in the eighteenth century, horrified at a picture with violet shadows because they have not yet learned to see the color violet; people to whom a pheasant tastes better if the cook has spent days preparing it, and to whom a cigarette case looks better if it is covered in renaissance ornament. And out in the country? Clothes and household goods all belong to earlier times. The peasant is not a Christian, he is still a heathen.

These people who lag behind are slowing down the cultural development of the nations and of humanity. As far as the economic aspect is concerned, if you have two people living next door to each other who have the same needs, the same aspirations, and the same income, but who belong to different cultural epochs, you will find the man of the twentieth century getting richer and richer, and the man of the eighteenth century poorer and poorer. I am assuming, of course, that in both cases their lifestyles reflect their attitudes. The man of the twentieth century needs much less capital to supply his needs, and can therefore make savings. The vegetables he likes are simply cooked in water and served with a knob of butter. They taste good to the other only if there are nuts and honey mixed in, and a cook has spent hours over them. Decorated plates cost more, while twentieth-century man likes his food on white crockery alone. The one saves money while the other throws it away. And it is the same with whole nations. Woe betide the people that lag behind in their cultural development. The English are getting richer, and we poorer . . .

The harm done by ornament to the ranks of the producers is even greater. Since ornament is no longer a natural product of our culture, but a symptom of backwardness or degeneracy, the craftsman producing the ornament is not fairly rewarded for his labor. The conditions among wood carvers and turners, the criminally low rates paid to embroiderers and lace makers are well-known. An ornamental craftsman has to work for twenty hours to reach the pay a modern worker earns in eight. In general, decoration makes objects more expensive, but despite that it does happen that a decorated object, with materials costing the same and demonstrably taking three times as long to produce, is put on sale at half the price of a plain object. The result of omitting decoration is a reduction in working hours and an increase in wages. A Chinese wood carver works for sixteen hours, an American laborer for eight. If I pay as much for a plain box as for one with ornamentation, the difference in labor time belongs to the worker. And if there were no ornaments at all—a state that will perhaps come about after thousands of years—we would need to work for only four hours instead of eight, since at the moment half of our labor is accounted for by ornamentation.

Ornament means wasted labor and therefore wasted health. That was always the case. Today, however, it also means wasted material, and both mean wasted capital.

As there is no longer any organic connection between ornament and our culture, ornament is no longer an expression of our culture. The ornament being created now bears no relationship to us, nor to any human being, or to the system governing the world today. It has no potential for development. Where is Otto Eckmann's ornamentation now, or that of van der Velde? In the past the artist was a healthy, vigorous figure, always at the head of humanity. The modern ornamental artist, however, lags behind or is a pathological case. After three years even he himself disowns his own products. Cultured people find them intolerable straight away; others become aware of it only after a number of years. Where are Otto Eckmann's works today? Where will Olbrich's be in ten years' time? Modern ornament has no parents and no offspring, no past and no future. Uncultivated people, for whom the greatness of our age is a closed book, greet it rapturously and then disown it after a short time.

Humanity as a whole is healthy, only a few are sick. But these few tyrannize the worker, who is so healthy he is incapable of inventing ornaments. They compel him to execute the ornaments they have invented, in a wide variety of different materials. The changing fashion *in* ornament results in a premature devaluation of the product of the worker's labor; his time and the materials used are wasted capital. I have formulated the following principle: *The form of an object should last, that is, we should find it tolerable as long as the object itself lasts.* I will explain: A suit will change its style more often than a valuable fur. A woman's ball outfit, intended for one night alone, will change its style more quickly than a desk. Woe betides us, however, if we have to change a desk as quickly as a ball outfit because we can no longer stand the old style. Then we will have wasted the money we paid for the desk.

Ornamental artists and craftsmen are well aware of this, and in Austria they try to show this deficiency in a positive light. They say, "A consumer who has furnishings he cannot stand after ten years, and thus is forced to refurnish his apartment every ten years, is better than one who buys something only when the old one becomes worn out with use. Industry needs that. The rapid changes in fashion provide employment for millions."

This seems to be the secret of the Austrian economy. When a fire breaks out, how often does one hear someone say, "Thank God! Now there is work for people again." Just set a house on fire, set the Empire on fire, and everyone will be rolling in money! Just keep on making furniture we chop up for firewood after three years, mountings we have to melt down after four, because even at auction they will not fetch a tenth of the cost of labor and materials, and we will get richer and richer!

Not only the consumer bears the loss, it is above all the producer. Nowadays, putting decoration on objects which, thanks to progress, no longer need to be decorated, means a waste of labor and an abuse of material. If all objects would last as long in aesthetic terms as they last physically, the consumer would be able to pay a price for them that would allow the worker to earn more money and work shorter hours. For an object from which I am convinced I will get full use until it is worn out I am quite happy to pay four times the price of another I could buy. I am happy to pay forty crowns for my shoes, even though there are shoes for ten in another shop. But in those trades that languish under the yoke of the ornamental artist, no value is put on good or bad workmanship. Work suffers because no one is willing to pay for it at its true value.

And that is a good thing too, since these ornamented objects are bearable only when they are shoddily produced. I find it easier to accept a fire when I hear it is only worthless rubbish that is being destroyed. I can enjoy the trumpery in the *Künstlerhaus* because I know it takes a few days to put it up and one day to tear it down. But throwing coins instead of stones, lighting a cigar with a bank note, crushing up and drinking a pearl, I find unaesthetic.

Only when these ornamented things have been made from the best material with the greatest care, and have taken up many man-hours of work, do they become truly unaesthetic. I have to admit I was the first to demand quality workmanship. Professor Hoffmann's interior for the Apollo Candle Factory shop in Vienna, done in pine with a colored stain fourteen years ago, is by no means as unbearable as his current designs. Or as unbearable as Hoffmann's designs will look in a further fourteen years' crime. My Café Museum, however, which opened at the same time as the shop, will be unbearable only when the carpentry work begins to fall apart.

A modern person, who regards ornament as a symptom of the artistic superfluity of previous ages and for that reason holds it sacred, will immediately recognize the unhealthy, the forced—painfully forced—nature of modern ornament. Ornament can no longer be produced by someone living on the cultural level of today. It is different for individuals and people who have not yet reached that level.

The ideal I preach is the aristocrat. What I mean by that is the person at the peak of humanity, who yet has a profound understanding of the problems and aspirations of those at the bottom. One who well understands the way the African works patterns into his cloth according to a certain rhythm, so the design appears only when the fabric is taken off the loom; likewise the Persian weaving his rug, the Slovak peasant woman making her lace, the old woman making marvelous needlework from silk and glass beads. The aristocrat lets them carry on in their own accustomed way; he knows the time they spend on their work is sacred to them. The revolutionary would go and tell them it was all pointless, just as he would drag an old woman away from the wayside shrine, telling her there is no God. But the atheist among the aristocrats still raises his hat when he passes a church.

My shoes are covered with decoration formed by saw-tooth patterns and holes. Work done by the shoemaker, work he has not been paid for. Imagine I go to the shoe-maker and say, "You charge thirty crowns for a pair of shoes. I will pay you forty-eight." It will raise the man to such a transport of delight he will thank me through his workmanship and the material used, making them of a quality that will far outweigh my extra payment. He is happy, and happiness is a rare commodity in his house. He has found someone who understands him, who respects his work, and does not doubt his honesty. He can already see the finished shoes in his mind's eye. He knows where the best leather is to be found at the moment, he knows which of his workers he will entrust with the task, and the shoes will have all the saw-tooth patterns and holes an elegant pair of shoes can take. And then I say, "But there is one condition. The shoes must be completely plain." I will drag him down from the heights of bliss to the depths of hell. He will have less work, and I have taken away all his pleasure in it.

The ideal I preach is the aristocrat. I can accept decoration on my own person if it brings pleasure to my fellow men. It brings pleasure to me, too. I can accept the African's ornament, the Persian's, the Slovak peasant woman's, my shoemaker's, for it provides the high point of their existence, which they have no other means of achieving. *We* have the art that has superseded ornament. After all the toil and tribulations of the day, we can go to hear Beethoven or *Tristan.* My shoemaker cannot. I must not take his religion away from him, for I have nothing to put in its place. But anyone who goes to the *Ninth* and then sits down to design a wallpaper pattern is either a fraud or a degenerate.

The disappearance of ornament has brought about an undreamed-of blossoming in the other arts. Beethoven's symphonies would never have been written by a man who had to dress in silk, velvet, and lace. Those who go around in velvet jackets today are not artists, but clowns or house painters. We have become more refined, more subtle. When men followed the herd they had to differentiate themselves through color, modern man uses his dress as a disguise. His sense of his own individuality is so immensely strong it can no longer be expressed in dress. Lack of ornamentation is a sign of intellectual strength. Modern man uses the ornaments of earlier or foreign cultures as he likes and as he sees fit. He concentrates his own inventive power on other things.

Reflective Text

REYNER BANHAM, "ORNAMENT AND CRIME: THE DECISIVE CONTRIBUTION OF ADOLF LOOS."

First Published in 1957

Everyone knows that Modern Architecture is undecorated. This concept is the layman's recognition check: flat roof, big windows, no decoration. It is also one of the great seminal half-truths that have now become rules of design morality. But how did this state of affairs come about? Did the spirit of the times command? Did the *Zeitgeist,* like a baroque angel, swoop down to stay a thousand pencils as they held poised above the beginning of an Ionic volute or an Art Nouveau lily?

In this particular case we can put these art-historical miasmas back where they belong, and recognize that they are the cloaks of ignorance. Ideas do not bumble about in the abstract, looking for somewhere to settle. They are formulated in the minds of men, and communicated from man to man. The *Zeitgeist* is primarily a record of our ignorance of the communications that took place in any particular epoch—grandiose statements of the order of "Perspective was not the discovery of anyone person, it was the expression of the whole era," are simply a roundabout way of admitting that we don't know to whom Brunelleschi talked before he talked to Manetti, and that we would rather not go to the labour of drawing up the family tree of personal contacts that runs from Brunelleschi to all the great perspectivists of the Quattrocento.

We are a bit too glib in presupposing diffuse cultural forces that act upon creative minds like the weather or the common cold, and a little too chary of conceding that some one specific person at some determined (if no longer determinable) moment must have been the first to conceive of central perspective, the undulating façade, architecture without ornament.

To us, now, the idea of an undecorated architecture has so nearly the status of a Mosaic commandment, to be flouted in practice but never queried in theory, that it is difficult to conceive of it as the thought of one man, and much easier to refer it back to the collective, unconscious of the pioneers of Modem design. But the surviving literary evidence from the first twenty years of this century does not reveal any widely diffused hostility to decoration. There were ideas like Significant Form that were later to reinforce such a hostility when it had taken hold; there was a certain suspicion of past styles of decoration; there was even a certain indifference to ornament, articulated by Geoffrey Scott and earlier by Auguste Choisy, as the feeling that ornament was something that one might do without if one's command of formal composition was sufficiently sure. But only in the writings of one man, the Viennese architect Adolf Loos, will one find a positive anathema on ornament.

Did Adolf Loos, then, beat ornament single-handed? He certainly thought so himself, for he wrote in the introduction to his book *Trotzdem*, published in 1930, "I have emerged victorious from my thirty years of struggle. I have freed mankind from superfluous ornament." This is an uncommonly big claim even for a big-talking movement like Modem Architecture, and it needs scrutiny. But scrutiny will be facilitated if we look first at the weapons with which he fought. The example of his buildings was not decisive—their exteriors are sometimes, but not always, plain; the interiors, though devoid of decorative objects for the most part, exhibit almost a milliner's sense of the decorative qualities of wood and marble, fair-face brick, turkey carpets, glass and metal. His doughtiest blows at ornament were struck in print, and the doughtiest of all in one single essay, published in 1908.

Its title is an eye-blacker for a start, *Ornament und Verbrechen:* Ornament and Crime. It brings the reader up with a jerk and sets his stock responses jangling. It is probably the first appearance of that pugnacious moral tone that was to characterize the writings of the Twenties and Thirties, and the opening paragraphs fully sustain this bourgeois-blasting, damn-your-delicate-feelings attitude.

This is still a tremendous performance nearly a half-century after its composition. . . . But it won't stand re-reading. This is *Schlagobers-Philosophie*, that whisks up into an exciting dish on the café table, and then collapses as you look at it, like a cooling soufflé. It is not a reasoned argument but a succession of fast-spieling double-takes and non-sequiturs holding together a precarious rally of clouds of witness—café-Feudalism, café-anthropology, café-criminology. The testimonies of these various witnesses don't really support one another, but they must have appeared convincing at the time, partly because they were all new and hot, but more especially for an overriding reason that will be discussed later. But Loos has no intention of giving the reader time to pick the argument to pieces, he wants to detail the poor response that the world made when presented with his "maxim."

"Men of the nineteenth century"—this must mean that the maxim had been enunciated in the [1890s] originally, and at that time, with Viennese Art Nouveau flour-ishing like a rain-forest, it must have sounded more mad than sad. Loos, however, followed it up with Old Testament rhetoric:

Then I said: Weep not. Behold the true greatness of our age, that it can no longer bring forth ornament. We have vanquished decoration and broken through into

> an ornamentless world. Behold. The time is at hand and fulfilment awaits us. Soon the pavements of our cities shall glisten like marble; Like Zion the holy city, the Capital of Heaven.

But no one thanked him. What had gone wrong? Most inevitably, he alleges an Imperialis plot: Certain reactionaries rejected his prophecies, the Austrian state continued to support and subsidize a reign of ornamental terror, retarding progress, making people wear felt boots instead of rational footwear because it had found that a backward people was easier to govern. Some citizens of the Austro-Hungarian Empire were so backward that they had not yet been converted to Christianity, would have been looked down on by the Goths and Visigoths. Happy the country that has no such stragglers! Happy America!

America for Loos, as for so many of the pioneers was the promised land of technology. Not a word about the Indian reservations or the hookworm belt nor the coloured slums of the Northern cities, which he must have seen on his visit to the U.S. Americans were his ideal Twentieth Century men.

What would he have made of a Cadillac economy, where undecorated goods are apt to be in an inaccessible luxury price-bracket, while ornamental products are within the reach of all but the most depressed strata of society? One can guess, for a few paragraphs later he sketches in a satirical draft of a high-obsolescence economy, where everything is highly decorated and thrown away almost as soon as it is made and everyone swims in wealth and well-being. But it is only a satirical view of a vulgar "Land of Cockayne." He is not envisaging it as a way of life that need be taken seriously, nor one that he wants any part in. He exhibits here that peasant streak so common in reformist aesthetes, and can see objects of use only as possessions whose market value must be maintained, not as equipment to be discarded when technically obsolete. Not for him the scrapping economy implicit in Futurism's "Every generation its own house," or Le Corbusier's "On jette, on remplace." In fairness one should note that he could accept expendability in trashy materials: "I can accept papier maché in an artists' club, run up in a couple of days, torn down when the exhibition is over. But to play ducks and drakes with golden sovereigns, to use banknotes to light cigars, to crush pearls and drink them—*das wirkt unästhetisch*."

But in skipping on thus far we have overpassed the vital paragraph that holds the historical key to "Ornament and Crime," and explains the instance of its writing and the immediate power of conviction that it undoubtedly possessed.

> Now that, ornament is no longer, organically integrated into our culture, it has ceased to be a valid expression of that culture. The ornament that is designed to-day has no relevance to ourselves, to mankind at large, nor to the ordering of the cosmos. It is unprogressive and uncreative.
>
> What has happened to the ornamental work of Otto Eckmann? What has happened to van de Velde? The artist used to stand for health and strength, at the

pinnacle of humanity, but the modern ornamentalist is either a cultural laggard or a pathological case. He himself is forced to disown his own work after three years. His products are already unbearable to cultured persons now, and will become so to others in a little time. . . . Modern ornament has neither forbears nor descendants, no past and no future.

That fixes him in time. Where other men of his day may have had an uneasy feeling that Art Nouveau was losing its impetus, he had a personal quarrel with Hoffmann and the *Wiener Sezession,* and any stick would serve to beat the *Wiener Werkstätte*. For all that, it took courage—truculence even—to launch these personal attacks at a time when the world reputation of both *Sezession* and *Werkstätte* were at their height, and had made Vienna a centre of artistic pilgrimage. On the other hand, the crack-up was already signaled. Long-witted operators like Peter Behrens were quietly sloughing off Art Nouveau, and that symptomatic young person Charles Edouard Jeanneret was, in the very year of "Ornament and Crime," telling Josef Hoffmann he could keep his *Werkstätte,* recognizing that it was no longer creative. In articulating his quarrel with the *Sezession,* Loos was polarizing the attitude of a generation to decoration, as surely as Marinetti in the next few months was to polarize its attitude to machinery. In a time of decision his was a decisive gesture.

The decision taken, his position was clear: all forms of cultural regression are crime and waste; ornament is cultural regression and must therefore be a waste and a crime; worse than that, sex-crime. With his position so clearly given, and in such forthright terms, it comes as a further shock to find him hedging the issue with soft options: "I address myself particularly to those natural aristocrats who stand at the summit of human progress, and yet have the deepest understanding of the needs and impulses of lesser men."

Then he goes on to relate a touching parable of the dismay of his shoemaker on being asked to make a pair of utterly plain shoes, even at a third over the price of the normally-ornamented model. Ornament, he says, is the culture of the poor, and we— aristocrats who have Beethoven and Wagner—have no right to deprive them of it. But a cultured man who goes to hear the Ninth Symphony and sits down to design a sampler is either a show-off or a degenerate.

In spite of the slight crescendo for the coda this is still a stingless tail, all passion spent. Nevertheless, "Ornament and Crime" is still good fighting talk. In its author's own eyes it ranks with *Architektur,* written a year later, as one of his two prime writings, but not necessarily as his unique blow against ornament. To revert to the introduction to *Trotzdem,* we find that it continues "Ornament was once synonymous with beautiful, but thanks to my life's work it now means inferior." Life's work, he says, and on the narrow stage of Austria this might be true, but on the wider screen of the Modern Movement at large much of his writing after 1900 went by default for lack of republication on foreign presses. It is on the reprinting history of "Ornament and Crime" that his claim to have liberated mankind must rest.

But it rests securely. Already in the Nineteen-teens it had attracted enough notice outside Vienna to earn republication, first in Herwarth Walden's expressionist magazine, *der Sturm,* in 1912, and then in Georges Besson's sprightly translation in *Les Cahiers d'Aujourdhui* in 1913.

These reprints brought Loos—and the essay—to the notice of an interested if restricted international readership. They also presumably brought Loos's ideas to the notice of the Futurist Sant'Elia, the first writer outside Vienna to be visibly influenced by them—Marinetti, the leader of the Futurists, had contacts with *der Sturm* as well as Parisian circles.

The French version was once more reprinted, unaltered, in No. 2 of *l'Esprit Nouveau.* One should remember that at this early date (March, 1920) *l'Esprit Nouveau* still had a third director beside Ozenfant and Le Corbusier, and while its appeal to those two for its relevance to architecture and design is obvious enough, its appeal to the third director, Paul Dermée, would be equally strong. For though he was a poet, he was also close in with the Dadaists, and one can imagine how gratefully any attempt to equate Beethoven with a cave artist, and a comfort-station muralist, would fall upon the ears of those who were trying to get the Morgue accepted as an object of sentimental interest and had already moustached the Mona Lisa. The reappearance of "Ornament and Crime" while Dada was still going full blast was uncommonly timely, and guaranteed it a favourable hearing at another moment of decision.

For this reprint appeared after Le Corbusier had finished with his flower-box-smothered house-projects of the war years, but before the Villa at Vaucresson that ushered in his new style. It was read, and of this we can be certain, by Erich Mendelsohn, between his first and second Dutch visits; after the decorated Luckenwald factory, and before the undecorated Sternefeld house. It appeared after Gropius's decorated Sommerfeld House had been designed, but before the "reformed" projects and the undecorated Jena theatre, and again we can safely posit communication between Paris and Germany. Riding hard behind this timely reappearance came the publication of Loos's first book of collected essays, *Ins Leere Gesprochen,* which covers the years 1897–1900 only, but shows him in his Plumbing-before-Art-work mood, and remains to this day better known and more widely read than *Trotzdem.*

For, by the time *Trotzdem* appeared, Loos had ceased to be timely. He caught no mood of disgust with *Art Nouveau,* nor any Dadaist mood of disgust with art in general. Not only had the mood changed, but the ideas he had pushed had now been so thoroughly absorbed and understood that they looked more like Laws of Nature than the Works of Man.

All his best ideas had been pirated by younger men. His advocacy of Thonet chairs and *Fauteuils Grandconfort "Maple"* had been so thoroughly taken over by Le Corbusier that Loos began to deride Thonet as *eine falsches Modell* in order to maintain some show of independence. But even the anti-ornament campaign had been plagiarized without acknowledgment, and in the introduction to *Trotzdem* he says, following what has been quoted already, "But even the echo as it answers believes the note to be its own, and that perfidious book *Die Form ohne Ornament*, published in Stuttgart in 1924, conceals my efforts even while it falsifies them."

He might well complain. *Form without Ornament* was the catalogue *de luxe* of a Werkbund exhibition that toured Germany in 1924–25. Its illustrations make a brisk start with Jena glass and Stuttgart soap, but then trail off through such objects as Breuer's early Bauhaus furniture until they wind up with products so arty that they can only be described as *Sezession ohne Ornament*. The impossible, as Loos had seen it, had taken place, and the fine art designers had climbed on the anti-ornamental bandwagon. Wolfgang Pfliederer says, in his introduction to this "perfidious" book, "If we survey the field of artistic handicraft today we find that it is not unified, but draws . . . from two sources . . . Technical form and Primitive form."

Technical Form and Primitive Form. Engineers and peasants had been identified by Loos in that other prime essay, *Architektur*, as the two good, clean form-givers who did not commit the crimes of architects and artists, and to suggest that they might be tributary to the artistic handicrafts was to turn his arguments upside down and inside out. Within three years he was dead anyhow, and rapidly passing into that special limbo of oblivion that is reserved for those who have ideas that are too good to belong to one man alone. He had settled the problem of ornament as Alexander settled the Gordian knot, shockingly but effectively, and his ideas had gained an empire wider than the Macedonian's wildest dream. It is impossible now to imagine how the Modern Movement might have looked as a decorated style, but it might have been just that, had not its creators had ringing in their ears Adolf Loos's challenging equation: Ornament equals Crime.

Philosophical Text

JOSEPH RYKWERT, "ORNAMENT IS NO CRIME."

First Published in 1975

There was a time when the painter and sculptor had a clear idea of their link with the architect: they were all three "visual" artists. The art of the painter and sculptor, however, was imitative of nature: that of the architect was only partially so. Architecture imitated, yes—but imitated culture. Monumental building reproduced the *necessary* forms of a primitive but rickety construction in permanent and noble materials. In so far as it came to imitating nature, it was the proportions of the human body which the architect abstracted in his measurements.

This view of the art of building, consecrated by theorists since Vitruvius (and he had drawn on much older sources) had an enormous vogue at the end of the eighteenth century. With a change of century came a change of attitude, shown by a double attack on the old view. Architecture, some said (with Goethe and the poets), did not imitate primitive construction: architecture imitated nature—the sacred wood, the cave-shrine. In this novel argument the old belief that architecture was based on the proportions of the human body (which had been the mainstay of the advocates of nature) was forgotten. But even this modified form of the natural argument was contradicted by a new and important breed, the Polytechnicians. Architecture, they maintained, did not imitate anything. Architecture was dressed-up construction. The Polytechnicians did not—at any rate at first—ever advocate that construction should appear shamelessly naked. Decency, propriety, convention—society in short—demanded that naked construction be covered, and that covering was ornament.

Ornament had once meant that which makes decent in supplying a missing essential. "Modesty," the French Academy dictionary defines, "is a great ornament of merit." That is not what the Polytechnicians meant. Ornament was not supplying that which was good in itself with its essential complement, but covering the unacceptable. The cover catered to trivial pleasure. Architecture was concerned primarily with necessity, and its true essential beauty depended on a direct and economic satisfaction of man's most urgent physical needs. The beauty of necessity satisfied reason alone; much as the beauty of association and sentiment could appeal only to the imagination. Here was a dichotomy which was to grow more divisive throughout the nineteenth century.

There were two kinds of architecture: that of the poets and that of the Polytechnicians. They often overlapped, and in any case the public came to consider them suitable for different kinds of building. The poets concentrated their attention on historical, and therefore nostalgic, ornament; the Polytechnicians maintained that if beauty must be specially catered for in building, it was through proportion. Not the old musical consonances of universal harmony, dear to Renaissance and Baroque theorists, but three different and separate kinds: that simply derived from the properties of materials, and that derived from economy which is the desire for the greatest possible simplicity of geometry (and justified their insistent use of the circle and square); and, as a mean, that old-fashioned kind of proportion which was associated with classical orders—and therefore with a repertory of decoration—and which was considered *useful* in that it would, by clothing structure with convention, spare the users of the building the shock of the unusual. This last proportion was thought to be of purely local application in Europe and the Mediterranean. Builders in Persia, China or India would have no call for this kind of packaging and could rely on materials and economy alone to furnish them with all they needed.

As the disciples of the Polytechnicians spread throughout Europe, to the Far East, to the American West and to Africa, they carried this doctrine with them. It is, of course, true that the nineteenth century was the great age of applied ornament. But as the century went on, the merely conventional nature of ornament was increasingly evident, and increasingly despised by any vital artist. Even those whose practice involved them in the most elaborate ornamental inventions theorised in terms which were not unsympathetic to the Polytechnicians. There should be no features about a building which are not necessary for convenience, one of them wrote; construction and propriety and all ornament should consist of the enrichment of the essential structure of a building. Such ideas now seem a strange justification for a full-blooded return to the imitation of English architecture in the late fifteenth century. But such theories were advanced as a justification of Gothic and classical, Hindu and Moorish and even Chinese. The appeal was ultimately to the polytechnic justification of ornament as a shock-absorbent package, particularly necessary in an age of structural innovation and functional specialising and diversifying. It was, however, self-destructive in the end, when the justification of ornament by convention would appear threadbare or even cynical. The process was expedited by another, and rather different development: throughout the nineteenth century, artists who had earlier been uprooted from their guilds and gathered into academies were schooled in the disciplines of taste. Art schools grew from the academies at the time when the Polytechnics were created. In the schools, artists shifted their attention from creating objects intended to edify, move or excite the spectator, and concentrated on an authentic expression of individual vision, in which the artist's relation to the spectator *through* the object became increasingly less important, as artists moved into that kingdom which has come to be known as Bohemia.

There were protests. The Pre-Raphaelites made stained glass and tapestries for William Morris. Puvis de Chavannes painted a fresco-cycle in the Paris Pantheon. But these were exceptions. The view of ornament as a conventional dressing was welded to a notion of style. A style was conceived from about the middle of the century onwards as a complete and integral "expression" of an epoch. It was, of course, most easily characterised by its surface features, its ornament.

Although various attempts had been made to devise a repertory of new ornament for the coming epoch, these were hampered by the kind of devaluation I have described. Some of the more adventurous innovators conceived an ideal point in time such as fifteenth-century England or Renaissance Italy to which architects might return, since it was a point of fusion; and took original development beyond it, first having achieved a satisfactory emulation of the chosen historical style.

The final attempt to create the total artistic vesture for the new age lasted about fifteen years in all. It had various names: Art Nouveau, Jugendstil, Stile Liberty and so on. At its height, one of the most influential architects of the time wrote: "there is no doubt that the point may and shall be reached when nothing visible will be created without receiving an *artistic* baptism."

It is a good description of tensions. But, of course, the aim was soon seen to be unattainable. And this gave rise to the final triumph of the Polytechnicians in a destructive attack on all ornament. It was summarised in the essay "Ornament and Crime" by the Austrian architect, Adolf Loos, which first appeared in 1908, the argument of which was insistently recapitulated through his work. To Loos pleasure in architecture is—ultimately—pleasure of the imagination; but it is the whole architectural object which must engage the imagination, having also satisfied reason, however. For Loos, the only ornament which is licit is that which expresses the maker's pleasure: of the upholsterer (mouldings and brass-work on furniture), of the nomadic carpet-weaver (patterns in oriental carpets), and the shoemaker (brogue shoes). It is an expression of the maker's pleasure, *not* a concession which indulges the user's eye. True pleasure in one's surroundings for the civilised man (defined by Loos as a man who listens to Beethoven's Ninth or to *Tristan)* is in the smooth texture of objects designed to perform their job with least fuss: the saddle, the smooth silver cigarette-case are examples obviously liked, as he liked the products of engineering and industry. They cater to the pleasures of reason and of the senses. Ornament—all art in fact—had its origin in the obscene, magical scrawl of the cave-dweller. The art of modern man is not concerned with the instinctive needs which were satisfied by such daubs, but is addressed to the higher faculties. In so far as architecture has to do with feeling and imagination, it is the whole mass of the building which does so, not any of its details.

Loos was not entirely consistent, but his attack was symptomatic, and was echoed by other writers. The sociologist Georg Simmel, for instance, writing in the same year as

Loos, in 1908, suggested that ornament, being related to the individuation of objects, may subsist in craft, but is out of place in industrial production, and must in any case be identified with the greatest possible "generalization" since style and elegance depend on the lack of individuality.

Within a matter of months of the publication of that fateful essay on Ornament and Crime, the man who Loos sometimes regarded as his arch-enemy was commissioned to design a theatre in Paris. This theatre was to be an epic building. Van de Velde recounts the story in circumstantial detail in his memoirs, though, he did not finish it of course: the original project was modified by Auguste Perret, who had been invited as a concrete expert, and ended by ousting van de Velde as van de Velde had ousted the previous architect, Roger Bouvard. The men who had maintained their part in the building, however, through the three architects' régimes were the painter Maurice Denis, a pupil of Cézanne, who had been commissioned from the outset of the whole enterprise to paint the auditorium ceiling (and acted as its impresario), and the sculptor, Antoine Bourdelle, who was to do the panels on the façade and the decorations of the foyer. The decorative continuity, which had been van de Velde's main preoccupation, was broken by Perret. For the flowing Art Nouveau lines, for the broken and coruscating surfaces, he substituted a smooth, severe, clipped, "French-classical" manner, much more to the taste of the committee which had originally commissioned the theatre than van de Velde's decorations. The divisions it marked between the articulations and the artists' works were also more to the taste of Bourdelle and Denis. And it marks a break in European taste from which there was no going back.

Perret, of course, had used ornament before, in the elaborate flower-design ceramic facing of his own flats in the rue Franklin, which was done in 1902–03; there, he already declared his independence of the current Art Nouveau linearities, his faith in a new material, reinforced concrete. He used it as a skeleton, inducing a modular severity which he chose to interpret in a "classical" fashion. But the abundant use of sculpture and painting in the Théâtre des Champs Elysées was not something he normally favoured; here it was part of the commission, and Bourdelle and Denis were there before him. He was to work with Denis again on the church of Our Lady at Raincy, done in 1922–23, where Denis was responsible for the coloured windows which fill the panels between the shorn and elongated classical colonettes. Although he went on designing churches based on the Raincy idea, this was the only other time he willingly collaborated with an artist of importance. "That which is beautiful does not need decoration, since it decorates," he used to say, according to an admirer: and so elided the problem. (Perret meant something more like "dignifies" or "gives decorum" than the English word "decorate.") And, of course, in the twenties a rather specious distinction grew up between the work of sculptors or painters, "works of art" used "decoratively" and the repetitive ornament produced by mere craftsmen. Perret did use both, and that in spite of his noble aphorism. He never wholly abjured the hammered and inlaid ornament of the shorn classicism I spoke of—even after the last war, in the reconstruction of Amiens and Le Havre, he did not renounce the detached colonnades, the apparatus of details derived from the style of *le grand siècle*. In the meanwhile, his old opponent van de Velde had become converted to a similar creed, if not a similar manner; the belief, as he put it, that "the rational conception produced the silex or cut onyx tools and weapons . . . [it] is the inexhaustible, and ever-cool source of all that strain, which—through the ages—has born witness to the existence and constant vitality of a style which never ages, which is and shall be of every age."

It was this ageless modern style which van de Velde was introducing to the Paris public by way of comment and almost of protest at the time of the decorative art exhibition in Paris in 1925. That exhibition was as much the apogee of Art Deco as the 1902 Turin show was of Art Nouveau. And the whole of what came to be called the Modern Movement was a protest against its pervasive influence.

Now the Modern Movement eschewed ornament with the greatest acerbity. But it did not quite dispense with the more or less 'decorative' work of art. Mies van der Rohe, the harshest of the Modern Movement formalists, not only employed sculptures by Kolbe and Lehmbruck as the only photographable inhabitants of his building, but also modelled the figures in his drawings on Lehmbruck's sculptures. Le Corbusier employed work by Jacques Lipschitz and by Léger, and in his later work—*faute de mieux* sometimes, as he himself knew—his own paintings and even sculptures. Of one building of that period, the Spanish pavilion at the Paris exhibition of 1937, little is remembered. But the painting which was specially done for it. Picasso's *Guernica*, has become the best-known single twentieth-century image. It also contained the mysterious painting by Miró (*Rebellious Catalan peasant* or *The Reaper*) and the mercury fountain by Calder, which stood before it, is fairly well known. The building itself deserved better than to become the Sistine Chapel of the twentieth century. But it is entirely dwarfed by the works of art which it sheltered, and which were in part commissioned by the architects and sometimes—as was the case with the mercury fountain—even attributed to them. Such buildings represent the upper tip of what you might call "architects' architecture" for the thirties. The minor masters were, of course, much more thorough in their eschewing of the visual "irrelevance." The generalised belief that whatever was beautiful did not need to decorate because it was itself *décor* was extended. It was beautiful because it served its purpose most directly. And therefore that which served its purpose most directly could in itself turn into an object *à émouvoir*; the archetype of such an object was, of course, the technological product, which had radically altered the means at the artists' disposal in the twentieth century. It had been regarded as a slave until the middle of the nineteenth, when it became an enemy. The volume of technological objects grew, however, and the dialogue with machine production altered in tone. The enemy of the nineteenth century became the master, the *deus* (doubly you might say) *ex machina*. God-created (as against man-created) nature became muted, trivialised. The menace to twentieth-century urban man was no longer drought, storm and flood. The great dangers came from a different nature: from the boom–crisis economy, from the methods of secret persuasion and of oppression, and from the omnipresent destructive forces we have devised: gases, bacteria, nerve-drugs in drinking-water, the BOMB; or even from the increasing malfunctioning of our ingenuities: pollution, overcrowding, jamming, the rising flood of detritus.

Artists were not able to absorb the technological product into their work and had therefore to account for it by irony: naming, indicating and quoting. It started gently with collage and frottage, and was speeded up by R. Mutt's famous fountain choice—of which so much has already been said. This attempt to absorb the industrial and exalt it into culture was a much more powerful and hazardous piece of magic than we can now realise. But the magic wore off (with the war), and had to be renewed. The efforts ranged from solipsist inflatable defiance to the total immersion of Ulm; from the admiring imitations of Tinguely to the rebarbative *longuers* of Warhol. The work of the artists stood apart from the rational normality of what was built and inhabited. Buildings increasingly became images of technical production, from which the world of the imagination was banished. But while the artist had less and less truck with society—and therefore with rationality—architects and designers strove earnestly to assimilate their procedure to that of the mechanic. In the heroic days of De Stijl, of the Russian Constructivists and, to some extent, in the later years of the Bauhaus, the very leap into the realm of quantity was exciting by the desperate nature of the exercise. Unfortunately, its consequence was anything but exhilarating. The pressing of all imaginative effort into the mould of pseudo-rationalism (of the particularly naïve positivist brand which went on in the late thirties and immediately after the war) has convinced the architect's most important clients, the world's various civil services and the boards of the large companies, that the answer to their problems in terms of what is now called "built form" (that is, architecture and building) will be a good social service provided that they are presented in tabulated form, and the quantities show some positive result, however dottily calculated. Hence the various products of "systems design" and its even dottier by-products (some of which, such as the work of the Ulm school) have even entered the murky penumbra of modern mythology.

Production is the result of our dialogue with nature: and the process of dialogue and production is what we call culture. Not an adequate definition perhaps, but it does something to tie up the diverse dictionary meanings of worship, tillage, selective breeding, training and education; and distinguishes it from the towny, even bourgeois qualities of civilisation. The truth is that technology is "Son of Culture," as they say in the titles of horror films, but culture has not learnt to take account of its vast offspring, at any rate not on a conscious level. The sad, playful attempts in the forties and fifties of our century to produce a generally acceptable and machine-based (as well as machine-made) ornament is a warning of the futility of any short-cuts. We are witnessing a similar and equally futile exercise just now: the revival of what has been called the "Cinema Style"; the ornamental jollities of Odeon cinemas and Lyons Corner Houses in this country aping the majority of twenties and early thirties skyscrapers in the U.S. But the revival raises the problem, which derives from a sub-cultural phenomenon: the shift in the social pattern of taste to a dictatorship of the working-class, more specifically the Anglo-Saxon working-class, which was exemplified by the cult of the Beatles and the Stones, and the graphic style of Alan Aldridge. The style is already past its peak, although its sources—the film strip-cartoon—are a permanent feature of our society, and cater for the same kind of irrational pleasure as the "Cinema Style": the pleasure which appeals through the medium of a market populism; the people like it because they buy it, *ergo* it is good in itself because the people are good. Yet the critical shift from a bourgeois to a working-class cultural mode has made the joys of cinema interiors seem exotically remote.

The attitude has its sociological and by implication (as often happens nowadays) its philosophical apologist in the work of an American sociologist, Herbert Gans, whose *Levittowners* has counterattacked the many critics of American suburbia. It concentrated on the life of a commercial suburban development, one of a successful chain based on mass-produced, relatively cheap housing (marketed in various styles for the same house) by a large industrial building contractor on the East Coast of the States. Levittown—as these suburbs are called—has become a slogan as well as a commercial enterprise. It covers the range of attitudes which maintains that everyone has the right to their life-style provided it is within their means and not actively anti-social; that no pundit has any right to tell them otherwise. And in particular not the planner and architect, whose real business is to provide a suitable packaging for the given life-style, including the ornamental patterns which the inhabitant may choose for himself.

Inevitably, too, the attitude acquired a high culture architect as its advocate. He is the triune person of Robert Venturi, Denise Scott-Brown and John Rauch. On his own, when Robert Venturi wrote *Complexity and Contradiction in Architecture* (1966), he replaced the Miesian paradox "Less is more" with the jibe "Less is a bore." His appeal against the purism of the old Modern Movement, against the uniformities and the boredom of the Masters was to an architecture of variety, and (as the title implied) of visual and volumetric complexity. Lutyens was quoted almost as often as Le Corbusier; and above all "Main Street," which had been the cynosure of so many "Purist" critics (Venturi attacked Peter Blake in particular), messy, disorderly, commercialised Main Street was *almost* all right.

His next step was perhaps foreseeable. If Main Street is almost all right, then it can be made wholly so by putting it in inverted commas. So that is what Venturi did. "Ugly and Ordinary" is how he describes the building he wishes to design. Note the inverted commas, however. Not ugly and ordinary, but "Ugly and Ordinary." These buildings are high culture, to be judged by the same criteria as "architects' architecture," just as the Rolling Stones put themselves between inverted commas when they made *Sympathy for the Devil* with Jean-Luc Godard.

The slogan of the ugly and the ordinary is not intended to be a critical judgment on their architecture, although it derives from a jury comment on a competition scheme of Venturi. Unfortunately, even in their second apologia, *Learning from Las Vegas* (1972), they do not offer a higher transcendental idea than variety as a justification for their approach. No idea there of variety for . . .? Variety is presented as good in itself, and the book sets as many posers as it answers.

Learning from Las Vegas was, you might say, the architectural tail of the comet which had Tom Wolfe as its flashing head. The analytical jeremiads which were the favoured U.S. kind of journalistic sociology, excellently purveyed by Vance Packard and William H. Whyte Jr., had its architectural equivalent in the post-Modern Movement style of Paul Rudolph. Naturally, he became the Venturis' favourite target. But architecture is more expensive than clothes or even customised motor cars, and architectural fashions follow behind other fashion manifestations which are cheaper, more volatile and more sensitive to the change of social tone.

The cult of Levittown as a representative of American suburban life combines the self-sufficiency and individualism of the generation which grew up in the fifties and early sixties and is now saddled with the universal paraphernalia of wife, children, mortgage and job. Levittown makes a premium of individuality within the suburban milieu. The variety which Venturi exalted in *Complexity and Contradiction* is available in Levittown, as it is on the Las Vegas strip, although it is a quite different product from the arcane complexities of Lutyens' plans.

But the counterposition of Las Vegas and of Levittown is interesting for another reason. The study done in *Learning from Las Vegas* deals *only* with the strip. Not a word is said of Las Vegas housing. Though if you look at the Venturis' plans of the town on which the strip is marked for your admiration, you will see that it is virtually square: and yet in the book, the parts of the town beyond the façades of the strip do not appear, except at the edge of one or two aerial photographs. Their attention is entirely focused on the eccentric volumes of the casinos and hotels: but even more, on their signs.

The variety of the neon and other electric signs is, of course, what continues to fascinate so many journalists as well as the architects and designers who make Las Vegas part of their grand tour. And yet Tom Wolfe, who had popularised it, also had, all those many years ago, a warning for them: his first hero of the Las Vegas adventure, whom he called "Raymond" and who—"although not a typical Las Vegas tourist"—is a "good example of the impact Las Vegas had on the senses," demonstrated that the impact, augmented by alternating doses of amphetamine and meprobamate (taken with alcohol), had induced a state of toxic schizophrenia.

The Venturis have now transferred their attention to the much more anodyne varieties of "customised" Levittown housing, which indicates a duality (unresolved and perhaps unresolvable) in approach. On the one hand is the public space of Las Vegas; on the other, the private one of the speculators' suburb. Variety is the one transcendent value to which they pay any service. Yet in the first book there was a pervading assumption that variety had no meaning without a unity to which it is subsumed.

In the later studies there is less talk of unity. In the Las Vegas study there is a crucial attempt to classify all building into two major classes: ducks, that is buildings which are three-dimensional, volumetric envelopes for a given function (a drive-in in the shape of a vast duck was illustrated in a book by Peter Blake, *God's Own Junkyard*, which he ridiculed); and "decorated sheds." Venturi maintains that most modern "architects' architecture" is "ducks" buildings in which the symbolic form is the organising principle of structure, volume and programme. While their validity in the past (Gothic cathedrals) is unquestioned, the Venturis propose as the type of a modern building the decorated shed, in which the shelter is dictated by utilitarian considerations, while the symbolic bits and pieces are stuck on to the front: façades, billboards or signs. Assertively, Venturi has carried his theory out in practice. Decorated sheds, "ugly and ordinary" is what he claims to build, though he also produces the occasional duck: there is after all no ban on ducks in his theory.

The dual classification, with its emphatic preference for the decorated shed, does, however, raise a most important issue; and it may be worth looking at one of their buildings in some detail to state it. This oldish scheme (1967) is useful since it embodies the approach at a level near parody. It is the competition design for the National Football Hall of Fame near the Rutgers Stadium in New Jersey. The scheme is a low (three-storey) vaulted gallery with an atrophied grandstand towards a playing field at the back; but the important feature is the vast electrified billboard (Bill-Ding-Board), the size of a full-size football pitch, more than twice the height of the hall proper, and running its full width. The triangular piazza in front, the building and the pitch are isolated from the surrounding roadways by a parking lot about twice the total area of piazza, building and pitch. The shed is therefore decorated with a vengeance; and isolated in the New Jersey urban sprawl in a way which makes it part of the suburban landscape, camouflaged indeed as an uncritical object among others. Here's the rub. This acceptance of the culture of the shed and the billboard, which *Learning from Las Vegas* has theorised, is an acceptance of the product of technology as the incarnation of some natural force immanent in machine production, it is therefore presented as being outside the critical, judging reach of any cultural criteria. In that way, the Venturi argument is strangely parallel to the Loos argument. Needs dictate the shed: the shed should not be transformed into "sculptured" volume which is more expensive and less directly related to their direct satisfaction. So far the argument has much in common with Loos' more sophisticated justification of engineering works against the tortuous effects of architects' insensitivity to the deeds of men and of nature. But the Venturi argument adds a rather heavy makeweight, which inverts the result. Since variety is an essential human need and buildings need in some way to say what they are, this extra need and the labelling requirement is fully satisfied by sticking the most varied matter on to the building itself: and you have the new architecture, which has moreover the great virtue of looking just like all other buildings.

So concerned are the Venturis to emphasise the unity of their buildings with all that surrounds them that the distinction between the "*almost* all right" of Main Street and the presumably "quite all right" of the Venturis' work is often blurred; though it is probably discernible in the way the ugly and ordinary have been complex and contradictory.

I say this without malice: it is the Venturis' favourite approval words which I have used to qualify their own work. Since they have become the best-known architectural office (among the younger ones) in the Anglo-Saxon world, the whole problem of ornament has now been identified with their formulation of it. But in fact it has been about for some time. Some ten years ago, the Zurich Kunstgewerbemuseum presented the argument for and against the thing visually, through an exhibition. And the problem has been re-appearing in quite different ways. Notoriously, certain architects as different as James Stirling (air-conditioning plant in the History Faculty Library at Cambridge) and Richard Rogers and Renzo Piano (service ducting on the exterior of the Centre Pompidou in Paris) have been using services in a way which suggests that they have formulated the problem, at least to themselves. More crucially, it has been explored by the Viennese group: St. Florian, Pichler, Abraham, Hollein and others. For lack of space, I shall arbitrarily take Hans Hollein as the representative of the group. He has none of the populist propensities of the Venturis, though he, too, is concerned with the ordinary, if not the ugly. In particular, he has elevated the method of ironic choice into an exercise which he has called "Everything is architecture." Among his media, he has included an atomiser for making "instant environment" and a box of varying pills for transforming environment "from inside yourself." Many of his more tangible projects involve the changing of some piece of technology (a sparking plug, an aircraft-carrier) into an enigmatic but architectonic object through a change of scale and context. These buildings are all ornament; the very thing that is anathema to the Venturis. In condemnation of such things, they quote an aphorism of Pugin's (from a book he published in 1843) deploring "ornaments that are actually constructed, instead of forming the decoration of construction." In fact, Pugin meant the aphorism to condemn "decorated sheds" of the kind dear to the Venturis, as the first part of that aphorism makes quite clear: "Architectural features are continuously tacked on to buildings with which they have no connection, merely for what is termed effect."

To tag "Eat Here" on to a cafe or diner is not what Pugin meant by "the decoration of construction" at all. What he did mean is that ornament must be integrated with the way the building is built, as well as the way it is used. The whole unity, as he conceived it, would then become a kind of social operation. This kind of building he set up against the decorated sheds which his contemporaries purveyed. For him then, as it is for me now, the problem of architectural form was not one of packaging: nor could problems of ornament be solved by "sticking" suitable labels on to neutral packaging.

And yet, at the formal level, both the Venturis and Hollein have something in common with an artist whose irony, whose sense of scale, have made him turn to con-structions which are—more or less—urban and monumental complexes: Claes Oldenburg. His technique has always been one of irony: the edible hardened, the metallic made floppy, the household or even the hand-held turned into a vast monument. But always, as he him-self has said, he is concerned with a reversal of expectation in his reshaping of the tangible (tangible–untouchable is a most important pair of opposites for him) commonplace.

This is where, perhaps, the Venturis' design is nearest to being critical, in the only sense which makes architecture worthwhile. Their buildings, unlike the creations of their more successful and more generalising contemporaries, are at their best eminently touchable. Hollein, too, is concerned with this bodily quality: almost obsessively. That may be the most important indicator of the way forward in architecture. And it is a way architects cannot take without the help of the painters and sculptors. If only because we must all acknowledge that, in a negative way at any rate, Loos was right: ornament, as the nineteenth-century architects and critics understood it, is wholly dead, beyond any hope of resurrection. We cannot rely on any kind of convention: the world of tangible form has to be learnt anew. Architects never think of buildings as tangible objects, except at the one direct point of contact, the door-handle. And yet buildings are not only enclosure; they are also extensions of ourselves, like clothing. But being more stable, more permanent, more important in fact, they are subject to the importuning demand that we, and by that I mean everybody, make of objects: that they should enhance, enrich, improve with our handling of them. This, it is increasingly clear, will not be done as long as there is a general social assumption that reasonable returns is all we require of products. On the contrary, they must engage our imagination. And they will not do so until architects and designers have really begun to learn the lessons which the painters and sculptors have to teach; and, moreover, have learnt to work together with them, make use of their work not only as analogue, but also as adornment. But such a development will only be valid if it is seen to be necessary, not gratuitous: as long as it will be seen not as a problem of ornament or not ornament, but as a problem of meaning.

Writing and Discussion Questions

ANALYSIS

1. What was Loos arguing for and against? What excerpt/quotation best represents this?
2. What was Banham arguing for and against? What excerpt/quotation best represents this?
3. What was Rykwert arguing for and against? What excerpt/quotation best represents this?

SYNTHESIS

1. Regarding concepts of ornament, discuss one major difference regarding Loos', Banham's, and Rykwert's texts.
2. Regarding concepts of ornament, discuss one primary commonality regarding Loos', Banham's, and Rykwert's texts.

SELF-REFLECTION

1. For each of the texts, discuss a major issue with which you most agree and most disagree; reflect upon why you hold these views.
2. Select a recent design project, or a current project on which you are working. Discuss the characteristics of the project in regards to ornament, in light of the discussion and texts introduced in this chapter. What attitudes regarding ornament does your work illustrate?

PROSPECTION

1. Select one of the texts listed in the bibliography for this chapter; locate and read it. To what degree is that text and the attitudes it represents still relevant to architecture today and in the near future?

2. What is the role of ornament in architecture today? Is ornament (i.e., aesthetic expression) predominantly a technological, cultural, economic, environmental, or artistic task; some combination of these; or something else? In other words, if a fourth text were added to this chapter, what would the argument be?

Other Readings on Ornament and Austerity

Alberti, Leon B. "Book VI," "Book VII," "Book VIII," and "Book IX," in *On the Art of Building in Ten Books*. J. Rykwert, N. Leach, and R. Tavernor, trans. (Cambridge: MIT Press, 1988), 154–319. First published 1452.

Bloomer, Kent. *The Nature of Ornament: Rhythm and Metamorphosis in Architecture* (New York: W. W. Norton & Company, 2000).

Brolin, Brent C. *Architectural Ornament: Banishment and Return* (New York: W. W. Norton & Co., 2000).

Harries, Karsten. "The Promise of Ornament," in *The Ethical Function of Architecture* (Cambridge: MIT Press, 1997), 50–68.

Hearn, M. Fil. "Decoration and the Integrity of Design," in *Ideas that Shaped Buildings* (Cambridge: MIT Press, 2003), 271–280.

Jones, Owen. *The Grammar of Ornament: Illustrated by Examples from Various Styles of Ornament* (New York: Dorling Kindersley, 2001).

Laugier, Marc-Antoine. "On the Decoration of Buildings," in *An Essay on Architecture*. W. Herrmann and A. Hermann, trans. (Los Angeles: Hennessey & Ingalls, Inc., 1977), 130–133. First published 1753.

Moussavi, Farshid and Kubo, Michael, eds. *The Function of Ornament* (New York: Actar, 2006).

Palladio, Andrea. "On the Ornaments of Doors and Windows," in *The Four Books on Architecture*. R. Tavernor and R. Schofield, trans. (Cambridge: MIT Press, 1997), 61–64. First published 1570.

Riegl, Alois. *Problems of Style: Foundations for a History of Ornament*. Evelyn Kain, trans. (Princeton: Princeton University Press, 1992). First published 1893.

Ruskin, John. "The Lamp of Beauty," in *The Seven Lamps of Architecture* (New York: Dover Publications, 1989), 103–147. First published 1849.

Schafter, Debra. *The Order of Ornament, the Structure of Style: Theoretical Foundations of Modern Art and Architecture* (Cambridge: Cambridge University Press, 2003).

Sullivan, Louis. "Ornament in Architecture," in *Kindergarten Chats and Other Writings* (New York: Dover Publications, 1979), 187–190. First published 1892.

Vitruvius, Marcus. "Book IV," in *The Ten Books on Architecture*. M. Morgan, trans. (New York: Dover, 1960), 99–126. First written 1st century B.C.E.

Wright, Frank L. "Integral Ornament," in *An American Architecture*. E. Kaufmann, ed. (New York: Bramhall House, 1955), 220–228.

Chapter 3

HONESTY and DECEPTION

FIGURE 3.1
Photograph of the exterior
perforated copper panels and
fenestration of the addition to
Sarphatistraat Offices of Het
Oosten, Amsterdam,
Netherlands (1996–2000).
Architect: Steven Holl.

FIGURE 3.2
Photograph taken from the
Dome of St. Peter's of the
trapezoidal and elliptical plan of
the Piazza of St. Peter's, Vatican
City, Rome, Italy (1656–1667).
Architect: Gian Lorenzo Bernini.

INTRODUCTORY DISCUSSION

1. Of the two images above, which better represents the concept of "honesty" in
    architecture? Which better represents "deception" in architecture? Why?
2. What are the various definitions and connotations of the terms "honesty" and
    "deception" in architecture? What are the characteristics of an architecture of
    honesty? What are the characteristics of an architecture of deception?
3. Which is more appropriate in architecture today, honesty or deception?

Introduction

As children, we are often taught that "honesty is the best policy," that lying is unethical. In contrast, we come to learn that some of the most enjoyable games and play activities are filled with deception, e.g., the game of hide-and-seek. We also learn that, in certain settings, surprise, mystery, and ambiguity are desirable. We learn that there is an art to using deception without breaking accepted rules of honesty. This may also be the case in architectural design.

Questions of "truth" in architecture became particularly prominent in the 19th century. Advancements in material and construction technologies were the primary catalysts, namely new forms of iron. Some architects and theorists, in favor of innovation, contended that new systems of construction would, and should, lead to new architectural spaces, uses, and forms. Others, supportive of traditional architecture, felt that technological advancements unsettled the clarity and objectivity of the discipline, a direct threat to the tenets of Classical architecture. Yet others supported hybridization, a combining of new and traditional architectural materials, technologies, and forms. It was the third group who faced the most fervent criticism, assailed from both the proponents of innovation and the proponents of tradition. Hybrid architecture was seen as "dishonest." John Ruskin, a traditionalist, and Eugène Emmanuel Viollet-le-Duc, a modernist, were among the most active architectural voices of the latter 19th century.

Ruskin and Viollet-le-Duc were contemporaries of one another. Ruskin, an English art and architectural theorist and critic, and Viollet-le-Duc, a French architect and architectural theorist and critic, both wrote about the importance of honesty in architecture and wrote against deception. Ruskin's major contribution to architectural theory was a collected set of essays, *The Seven Lamps of Architecture*, first published in 1849. In "The Lamp of Truth," the *original text* for this chapter, Ruskin articulated three types of deceits: structural deceits, surface deceits, and operative deceits. Structural deceits occurred in several forms: members, such as columns, that appear to serve a structural role but do not; the concealment of primary structural members; structural members that appear too weak or "emaciated"; the use of architectural forms that do not convey (or worse, contradict) the vertical or horizontal forces at work; and the use of iron as a reinforcement for masonry. Surface deceits occur when one material is painted to appear as if another material, e.g., painting wood to look like marble; or when using more desirable materials, e.g., marble, as thin veneers attached to less valuable materials, e.g., brick. Operative deceits, in the words of Ruskin, resulted from "the substitution of cast or machine work for that of the hand," especially the substitution of hammered iron for cast iron. Ruskin did, however, note exceptions to each of the architectural "sins" he discussed. Painting, for example, was acceptable as long as it was integrated with the architectural form and that the architecture is clearly identified as being painted (such as the ceiling of the Sistine Chapel). Likewise, he acknowledged that concealing some structural elements and material assemblies may be necessary: "The architect is not *bound* to exhibit structure, nor are we to complain of him [or her] for concealing it." This illustrates that, in architecture, the boundaries of honesty and deception are not easily delineated, even for adamant proponents of "truth" like Ruskin. This opened room for debate, especially in regards to the use of contemporary building materials.

Like Ruskin, structural and material honesty and deception were themes discussed by Viollet-le-Duc in a series of lectures later titled *Discourses on Architecture*, first published in 1863. Where Ruskin showed concern and trepidation regarding the use of new materials, Viollet-le-Duc asserted that the use of contemporary materials and technologies contributed to making an architecture of "originality" and "of the present day." These themes were especially prevalent in "Lecture X: On Method," the *reflective text* for this chapter. Here, Viollet-le-Duc stressed two aspects of architectural design: architects "must be true in respect of the programme, and true in respect of the constructive processes." To ensure these, Viollet-le-Duc recommended a four-step design methodology that closely followed theories put forth by philosopher René Descartes:

1. To accept as true only that which could be proven as such, and to proceed with factual, rigorous logic.
2. To divide the project/problem into as many parts as possible, or what Viollet-le-Duc described as "analysis pushed to its extreme limits."
3. To begin with the concepts or "objects which are simplest and most easy to understand" and to progress incrementally toward more complex, synthetic, and "composite" knowledge and architecture.[1]
4. To review and examine "every field of inquiry" applicable to the project in order to "be certain of omitting nothing."

1. In this case, "composite" architecture referred to the synthesis of the aforementioned—program and construction—not to stylistic or formal composites, which Viollet-le-Duc adamantly opposed.

The refinement, transformation, and bringing together of materials into built form is a longstanding discussion in architecture. It is a theme encapsulated in Fil Hearn's "Truth to the Medium: Using Materials," the *philosophical text* of this chapter: Hearn, in addition to discussing the relationships between the theories of Ruskin and Viollet-le-Duc, discussed the diverse attitudes regarding material and construction in the 19th and 20th centuries.

As demonstrated by Hearn, there are diverse forms of expressing, suppressing, or obscuring architectural structures and materials.

Since the mid-19th century, the number of materials and construction technologies available to architects has grown exponentially. New materials have allowed for a variety of new structures, forms, and effects. Once-heavy materials have become light; opacity and transparency have given way to translucency; and structure, space, and form have become increasingly separate from one another. By way of what appears to be an architectural game, the line between honesty and deception has become more ambiguous. We are also left to question which is more desirable: honesty or deception?

Original Text

JOHN RUSKIN, "THE LAMP OF TRUTH."

First Published in 1849

We are too of much in the habit of looking at falsehood in its darkest associations, and through the colour of its worst purposes. That indignation which we profess to feel at deceit absolute, is indeed only at deceit malicious. We resent calumny, hypocrisy, and treachery, because they harm us, not because they are untrue. Take the detraction and the mischief from the untruth, and we are little offended by it; turn it into praise, and we may be pleased with it. And yet it is not calumny nor treachery that do the largest sum of mischief in the world; they are continually crushed, and are felt only in being conquered. But it is the glistening and softly spoken lie; the amiable fallacy; the patriotic lie of the historian, the provident lie of the politician, the zealous lie of the partizan, the merciful lie of the friend, and the careless lie of each man to himself, that cast that black mystery over humanity, through which we thank any man who pierces, as we would thank one who dug a well in a desert; happy, that the thirst for truth still remains with us, even when we have willfully left the fountains of it. . . .

We may not be able to command good, or beautiful, or inventive, architecture; but we *can* command an honest architecture. . . .

Architectural Deceits are broadly to be considered under three heads:

1st. The suggestion of a mode of structure or support, other than the true one. . . .

2nd. The painting of surfaces to represent some other material than that of which they actually consist. . . .

3rd. The use of cast or machine-made ornaments of any kind.

Now, it may be broadly stated, that architecture will be noble exactly in the degree in which all these false expedients are avoided. Nevertheless, there are certain degrees of them, which, owing to their frequent usage, or to other causes, have so far lost the nature of deceit as to be admissible; as, for instance, gilding, which is in architecture no deceit, because it is therein not understood for gold; while in jewellery it is a deceit, because it is so understood, and therefore altogether to be reprehended. So that there arise, in the application of the strict rules of right, many exceptions and niceties of conscience; which let us as briefly as possible examine.

1ST. STRUCTURAL DECEITS[2]

I have limited these to the determined and purposed suggestion of a mode of support other than the true one. The architect is not *bound* to exhibit structure; nor are we to complain of him for concealing it, any more than we should regret that the outer surfaces of the human frame conceal much of its anatomy; nevertheless, that building will generally be the noblest, which to an intelligent eye discovers the great secrets of its structure, as an animal form does, although from a careless observer they may be concealed. In the vaulting of a Gothic roof it is no deceit to throw the strength into the ribs of it, and make the intermediate vault a mere shell. Such a structure would be presumed by an intelligent observer, the first time he saw such a roof; and the beauty of its traceries would be enhanced to him if they confessed and followed the lines of its main strength. If, however, the intermediate shell were made of wood instead of stone, and whitewashed to look like the rest—this would, of course, be direct deceit, and altogether unpardonable.

There is, however, a certain deception necessarily occurring in Gothic architecture, which relates, not to the points, but to the manner, of support. The resemblance in its shafts and ribs to the external relations of stems and branches, which has been the ground of so much foolish speculation, necessarily induces in the mind of the spectator a sense or belief of a correspondent internal structure; that is to say, of a fibrous and continuous strength from the root into the limbs, and an elasticity communicated *upwards,* sufficient for the support of the ramified portions. The idea of the real conditions, of a great weight of ceiling thrown upon certain narrow, jointed lines, which have a tendency partly to be crushed, and partly to separate and be pushed outwards, is with difficulty received; and the more so when the pillars would be, if unassisted, too slight for the weight, and are supported by external flying buttresses, as in the apse of Beauvais, and other such achievements of the bolder Gothic. Now, there is a nice question of conscience in this, which we shall hardly settle but by considering that, when the mind is informed beyond the possibility of mistake as to the true nature of things, the affecting it with a contrary impression, however distinct, is no dishonesty, but, on the contrary, a legitimate appeal to the imagination. For instance, the greater part of the happiness which we have in contemplating clouds, results from the impression of their having massive, luminous, warm, and mountain-like surfaces; and our delight in the sky frequently depends upon our considering it as a blue vault. But, if we choose, we may know the contrary, in both instances and easily ascertain the cloud to be a damp fog, or a drift of snow flakes; and the sky to be a lightless abyss. There is, therefore, no dishonesty, while there is much delight, in the irresistibly contrary impression. In the same way, so long as we see the stones and joints, and are not deceived as to the points of support in any piece of architecture, we may rather praise than regret the dexterous artifices which compel us to feel as if there were fibre in its shafts and life in its branches. Nor is even the concealment of the support of

2. *Aesthetic* deceits, to the eye and mind, being all that are considered in this chapter— not practical roguery.

the external buttress reprehensible, so long as the pillars are not sensibly inadequate to their duty. For the weight of a roof is a circumstance of which the spectator generally has no idea, and the provisions for it, consequently, circumstances whose necessity or adaptation he could not understand. It is no deceit, therefore, when the weight to be borne is necessarily unknown, to conceal also the means of bearing leaving only to be perceived so much of the support as is indeed adequate to the weight supposed. For the shafts do, indeed, bear as much as they are ever imagined to bear, and the system of added support is no more, as a matter of conscience, to be exhibited, than, in the human or any other form, mechanical provisions for those functions which are themselves unperceived.

But the moment that the conditions of weight are comprehended, both truth and feeling require that the conditions of support should be also comprehended. Nothing can be worse, either as judged by the taste or the conscience, than affectedly inadequate supports–suspensions in air, and other such tricks and vanities.[3]

With deceptive concealments of structure are to be classed, those still more blameable, deceptive assumptions of it—the introduction of members which should have, or profess to have, a duty, and have none. One of the most general instances of this will be found in the form of the flying buttress in late Gothic. The use of that member is, of course, to convey support from one pier to another when the plan of the building renders it necessary or desirable that the supporting masses should be divided into groups; the most frequent necessity of this kind arising from the intermediate range of chapels or aisles between the nave or choir walls and their supporting piers. The natural, healthy, and beautiful arrangement is that of a steeply sloping bar of stone, sustained by an arch with its spandril carried farthest down on the lowest side, and dying into the vertical of the outer pier; that pier being, of course, not square, but rather a piece of wall set at right angles to the supported walls, and, if need be, crowned by a pinnacle to give it greater weight. . . . In later Gothic the pinnacle became gradually a decorative member, and was used in all places merely for the sake of its beauty. There is no objection to this; it is just as lawful to build a pinnacle for its beauty as a tower; but also the *buttress* became a decorative member; and was used, first, where it was not wanted, and, secondly, in forms in which it could be of no use, becoming a mere tie, not between the pier and wall, but between the wall and the top of the decorative pinnacle, thus attaching itself to the very point where its thrust, if it made any, could not be resisted. . . . There are hardly any of the magnificent and serene methods of construction in the early Gothic, which have not, in the course of time, been gradually thinned and pared away into these skeletons, which sometimes indeed, when their lines truly follow the structure of the original masses, have an interest like that of the fibrous framework of leaves from which the substance has been dissolved, but which are usually distorted as well as emaciated, and remain but the sickly phantoms and mockeries of things that were. . . .

Perhaps the most fruitful source of these kinds of corruption which we have to guard against in recent times, is one which, nevertheless, comes in a "questionable shape," and of which it is not easy to determine the proper laws and limits; I mean the use of iron.

3. Four lines are here suppressed, of attack by Mr. Hope on St. Sophia, which I do not now choose to ratify, because I have never seen St. Sophia; and of attack by myself on King's College Chapel, at Cambridge, which took no account of the many charming qualities possessed through its faults, nor of its superiority to everything else in its style.

The definition of the art of architecture . . . is independent of its materials. Nevertheless, that art having been, up to the beginning of the present century, practised for the most part in clay, stone, or wood, it has resulted that the sense of proportion and the laws of structure have been based, the one altogether, the other in great part, on the necessities consequent on the employment of those materials; and that the entire or principal employment of metallic framework would, therefore, be generally felt as a departure from the first principles of the art. Abstractedly there appears no reason why iron should not be used as well as wood; and the time is probably near when a new system of architectural laws will be developed, adapted entirely to metallic construction. But I believe that the tendency of all present sympathy and association is to limit the idea of architecture to non-metallic work; and that not without reason.[4] For architecture being in its perfection the earliest, as in its elements it is necessarily the first, of arts, will always precede, in any barbarous nation, the possession of the science necessary either for the obtaining or the management of iron. Its first existence and its earliest laws must, therefore, depend upon the use of materials accessible in quantity, and on the surface of the earth; that is to say, clay, wood, or stone: and as I think it cannot but be generally felt that one of the chief dignities of architecture is its historical use, and since the latter is partly dependent on consistency of style, it will be felt right to retain as far as may be, even in periods of more advanced science, the materials and principles of earlier ages.

But whether this be granted me or not, the fact is, that every idea respecting size, proportion, decoration, or construction, on which we are at present in the habit of acting or judging, depends on presupposition of such materials: and as I both feel myself unable to escape the influence of these prejudices, and believe that my readers will be equally so, it may be perhaps permitted to me to assume that true architecture does not admit iron as a constructive material, and that such works as the cast-iron central spire of Rouen Cathedral, or the iron roofs and pillars of our railway stations, and of some of our churches, are not architecture at all. Yet it is evident that metals may, and sometimes must, enter into the construction to a certain extent, as nails in wooden architecture, and therefore, as legitimately, rivets and solderings in stone; neither can we well deny to the Gothic architect the power of supporting statues, pinnacles, or traceries by iron bars; and if we grant this, I do not see how we can help allowing Brunelleschi his iron chain around the dome of Florence, or the builders of Salisbury their elaborate iron binding of the central tower. If, however, we would not fall into the old sophistry of the grains of corn and the heap, we must find a rule which may enable us to stop somewhere. This rule is, I think, that metals may be used as a *cement,* but not as a *support.* For as cements of other kinds are often so strong that the stones may easier be broken than separated, and the wall becomes a solid mass, without for that reason losing the character of architecture, there is no reason why, when a nation has obtained the knowledge and practice of iron work, metal rods or rivets should not be used in the place of cement, and establish the same or a greater strength and adherence, without in any wise inducing departure from the types and system of architecture before established; nor does it make any difference, except

4. "Present" (*i.e.* of the day in which I wrote), as opposed to the ferruginous temper which I saw rapidly developing itself, and which, since that day, has changed our merry England into the Man in the Iron Mask.

77

as to sightliness, whether the metal bands or rods so employed be in the body of the wall or on its exterior, or set as stays and cross-bands; so only that the use of them be always and distinctly one which might be superseded by mere strength of cement; as for instance if a pinnacle or mullion be propped or tied by an iron band, it is evident that the iron only prevents the separation of the stones by lateral force, which the cement would have done, had it been strong enough. But the moment that the iron in the least degree takes the place of the stone, and acts by its resistance to crushing, and bears superincumbent weight, or if it acts by its own weight as a counterpoise, and so supersedes the use of pinnacles or buttresses in resisting a lateral thrust, or if, in the form of a rod or girder, it is used to do what wooden beams would have done as well, that instant the building ceases, so far as such applications of metal extend, to be true architecture.[5]

The limit, however, thus determined, is an ultimate one, and it is well in all things to be cautious how we approach the utmost limit of lawfulness; so that, although the employment of metal within this limit cannot be considered as destroying the very being and nature of architecture, it will, if extravagant and frequent, derogate from the dignity of the work, as well as (which is especially to our present point) from its honesty. For although the spectator is not informed as to the quantity or strength of the cement employed, he will generally conceive the stones of the building to be separable; and his estimate of the skill of the architect will be based in great measure on his supposition of this condition, and of the difficulties attendant upon it: so that it is always more honourable, and it has a tendency to render the style of architecture both more masculine and more scientific, to employ stone and mortar simply as such, and to do as much as possible with their mere weight and strength, and rather sometimes to forego a grace, or to confess a weakness, than attain the one, or conceal the other, by means verging upon dishonesty. . . .

2ND. SURFACE DECEITS

These may be generally defined as . . . inducing the supposition of some form of material which does not actually exist; as commonly in the painting of wood to represent marble, or in the painting of ornaments in deceptive relief. . . . But we must be careful to observe, that the evil of them consists always in definitely attempted *deception*, and that it is a matter of some nicety to mark the point where deception begins or ends.

Thus, for instance, the roof of Milan Cathedral is seemingly covered with elaborate fan tracery, forcibly enough painted to enable it, in its dark and removed position, to deceive a careless observer. This is, of course, gross degradation; it destroys much of the dignity even of the rest of the building, and is in the very strongest terms to be reprehended.

The roof of the Sistine Chapel has much architectural design in grisaille mingled with the figures of its frescoes; and the effect is increase of dignity.

In what lies the distinctive character?

In two points, principally:—The first, that the architecture is so closely associated with the figures, and has so grand fellowship with them in its forms and cast shadows,

5. Again the word "architecture," used as implying perfect . . . authority over materials. No builder has true command over the changes in the crystalline structure of iron, or over its modes of decay. The definition of iron by the Delphic oracle, "calamity upon calamity" (meaning iron on the anvil), has only been in these last days entirely interpreted: and from the sinking of the "Vanguard" and "London" to the breaking Woolwich Pier into splinters— two days before I write this note, the "anarchy of iron" is the most notable fact concerning it.

that both are at once felt to be of a piece; and as the figures must necessarily be painted, the architecture is known to be so too. There is thus no deception.

The second, that so great a painter as Michaelangelo would always stop short, in such minor parts of his design, of the degree of vulgar force which would be necessary to induce the supposition of their reality; and, strangely as it may sound, would never paint badly enough to deceive. . . .

Evidently, then, painting, confessedly such, is no deception; it does not assert any material whatever. Whether it be on wood or on stone, or, as naturally will be supposed, on plaster, does not matter. Whatever the material, good painting makes it more precious; nor can it ever be said to deceive respecting the ground of which it gives us no information. To cover brick with plaster, and this plaster with fresco, is, therefore, perfectly legitimate; and as desirable a mode of decoration, as it is constant in the great periods. Verona and Venice are now seen deprived of more than half their former splendour; it depended far more on their frescoes than their marbles. The plaster, in this case, is to be considered as the gesso ground on panel or canvas. But to cover brick with cement, and to divide this cement with joints that it may look like stone, is to tell a falsehood; and is just as contemptible a procedure as the other is noble.

It being lawful to paint then, is it lawful to paint everything? So long as the painting is confessed—yes; but if, even in the slightest degree, the sense of it be lost, and the thing painted be supposed real—no. Let us take a few instances. In the Campo Santo at Pisa, each fresco is surrounded with a border composed of flat coloured patterns of great elegance—no part of it in attempted relief. The certainty of flat surface being thus secured, the figures, though the size of life, do not deceive, and the artist thenceforward is at liberty to put forth his whole power, and to lead us through fields, and groves, and depths of pleasant landscape, and soothe us with the sweet clearness of far off sky, and yet never lose the severity of his primal purpose of architectural decoration.

In the Camera di Correggio of San Lodovico at Parma, the trellises of vine shadow the walls, as if with an actual arbour; and the groups of children, peeping through the oval openings, luscious in colour and faint in light, may well be expected every instant to break through, or hide behind the covert. The grace of their attitudes, and the evident greatness of the whole work, mark that it is painting, and barely redeem it from the charge of falsehood; but even so saved, it is utterly unworthy to take a place among noble or legitimate architectural decoration.

In the cupola of the duomo of Parma the same painter has represented the Assumption with so much deceptive power, that he has made a dome of some thirty feet diameter look like a cloud-wrapt opening in the seventh heaven, crowded with a rushing sea of angels. Is this wrong? Not so: for the subject at once precludes the possibility of deception. We might have taken the vines for a veritable pergola, and the children for its haunting ragazzi; but we know the stayed cloud and moveless angels must be man's work; let him put his utmost strength to it, and welcome; he can enchant us, but cannot betray.

We may thus apply the rule to the highest, as well as the art of daily occurrence, always remembering that more is to be forgiven to the great painter than to the mere decorative workman; and this especially, because the former, even in deceptive portions, will not trick us so grossly; as we have just seen in Correggio, where a worse painter would have made the thing look like life at once. There is, however, in room, villa, or garden decoration, some fitting admission of trickeries of this kind, as of pictured landscapes at the extremities of alleys and arcades, and ceilings like skies, or painted with prolongations upwards of the architecture of the walls, which things have sometimes a certain luxury and pleasureableness in places meant for idleness, and are innocent enough as long as they are regarded as mere toys.

Touching the false representation of material, the question is infinitely more simple, and the law more sweeping; all such imitations are utterly base and inadmissible. It is melancholy to think of the time and expense lost in marbling the shop fronts of London alone, and of the waste of our resources in absolute vanities, in things about which no mortal cares, by which no eye is ever arrested, unless painfully, and which do not add one whit to comfort, or cleanliness, or even to that great object of commercial art—conspicuousness. But in architecture of a higher rank, how much more is it to be condemned! I have made it a rule in the present work not to blame specifically; but I may, perhaps, be permitted, while I express my sincere admiration of the very noble entrance and general architecture of the British Museum, to express also my regret that the noble granite foundation of the staircase should be mocked at its landing by an imitation, the more blameable because tolerably successful. The only effect of it is to cast a suspicion upon the true stones below, and upon every bit of granite afterwards encountered. . . .

Painting, however, is not the only mode in which material may be concealed, or rather simulated; for merely to conceal is, as we have seen, no wrong. Whitewash, for instance, though often (by no means always) to be regretted as a concealment, is not to be blamed as a falsity. It shows itself for what it is, and asserts nothing of what is beneath it. Gilding has become, from its frequent use, equally innocent. It is understood for what it is, a film merely, and is, therefore, allowable to any extent: I do not say expedient: it is one of the most abused means of magnificence we possess, and I much doubt whether any use we ever make of it, balances that loss of pleasure, which, from the frequent sight and perpetual suspicion of it, we suffer in the contemplation of any thing that is verily of gold. I think gold was meant to be seldom seen, and to be admired as a precious thing; and I sometimes wish that truth should so far literally prevail as that all should be gold that glittered, or rather that nothing should glitter that was not gold. Nevertheless, Nature herself does not dispense with such semblance, but uses light for it; and I have too great a love for old and saintly art to part with its burnished field, or radiant nimbus; only it should be used with respect, and to express magnificence, or sacredness, and not in lavish vanity, or in sign painting. Of its expedience, however, any more than that of colour, it is not here the place to speak; we are endeavouring to determine what is lawful, not what is desirable. Of other and less common modes of disguising surface, as of powder of lapis lazuli, or mosaic imitations of coloured stones, I need hardly speak. The rule will apply to all alike, that whatever is pretended, is wrong; commonly enforced also by the exceeding ugliness and insufficient appearance of such methods, as lately in the style of renovation by which half the houses in Venice have been defaced, the brick covered first with stucco, and this painted with zigzag veins in imitation of alabaster. But there is one more form of architectural fiction, which is so constant in the great periods that it needs respectful judgment. I mean the facing of brick with precious stone.

It is well known, that what is meant by a church's being built of marble is, in nearly all cases, of only that a veneering of marble has been fastened on the rough brick wall, built with certain projections to receive it; and that what appear to be massy stones, are nothing more than external slabs.

Now, it is evident, that, in this case, the question of right is on the same ground as in that of gilding. If it be clearly understood that a marble facing does not pretend or imply a marble wall, there is no harm in it; and as it is also evident that, when very precious stones are used, as jaspers and serpentines, it must become, not only an extravagant and vain increase of expense, but sometimes an actual impossibility, to obtain mass of them enough to build with, there is no resource but this of veneering; nor is there any thing to be alleged against it on the head of durability, such work having been by experience found to last as long, and in as perfect condition, as any kind of masonry. It is, therefore, to be considered as simply an art of mosaic on a large scale, the ground being of brick, or any other material; and when lovely stones are to be obtained, it is a manner which should be thoroughly understood, and often practised. Nevertheless, as we esteem the shaft of a column more highly for its being of a single block, and as we do not regret the loss of substance and value which there is in things of solid gold, silver, agate, or ivory; so I think that walls themselves may be regarded with a more just complacency if they are known to be all of noble substance; and that rightly weighing the demands of the two principles of which we have hitherto spoken——Sacrifice and Truth,—we should sometimes rather spare external ornament than diminish the unseen value and consistency of what we do; and I believe that a better manner of design, and a more careful and studious, if less abundant, decoration would follow, upon the consciousness of thoroughness in the substance. . . . It is thus true that there is no falsity, and much beauty, in the use of external colour, and that it is lawful to paint either pictures or patterns on whatever surfaces may seem to need enrichment. But it is not less true, that such practices are essentially unarchitectural. . . . The true colours of architecture are those of natural stone, and I would fain see these taken advantage of to the full. Every variety of hue, from pale yellow to purple, passing through orange, red, and brown, is entirely at our command; nearly every kind of green and grey is also attainable; and with these, and pure white, what harmonies might we not achieve? Of stained and variegated stone, the quantity is unlimited, the kinds innumerable; where brighter colours are required, let glass, and gold protected by glass, be used in mosaic—a kind of work as durable as the solid stone, and incapable of losing its lustre by time—and let the painter's work be reserved for the shadowed loggia and inner chamber. . . .

3RD. OPERATIVE DECEITS

The last form of fallacy which it will be remembered we had to deprecate, was the substitution of cast or machine work for that of the hand, generally expressible as Operative Deceit.

There are two reasons, both weighty, against this practice: one, that all cast and machine work is bad, as work; the other, that it is dishonest. Of its badness I shall speak in another place, that being evidently no efficient reason against its use when other cannot be had. Its dishonesty, however, which, to my mind, is of the grossest kind, is, I think, a sufficient reason to determine absolute and unconditional rejection of it.

Ornament, as I have often before observed, has two entirely distinct sources of agreeableness: one, that of the abstract beauty of its forms, which, for the present, we will suppose to be the same whether they come from the hand or the machine; the other, the sense of human labour and care spent upon it. . . . The worth of a diamond is simply the understanding of the time it must take to look for it before it is found; and the worth of an ornament is the time it must take before it can be cut. . . . I suppose that hand-wrought ornament can no more be generally known from machine work, than a diamond can be known from paste; nay, that the latter may deceive, for a moment, the mason's, as the other the jeweller's, eye; and that it can be detected only by the closest examination. Yet exactly as a woman of feeling would not wear false jewels, so would a builder of honour disdain false ornaments. The using of them is just as downright and inexcusable a lie. You use that which pretends to a worth which it has not; which pretends to have cost, and to be, what it did not, and is not. . . . Nobody wants ornaments in this world, but every body wants integrity. . . . Leave your walls as bare as a planed board, or build them of baked mud and chopped straw, if need be; but do not rough-cast them with falsehood.

This, then, being our general law, and I hold it for a more imperative one than any other I have asserted; and this kind of dishonesty the meanest, as the least necessary;[6] for ornament is an extravagant and inessential thing; and therefore, if fallacious, utterly base—this, I say, being our general law, there are, nevertheless, certain exceptions respecting particular substances and their uses.

Thus in the use of brick: since that is known to be originally moulded, there is no reason why it should not be moulded into diverse forms. It will never be supposed to have been cut, and, therefore, will cause no deception; it will have only the credit it deserves. In flat countries, far from any quarry of stone, cast brick may be legitimately, and most successfully, used in decoration, and that elaborate, and even refined. . . . But I believe no cause to have been more active in the degradation of our national feeling for beauty than the constant use of cast-iron ornaments. The common iron work of the middle ages was as simple as it was effective, composed of leafage cut flat out of sheet iron, and twisted at the workman's will. No ornaments, on the contrary, are so cold, clumsy, and vulgar, so essentially incapable of a fine line or shadow, as those of cast-iron; and while, on the score of truth, we can hardly allege any thing against them, since they are always distinguishable, at a glance, from wrought and hammered work, and stand only for what

6. Again too much fuss and metaphysics about a perfectly simple matter; inconclusive besides, for the dishonesty of machine work would cease, as soon as it became universally practised, of which universality there seems every likelihood in these days. The subject was better treated subsequently in my address to the art-students of Mansfield; which I hope presently to reprint, and sum the conditions of verdict, in the preface to the new edition of my "Political Economy of Art."

they are, yet I feel very strongly that there is no hope of the progress of the arts of any nation which indulges in these vulgar and cheap substitutes for real decoration. Their inefficiency and paltriness I shall endeavour to show more conclusively in another place; enforcing only, at present, the general conclusion that, if even honest or allowable, they are things in which we can never take just pride or pleasure, and must never be employed in any place wherein they might either themselves obtain the credit of being other and better than they are, or be associated with the thoroughly downright work to which it would be a disgrace to be found in their company.

Such are, I believe, the three principal kinds of fallacy by which architecture is liable to be corrupted.

Reflective Text

EUGÈNE-EMMANUEL VIOLLET-LE-DUC, EXCERPTS
FROM *DISCOURSES ON ARCHITECTURE*.

First Published in 1863

PREFACE

This is what I propose . . . in [the] treating of Architecture: to inquire into the reason of every form,—for every architectural form has its reason; to point out the origin of the various principles that underlie them, and to trace the logical consequences of those principles, analysing their most typical developments so as to exhibit them with their merits and defects; and, finally, to call attention to the application which can be made of the principles of ancient Art to the requirements of the present day. . . . I must insist upon it that if any of my readers are disposed to believe that I am maintaining principles favourable to one school rather than another, they are mistaken, and my lectures will prove them to be so. I have not taken pen in hand to promote the triumph of a system or to refute theories; I leave this task to those who, while they fancy themselves defending the interests of Art, are for the most part only obeying the passions of the moment. I am contemplating a different object,—the knowledge of the True. . . .

**LECTURE X: ARCHITECTURE IN THE NINETEENTH CENTURY:
IMPORTANCE OF METHOD**

We must not shrink from recognising the fact that in architecture, shackled as we are by prejudice and traditions, and accustomed to confusion, both ideas and principles are wanting to us. The more our buildings are loaded with details, and the richer they are through the variety of their constituent elements, the more do they betray forgetfulness of great principles and the absence of ideas in the artists who contribute to their erection. . . .

Since the Revolution of the last century we have entered on a transitional phase; we are investigating, searching into the past, and accumulating abundance of materials, while our means and appliances have been increased. What then is wanting to enable us to give an original embodiment and form to so many various elements? Is it not simply method that is lacking? In the arts, as in the sciences, the absence of method, whether we are engaged in investigating or in attempting to apply the knowledge we have acquired, occasions an embarrassment and confusion proportional to the increase of our resources; the abundance becomes an obstruction. Every transitional period however must have a limit; it must tend towards an aim of which we get a glimpse only when, weary of searching through a chaos of ideas and materials brought from every quarter, we set to work to disentangle certain principles from this disorderly mass,—to develop and apply them by the help of a determinate method. This is the work that devolves upon us, and to which we should devote ourselves with uncompromising persistency— struggling against those deleterious elements which are invariably engendered during all transitional periods, just as miasmas exhale from matter in a state of fermentation.

The arts are diseased; architecture is dying in the midst of prosperity, notwith- standing the presence of energetic vital principles; it is dying of excesses and a debilitating régime. The more abundant the stores of our knowledge, the more strength and rectitude of judgment is needed to enable us to make a productive use of them, and the more necessary is it to recur to rigorous principles. The disease from which architectural art suffers dates from a remote period; it has not been developed in a single day; we see it increasing from the sixteenth century to our own times; from the time when, after a very superficial study of the architecture of ancient Rome—certain of whose externals were made objects of imitation—our architects ceased to make the alliance of the form with the requirements and the means of construction the chief consideration. Once out of the way of truth, architecture has been more and more misled into degenerating paths. Endeavouring at the commencement of the century to reproduce the forms of classical antiquity, without taking any trouble to analyse and develop their principles, it has been incessantly hastening to its decay. Then, in the absence of the light which reason alone can furnish, it has endeavoured to connect itself with the Middle Ages and the Renaissance; but still only superficially adopting certain forms without analysing them or recurring to their causes, seeing nothing but the effects, it has become *Neo-Greek, Neo-Roman, Neo- Gothic*; it has sought its inspiration in the caprices of the age of Francis I., the pompous style of Louis XIV., and the decadence of the seventeenth century; it has become the slave of fashion to such a degree, that in the bosom of the *Académie des Beaux Arts*,—that classic domain, as it is esteemed,—we have seen designs made presenting the most grotesque medley of styles, fashions, epochs, and means of construction, but not suggesting the least symptom of originality. The reason is that originality is impossible apart from truth. Originality results from the direct irradiation of truth on an individual mind; and though the truth be one, the medium which receives has a refraction happily as infinitely varied as humanity itself. So that whatever efforts may have been made in recent times to bring together such a number of styles and influences, and to satisfy all the caprices of the moment, that which strikes us most in all our modern public buildings is their monotony.

There are in architecture—if I may thus express myself—two indispensable modes in which truth must be adhered to. We must be true in respect of the programme, and true in respect of the constructive processes. To be true in respect of the programme is to fulfill exactly, scrupulously, the conditions imposed by the requirements of the case. To be true in respect of the constructive processes is to employ the materials according to their qualities and properties. What are regarded as questions purely belonging to art, symmetry and external form, are only secondary conditions as compared with those dominant principles. . . .

It is therefore of essential importance to apply a rigorous method to this knowledge of the arts of the past; and I do not know that we can do better in this matter than to abide by the four principles of Descartes, and which he deemed sufficient, "provided," he remarked, "that I made a firm and constant resolution not to neglect them in a single instance." The first, he adds, "was never to receive anything as true which I did not clearly know to be so, *i.e.* carefully to avoid precipitancy and prepossession, and not to include more in my conclusions than what presented itself so clearly and distinctly to my mind that I had no reason to doubt it."

"The second, to divide each of the problems I was investigating into as many portions as possible, or as should be requisite for a complete solution."

"The third, to follow a certain order in my thoughts, beginning with those objects which are simplest and most easy to understand, and ascending as by gentle degrees to the knowledge of the most composite,—supposing an order even in the case of those which do not appear naturally consecutive."

"The last, to make such complete enumerations and general reviews in every field of inquiry as that I should be certain of omitting nothing."

No wiser precepts have been uttered, nor any more applicable to the present subject. If we follow these precepts in the study and practice of art, we shall discover an architecture appropriate to our age, or at least we shall prepare the way for those who follow us; for an art is not made in a day. In fact, if we bring to the study of the arts of the past a spirit of examination sufficiently earnest and enlightened to distinguish the false from the true, and to deduce primordial principles from traditions, we shall in the first place have cleared those arts from the various influences that have successively modified their expression, and we shall succeed in finding those expressions which best accord with immutable principles; we shall then consider these expressions—or forms, if we prefer the term—as those which are nearest the truth. . . .

From a large collection of examples . . . it becomes possible to ascertain what are the forms suitable to such or such a structure; we no longer run the risk of getting into that confusion of styles, methods, and forms which renders most of our modern edifices incomprehensible and repulsive. A certain school, weary of the more or less faithful imitations that have been produced of the various styles of architecture anterior to our age, considers it possible to compose a new architecture by selecting from all of them what has appeared good; this is a dangerous error. A *macaronic* style cannot be a new style. Its adoption gives proof of nothing more than dexterity, intelligence, and acquirements of no great profundity; it is never the manifestation of a principle or an idea. Compositions of this kind, even the most successful, remain isolated, sterile works, incapable of being the origin of a new epoch in the arts. Only simple principles are productive; and it may be remarked that the simpler they are the more beautiful and varied are their products. . . .

PRECEPT 1

Let us return to the precepts given by Descartes: "Never to receive anything as true unless it has been evidently recognised as such." If this precept is applicable to Philosophy, it is still more so to an art such as architecture, which rests on laws of matter or laws purely mathematical. *It is true* that a great hall, a very long, wide, and lofty interior, ought to be lighted by windows larger than those which suffice for an ordinary room; the contrary is false. *It is true* that a portico supported by arcades or columns, is built for the purpose of sheltering persons from rain, sun, and wind; the relations between the height and width of this portico ought therefore to be such as will afford protection against atmospheric agencies; the contrary is false. *It is true* that a door ought to be made for the purpose of going into a building or going out of it; the width of such door ought therefore to be accommodated to the greater or smaller number of persons who have occasion to go in or out; but however dense a crowd may be, the persons composing it are always under seven feet in height; or, supposing them to carry lances, banners, canopies, or flags, even with these accessories, they will not require a height of much more than five or six yards; to make a door five yards wide and ten high is therefore absurd. *It is true* that a column is a support,—not a decoration, like a frieze or an arabesque; if then you have no occasion for columns, I cannot understand why you furnish your façades with them. *It is true* that a cornice is intended to keep the water from the face of the wall: if therefore you put a projecting cornice in an interior, I cannot but say that it is unmeaning. *It is true* that a staircase is necessary for reaching the upper stories of a building: that this staircase is not a place of rest but of passage, and that if you give it a relative importance out of proportion to the apartments to which it leads, you may produce a magnificent flight of steps, but you commit an absurdity. *It is true* that the thing which supports should be proportioned to the thing supported, and that if you build a stone wall or pier two or three yards in thickness to carry floors that would be easily supported by a wall one yard in thickness, you produce a work that cannot be justified by reason, which satisfies neither my eyes nor my understanding, and wastes costly materials. *It is true* that vaulting ought to be maintained by buttresses, whatever form you give them; but it is a falsity to introduce salient pilasters, engaged columns, and buttresses, if there are no thrusts to which resistance must be opposed. It is needless, I think, to continue this parallelism. Following this simple method of reasoning, of which anyone may see the force without being versed in architectural art, and passing in review the styles of architecture adopted by the ancients, in the Middle Ages, and in modern times, it will be easy to assign them their true value.

We shall see that the Greeks (taking into account their social condition and the climate in which their buildings were erected) remained faithful to those primitive principles which originated in mere good sense; that the Romans often deviated from them; that the lay architects of the French school of the twelfth and thirteenth centuries rigorously observed them and that we have almost abandoned them. We may therefore class the various styles of architecture and the studies relating to the monuments produced by them according to that first precept, which is based on the true expression of the requirements and necessities of the structure. Thus a house at Pompeii of insignificant dimensions, the gate of a city, a fountain or a well, may sometimes possess a value superior in point of art to that of a palace. Being thus able to separate the true from the false, we shall succeed after mature examination in recognising the various modes of expressing it employed by our predecessors: for in architecture truth is not sufficient to render a work excellent; it is necessary to give to truth a beautiful or at least appropriate form,—to know how to render it clear, and to express it felicitously;—indeed, in the arts, although we make use of the most rigorous and logical reasoning, we often continue obscure and unpleasing, we may, in fact, produce what is ugly. But while conceptions based on the soundest reason sometimes produce only repulsive works, true beauty has never been attainable without the concurrence of those invariable laws which are based on reason. To every work that is absolutely beautiful there will be always found to correspond a principle rigorously logical.

PRECEPT 2

Having first directed our course of study in conformity with this primary principle, let us pass to the second: "to divide," says Descartes, "each of the problems I was investigating into as many portions as possible, or as should be requisite for a complete solution." We remain here still on the domain of speculative study; we are engaged with analysis pushed to its extreme limits. In fact, if we examine ancient buildings, we find them to be complete, finished, composite works. We are obliged, if we would understand them in all their parts, to proceed in an order the reverse of that in which they were produced. Their author proceeded from his primitive conception to the execution in its final form,—from the programme and the means at disposal to the result; *we* must start from the ultimate result and ascertain successively the design and the programme and means of execution; we must dissect the edifice, as it were, and verify the more or less complete relations that exist between that apparent result which first engages our attention and the hidden methods and reasons that have determined its form. This second part of our studies, which is long, irksome and arduous, is the best exercise we could engage in if we would learn to design, to create. To arrive at synthesis we must necessarily pass through analysis. . . . Since our modern civilisation is very complicated, while it is desirable to commence our studies with the analysis of the simplest works of classical antiquity, we must not stop there; we must certainly go on to analyse more complete works, and learn how in former ages architects succeeded in solving problems more and more extensive in their bearing, encumbered with details and replete with difficulties; and in raising buildings possessing, if I may so express myself, an organism much more delicate, and especially more complicated.

To insist on limiting the studies by which architects are to be trained, to certain monuments of classical antiquity which have not even come down to us in their complete state, or to more or less successful imitations of those monuments, is not the way to obtain what is asked for everywhere—an architecture of the nineteenth century. It is better to take account of that long series of efforts which have developed new principles and methods, and to consider all human labour as a chain whose links are connected in logical order.

PRECEPT 3

The third precept introduces us to the application of principles, for its import is that we should "follow a certain order in our thoughts, beginning with those objects which are simplest and most easy to understand, and ascending as by gentle degrees to the knowledge of the most composite,—supposing an order even in the case of those which do not appear naturally consecutive." In fact, if by analysis we have proceeded from the compound to the simple—from the complete work—the apparent result to the means and causes that have produced this result,—it will become easier, when we are desirous of designing in our turn, to proceed in order, and to give precedence to fundamental considerations with a view to reach the consequences that will follow from them. The fundamental points of consideration in architecture,—those which decide everything else,—are none other than the programme and the material means of execution. The programme is only the statement of the requirements. As regards the means of execution, they are various; they may be restricted or extensive; whatever they are, we must know them and take account of them: the same programme may be complied with by the use of very different means, according to the locality, the materials, and the resources at our disposal.—Great Assembly Halls to hold two thousand persons have to be built in different localities. But at *A* we are furnished with materials of superior quality; considerable sums are placed at our disposal; we have durable stone—marble or granite. At *B* we can procure only brick and wood; our resources are at a minimum. Shall we give these two halls the same superficial extent? Evidently we must, since we have to accommodate two thousand persons at both *A* and *B*. Shall we make them alike in appearance? Certainly not, since the means at our disposal at *B* are not the same as we have at *A*. While thus complying with the same programme we shall have to adopt two very different methods of architecture, for if, having only brick and deal, we simulate a structure of stone or marble, by means of stucco and paint; we make a very sorry use of art. Compliance with a programme and the determining of a plan of structure are not enough to produce a work of art; a form is also requisite. The programme as well as the structure will exert an influence on the form; but while scrupulously respecting the first, and paying attention to the second, we may nevertheless adopt very diverse forms. And which is the one most appropriate to our civilization? Probably that which is most supple and pliable; that which will lend itself the most readily to the infinitely varied details of our excessively complicated life. . . .

Applying the third precept of Descartes in designing, the programme being satisfied and the structure determined, what have we to do in proceeding from the simple to the compound? 1st, We must know at the outset the nature of the materials to be employed; 2dly, We must give these materials the function and strength required for the result, and the forms which most exactly express that function and strength; 3dly, We must adopt a principle of unity and harmony in this expression,—that is, a scale, a system of proportion, a style of ornamentation related to the destination of the structure and having a definite signification, as also the variety indicated by the diverse nature of the requirements to be complied with.

What then is implied in an acquaintance with the materials to be employed in a building? Is it to know whether the stone will resist frost or not? Whether it will bear a certain pressure or not? Is it to be acquainted with the fact that wrought-iron will endure considerable tension, while cast-iron is rigid? Yes, certainly; but it implies more than this. It is to know the effect that can be produced by the use of these materials, according to certain conditions; a stone placed on end, or a monostyle, has a quite different meaning for the eye from that of an erection in courses; a casing of great slabs does not produce the effect of a facing of small flat bedded stones. An arch consisting of extradossed stones has an appearance quite different from that of an arch of notched voussoirs. A jointed lintel has not the strong look of a monolithic lintel. An archivolt of similar section built in several concentric rings, possesses other qualities and produces a different impression from those resulting from one built in a single ring. A perfectly close-jointed masonry, such as that of the Greeks and Romans, suits forms that cannot be made consistent with a masonry between whose joints there is a layer of mortar. Three stones with mouldings, forming a door or window casing, environed by a plastered wall, answer to a necessity, and consequently exhibit an architectural form that is comprehensible and has a good effect; but a casing jointed in horizontal courses shocks reason and the eye. In the same way stone-jointing, which does not coincide with the various architectural members, whose beds are not placed immediately above and below the string-courses, socles, base-mouldings, etc., destroys the effect which a design should produce. To give the materials the function and strength suitable to their purpose, and the forms that most exactly express this function and strength, is one of the most important points in design. We can give a special style, a distinction, to the simplest structure, if we know how to employ the materials exactly in accordance with their purpose. A simple band of stone, placed in a wall, thus becomes an expression of art. A column, a pillar, shaped with due regard to the resisting power of the material in relation to what it has to sustain, cannot fail to satisfy the eye. Similarly a capital whose contour is designed with due regard to that which surmounts it and the function it performs, always assumes a beautiful form. A corbelling which plainly shows its purpose, will always produce a better effect than an undecided form which hides the strength needed by this architectural member. The adoption of a principle of unity and harmony in the expression of the various requirements indicated in a programme,—that is to say, a scale, a system of proportion, a style of ornamentation in harmony with the purpose of this structure, which has a meaning, and which also displays the variety proper to the diverse nature of the requirements to be satisfied,— this is the point in architectural design in which the intelligence of the artist develops itself. When the conditions of the programme have been satisfied, and the system of construction has been determined, when we have been able to apply in our methods a sound process of reasoning, so as to do neither too much nor too little, and to assign to each class of materials the function, appearance, or, if we choose to call it so, the form suitable to its properties and use, we must search for and discover those principles of unity and harmony which should govern every work of art. This is the rock on which nearly all our architects, since the sixteenth century, have made shipwreck; they have either sacrificed the requirements, and the judicious employment of the materials to a form that is symmetrical without being rational, or they have not known how to give an appearance of unity, a *oneness* of conception to the buildings, while satisfying the programme and employing the material judiciously. But since that epoch the first of these defects has certainly been the most frequent, and the one against which architects have been least on their guard. . . .

"This principle of unity and harmony in the expression of the various requirements indicated in a programme" is therefore neither symmetry nor uniformity; still less is it an undigested medley of various styles and forms of which it is impossible to give a rational explanation, even if such a medley were skillfully composed: it is in the first place a rigorous observation of the scale. But what is the scale? It is the relation of all the parts to unity. The Greeks adopted as their scale, not an absolute, but a relative unity,—what is called the *module*; this becomes evident in studying their temples; for it is certain that in their private dwellings the Greeks kept in view the absolute scale, which is the human stature. But regarding it as relative, the scale, by the very fact that it was the module,—that is, a component unity,—established a harmonious relation between the parts and the whole in every building. The Greek temple on the large scale is simply the small one viewed through a magnifying glass. The parts and the whole, in the smaller as in the larger, present the same harmonious relations; a perfectly logical method when the *order* alone constituted the building. We find the Romans, who had to satisfy programmes much more extensive and complicated than those of the Greeks, adopting in their buildings the absolute scale, that is, an invariable unity; only instead of taking the human stature for this invariable unity, it is an *ordonnance* with which they start. In their large scale edifices there is always a small order which serves as a scale, and gives an idea of the real dimension of the whole. . . .

In the best periods of Classic art, the ornamentation, which forms an important part of architectural design, was never anything more than the embellishment of the body after the latter had been completely formed. Now, the ancients employed two modes of ornamentation. The one consisted in not contravening the form adopted, but clothing it with a kind of drapery more or less rich: this was the system employed by the Egyptians, among whom the ornamentation, properly so called (statuary excepted) never presented a projecting outline,—a relief,—but contented itself with enveloping the geometric form as would an embroidered stuff, a diapered covering. The other, on the contrary, was, as it were, independent of the architectural form; it was attached or applied to it, modifying by its projections the particular shape of that form. It was then no longer a drapery spread over the form; it consisted of flowers, leaves, ornaments in relief, designs borrowed from the vegetable and animal kingdoms. . . .

The attempt to reconcile the two systems just described, in architectural design,— that is, embroidering the architectural form in one part and attaching ornaments in another,—is a sin against unity; it is rendering the two systems mutually injurious.

PRECEPT 4

"In the last place," says Descartes, "to make everywhere enumerations so complete and reviews so comprehensive that I may be sure of having omitted nothing." This precept is applicable to studies generally, but still more to the case of architectural design; for it is in the consideration of the programme, of the requirements to be met and of the means supplied that it is desirable to undertake those "so comprehensive reviews." It is not enough to have succeeded in conveniently disposing the services of a public building or a private dwelling; to have succeeded in giving these arrangements the aspect befitting each of them; there must be a connection between the parts: there must be a dominant idea in this assemblage of services; the materials must be judiciously employed, according to the qualities; there must be no excess on the side of strength or slightness; the materials used must indicate their function by the form we give them; stone must appear as stone, iron as iron, wood as wood; and these substances, while assuming forms suitable to their nature, must be in mutual harmony. . . . "The so complete enumerations" of what has been done before our time, especially by the mediæval architects, are therefore useful if we would advance and not fall below the works of our predecessors; for, I say once more, it would seem as if those men had a presentiment of the appliances which our age affords. There is in the works of our French mediæval architects of the secular school, at the time of its first development, such complete cohesion, so close a connection between the requirements, the means, and the architectural form; there is such an abundance of resources provided for the solution of the numerous difficulties inherent in the complicated requirements of our civilisation, that nowhere else could we find a precedent more fitted to facilitate the task we have to perform. To attempt in the present day to find in the good architecture of Greek or even Roman antiquity anything more than valuable instruction in a few very simple principles applied with inflexible logic; to attempt to copy, imitate, or even to get ideas from the forms given by the expression of those principles, is gratuitously to involve ourselves in inconsistencies the more glaring as our requirements become more complicated and our resources more extensive. During the seventeenth century, so great was the enthusiasm for Roman architecture that every imaginable inconvenience was put up with for the sake of being Roman. . . . Of what use then to us are those incessantly copied, and moreover badly copied, Classic forms? What business have we with them? They embarrass us artists; they have not the adaptability demanded by modern requirements; they are very expensive; they have very little interest for the public; they cut the strangest figure amid certain modern arrangements which we are obliged to adopt; they have the disadvantage of perpetually contravening our habits and methods of building. Why then this persistence in retaining them, or rather in so misapplying them? . . .

If we want to have an architecture of our own time, let us first provide that the architecture shall be ours, and not seek everywhere else than in the bosom of our own social state for its forms and arrangements. That our architects should be acquainted with the best examples of what has been done before us, and in analogous conditions, is highly desirable, provided they unite with this knowledge a good method and a critical spirit. That they should know how the arts of former times faithfully reflected the social conditions amid which they were developed is also most desirable, provided that this knowledge does not lead to an unconsidered imitation of forms that are often foreign to our usages. But that, under pretext of maintaining such or such a doctrine, or perhaps merely for the sake of not troubling the repose of some twenty individuals, we fail to deduce the practical results from those studies which could be gained by paying regard to principles rather than to forms, is reprehensible. The architect must not only be well informed, but must make use of his knowledge, and must derive something from his own powers; he must determine to ignore the commonplace notions which, with a persistence worthy of a nobler cause, have for nearly two centuries been promulgated respecting architectural art.

The architecture we desiderate must take account of the ideas of progress proper to the age,—subjecting those ideas to a harmonious system sufficiently pliant to lend itself to all the modifications, and even consequences of progress; it cannot therefore confine itself to the study and application of purely conventional formulas; for instance, those relating to the orders, or those derived from what are called the laws of symmetry. . . .

If we seriously desire to invent an architecture, the first condition to be fulfilled is not to deceive, either in the general design or in that of the smallest details of the building to be erected. Certainly, in the present day, the determination to be absolutely sincere would produce very novel and probably very fascinating results. Besides, we should thus be putting ourselves in perfect accord with the methods pursued in the good periods of antiquity; we should be making ourselves really classic, in the sense of obeying the invariable laws of art. Having at our disposal novel materials, having machines formerly unknown, powerful appliances much more developed and complicated than those of the Ancients, a tolerably complete acquaintance with what has been effected amid various civilisations in the past, and with all this, a determination to be sincere,—to comply absolutely with the requirements, to take the materials for what they are and for what they will allow us to attempt, having regard to their properties, making some little use of science and a good deal of our reason, seeking, above all, to forget false doctrines, and to put aside some prejudices, we might then be able to lay the foundation of an architecture of our time; and if we did not discover it immediately, we should at least be preparing the way for our successors.

Philosophical Text

FIL HEARN, "TRUTH TO THE MEDIUM: USING MATERIALS."

First Published in 1996

Building materials in the modern era assumed a significance in architectural theory that they had not possessed in the past. This change was due to the fact that a multiplicity of materials, newly available due to industrial production, both imposed and invited new ways of building. The choice of materials, then, became much more than a matter of decorum and expense; it became inextricably related to the conception of the design itself. In the theory of architectural conventions, discussion of the use of materials (usually wood, stone, bricks, and rubble and mortar, as well as the secondary stuff of buildings) had been limited mainly to their procurement and proper handling in traditional structural systems. But in the theory of principles, such lore was relegated to the realm of practice. Instead, it became necessary to consider their appropriate use with respect to the site, plan, structural system, and decor—always taking care to honor the physical properties of each substance.

RUSKIN

No theorist writing on the principles governing materials in architecture has had a greater appreciation for the inherent qualities of building matter than John Ruskin. For him the difference between the color and texture of limestone and those of granite or marble was a matter of great import, both for the appearance of a building and for its effectiveness as an element of the built environment. He could equally concern himself with the varieties of brick, for which a number of different colors and textures were available. This sensitivity made him appreciate different techniques of masonry and patterns of bricklaying, and the artistic value of combining types of stone or brick to introduce color patterns. Indeed, his absorption in the *matière* of buildings and in the capacity of materials to establish poetic atmosphere made him the grand romantic on the subject in all the literature of architectural theory.

Ruskin forcefully and memorably inaugurated this perspective on materials when he raised the issue of their honest use. In doing so he set the agenda for their principled employment for the whole modern era. First, no matter which materials are used they should never be other than the highest grade. If the client cannot afford the highest grade of the costliest materials suitable for the purpose, the best quality of a less expensive medium should be chosen. Second, no material should ever be disguised as another, most especially if the substitute is cheaper, although an exception should be allowed if the disguising material patently could not be the actual one through and through. Examples he cited are the gilding of a decorative feature, such as a carved capital, or the covering of a brick wall with plaster and fresco painting. Third, a material should never be used for structural purposes that are contrary to its inherent physical properties. For instance, stone, which has a great capacity for compression but very little for tension, makes an excellent supporting pillar but not a spanning beam. It can, however, be made to cover an appreciable distance in the form of an arch. Fourth, a structural element should not be made in a given material with a technique that has not traditionally been used for that purpose. Thus, a foliate capital that would normally be carved of stone should not be cast in iron, because it will not have the crispness produced by the chisel. Fifth, a material that has not acquired the dignity of traditional use in august architecture should be avoided. Namely, new industrially produced materials such as cast iron should be avoided in polite circumstances. (Proscription of nontraditional materials is the one tenet of Ruskin's principles for materials that was retrograde.)

The aggregate imperative of all these principles is the doctrine of "truth to the medium." It carries with it the corollary of urging fine workmanship, whether or not the result will be in plain view. On the other hand, exquisite craftsmanship should not be wasted in a location where it cannot be clearly seen and justly appreciated. The main point is that the effectiveness of materials in the appearance of a building depends upon the quality of the workmanship. In this regard, Ruskin generally disapproved of machine production of building elements, favoring instead the minute variations introduced by the human hand. Equally, he preferred a building to be constructed from one basic material, usually traditional stone or brick, rather than mixing them according to the various roles the elements would play, in the design as a whole. In this reservation he was, of course, failing to recognize that modern structural needs would soon outstrip the capacity of traditional materials to perform every requisite task.

The implications of his principles were profound, with both conservative and progressive effects. The moral associations with fine workmanship and production by hand inspired William Morris in his founding of the Arts and Crafts movement, originally intended as a progressive antidote to bad quality in industrial production. In time, however, this movement became rather precious and rarefied, even reactionary in character. Yet in the end even this conservative trend paradoxically exerted a progressive influence by encouraging total environment design, first manifested in the Art Nouveau movement and then in the Bauhaus. The motive to make everything well, with good design had first extended to wallpaper, rugs, and furniture, but by the end of the nineteenth century it also encompassed dishes, flatware, and even the clothing of a building's inhabitants.

The vein that was progressive from the outset, the one in which principled use of materials impinged upon the formulation of structure, permanently obligated architects to be on guard against infractions of design integrity. Ruskin's ideas either spread so pervasively that their source soon lost identity or their source was deemed so obvious that attribution seemed unnecessary, but they lived on without acknowledgment in the writings of virtually every theorist of the modern era.

VIOLLET-LE-DUC

Viollet-le-Duc is almost certainly one of the theorists indebted to Ruskin. Although he couched his theory under the blanket of rationalism, his principles regarding materials overlap those that Ruskin subsumed under morality. He held that materials should not appear to have been worked in a manner different from the way they actually were. He cited as an instance the scoring of a single piece of stone, set as lintel, to look instead as if it is made up of the separate voussoirs of a straight arch. He urged that as nearly as possible materials should be made ready for construction at their place of production, to avoid bringing an excess to the building site, costly in the first instance to transport in and, costly again to take away as waste. Radically progressive in outlook, he welcomed, even fostered, the availability of new materials that could perform a structural task better than a traditional one. He also advocated the posing of structural problems that would challenge manufacturers to produce new materials or new formats for existing materials.

A very strong reason for accepting new materials to perform various structural tasks was that their inherent virtues could be exploited to make the structure more efficient and the building more commodious. For instance, in a scheme for a hypothetical market hall with masonry load-bearing walls he sought to demonstrate the improvements that would be made possible by substituting nontraditional for traditional materials. He proposed substituting diagonal cast-iron struts for stone piers in a vehicular pass-through, iron beams for wooden ones overhead, curved terra-cotta vaulting panels for planks between the beams, and glazed iron framing for heavy masonry in an awning over the sidewalk.

More generally, Viollet-le-Duc advocated using structural iron rather than masonry alone because it would permit architects to make larger spaces with lighter and stronger construction. In that advocacy resided the principle of economy of means, more readily achievable when the most efficient material to do a given job has been specified. If these materials could be industrially produced by machines, all the better, for that would ensure greater uniformity of quality and reduced labor cost, thus bringing down the expense for construction. In all this there was an implicit assumption that the role of materials in architecture is a means toward an end, whereas for Ruskin—for whom their visual qualities were so palpable—they were also ends in themselves.

SCHEERBART

The prescription of industrially produced materials reached its apogee in Paul Scheerbart's celebration of glass in his manifesto *Glasarchitektur* (Berlin, 1914). Explicitly taking for granted the use of structural frames made either of iron or of reinforced concrete, he advocated their enclosure with glass, mainly sheets of plate glass but of other types as well. To be proof against decay and fire were two of the important justifications, but his principal motive was the creation of a socially and aesthetically revolutionary architecture.

Scheerbart was acutely aware that for human beings to live in virtually transparent buildings would drastically change their sense of relationship both to buildings and to the natural world outside the confines of a room. Not only would placement of furnishings against the wall no longer be appropriate in a room, but the natural environment of the outdoors would also be constantly in proximity. Equally, he was aware that it would alter people's sense of living in the world when they were on view behind transparent walls. In both instances he foresaw an advance in human culture as a result. In order to achieve this he recognized that there were practical problems to be overcome, one of the most pressing of which would be climatic comfort. Toward this end he foresaw the need for double glazing, with provision for heating and cooling in the interval between panes. He also saw in that interval a place where internal lighting could be accommodated.

But he was mainly enchanted with the notion that a built environment of "crystal" buildings would be aesthetically gratifying. He was, in addition, particularly interested in exploiting the opportunities to employ both colored light and colored glass, invoking the precedent of Gothic architecture for its use of stained glass as well as its emphasis on large-scale glazing in principle. He envisioned whole cityscapes of buildings illumined at night with colored light, colored-glass trains moving through the landscape, and airplanes with colored lights flying through the sky. But not all of Scheerbart's glass would be transparent: he advocated the use of translucent glass brick and opaque ceramic tile, brightly colored, as well. Virtually every surface could be made of or covered with some type of glass product.

The value of his prophecy is that, having been generated outside the spheres of the architectural profession, its originality had not been hampered by the confines of recognized practice. His leap of imagination provided the first fundamentally new structural image in the theory of architecture, one that opened a whole new conceptual world. Given his distance from the mainstream of society, by dint of his radical eccentricity, Scheerbart's contribution might well have been lost had he not been a close friend of Bruno Taut, who took upon himself the task of realizing this vision in his glass pavilion for the 1914 Werkbund Exhibition in Cologne. Thereby did this manifesto reach avant-garde architects in Berlin (such as Mies van der Rohe, in his epoch-making, unbuilt projects of 1921 and 1922 for a glass skyscraper) and, through them, the rest of the world. Eventually it became the dominant vision for large-scale modernist architecture everywhere.

WRIGHT

Frank Lloyd Wright's theory of materials, which combined and intensified those of Ruskin and Viollet-le-Duc, together with ideas from Japan, was set out in two different contexts and consists of two distinct groups of ideas. The earlier ideas, most strikingly realized in the original construction of Taliesin (1911), were first set out in his series of articles titled "In the Cause of Architecture," in *Architectural Record* in 1908, and colorfully enhanced in accounts of specific buildings in the *Autobiography*, of 1932. The later ideas appeared in two series of articles in *Architectural Record*, one continuing "In the Cause of Architecture," in 1927, and the other titled "The Meaning of Materials," in 1928.

Taliesin represents probably the most radical commitment to the natural expression of materials in Western architecture. Wright constructed it of stone and slate from quarries near the site. The stone was neatly cut into rectangular slabs of varying size and thickness, but it was left rough on the outward-facing surface and set in nonuniform courses in which random stones also project beyond the standard surface plane. The effect is of a masonry that belongs to the earth and suggests the natural layering of the stone in its quarry. The house itself is irregularly composed and famously hugs the brow of the hill rather than sitting atop it as if on a pedestal. The roof is covered with thick, roughly cut slates and has no gutters, so that rain can be seen dripping off it and icicles can hang from it all around. The rusticity of the setting has been carefully maintained; the big trees and the lawn and flower beds are kept as informal as possible.

On the interior the materials are left undisguised in their natural state, for the most part repeating the exterior treatments. Where there is wood, it is merely stained or finished with nothing more than sealant and a coat of wax. Where there is plaster, it is left untreated or given a stain wash. Where there is stone, it remains bare (the same was done elsewhere with brick walls). It is hard to imagine a more starkly honest expression of the character of the materials throughout the building, or a more straightforward application of them to the structural format. The project as a whole combines a natural exploitation of the site, a natural articulation of the plan and structure, and a natural handling of the materials. Beyond ice igloos and grass huts, it is as organic as architecture can reasonably be.

Wright's later essays take up rather different matters, discussing the use of steel, concrete, stone, wood, glass, and kiln-fired materials such as brick and terra-cotta tile. For the most part they are poetic musings about the materials and the ways, satisfactory or otherwise, in which the traditional ones have been used in the past. But their importance lies in having raised the visionary issue of how materials, through the use of machines to produce or refine them, can be wrought in a fundamentally new artistic expression. Wright's concern was to work materials with optimum honesty so as to devise inherently artistic structure. He was confident that forms unanticipated by any architecture of the past could be produced. He did not have a specific vision of them in mind, but he counted on young architects to intuit what those forms might be. The final essay, of 1928, was about the creation of poetic form, achieving beauty in architecture by working with principles. (Is it unfair to point out that Le Corbusier had called for a poetry of form in *Vers une architecture*, the English translation of which had appeared in 1927?)

LE CORBUSIER

For Le Corbusier, the theory of materials had nothing to do with the inherent artistic qualities of one building substance as opposed to another. Rather, he concentrated on the handling of materials and their role in the erection of a structure. His pronouncements on the subject were sparse, appearing mainly in discussion of his own hypothetical buildings in the penultimate chapter of *Vers une architecture.* Contrary to Wright, he did not care about the natural qualities of wood and stone and even regarded their color and pattern variations as a defect. Accordingly, he championed the use of manufactured materials, the more artificial and standardized the better. Taking the rationalist position of Viollet-le-Duc to its ultimate conclusion, he proposed the industrial production of all materials in assembly-ready units of standard dimensions. Construction at the site could then be mostly a matter of assembling prefabricated elements. He welcomed the development of new materials in the laboratory, where they could be tested and proved prior to practical adoption, and regretted that all traditional materials and construction methods could not be replaced. The introduction of machines was urged wherever they could be employed, in the creation of artificial substances, in the prefabrication of units, and in work on the site. Such a position was embraced by European modernists in general and did not seem to require detailed restatement by Gropius or others. The modernist outlook marked the apogee of Viollet-le-Duc's rationalist approach.

The romantic, Ruskinian view of materials did have a resurgence of sorts after World War II in the brutalist movement, of which, ironically, Le Corbusier was the primary instigator. It was, however, a theory that Ruskin himself might have deplored, for it fostered a bluntly primitive aesthetic expression, one that embraced ordinary materials and eschewed traditional ideas of beauty in their manipulation. Indeed, it was at heart an anti-art movement. The use of concrete was at the heart of the matter—that is, poured-in-place, metal-reinforced concrete. As Le Corbusier himself wrote apropos his own work in the postwar period, the availability and cheapness of concrete dictated its use in large projects, and technical limitations on the part of the workforce necessitated a tolerance for rough finish. To be sure, lack of maintenance during the war years had exposed the vulnerability of machine-style finishes to the elements and brought their appropriateness into question. But in the construction of his major new buildings, Le Corbusier had discovered the visual expressiveness of the ridges left in the surface of concrete by its oozing into the intervals between planks of the wooden forms. Together with the thick, simplified forms encouraged by the medium of poured concrete, this new approach promised a novel expression of force and vigor. (No one said so, but it aspired to Ruskin's concept of the sublime.) More importantly, it provided for the medium of concrete a visual manifestation of its having been poured into a mold, hence a testament to its most authentic technical handling.

NEW BRUTALISM AND ITS PROGENY

Brutalist architecture was preeminently the architecture of poured-in-place concrete. Indeed, the very name brutalist refers to the French word for concrete, namely *béton brut*. The impulse to define this assertive primitivism theoretically and declare it a new movement came not from Le Corbusier but from young English architects—such as Peter and Alison Smithson, and later James Stirling and Denys Lasdun. As their spokesman, critic-historian Reyner Banham, explained in his eponymous article in *Architectural Review* of 1955, the movement was largely a radical expression of honesty in both structure and the use of materials, consciously intended as a social and political statement. In general its adherents advocated a much earthier and more boldly articulated architecture than that fostered by the modernist movement. Its novelty lay more in the way plans were developed and materials used than in its structural conception, but those special emphases were sufficient to produce a very different appearance from that of the Villa Savoye or the Bauhaus.

An aspect of the new honesty was to employ materials of ordinary provenance. It became a matter of principle to specify catalog items rather than custom-made ones and to prefer humble materials to those with elite associations. Hence, not only rough concrete but also industrial brick and terra-cotta tile were adopted. Glass was used in smaller, cheaper panes rather than in expensive sheets, and ordinary hardware was preferred to elegant. A typical example was James Stirling and James Gowan's industrial-tile, steel, and glass Leicester University Engineering Laboratory, completed in 1962, already discussed in connection with plan and structure. A poured concrete example was Denys Lasdun's National Theater, completed 1975, on London's South Bank. Its boldly blocky forms of exposed concrete, inside as well as out challenged with their no-nonsense informality all established notions about theater going as an elite social activity. Such an alteration of implicit social expression was the general intention behind brutalist buildings everywhere; as the mode was being adopted for museums, libraries, university buildings, government centers, and apartment complexes. For that very reason the movement did not make much impact on corporate headquarters and shopping malls.

High tech, as a transmogrification of new brutalism, maintains just as rigorously the principle of honesty, but it resubscribes to rationality as well. By way of contrast to its immediate predecessor, it has exchanged the expression of ruggedness for one of sleek sophistication. It accepts only the machine-made and, insofar as possible, the prefabricated, as seen in Renzo Piano and Richard Rogers's Pompidou Center, Paris, of the mid-1970s. Materials that are hard, smooth, and shiny are preferred to anything that is otherwise, which means a bias toward metal, glass, and some plastics. Although high tech design favors the use of standardized building elements, the parts almost always have to be specially manufactured for a particular project. Relentlessly urban, even when situated in the countryside, high tech materials denote the cutting edge of modernity. They achieve, even celebrate, the aims of the early modernists in the expression of technology. But, unlike the modernists, high tech practitioners often use unorthodox colors, or unexpected combinations of colors or finishes, in order to be lighthearted or witty.

Writing and Discussion Questions

ANALYSIS

1. What was Ruskin arguing for and against? What excerpt/quotation best represents this?
2. What was Viollet-le-Duc arguing for and against? What excerpt/quotation best represents this?
3. What was Hearn arguing for and against? What excerpt/quotation best represents this?

SYNTHESIS

1. Regarding concepts of honesty and deception, discuss one major difference regarding Ruskin's, Viollet-le-Duc's, and Hearn's texts.
2. Regarding concepts of honesty and deception, discuss one primary commonality regarding Ruskin's, Viollet-le-Duc's, and Hearn's texts.

SELF-REFLECTION

1. For each of the texts, discuss a major issue with which you most agree and most disagree; reflect upon why you hold these views.
2. Select a recent design project, or a current project on which you are working. Discuss the characteristics of the project in regards to honesty and deception, in light of the discussion and texts introduced in this chapter. What attitudes regarding honesty and deception does your work illustrate?

PROSPECTION

1. Select one of the texts listed in the bibliography for this chapter; locate and read it. To what degree is that text and the attitudes it represents still relevant to architecture today and in the near future?
2. What is the role of honesty and deception in architecture today? Is honesty and deception predominantly about the expression of structure, the relationship between interior and exterior, the expression of the goals and challenges of the architect; some combination of these; or something else? In other words, if a fourth text were added to this chapter, what would the argument be?

Other Readings on Honesty and Deception

Benedikt, Michael. *For an Architecture of Reality.* (Santa Fe: Lumen Books, 1992).

Caldwell, Michael. *Strange Details.* (Cambridge: MIT Press, 2007).

Frampton, Kenneth. *Studies in Tectonic Culture: The Poetics of Construction in Nineteenth and Twentieth Century Architecture.* (Cambridge: MIT Press, 2001).

Gropius, Walter. *The New Architecture and the Bauhaus.* P. Morton Shand, trans. (Cambridge: MIT Press, 1965).

Grudin, Robert. *Design and Truth* (Yale University Press, 2010).

Leatherbarrow, David, and Mastafavi, Mohsen. *Surface Architecture.* (Cambridge: MIT Press, 2002).

Papadakis, Andreas, ed. *New Architecture 5: Truth, Radicality, and Beyond in Contemporary Architecture.* (London: Andreas Papadakis, 2000).

Ringbom, Sixten. *Stone, Style, and Truth: The Vogue for Natural Stone in Nordic Architecture, 1880–1910.* (Helsinki: Suomen Muinaismuistoyhdistys, 1987).

Rowe, Colin, and Slutzky, Robert. "Transparency: Literal and Phenomenal." *Perspecta,* 8 (1963): 45–54.

Schumacher, Thomas. "The Skull and the Mask: The Modern Movement and Dilemma of the Façade." *Cornell Journal of Architecture,* 3 (1987): 5–11.

Wilson, Colin St. John. *Architectural Reflections: Studies in the Philosophy and Practice of Architecture.* (Manchester: Manchester University Press, 2000). First published 1992.

Chapter 4

MATERIAL and IMMATERIAL

FIGURE 4.1
Photograph of the entry to Thorncrown Chapel, including interior cross bracing, Eureka Springs, Arkansas, United States (1979–1980). Architect: E. Fay Jones.

FIGURE 4.2
Photograph at dusk of the addition to the Nelson-Atkins Museum of Art, Kansas City, Missouri, United States (1999–2007). Architect: Steven Holl.

INTRODUCTORY DISCUSSION

1. Of the two images above, which better represents "material" expression in architecture? Which better represents the concept of "immaterial" architecture? Why?

2. What are the various definitions and connotations of the terms "material," "materiality," "immaterial," and "immateriality" in architecture? What are the characteristics of an architecture of materiality? What are the characteristics of an architecture of immateriality?

3. Which is more appropriate in architecture today, materiality or immateriality?

Introduction

Architects—from Vitruvius to Le Corbusier, Alberti to Wright, and Viollet-le-Duc to Kahn—have discussed the importance of materiality in architecture. Since the beginning of architectural history, designers and builders articulated both practical and theoretical principles on how materials are to be procured, refined, stored, and assembled. Architecture is, of course, the putting together of materials: stone, wood, brick, etc. Throughout much of architectural history, architects focused on qualities of solidity, permanence, and heaviness. In opposition, new materials have enabled new qualities: Can buildings be more transparent, maybe ghostly or invisible? Can buildings become lighter, maybe able to float? Can buildings be made to move, maybe daily? Exemplified by Diller and Scofidio's "Blur Building" at the 2002 Swiss Expo, where the primary building material was fog, the exploration of "immateriality" in architecture is relatively new.

Building upon Vitruvius' work, Leon Battista Alberti wrote at length about materials and construction in "Book III" of *The Art of Building in Ten Books*, the *original text* for this chapter. Alberti articulated the properties and procurement of various building materials: timber, stone, brick, lime, and sand. He described how to "properly" refine these materials, and to utilize them in construction. Beginning with the foundation, and moving on to discussions of walls, roofs, and "pavements" (i.e., flooring), Alberti delivered a systemic guide for constructing public buildings, predominantly based on objective, practical, empirical, and technical expertise. Durability, much more than aesthetics, was Alberti's primary concern throughout the first half of his *Ten Books*, developing a seamless translation from raw material—the natural properties of stone, wood, etc.—to built form. This parallels Louis Kahn's famous dialogue with a brick, where he asks the brick what it wants to be, and the brick, in Kahn's words, says, "I like an arch."[1]

Finnish architect and theorist Juhani Pallasmaa saw the process of construction not only as an extension of material properties but also as an extension of the human body. In *The Eyes of the Skin: Architecture and the Senses*, the *reflective text* for this chapter, Pallasmaa asserted, "Construction in traditional cultures is guided by the body in the same way that a bird shapes its nest by movements of its body. Indigenous clay

1. This conversation appears in the 2003 documentary film *My Architect*, directed by Kahn's son Nathaniel Kahn.

and mud architectures in various parts of the world seem to be born of the muscular and haptic senses." Pallasmaa utilized this conceptualization to critique what he viewed as an overreliance on the visual, rather than tactile, sense in architectural design. According to Pallasmaa, inhabitants become "spectators," experiencing architecture as an image, which results in a loss of intimate, tactile, bodily connection to the work. Pallasmaa added, "The current over-emphasis on the intellectual and conceptual dimensions of architecture contributes to the disappearance of its physical, sensual and embodied essence," and that contemporary architecture needed to intensify material qualities of weight, texture, and time.[2]

This heightened interest in "materiality"—the experienced "reality" of materials—led to a search for complementary properties of "immateriality." Architects sought ways to bring "material" properties, such as heaviness or opacity, together with "immaterial" properties, such as lightness or translucency, what Jonathan Hill, in 2006, described as "an architecture that fuses the immaterial and the material . . . so that they are in conjunction not opposition." In *Immaterial Architecture*, the *philosophical text* for this chapter, Hill asserted, "Architecture is expected to be solid, stable and reassuring—physically, socially and psychologically. Bound to each other, the architectural and the material are considered inseparable. But . . . the immaterial is as important to architecture as the material and has as long a history." Furthermore, Hill contended that immateriality was a question of individual perception; "the user decides whether architecture is immaterial" or not. Is a particular architecture theoretically material/immaterial—e.g., historically significant, etc.? Is a particular architecture physically material/immaterial—e.g., tactilely engaging, etc.?

New architectural materials are being invented at a rapid rate. The combined material properties of some of these materials are highly unexpected. Nicknamed "solid smoke," aerogel, for example, is a solid compound that is translucent, has an exceedingly high insulating value, is fire retardant, has a high load-bearing capacity, and is only twice the density of air. In a more extreme sense, scientists have recently produced new elements so unstable that they exist for mere milliseconds and their properties are not yet fully understood. For instance, the creation of elements such as *ununseptium* in 2010, the 117th item on the Periodic Table of Elements, suggests the generation of "an array of strange new materials with as yet unimagined scientific and practical uses."[3] Radical new materials like this will invariably change architectural space and form. While it is interesting to speculate how architecture will change because of material innovation, it may be more intriguing to question how human perception will change as we live, work, and play in these new material and immaterial environments.

2. These concepts were part of the emergence of the larger architectural realm known as "phenomenology." Phenomenology was originally an early twentieth-century paradigm of philosophy that focused on the first-person experience. Phenomenology entered architecture through two primary paths. First, prominent philosophers extended their philosophies to include architecture. Martin Heidegger's mid-twentieth-century essay entitled "Building, Dwelling, Thinking" is one definitive example. Second, twentieth-century architects began reading and incorporating various philosophical texts and concepts into their built and written works. In addition to Pallasmaa, late twentieth- and early twenty-first-century architects—such as, Peter Zumthor, Tadao Ando, and Steven Holl—focused on sensory perceptions of space and material, e.g., tactility, acoustics, kinesthesia, etc. For a straightforward explanation of phenomenology, see the *Stanford Encyclopedia of Philosophy* website: http://plato.stanford.edu/entries/phenomenology/.

3. James Glanz, "Scientists Discover Heavy New Element," *The New York Times*, April 6, 2010, http://www.nytimes.com/2010/04/07/science/07element.html, retrieved February 1, 2011.

Original Text

LEON BATTISTA ALBERTI, EXCERPTS FROM
THE ART OF BUILDING IN TEN BOOKS.

First Published in 1486

MATERIALS

In my opinion, the labor and expense of building should not be undertaken lightly: apart from everything else that may be at stake, one's esteem and good name may suffer. A well-constructed building will enhance the renown of anyone who has invested understanding, attention, and enthusiasm in the matter; yet equally, should the wisdom of the designer or the competence of the workman be found wanting anywhere, it will greatly detract from his reputation and good name. Merits and defects are particularly obvious and striking in public buildings, though (for some reason, I do not understand) criticism of impropriety is more readily given than approval for a work elegantly constructed and with no imperfections. It is remarkable how some natural instinct allows each of us, learned and ignorant alike, to sense immediately what is right or wrong in the execution and design of a work. . . . If presented with anything in any way inadequate, unstable, redundant, useless, or imperfect, we are immediately struck by the desire to make it more agreeable.
. . .

For this reason I will always commend the time-honored custom, practised by the best builders, of preparing not only drawings and sketches but also models of wood or any other material. These will enable us to weigh up repeatedly and examine, with the advice of experts, the work as a whole and the individual dimensions of all the parts, and, before continuing any farther, to estimate the likely trouble and expense. Having constructed these models, it will be possible to examine clearly and consider thoroughly the relationship between the site and the surrounding district, the shape of the *area*, the number and order of the parts of a building, the appearance of the walls, the strength of the covering, and in short the design and construction of all the elements.
. . .

In particular, great attention should be paid to ensure that the design of the roof is the best possible. For unless I am mistaken, the roof of its very nature was the first of all building elements to provide mankind with a place of shelter: so much so that it was for the sake of the roof that the need arose not only for the wall and all that goes with it, but also for anything constructed below ground, such as water conduits, rainwater channels, sewers, and the like. From my own not inconsiderable experience in these matters, I am aware of the difficulties encountered in executing a work in such a manner that it marries practical convenience with dignity and grace, so that, among other commendable advantages, these parts are imbued with a refined variety, in accordance with the demands of proportion and harmony: that really is difficult! . . .

We shall now deal with the materials suitable for constructing buildings, and we shall relate the advice handed down to us by the learned men of the past, in particular Theophrastus, Aristotle, Cato, Varro, Pliny, and Vitruvius: for such knowledge is better gained through long experience than through any artifice of invention. . . .

It would be most convenient, I believe, to follow the natural order and begin with the material that man first used for building; this, unless I am mistaken, was timber from trees felled in the forest. . . .

TIMBER

The ancients, then, especially Theophrastus, recommended that trees, in particular the fir, the pitch tree, and the pine, should be felled as soon as they germinate and begin to send out young shoots, in that the high quantity of sap produced at that time will facilitate the removal of the bark. Yet they recommended that other trees, such as the maple, elm, ash, and linden, should be cut down after the vintage. Likewise they maintained that the oak would be prone to worms if felled in spring, but would suffer no defect and would not split if felled in winter. Equally relevant is their observation that timber felled in winter, when Boreas is blowing, will burn beautifully and almost without smoke, although still green, showing that the sap it contains is not raw but well absorbed.

Vitruvius prefers that timber be felled from the beginning of autumn until Favonius blows. Yet in the words of Hesiod: Reap the crops when the sun hangs over your head with raging heat and gives men a dusky tan; but do not fell the trees until their leaves begin to drop. But this is Cato's advice on the matter: "Fell timber, if it is oak, during the solstice; for in the winter it is always ready. Fell all other timber when it is mature, if it bears seeds, or if not, whenever you wish; fell any whose seed is both green and ripe, when the seed falls, and the elm, when its leaves fall." . . .

Once the timber has been cut, it should be laid down away from the severities of the sun or the harshness of the wind; above all, wood with an inherent tendency to split ought to be particularly well shaded. This was the purpose behind the ancient architects' practice of smearing the wood with dung, usually of oxen. Theophrastus argues that the reason for this was to close up the pores to force any congealed gum and any moisture that had built up to seep along the marrow and evaporate, so that the process of drying imparted a more even density to the whole length. It is also believed that timber will dry out better if stood upside down. . . .

These are the trees whose wood is reckoned most useful for the construction of buildings: the turkey oak, common oak, bay oak, winter oak, poplar, linden, willow, alder, ash, pine, cypress, oleaster, olive tree, chestnut tree, larch, box tree, likewise the cedar, ebon tree, and the vine. Each has a different character and so is best suited to a different use. Some fare better when exposed to the sky, others keep better in shadow; some flourish in the open air, others grow hard in water, and others last longer underground. Therefore, while some are more suitable for lamination, paneling, statues, and internal furnishing, others make better posts and beams, and others strong supports for terraces and roofs.

In particular, the alder makes the very best stakes for restraining rivers and marshes, and is very resistant to moisture, although it will not last long when exposed to air and sun. The winter oak, on the other hand, has little resistance to water. The elm hardens if left in the open, but elsewhere splits and does not last long, whereas the pitch tree and the pine, if buried underground, last for ever. The bay oak, being a hard, sinewy, dense wood, with only the smallest of pores, does not absorb moisture and is therefore thoroughly suitable for any work underground; it is most usefully employed for bearing weights and makes extremely strong columns. Yet, although it has such innate natural strength that it cannot be drilled unless it is soaked, above ground it is said to be less reliable, and apt to crack and warp, while even in seawater it may be easily ruined. This will not happen to the olive or the holm oak or the oleaster (which are very like the bay oak in other ways) when soaked in water. The common oak does not deteriorate with age, but retains its sap as if it were young. The beech and the walnut tree never rot in water and are counted among the most suitable for use underground. The cork tree, meanwhile, the wild pine, mulberry, maple, and elm are not unsuitable for columns. . . .

To sum up . . . trees that do not bear fruit are more robust than those that do, and . . . wild trees, uncultivated by hand or steel, are hardier than domestic ones. . . .

STONE

We have also to prepare the stone to be used in the walls. There are two kinds of stone, one to be used as aggregate in mortar, the other suitable for the structure of the building. . . .

White stone is easier to handle than dark, and translucent more workable than opaque, but the closer a stone resembles salt, the harder it is to work. If a stone is coated with shining sand, it will be coarse; if sparkling with gold particles, stubborn; if it is, as it were, flecked with black, unmanageable. Stones dappled with polygonal markings are more solid than those with circular ones; and the smaller the markings on a stone, the greater the weight it can bear; the purer and clearer the color, the longer it will last; and the fewer veins it has, the sounder it will be; and the closer the color of the veins to that of the surrounding stone, the more uniform its structure; while the thinner the veins, the more capricious the stone will be; the more tortuous and twisted they are, the more troublesome; the more knotted, the more refractory. The veins most likely to crack are those whose center is streaked with the color of red clay, or the ochre of rot, followed by those tinted in places with a pale, faded grass color; but the most awkward of all are veins that have taken on the blue color of ice. A large number of veins means that a stone will be unreliable and apt to split, while the straighter the veins, the less trustworthy it will be.

The sharper and cleaner the edge of the pieces into which the stone breaks, the more compact it is; while the smoother their surface, the easier the stone will be to work. But those with rough surfaces will prove more awkward the whiter their color, whereas with dark stone, the closer the grain, the greater its resistance to the iron blade. With stone of inferior quality, the greater its porosity, the hardest is; and the longer it takes to dry out, when soaked all over with water, the coarser it is. A heavy stone will be more solid and easy to polish than a light one, and a light one will be more friable. A stone that rings out when struck will be denser than one that does not. Any stone that produces a sulphur-like smell when rubbed will be stronger than one that does not; finally, the greater its stubbornness to the chisel, the more rigid and steadfast a stone will be against the assaults of the weather. . . .

It is agreed that the ancients were quite willing to use bricks instead of stone. I do believe that men were first prompted by necessity, in the absence of other suitable material, to build in brick. Noticing both how easy this method of construction was and how practical, graceful, solid, and reliable, they proceeded to use brick for other buildings, and even royal palaces. Finally, whether by accident or by careful investigation, they discovered that fire strengthened and hardened bricks, and went on to construct everything of earthenware. Indeed, from what I have observed from studying very ancient structures, I would be so bold as to state that there is no building material more suitable than brick, however you wish to employ it, though it must be baked rather than raw, and the correct methods of molding and firing must be strictly followed. . . .

It is useful to note here the opinion that a whitish, chalky clay makes very good bricks; likewise reddish clay and the so-called masculine sand. It is advisable to avoid clay that is sandy or full of gravel; but above all, clay containing pebbles ought to be discarded utterly: clay of this type tends to warp and crack during firing and to break up afterward by itself.

Freshly dug clay should not be used to make bricks, they say: rather the clay should be dug in the autumn, allowed to macerate throughout the winter, and not used for making bricks until the beginning of spring. If bricks are made during winter, obviously the frost will split them, or, if during summer, the intense heat will crack them as they dry. But if it is absolutely necessary to make them during the cold of winter, they should be covered immediately with a layer of very dry sand, and if in the heat of the summer, with damp straw: stored in this way they will neither crack nor warp.

Some prefer bricks to be glazed. If so, sandy clay or clay that is too thin and dry ought to be strenuously avoided, as this will absorb the glaze; instead, glazed bricks should be made of a white, chalky, rich clay. The bricks must be thin: if they are too thick, they will not bake properly and will be liable to crack. But if thick ones are required, the problem may on the whole be avoided if a number of holes are spiked here and there through the middle: these will act as vents and will improve the drying out and firing of the bricks by allowing moisture and vapor to escape. . . .

Bricks, they say, should be polished either immediately after their removal from the kiln and before they have been wetted, or after they have been wetted and before they have dried out; for once they have been dampened and allowed to dry out again, they become so hard that they will blunt or wear down the edge of any tool; but, in our opinion, they are easier to rub smooth as soon as they have been made, and while they are still warm. . . .

In my concern for brevity I should not neglect to mention that whatever has been said about bricks applies equally to pantiles and plaintiles on the roof, and to earthenware piping, in short to any pottery or earthenware work.

So much for stone; we must now deal with lime. . . .

LIME

The lime most highly praised by ancient architects is produced from extremely hard and compact stone, preferably white: it is thought suitable for many types of work and is particularly solid when used in vaulting. Their next preference is for lime made from stone which is porous, but neither light nor crumbly; this they consider the best for plastering, being easier to fashion and imparting a more splendid finish to the work. In Gaul I have seen that architects use lime extracted solely from dark, round, hard stones found in riverbeds, which give the impression of being flint; nonetheless this lime has certainly shown itself strong and very lasting in both stone and brick buildings. . . .

Any quarried stone will make better lime than that gathered from the ground; a shady, damp quarry will contain better stone than a dry one; and lime from white stone, rather than dark, will be easier to plaster. . . .

There is another type of lime called gypsum; this is also made by roasting stone, although they say that in Cyprus and Thebes gypsum may be dug from the very surface of the ground, ready roasted by the sun. However, stone that produces gypsum is quite different from that which produces lime, since it is very soft and friable, with the exception of that quarried in Syria, which is extremely hard. Further, stone for gypsum needs to be roasted for no more than twenty hours, whereas that for lime needs at least sixty. I have observed that there are four types of gypsum to be found in Italy: two translucent and two opaque. Of the two that are translucent, one resembles lumps of alum, or rather alabaster: this is called "squameola," as it consists of very slender scales attached and pressed together like thin layers; the other is also scaly, but more closely resembles dark salt than alum. Both of the opaque varieties resemble dense chalk, although one is whitish and very pale, and the other a pallid color tinged with red. The latter two are denser than the former, and of these the reddish one grips better. Of the first two, the purer one makes more lustrous stucco for cornices and figurines. A type of gypsum is to be found near Rimini that is so compacted that it gives the impression of being marble or alabaster: I have had this sawn into slabs that make excellent facing. I should not forget to mention that all forms of gypsum must be pounded with wooden mallets and crushed into powder; this should be piled up and stored in a dry place, but once brought out, it ought to be mixed with water immediately and put to use without delay.

Lime is the opposite: it does not need to be crushed, but may be soaked while still in lumps; indeed it should be allowed to soften in water for a good while before being mixed, especially if intended for plastering, so that any lumps not baked thoroughly enough by the fire will dissolve. If it is used too soon, before it has been properly steeped and softened, it may still contain some small half-roasted stones, which might with time begin to rot, soon developing blisters which disfigure the finish. It should be added here that lime ought not to be soaked by a single dousing, but ought to be dampened gradually with several sprinklings, until it is evenly saturated. It should then be left on its own, mixed with nothing else, in a damp, shady place with nothing but a layer of sand to protect it, until the process of time has fermented it into a more fluid paste. It is certain that this lengthy fermentation greatly improves the lime. We have ourselves seen lime that has been recently discovered in an old deserted cave, left for more than five hundred years, as numerous indications make abundantly clear, which stayed damp and viscous, and so mature that it was far softer than honey or the marrow in bones. Surely there is nothing else to be found more suitable for whatever purpose. Lime prepared in this way requires twice the sand as when mixed freshly slaked.

In this respect, then, lime and gypsum are different, though in other ways they are similar. . . .

SAND

Since in order to build, not only lime is needed but also sand, we must now deal with the latter.

There are three kinds of sand: that which comes from pits, that from rivers, and that from the sea. The best is from pits. This comes in several varieties: black, white, red, carbuncular, and gravelly.

. . .

Of all these types of pit sand the carbuncular is the favorite, although I notice that red sand was not the last choice for public buildings in Rome. White sand is the worst type of pit sand. Gravelly sand makes a very suitable infill for foundations. Next, in order of preference, comes fine, gravelly sand, especially if the grains are sharp and quite free of soil, as is the variety found in great abundance in the territory of the Vilumbrians. After that comes sand extracted from riverbeds, once the top layer has been removed. The most useful river sand comes from streams, and of these the best is provided by mountain streams with steep gradients. Sand extracted from the sea is considered the worst, although any that is black or vitreous is not entirely unacceptable.

. . .

There are many differences among the various types of sand. Sea sand is difficult to dry: saltiness makes it soluble, so that it is always prone to take up moisture and dissolve; it is therefore unsuitable and unreliable for bearing weights. River sand is damper than pit sand and therefore easier to mold and more suitable for plastering. Pit sand, being fatter, holds together much better, although it tends to crack and therefore is more suitable for vaulting than for plastering.

But the best sand of any kind will be one that crackles when rubbed or crushed in the hand, and when gathered in a clean garment leaves no stain, nor residue of soil. On the other hand, a sand smooth in texture, without any harshness, and of a color and smell like those of a clayey soil will not be good, nor will any variety which when stirred in water leaves it turbid and muddy, nor will one that is covered by grass as soon as it is spread on the ground. It will be no good if, once procured, it is left in the open for a long time exposed to the sun, the moon, and the frost: this leaves it earthlike and rotten, and therefore quite capable of producing shrubs and wild fig trees, but with little strength for holding buildings together. . . .

SUMMARY

. . . To conclude, then, not every place will have the same supply of stone, sand, and so on, since the quality and quantity of natural resources vary from place to place. And so use should be made of whatever is available, and care must be taken to ensure, first, that only the most manageable and convenient materials are procured, and second, that in the process of construction all the right materials are used in the right places.

Having procured the materials mentioned above—that is, timber, stone, lime, and sand—it remains now to deal with the method and manner of construction.

ON CONSTRUCTION

The whole method of construction is summed up and accomplished in one principle: the ordered and skilful composition of various materials, be they squared stones, aggregate, timber, or whatever, to form a solid and, as far as possible, integral and unified structure. A structure may be said to be integral and unified when the parts it contains are not to be separated or displaced, but their every line joins and matches.

We need to consider, therefore, which are the primary parts of the structure, their order, and the lines of which they are composed. It is not difficult to discover the parts that make up the structure: clearly they are the top and bottom, the right and left, the front and back, and all that lies in between; but not everyone will comprehend their specific characteristics and why each is different.

The construction of a building does not entail just setting stone on stone, and aggregate on aggregate, as the ignorant may imagine; for, because the parts are different, so too the materials and methods of construction vary quite radically. The foundations need to be treated one way, the girdle and cornices another, and the corners and lips of openings yet another, while the outer skins of a wall must be treated differently from the infill of the middle. We must now inquire what is appropriate in each case.

In this we shall follow, as we mentioned above, the same order as those who are to undertake the work with their own hands; we shall begin, therefore, with the foundations. The foundations, unless I am mistaken, are not part of the structure itself; rather they constitute a base on which the structure proper is to be raised and built. For if an *area* could be found that was thoroughly solid and secure—of stone, for example, as may be found often around Veioi—there would be no need to lay down foundations before raising the structure itself. . . .

FOUNDATIONS

A foundation—that is to say, "a going to the bottom" —and a trench will be necessary wherever a pit must be dug to reach solid ground, as is the case almost everywhere. . . .

The ancients used to say, "Dig until you reach solid ground, and God be with you." The ground has many layers, some sandy, some gravelly, others stony, and so on; and below these, its position ever changing and uncertain, lies a hard, compact layer of earth, extremely suitable for bearing the weight of buildings. The nature of this layer may itself vary, there being scarcely any similarities between the various types: some may be hard, almost impregnable to iron, others thick, some black, others white (the latter are commonly thought the weakest of all), some composed of clay, others of tufa, and others of a mixture of gravel and clay. Nothing can be said for certain as to which of these is best, except that any that resist iron, or scarcely dissolve when immersed in water, can be recommended. . . .

Advice should be sought from those with any knowledge and experience in the matter, be they local residents or nearby architects: through their acquaintance with existing buildings or their daily experience in constructing new ones, they will have acquired a ready understanding of the nature and quality of the local soil. . . .

The design of the foundations must vary therefore according to the site. Some sites may be up high, others down low, and others in between these, such as slopes, for example; then again, some may be parched and arid, especially mountain ridges and summits, and others utterly saturated and damp, such as those which lie on the coast, by a lagoon, or in a valley. Others may remain neither totally dry nor utterly wet, because they are positioned on a slope, which is true for any place where water does not remain still and stagnant but always runs downhill. . . .

Before you start any excavation, it is advisable to mark out all the corners and sides of the *area*, to the correct size and in the right place several times, with great care. . . .

In setting out the foundations, it should be noted that the base of the wall and the plinth (which are also considered part of the foundations) must be somewhat wider than the proposed wall. . . .

On some occasions, either to reduce costs or to avoid an insecure stretch of ground along the way, it may be better not to construct a solid work along a single, continuous trench, but to leave spaces between, as though only making foundations for pillars or columns; arches are then constructed from one pillar to the next, and the rest of the wall is raised on top. Here we must follow the same principle mentioned elsewhere, but the greater the intended load, the wider and firmer should be the foundations and footings. . . .

Once the foundations are laid, the walls may follow directly. . . .

WALLS

The difference between the footings and the wall proper is this: the footings are supported by both sides of the trench and may be one mass of rubble alone, whereas the wall is composed of many parts, as I shall now explain. The main parts of the wall are these: the lower, that is to say the section immediately above the infill of the foundations (this we may possibly call the podium, or platform); the middle, which encompasses and encases the wall (known as the apron); and the upper, the collar around the top of the wall (called the cornice).

Among the other important, perhaps even more important, parts of the wall are the corners and inherent or additional elements such as piers, columns, and anything else that acts as a column and supports the trusses and roof arches. These all come under the description of bones. So too the lips on either side of openings, which share the characteristics of both corner and column. Also included in the bones are the coverings to the openings, that is, the beams, whether straight or arched: for I call an arch nothing but a curved beam, and what is a beam but a column laid crossways? The zone stretching between these primary parts is referred to appropriately as "paneling."

Throughout the wall there should be something common to all the above-mentioned parts; by this I mean the infill and the twin skins or shells on either side, one to keep the wind and the sun out, the other to protect the *area* within. The design of both infill and shell will vary according to the method of construction.

These are the kinds of construction: ordinary, reticulated, and irregular. . . .

Ordinary construction involves using stones (standard or, preferably, large-size) that have been cut square, and bonding these in a regular fashion along vertical and horizontal lines; there can be no method of construction stronger or more steadfast than this.

Reticulated construction involves using standard or, preferably, small-sized stones that have been cut square; these are laid not flat, but at an angle with their faces set flush and vertically aligned.

In irregular stonework, irregular stones are laid with each side, as far as its shape will allow, fitting closely into the sides of adjoining stones. This is the method of bonding used in the construction of flint roads.

However, the method of construction to be used will depend on the situation. For the facing of a plinth, for example, we will use nothing but extremely large, hard stone, cut square. Since the structure must be as solid and firm as possible, as we said earlier, then surely this part of the wall requires greater strength and stability than any other. In fact, if at all possible, it should consist of a single stone, or at least of only so many as may give it the soundness and durability closest to that of a single one. The question of how to handle and transport these huge stones is related principally to ornament, and will be dealt with in the appropriate place.

Build your wall, advises Cato, of solid stone and good mortar to at least one foot above the ground. As for the rest of the wall, you may even use unbaked bricks, if you so wish. The reason for this is obvious: this part of the wall is liable to be eroded by rain dripping from the roof. But if we inspect the buildings of the ancients, we will notice that not only in this country but everywhere else, the bases of well-constructed buildings are made of hard stone. . . .

It is advisable therefore, when laying stones, especially where the wall needs to be most robust, to ensure that only the strongest side, which will deteriorate the least, is exposed to the onslaught of the elements. It is best not to set the stones on their sides with the grain standing upright, as the weather will cause them to deteriorate in this position; rather, lay them flat, so that pressure from the load above will prevent them from splitting. Whichever side was hidden facing inward when the stone was in the quarry should now be exposed to the open; it will be richer in natural juices and stronger. But in any quarried stone the most resistant surface will be the one that has been cut not along the grain of the stone but transversely across it.

Moreover, the corners throughout the building need to be exceptionally strong, and so must be solidly constructed. In fact, unless I am mistaken, each corner represents half of the building, in that damage to one of the corners will inevitably entail the destruction of two of the sides. And a closer inspection will undoubtedly reveal that in almost every building where deterioration has set in, a structural weakness in one of the corners will have been responsible. Therefore it was sound practice that the ancients should have made their walls considerably thicker at the corner than elsewhere, and would add pilasters to reinforce the corners in colonnaded porticoes.

The reason why the corners need to be so strong is not only to enable them to support the roof—indeed, that is the task of the columns rather than the corners—but mainly to help them keep the walls in position and prevent them from leaning away from the vertical in either direction. The cornerstones should be extremely hard and long, therefore, so that they extend into the adjoining wall like the elbow joint of an arm, and they should be wide enough relative to the depth of the wall to avoid the need for any infill. The bones within the wall and around the openings should be treated in the same way as the corners, and strengthened according to the size of the load they may have to bear. It is most important that there be a system of claws—that is, stones projecting into each side in alternate courses—as a kind of armrest that supports the remaining paneling.

The paneling consists of two components, which, as we mentioned above, are common to the whole wall: the skin and the infill. There are two types of skin, the inner and the outer. If the outer skin is made of hard stone, the durability of the building will be improved. I do not care how you prefer to construct the rest of the paneling—whether it be of reticulated or irregular stonework—so long as you protect it from the fierce hostility of the sun, the vexing winds, the fire and frost, by a layer of stone having great natural resistance to assault, pressure, and injury. . . .

In my opinion, one of the most important rules to be followed is that once it has been started, a wall should be built level and uniform round the whole structure, so that one side should not have large stones and the other small ones. For it is said that any imposed weight will put pressure on the structure, and the drying mortar have less grip, inevitably leading to cracks in the wall.

Yet I have no objections to your using soft stone for the inner skin and all of the wall facing. But whatever kind of stone is used, the skin inside and outside alike must be raised vertically and in line. It must follow the outline of the *area* exactly, without bulging out or caving in anywhere, or wavering at all: it should be straight and properly constructed throughout.

If during construction you apply the first layer of plaster to the wall while it is still fresh, whatever you add subsequently by way of rendering or stucco work will prove permanent.

There are two types of infill: one consisting of aggregate piled in to fill the gap between the two skins, the other simply consisting of common but rough stone, providing a structural center rather than just acting as infill. Both types seem to have been invented for the sake of economy, in that small, common stone of any kind is all that is required for this part of the wall. For if there were a ready supply of large, square-cut stone available, surely nobody would be willing to use small stone chips.

And herein lies the difference between the paneling and the bones: with the former, the skins are filled with stone chippings and any rubble that is available—a quick task involving little more than shoveling; with the latter, irregular stones are never or only very seldom included, but ordinary-bond stonework is used to bind together the whole thickness of the wall.

I would prefer, for the sake of durability, to have each course of the whole wall composed entirely of squared stone; but however you decide to fill the gap between the two skins, as much care as possible should be taken to ensure that the courses on either side are bonded together and level. It is important also to include a number of ordinary stones, not too far apart, spanning across the wall, from the inside of one skin to the outside of the other; connecting both skins to prevent the two outer surfaces that frame the work from bulging out when the infill is poured in. . . .

A number of courses of large stone should be included to act as bonds, and tie outer shell to inner, and bone to bone, just like those we mentioned that were to be inserted every five feet. There are other bonds—and these of great importance—which stretch the whole length of the wall and are intended to hold in the corners and support the work. The latter are less frequent, and I cannot recall having seen more than two or, occasionally, three in a single wall. Their main seat and place is to act as a cornice to clasp the top of the wall with a ledge of strong stones. The next rung runs immediately over the openings. Equally, they made sure that the podium at the bottom did not lack a decent cornice. Where the more common bonds, those every five feet, are more frequent, thinner stones are not amiss. But with the second type, known as cornices, because they are less frequent and the role they play more prominent, it is best to make the stones correspondingly stronger and thicker. But with either category, in general the longest, thickest, and strongest stone is required. The smaller bonds should be set square and flush with the rest of the wall; but the others should project from the façade like cornices. And their extremely long and wide stones should be set exactly level, and well connected between courses, so that those above cover the ones below like a pavement. This is how the stones should be laid: each fresh stone should be laid to fit tightly and neatly on those below, its center resting immediately above their joint and its surface spread evenly over the two. Although this pattern of laying stones should be practiced throughout the work, it is even more important that it is followed in bonds of this kind. . . .

When constructing the cornice, none of the rules for bonds that we have so far mentioned should be overlooked, since it, too, binds the wall tightly together: only the firmest stone should be included, the blocks should be extremely long and wide, the joints continuous and well formed, and each course laid perfectly level and square as required. Its position demands that the cornice be treated with a great deal of care and attention, in that it binds the work together at a point where it is most likely to give way, and in addition acts as a roof to the wall below. Hence the saying: For walls of unbaked brick make a cornice of baked brick; this will cover and protect them from the damage of rain dripping from rooftops and eaves. For this reason ensure that every sort of wall is made with a firm cornice, serving as a covering, to prevent damage by rain. . . .

Enough about the wall; I come now to the roof. . . .

ROOFS
Some roofs are exposed to the sky and others not; of these some may be composed of straight lines, others of curved ones, and others of a mixture of the two. A further dis-

tinction, which is appropriate here, is that a roof may be built either of timber or of stone. We shall begin our discussion by establishing exactly which features are common to the design of all roofs. They are the bones, muscles, infill paneling, skin, and crust, and can be recognized in any roof just as in any wall. . . .

To begin with timber roofs composed of straight lines. In order to support the roof it is necessary to lay strong beams spanning from wall to wall. And, as we have just mentioned, there is no doubt that beams are columns laid crossways. Where bones should be, there is a beam. But, if finance permitted it, would not anyone prefer to make the work as strong as possible, of solid bone, so to speak, by making the columns continuous and linking all the beams together? We must take costs into account, however, and reckon anything that can be dispensed with without impairing the structural stability of the work superfluous. Therefore spaces are left between the beams, then cross-beams are added, and from these span the lathing and anything else similar. Each of these can quite acceptably be considered ligaments. To these are added planks, or wider boards, which surely take the place of infill paneling. Equally, the pavement or the tiling undeniably serves as the outside skin, whereas the ceiling above our heads serves as the inside one. . . .

The beam must be perfectly intact and sound, quite free of any defect, especially midway along its length. If you position your ear at one end, and the other end is struck several ringing blows that sound dull and flat, this is a sure indication that the inside is diseased. Any beam containing knots should be rejected, especially if the knots are frequent or clustered together. The part closest to the marrow should be planed and laid upwards, whereas the lower surface of the beam should be stripped of bark or planed as little as possible. But any side with any defect running across it should be set on top. If any side has a crack running right down its length, it should not be left as one of the vertical surfaces, but be made the top or better the bottom. If you need to bore through a beam or perhaps to make notches in it, spare the central part of its length, and do not harm the lower surface. . . .

If, however, the trees are too small to make a complete beam out of a single trunk, join several together into a composite beam, in such a manner that they acquire the inherent strength of an arch, that is, so that the load will not compress the upper line of the composite beam nor stretch the lower line, which should act like a cord, to hold the trunks in tension, their opposing faces notched into one another. . . .

I shall now turn to the covering of the roof. If I judge correctly, surely the most ancient function of the whole building was to provide a shelter from the burning sun and the storms raging down from heaven. And it is not the wall, nor the *area,* nor any other part that is responsible for maintaining this service for you, but primarily, as must be obvious, the outer membrane of the roof; yet, despite all the determination and skill that man has invested in his attempt to strengthen and reinforce it against the assaults of the weather, he has scarcely succeeded in protecting it as much as necessity demands. Nor do I imagine that this would be easy, faced as it is with the unremitting barrage not only of rain but also of ice and heat, and, most harmful of all, wind. Could anyone possibly hold out against enemies so relentless and so fierce for any great length of time? As a result, some decay straightaway, others crumble, others weigh down the wall, others split and fall apart, and others are washed away, so that no metal, however invincible it might otherwise prove against the ravages of the weather, could here possibly endure so continuous an onslaught. . . .

Nevertheless, of all the techniques man has tried, his wit and energy have yet to discover anything more suitable than earthenware tiles. Frost will cause paviors' work to roughen, split, and settle; lead melts under the heat of the sun; copper, if laid in heavy plates, is costly, and if thin, may be damaged by the wind, and worn and eaten away by verdigris. . . .

There are two kinds of tile: one is flat, measuring a foot in width by a cubit in length, with a rough ridge on either side a ninth of the width; the other is curved like the greaves that protect the legs; both are wider where they receive the flowing rain and narrower where they throw it off. But flat tiles are better, in that they can be joined in line and perfectly level without dipping on one side, and without any valleys, ridges, gaps, or anything to obstruct the rain as it runs off. If the surface of the roof covers a vast expanse, larger tiles will be required; otherwise the channels will be insufficient and the rivulets of rainwater will overflow. To prevent gales from dislodging the tiles, I would recommend that, particularly in public works, they be set firm in a bed of lime. In private ones, though, it will be sufficient simply to reinforce the guttering against the wind, in that it is easier to repair broken tiles, if they are not bedded.

There is another very suitable type of roof covering. With wooden roofs, instead of boarding, earthenware panels are fixed with gypsum to the transverse lathing; on top of these are laid plain-tiles held in position with lime. This produces a work with great resistance to fire, and one that is extremely convenient for the inhabitants; it will be even cheaper if, instead of panels, Greek reeds are laid and held down with lime.

Tiles that are to be fixed with lime, especially those for public works, should not be used until they have been exposed to the frost and sun for at least two years; if a weak one is laid in position, it cannot be removed without a great deal of effort. . . .

PAVEMENTS

I now come to deal with the pavement, since it shares the same characteristics as the roof. Some are exposed to the sky, some are built of composite beams, and others not. But in each case the surface onto which they are laid must be solid and exact in its lines.

A surface exposed to the sky should have a fall of at least two inches in every ten feet. It should be so designed that the water running off is either collected in cisterns or drawn off into drains. If the water cannot be emptied into the sea or a river, find suitable places to dig wells deep enough to reach running water, then fill up the holes with pebbles. If even this is not possible, the final advice is to make a generous pit, throw in some coal, then fill it up with sand. This will absorb and remove any superfluous water.

If the *area* consists of piled-up earth, it must be leveled off accurately and covered with a layer of rubble rammed into place. But if the surface has a composite timber base, then further boarding should be laid crossways, rammed down, and covered with rubble to a depth of one foot. Some think that a layer of broom or fern should be laid as a base to prevent damage to the timber from its coming into contact with any lime. If the rubble is new, mix it three parts to one with lime; if old, five to two. Once it has been laid, it must be consolidated by being continually beaten with beetles. A pulp consisting of crushed tiles mixed three to one with sand is then laid over this to a depth of six inches. Finally, arrangements of marble or herringbone tiles or mosaic should be laid on top, in line and level. The work will be better protected if a layer of tiles bonded with lime, soaked in oil, is set between the hardcore and the dough. . . .

Pavements rejoice in being laid in damp and humid conditions, and remain stronger and more intact in the shade and the damp. They are most vulnerable to infirm soil, and also to being dried out too quickly. Just as the earth in the fields, which hardens with continual rain, likewise pavements, if they are kept saturated, will be welded together into a single, complete solid. Wherever rain drips from the drainpipes of the roof onto the pavement, the crust must be made of sound and very solid stone, to prevent the continual malice, so to speak, of the falling drops from wearing away and impairing it.

With pavements laid on top of framed wooden floors, care must be taken to ensure that the bones that provide the support are robust enough and that they all have the same strength. Otherwise, if any point in a wall or beam is stronger than the rest, there the pavement will split and be damaged. The strength and vitality of timber does not always remain constant, but varies with the conditions: timber will soften in the damp, but it will regain its rigidity and strength in the dry; and so, clearly, if any of the weaker parts strain and subside under the weight, the pavement will split. But enough on this subject.

There is, however, one pertinent consideration that I would not wish to pass over. The digging of the foundations and their infilling, the raising of the wall and the laying of the covering, should all be conducted at different times of the year and under different climatic conditions. The best moment to dig foundations is at the time of the Dog Star or during autumn itself, when the ground is dry and there is no water to flow into the trenches to impede the work. It is not at all unsuitable to fill in the foundations at the beginning of spring, especially if they are deep, as the earth will stand by and give them sufficient protection from the heat of the summer. The beginning of winter, however, is by far the best time to fill them in, except in polar regions and other cold places, where they will immediately freeze rather than set. The wall also dislikes excessive heat, biting cold, sudden frost, and, above all, northerly winds. The vault prefers an even and temperate climate, until the work has gained sufficient strength and has hardened.

The most opportune time to set the outer shell is at the rising of the Pleiades, and, in general, any period when Auster is blowing strong and full of moisture, because if the surface to which you apply the skin or rendering is not thoroughly damp, it will not adhere, but will peel, tear, and come away everywhere, leaving the work disfigured and full of blemishes.

Reflective Text

JUHANI PALLASMAA, EXCERPTS FROM *THE EYES OF THE SKIN*.

First Published in 1996

RETINAL ARCHITECTURE AND THE LOSS OF PLASTICITY

It is evident that the architecture of traditional cultures is also essentially connected with the tacit wisdom of the body, instead of being visually and conceptually dominated. Construction in traditional cultures is guided by the body in the same way that a bird shapes its nest by movements of its body. Indigenous clay and mud architectures in various parts of the world seem to be born of the muscular and haptic senses more than the eye. We can even identify the transition of indigenous construction from the haptic realm into the control of vision as a loss of plasticity and intimacy, and of the sense of total fusion characteristic in the settings of indigenous cultures.

The dominance of the sense of vision pointed out in philosophical thought is equally evident in the development of Western architecture. Greek architecture, with its elaborate systems of optical corrections, was already ultimately refined for the pleasure of the eye. However, the privileging of sight does not necessarily imply a rejection of the other senses, as the haptic sensibility, materiality and authoritative weight of Greek architecture prove; the eye invites and stimulates muscular and tactile sensations. The sense of sight may incorporate, and even reinforce, other sense modalities; the unconscious tactile ingredient in vision is particularly important and strongly present in historical architecture, but badly neglected in the architecture of our time.

Western architectural theory since Leon Battista Alberti has been primarily engaged with questions of visual perception, harmony and proportion. Alberti's statement that "painting is nothing but the intersection of the visual pyramid following a given distance, a fixed centre and a certain lighting" outlines the perspectival paradigm which also became the instrument of architectural thinking.[4] Again, it has to be emphasised that the conscious focusing on the mechanics of vision did not automatically result in the decisive and deliberate rejection of other senses before our own era of the omnipresent visual image. The eye conquers its hegemonic role in architectural practice, both consciously and

4. Leon Battista Alberti, as quoted in David M. Levin, *Modernity and the Hegemony of Vision* (Berkeley: University of California Press, 1993), 64.

unconsciously, only gradually with the emergence of the idea of a bodiless observer. The observer becomes detached from an incarnate relation with the environment through the suppression of the other senses, in particular by means of technological extensions of the eye, and the proliferation of images. As Marx W. Wartofsky argues, "the human vision is itself an artifact, produced by other artifacts, namely pictures."[5]

The dominant sense of vision figures strongly in the writings of the modernists. Statements by Le Corbusier—such as: "I exist in life only if I can see";[6] "I am and I remain an impenitent visual—everything is in the visual";[7] "One needs to see clearly in order to understand";[8] ". . . I urge you to *open your eyes*. Do you open your eyes? Are you trained to open your eyes? Do you know how to open your eyes, do you open them often, always, well?";[9] "Man looks at the creation of architecture with his eyes, which are 5 feet 6 inches from the ground";[10] and, "Architecture is a plastic thing. I mean by 'plastic' what is seen and measured by the eyes"[11]—make the privileging of the eye in early modernist theory very clear. Further declarations by Walter Gropius—"He [the designer] has to adapt knowledge of the scientific facts of optics and thus obtain a theoretical ground that will guide the hand giving shape, and create an objective basis"[12]—and by Laszlo Moholy-Nagy—"The hygiene of the optical, the health of the visible is slowly filtering through"[13]—confirm the central role of vision in modernist thought.

Le Corbusier's famous credo, "Architecture is the masterly, correct and magnificent play of masses brought together in light,"[14] unquestionably defines an architecture of the eye. Le Corbusier, however, was a great artistic talent with a moulding hand, and a tremendous sense of materiality, plasticity and gravity, all of which prevented his architecture from turning into sensory reductivism. Regardless of Le Corbusier's Cartesian ocularcentric exclamations, the hand had a similar fetishistic role in his work as the eye. A vigorous element of tactility is present in Le Corbusier's sketches and paintings, and this haptic sensibility is incorporated into his regard for architecture. However, the reductive bias becomes devastating in his urbanistic projects.

In Mies van der Rohe's architecture a frontal perspectival perception predominates, but his unique sense of order, structure, weight, detail and craft decisively enriches the visual paradigm. Moreover, an architectural work is great precisely because of the oppositional and contradictory intentions and allusions it succeeds in fusing together. A tension between conscious intentions and unconscious drives is necessary for a work in order to open up the emotional participation of the observer. "In every case one must achieve a simultaneous solution of opposites," as Alvar Aalto wrote.[15] The verbal statements of artists and architects should not usually be taken at their face value, as they often merely represent a conscious surface rationalisation, or defence, that may well be in sharp contradiction with the deeper unconscious intentions giving the work its very life force.

With equal clarity, the visual paradigm is the prevailing condition in city planning, from the idealised town plans of the Renaissance to the Functionalist principles of zoning and planning that reflect the "hygiene of the optical." In particular, the contemporary city is increasingly the city of the eye, detached from the body by rapid motorised movement,

5. As quoted in Martin Jay, *Downcast Eyes: The Denigration of Vision in Twentieth-Century French Thought* (Berkeley: University of California Press, 1994), 5.

6. Le Corbusier, *Precisions* (Cambridge: MIT Press, 1991), 7.

7. Pierre-Alain Crosset, "Eyes Which See," *Casabella*, 531–532 (1987): 115.

8. Le Corbusier, *Precisions*, 231.

9. Ibid., 227.

10. Le Corbusier, *Towards a New Architecture* (London: Architectural Press, 1959), 164.

11. Ibid., 191.

12. Walter Gropius, *Architektur* (Frankfurt: Fischer, 1956), 15–25.

13. As quoted in Susan Sontag, *On Photography* (New York: Penguin Books, 1986), 96.

14. Le Corbusier, *Towards a New Architecture*, 31.

15. Alvar Aalto, "Taide ja Tekniikka" [Art and Technology], in *Alvar Aalto: Luonnoksia* [Sketches], eds. Alvar Aalto and Göran Schildt (Helsinki: Otava, 1972), 87.

or through the overall aerial grasp from an airplane. The processes of planning have favoured the idealising and disembodied Cartesian eye of control and detachment; city plans are highly idealised and schematised visions seen through *le regard surplombant* (the look from above), as defined by Jean Starobinski,[16] or through "the mind's eye" of Plato.

Until recently, architectural theory and criticism have been almost exclusively engaged with the mechanisms of vision and visual expression. The perception and experience of architectural form has most frequently been analysed through the gestalt laws of visual perception. Educational philosophy has likewise understood architecture primarily in terms of vision, emphasising the construction of three-dimensional visual images in space.

AN ARCHITECTURE OF VISUAL IMAGES

The ocular bias has never been more apparent in the art of architecture than in the past 30 years, as a type of architecture, aimed at a striking and memorable visual image, has predominated. Instead of an existentially grounded plastic and spatial experience, architecture has adopted the psychological strategy of advertising and instant persuasion; buildings have turned into image products detached from existential depth and sincerity.

David Harvey relates "the loss of temporality and the search for instantaneous impact" in contemporary expression to the loss of experiential depth.[17] Fredric Jameson uses the notion of "contrived depthlessness" to describe the contemporary cultural condition and "its fixation with appearances, surfaces and instant impacts that have no sustaining power over time."[18]

As a consequence of the current deluge of images, architecture of our time often appears as mere retinal art of the eye, thus completing an epistemological cycle that began in Greek thought and architecture. But the change goes beyond mere visual dominance; instead of being a situational bodily encounter, architecture has become an art of the printed image fixed by the hurried eye of the camera. In our culture of pictures, the gaze itself flattens into a picture and loses its plasticity. Instead of experiencing our being in the world, we behold it from outside as spectators of images projected on the surface of the retina. David Michael Levin uses the term "frontal ontology" to describe the prevailing frontal, fixated and focused vision.[19]

Susan Sontag has made perceptive remarks on the role of the photographed image in our perception of the world. She writes, for instance, of a "mentality which looks at the world as a set of potential photographs,"[20] and argues that "the reality has come to seem more and more what we are shown by camera,"[21] and that "the omnipresence of photographs has an incalculable effect on our ethical sensibility. By furnishing this already crowded world with a duplicate one of images, photography makes us feel that the world is more available than it really is."[22]

As buildings lose their plasticity, and their connection with the language and wisdom of the body, they become isolated in the cool and distant realm of vision. With

16. As quoted in Jay, *Downcast Eyes*, 19.
17. David Harvey, *The Condition of Postmodernity* (Malden: Blackwell Publishing, 1990), 58.
18. Fredric Jameson, as quoted in ibid., 58.
19. Levin, *Modernity*, 203.
20. Sontag, *On Photography*, 7.
21. Ibid., 16.
22. Ibid., 24.

the loss of tactility, measures and details crafted for the human body—and particularly for the hand—architectural structures become repulsively flat, sharp-edged, immaterial and unreal. The detachment of construction from the realities of matter and craft further turns architecture into stage sets for the eye, into a scenography devoid of the authenticity of matter and construction. The sense of "aura," the authority of presence, that Walter Benjamin regards as a necessary quality for an authentic piece of art, has been lost. These products of instrumentalised technology conceal their processes of construction, appearing as ghostlike apparitions. The increasing use of reflective glass in architecture reinforces the dreamlike sense of unreality and alienation. The contradictory opaque transparency of these buildings reflects the gaze back unaffected and unmoved; we are unable to see or imagine life behind these walls. The architectural mirror, that returns our gaze and doubles the world, is an enigmatic and frightening device.

MATERIALITY AND TIME

The flatness of today's standard construction is strengthened by a weakened sense of materiality. Natural materials—stone, brick and wood—allow our vision to penetrate their surfaces and enable us to become convinced of the veracity of matter. Natural materials express their age and history, as well as the story of their origins and their history of human use. All matter exists in the continuum of time; the patina of wear adds the enriching experience of time to the materials of construction. But the machine-made materials of today—scaleless sheets of glass, enamelled metals and synthetic plastics—tend to present their unyielding surfaces to the eye without conveying their material essence or age. Buildings of this technological age usually deliberately aim at ageless perfection, and they do not incorporate the dimension of time, or the unavoidable and mentally significant processes of aging. This fear of the traces of wear and age is related to our fear of death.

Transparency and sensations of weightlessness and flotation are central themes in modern art and architecture. In recent decades, a new architectural imagery has emerged, which employs reflection, gradations of transparency, overlay and juxtaposition to create a sense of spatial thickness, as well as subtle and changing sensations of movement and light. This new sensibility promises an architecture that can turn the relative immateriality and weightlessness of recent technological construction into a positive experience of space, place and meaning.

The weakening of the experience of time in today's environments has devastating mental effects. In the words of the American therapist Gotthard Booth, "nothing gives man fuller satisfaction than participation in processes that supersede the span of individual life."[23] We have a mental need to grasp that we are rooted in the continuity of time, and in the man-made world it is the task of architecture to facilitate this experience. Architecture domesticates limitless space and enables us to inhabit it, but it should likewise domesticate endless time and enable us to inhabit the continuum of time.

The current over-emphasis on the intellectual and conceptual dimensions of architecture contributes to the disappearance of its physical, sensual and embodied

23. From a conversation with Professor Keijo Petäjä in the early 1980s; the source is unidentified.

essence. Contemporary architecture posing as the avant-garde, is more often engaged with the architectural discourse itself and mapping the possible marginal territories of the art than responding to human existential questions. This reductive focus gives rise to a sense of architectural autism, an internalised and autonomous discourse that is not grounded in our shared existential reality.

Beyond architecture, contemporary culture at large drifts towards a distancing, a kind of chilling de-sensualisation and de-eroticisation of the human relation to reality. Painting and sculpture also seem to be losing their sensuality; instead of inviting a sensory intimacy, contemporary works of art frequently signal a distancing rejection of sensuous curiosity and pleasure. These works of art speak to the intellect and to the conceptualising capacities instead of addressing the senses and the undifferentiated embodied responses. The ceaseless bombardment of unrelated imagery leads only to a gradual emptying of images of their emotional content. Images are converted into endless commodities manufactured to postpone boredom; humans in turn are commodified, consuming themselves nonchalantly without having the courage or even the possibility of confronting their very existential reality. We are made to live in a fabricated dream world.

I do not wish to express a conservative view of contemporary art in the tone of Hans Sedlmayr's thought-provoking but disturbing book *Art in Crisis*.[24] I merely suggest that a distinct change has occurred in our sensory and perceptual experience of the world, one that is reflected by art and architecture. If we desire architecture to have an emancipating or healing role, instead of reinforcing the erosion of existential meaning, we must reflect on the multitude of secret ways in which the art of architecture is tied to the cultural and mental reality of its time. We should also be aware of the ways in which the feasibility of architecture is being threatened or marginalised by current political, cultural, economic, cognitive, and perceptual developments. Architecture has become an endangered art form.

THE REJECTION OF ALBERTI'S WINDOW

The eye itself has not, of course, remained in the monocular, fixed construction defined by Renaissance theories of perspective. The hegemonic eye has conquered new ground for visual perception and expression. The paintings of Hieronymus Bosch and Pieter Bruegel, for instance, already invite a participatory eye to travel across the scenes of multiple events. The 17th-century Dutch paintings of bourgeois life present casual scenes and objects of everyday use which expand beyond the boundaries of Albertian window. Baroque paintings open up vision with hazy edges, soft focus and multiple perspectives, presenting a distinct, tactile invitation and enticing the body to travel through the illusory space.

An essential line in the evolution of modernity has been the liberation of the eye from the Cartesian perspectival epistemology. The paintings of Joseph Mallord William Turner continue the elimination of the picture frame and the vantage point begun in the Baroque era; the Impressionists abandon the boundary line, balanced framing and

24. Hans Sedlmayr, *Art in Crisis: The Lost Centre* (London: Hollis & Carter, 1957).

perspectival depth; Paul Cézanne aspires "to make visible how the world touches us";[25] Cubists abandon the single focal point, reactivate peripheral vision and reinforce haptic experience, whereas the colour field painters reject illusory depth in order to reinforce the presence of the painting itself as an iconic artifact and an autonomous reality. Land artists fuse the reality of the work with the reality of the lived world, and finally, artists such as Richard Serra directly address the body as well as our experiences of horizontality and verticality, materiality, gravity and weight.

The same countercurrent against the hegemony of the perspectival eye has taken place in modern architecture regardless of the culturally privileged position of vision. The kinesthetic and textural architecture of Frank Lloyd Wright, the muscular and tactile buildings of Alvar Aalto, and Louis Kahn's architecture of geometry and gravitas are particularly significant examples of this.

A NEW VISION AND SENSORY BALANCE
Perhaps, freed of the implicit desire of the eye for control and power, it is precisely the unfocused vision of our time that is again capable of opening up new realms of vision and thought. The loss of focus brought about by the stream of images may emancipate the eye from its patriarchal domination and give rise to a participatory and empathetic gaze. The technological extensions of the senses have until now reinforced the primacy of vision, but the new technologies may also help "the body . . . to dethrone the disinterested gaze of the disincarnated Cartesian spectator."[26]

Martin Jay remarks: "In opposition to the lucid, linear, solid, fixed, planimetric, closed form of the Renaissance . . . the baroque was painterly, recessional, soft-focused, multiple, and open."[27] He also argues that the "baroque visual experience has a strongly tactile or haptic quality, which prevents it from turning into the absolute ocularcentrism of its Cartesian perspectivalist rival."[28]

The haptic experience seems to be penetrating the ocular regime again through the tactile presence of modern visual imagery. In a music video, for instance, or the layered contemporary urban transparency, we cannot halt the flow of images for analytic observation; instead we have to appreciate it as an enhanced haptic sensation, rather like a swimmer senses the flow of water against his/her skin.

In his thorough and thought-provoking book *The Opening of Vision: Nihilism and the Postmodern Situation*, David Michael Levin differentiates between two modes of vision: "the assertoric gaze" and "the aletheic gaze."[29] In his view, the assertoric gaze is narrow, dogmatic, intolerant, rigid, fixed, inflexible, exclusionary and unmoved, whereas the aletheic gaze, associated with the hermeneutic theory of truth, tends to see from a multiplicity of standpoints and perspectives, and is multiple, pluralistic, democratic, contextual, inclusionary, horizontal and caring.[30] As suggested by Levin, there are signs that a new mode of looking is emerging.

Although the new technologies have strengthened the hegemony of vision, they may also help to re-balance the realms of the senses. In Walter Ong's view, "with telephone,

25. Maurice Merleau-Ponty, "Cezanne's Doubt," in *Sense and Non-Sense* (Evanston: Northwestern University Press, 1964), 19.
26. Jay, in Hal Foster, *Vision and Visuality* (Seattle: Bay Press, 1988), 18.
27. Ibid., 16.
28. Ibid., 17.
29. David M. Levin, *The Opening of Vision—Nihilism and the Postmodern Situation* (New York: Routledge, 1988), 440.
30. Ibid.

radio, television and various kinds of sound tape, electronic technology has brought us into the age of 'secondary orality.' This new orality has striking resemblances to the old in its participatory mystique, its fostering of communal sense, its concentration on the present moment."[31]

"We in the Western world are beginning to discover our neglected senses. This growing awareness represents something of an overdue insurgency against the painful deprivation of sensory experience we have suffered in our technologised world," writes the anthropologist Ashley Montagu.[32] This new awareness is forcefully projected by numerous architects around the world today who are attempting to re-sensualise architecture through a strengthened sense of materiality and hapticity, texture and weight, density of space and materialised light.

31. Walter J. Ong, *Orality and Literacy: The Technologizing of the Word* (London: Methuen & Co., 1982), 136.

32. Ashley Montagu, *Touching: The Human Significance of the Skin, 3rd Ed.* (New York: Harper Paperbacks, 1986), XIII. First published in 1971.

Philosophical Text

JONATHAN HILL, EXCERPTS FROM *IMMATERIAL ARCHITECTURE*.

First Published in 2006

INTRODUCTION: IMMATERIAL/MATERIAL

The view from my first home extended across fields for three miles to the north. In the distance was a row of electricity pylons. Against the familiar grey sky the grey pylons were invisible. Very occasionally, when light chanced on steel, the pylons would briefly flicker and then disappear. Physically unchanging, the pylons were as seasonal as the fields.

For many an architect or writer, ideas and concerns evolve over time, from project to project. Strategies, forms and materials that first appear in one design develop and mutate in another. Characters, narratives and events that first appear in one book grow and change in another. In *Actions of Architecture: Architects and Creative Users* I write:

> The word architecture has a number of meanings. For example, it is a subject, practice, and a certain type of object and space, typically the building in the city. . . . I consider each of these definitions but focus on another: architecture is a certain type of object and space used. Within the term "use" I include the full range of ways in which buildings and cities are experienced, such as habit, distraction and appropriation.[33]

Architecture is expected to be solid, stable and reassuring—physically, socially and psychologically. Bound to each other, the architectural and the material are considered inseparable. But *Immaterial Architecture* states that the immaterial is as important to architecture as the material and has as long a history. . . .

There are many ways to understand immaterial architecture. As an idea, a formless phenomenon, a technological development towards lightness, a *tabula rasa* of a capitalist economy, a gradual loss of architecture's moral weight and certitude or a programmatic

33. Jonathan Hill, *Actions of Architecture: Architects and Creative Users* (London: Routledge, 2003), 2.

focus on actions rather than forms. I recognize each of these models but concentrate on another. Focusing on immaterial architecture as the perceived absence of matter more than the actual absence of matter,[34] I devise new means to explore old concerns: the creativity of the architect and the user. The user decides whether architecture is immaterial. But the architect, or any other architectural producer, creates material conditions in which that decision can be made. . . .

Immaterial Architecture advocates an architecture that fuses the immaterial and the material, and considers its consequences, challenging preconceptions about architecture, its practice, purpose, matter and use . . . so that they are in conjunction not opposition. . . .

CONCLUSION: IMMATERIAL-MATERIAL

IMMATERIAL ARCHITECTURE

Western discourse depends on the binary opposition of terms—one superior, the other inferior—that are assumed to be separate and distinct, one "*external* to the other,"[35] such as immaterial philosophy and material architecture. But such terms are in fact inter-dependent and inseparable, undermining dualistic discourse. Architecture is built into philosophy, whether in spatial metaphors such as interior and exterior or in references to philosophical discourse as a sound edifice built on solid foundations. But to protect its status philosophy must conceal its dependence on architecture. Philosophy "attempts to subordinate architecture precisely because it is so indebted to it. Philosophical discourse is only able to preserve the image of architecture with which it organizes and describes itself by veiling its indebtedness to that image," writes Wigley.[36]

Hidden within one another, the terms material and immaterial blur and slip, questioning other terms such as intellectual and manual, form and formless, real and virtual. One familiar meaning of the immaterial refers to the realm of ideas. Few people today agree with Plato that matter is modelled on ideal forms, but associating the immaterial with the intellectual is common. Countering Plato's coupling of ideas and forms the immaterial is sometimes associated with the formless, from which some of its fascination derives. But the formless is not absence of order, it is order that is unacceptable.[37]

My concern is not the immaterial alone or the immaterial in opposition to the material. Instead, I advocate an architecture that embraces the immaterial and the material. Since the eighteenth century ideas have more often been grounded in experience and interpretations have more often been personal. The immaterial architecture I propose is less the absence of matter than the perceived absence of matter.[38] Whether architecture is immaterial is dependent on perception, which involves creative interpretation, fictions rather than facts. Gregory writes that "visual and other perception is intelligent decision-taking from limited sensory evidence. The essential point is that sensory signals are not adequate for direct or certain perceptions, so intelligent guesswork is needed for seeing

34. In this book I mostly use the familiar architectural understanding of matter as a material rather than matter as energy, which is discussed in "Chapter 2: Hunting the Shadow."
35. Jaques Derrida, *Of Grammatology*, trans. Gayatri Chakravorti (Baltimore: Johns Hopkins University Press, 1976), 157.
36. Mark Wigley, *The Architecture of Deconstruction: Derrida's Haunt* (Cambridge: MIT Press, 1995), 14.
37. Mary Douglas, *Purity and Danger* (London: Routledge & Kegan Paul, 1966) 104.
38. Explored especially in "Index of Immaterial Architectures."

39. Richard Gregory, *Eye and Brain: The Psychology of Seeing* (Oxford: Oxford University Press, 1998), 5.

40. Ibid., 10.

41. Richard Andrews and Chris Bruce, "1992 Interview with James Turrell," in *James Turrell: Sensing Space*, eds. Richard Andrews and Chris Bruce (Seattle: University of Washington Henry Art Gallery, 1992), 48.

42. Juhani Pallasmaa, *The Eyes of the Skin: Architecture and the Senses* (London: Academy Editions, 1996), 29.

43. Use can be a reaction to habit, result from the knowledge learned through habit, or be based on habit, on a conscious and evolving deviation from established behaviour.

44. For a discussion of the juxtaposition of the senses, refer to "Index of Immaterial Architecture: Nordic Light" and "Silence."

45. Karl Marx and Friedrich Engels, "Manifesto of the Communist Party," in *Marx-Engels Reader, 2nd Ed.*, ed. Robert Tucker (New York: W. W. Norton & Co., 1978), 476.

46. David Sibley, "Comfort Anxiety and Space," in *Architecture— the Subject is Matter*, ed. Jonathan Hill (London: Routledge, 2001), 108.

47. Ibid., 115.

48. Sigmund Freud, "The 'Uncanny'," in *The Standard Edition*, trans. Alix Strachey (New York: Vintage, 1999), 233. First published in 1919. This is a quotation from a dictionary, Daniel Sanders, *Wörtenbuch der Deutschen Sprache*, 1860.

49. Hilde Heynen, *Architecture and Modernity: A Critique* (Cambridge: MIT Press, 1999), 233.

objects."[39] Consequently, permeated by memory, "perceptions are hypotheses. This is suggested by the fact that retinal images are open to an infinity of interpretations."[40] Binding immaterial architecture to perception focuses attention on the "capacity to just perceive one perceiving"[41] and the relations between architectural objects, spaces and users.

Pallasmaa writes that "Instead of mere vision . . . architecture involves realms of sensory experience which interact and fuse into each other."[42] The appreciation of immaterial architecture is especially complex, and a challenge to the familiar experience of architecture.[43] The richness of the user's experience of any building depends on awareness of all the senses, but immaterial architecture may trigger a sense more often associated with the immaterial, such as smell, and question one more often associated with the material, such as touch. The experience of immaterial architecture is based on contradictory sensations, and is appropriate to an active and creative engagement with architecture. The complexity of the whole experience depends upon the user's interpretation of what is present and absent. To experience the full character of the juxtaposition requires, therefore, an understanding of the conflict, whether pleasurable or not, and speculation on an imagined space or object.[44]

IMMATERIAL HOME

The statement "All that is solid melts into air" encapsulates the force of a capitalist society that, in expanding cycles of destruction, production and consumption, undermines all that is assumed to be solid, such as the home.[45] But in undermining the safety of the home, a capitalist society feeds desire for a home that is evermore safe. Sibley argues that while the apparent stability of the home may provide gratification it can also, simultaneously, create anxiety because the security and spatial purification the home offers can never be fully achieved. Often the consequence is an increasingly intense need for stability not an awareness of its limits: "Generally, anxieties are expressed in the desire to erect and maintain spatial and temporal boundaries. Strong boundary consciousness can be interpreted as a desire to be in control and to exclude the unfamiliar because the unfamiliar is a source of unease rather than something to be celebrated."[46] Referring to Sigmund Freud's 1919 essay on the uncanny, Sibley adds that "this striving for the safe, the familiar or *heimlich* fails to remove a sense of unease. I would argue that it makes it worse."[47] However, Freud offers another meaning of *heimlich*: "Concealed, kept from sight, so that others do not get to know about it."[48] Striving for the familiar is ineffective because the home can never be safe enough and the *heimlich* is not what it seems. Heynen writes:

> It is not without reason that dwelling is the key metaphor that Freud uses in his reflection on the uncanny. According to Freud, the most uncanny experience occurs in environment that is more familiar to us, for the experience of the uncanny has to do with the intertwining of heimlich (what is of the house, but also what is hidden) and unheimlich (what is not of the house, what is therefore in a strange way unconcealed yet concealed).[49]

The uncanny is experienced when something familiar is repressed but returns as unexpected and unfamiliar.[50] One is at home but out of place.

Sibley does not reject all attempts to construct a stable order. Instead he argues for the merits of both defined boundaries and spatial porosity. As an example he considers the child's experience of the home. He writes that the:

> negative view of strongly classified environments fails to take account of evidence from research in group therapy that children (and adults) need firm boundaries in order to develop a secure sense of self. If members of a family "live in each other's laps," in a boundary-less, weakly classified home, or they are "enmeshed" as Salvador Minuchin put it, there is a danger that children, in particular, will not develop a sense of autonomy.[51]

When it is identified with the formless, the immaterial is associated with all that appears to threaten society, architecture and the home, whether insidious disorder inside or lurking danger outside. But the threat of the immaterial is imagined as much as it is real. The desire for an architecture that is safe and secure can never be fulfilled. Instead, it may increase anxiety and further desire for an architecture that is evermore safe. Replacing a static and material architecture with one that is fluid and immaterial is no solution, however. Instead, compatibility between the spaces of a home and the habits of its occupants is desirable. A tightly structured group of people occupying a loose spatial configuration will create tension and anxiety, as will the opposite. However, matching users to spatial configurations fails to take account of changing users and changing needs.[52] Instead, a home must have the potential to be both spatially tight and loose. To accommodate evolving conceptions of the individual and society architecture must engage the material and the immaterial, the static and the fluid, the solid and the porous. An architecture that is immaterial and spatially porous, as well as solid and stable where necessary, will not change established habits. Rather it may offer those habits greater flexibility.[53]

IMMATERIAL PRACTICE

The practice of architects is expected to be as solid and reassuring as their buildings. With regard to immaterial architecture, therefore, architects are understandably cautious. An architect who persuades a client of the merits of an architecture that is insubstantial and unpredictable still faces numerous difficulties to see it built, such as building regulations and contractual liability. On a more fundamental note, immaterial architecture revels in qualities—the subjective, unpredictable, porous and ephemeral—that are contrary to the solid, objective and respectable practice expected of a professional.

The stability of architects' practice is a myth, however. Cousins states that the discipline of architecture is weak because it involves not just objects but relations between subjects and objects.[54] As the discipline of architecture is weak, so too is the practice of

50. The uncanny is a perception not a property of a space.

51. Sibley, "Comfort Anxiety and Space," 116; and Salvador Minuchin, *Families and Family Therapy* (London: Tavistock, 1974).

52. One failing of functionalism is that it assumes that needs do not change.

53. Discussed further in "Index of Immaterial Architectures."

54. Mark Cousins, "Building an Architect," in *Occupying Architecture*, ed. Jonathan Hill (London: Routledge, 1998), 13–22.

architects. But, weak is not pejorative here. Rather it is the strength to be fluid, flexible and open to conflicting perceptions and opinions. The practice of architects needs to confidently reflect the nature of the architectural discipline. Architecture must be immaterial and spatially porous, as well as solid and stable where necessary; and so should the practice of architects.

In this book I refer to the architect caught between the immaterial idea and the material object, the creative artist and the solid professional. In the discourse and practice of architects, the older meaning of design, as drawing ideas, and the newer meaning of design, as drawing appliances, are both in evidence, except that ideas are now understood as provisional not universal. Professionalism fits the newer conception of design in particular, and is less compatible with design as it was first conceived. A profession's claim to a monopoly depends upon superior expertise and competence; it is neither expected nor paid to generate ideas. But the architectural profession is unusual in that it claims to be innovative. Architects' claim that only they produce buildings that deserve to be called architecture uncomfortably fuses the desires of an artist and the needs of a professional. Other architectural producers, such as artists, are as dependent on the status of immaterial ideas but may face less pressure to produce solid objects from a solid practice. Immaterial architecture is an especially poignant and rewarding challenge for architects because it forcefully confronts what they practice and produce.

IMMATERIAL BOOK

In the Renaissance the building was connected to the immaterial through the ideas it presented, which had much to do with form and little to do with matter. Weston remarks that later "The Classical view that forms were independent of matter was no longer tenable, and from the early eighteenth century onwards scientists and engineers began to devote increasing attention to understanding and quantifying properties of materials."[55] In the nineteenth century the assumption that a particular tectonic language is innate within each material became familiar in architectural discourse. Semper was particularly influential in its development: "In the first place, every work of art should reflect in its appearance, as it were, the material as physical matter . . . In this way we may speak of a wood style, a brick style, an ashlar style, and so forth."[56] Giving it positive value and an active role, Semper undermines the long philosophical tradition that disregards matter. Influenced by Semper, Loos states that "Every material possesses its own language of forms, and none may lay claim for itself to the forms of another material."[57] However, Loos' discourse on the relations between materials and forms is reductive in comparison to that of Semper, who stresses the transfer of an idea from one material to another, with some modification to both, to the point that "men in times of high artistic development also *masked the material of the mask*".[58] Alois Riegl notes that "Wheras Semper did suggest that material and technique play a role in the genesis of art forms, the Semperians jumped to the conclusion that all art forms were always the direct product of materials and techniques."[59] Modernism encapsulates this simplification in the phrase

55. Richard Weston, *Materials, Form and Architecture* (London: Laurence King, 2003), 70.

56. Gottfried Semper, "On Architectural Styles," in *The Four Elements of Architecture and Other Writings* trans. Harry Francis Mallgrave and Wolfgang Herrmann (Cambridge: Cambridge University Press, 1989), 269. First published in 1851.

57. Adolf Loos, "The Principle of Cladding," in *Spoken into the Void*, trans. Jane O. Newman and John H. Smith (Cambridge: MIT Press, 1987), 66.

58. Gottfried Semper, *Der Stil in den Technischen und Tektonischen Künsten oder Praktische Ästhetik* (Frankfurt: Verlag, 1860), 257.

59. Alois Riegl, *Problems of Style: Foundations for a History of Ornament*, trans. Evelyn Kain (Princeton: Princeton University Press, 1992), 4.

"truth to materials." Here the material speaks and the architect responds, as in Louis Kahn's remark—both comical and thoughtful—that "When you are designing in brick, you must ask brick what it wants or what it can do."[60] Rather than coupling tectonics to materials, I argue for the interdependence of the subject, method and matter of architecture. What then are the subject, method and matter of an architectural book?

In Benjamin's *The Arcades Project*, montage is the subject, method and matter.[61] Unfinished at the time of his death, Benjamin initially intended to construct *The Arcades Project* from the juxtaposition of fragmentary quotations from the nineteenth century. His second 1935 draft is an example of ambiguous montage.[62] With a grid of holes punched through its pages front and back, *Chora L Works: Jacques Derrida and Peter Eisenman* explores the idea that the absence of material is not necessarily the same as the absence of meaning.[63] The presence of holes is formed by the absence of paper. Each hole marks the absence of a section of the text but not an absence in meaning because the reader can either identify the missing word or select a new one. In "The Death of the Author" Roland Barthes recognizes that the journey from author to text to reader is never seamless or direct. Questioning the authority of the author, he states that reading can be a creative activity that constructs a text anew, and argues for a writer aware of the creativity of the reader.[64] *The Arcades Project, Chora L Works* and "The Death of the Author" address the creative role of the reader in the formulation of the text through the creation of gaps, interpretative and literal.[65]

Like other books this one is made of ink and paper. As my principal concern is the perception of the material as immaterial, the immaterial is conjured forth not by a lighter paper or holes cut into its surface but by the ideas of the reader, formulating immaterial architectures from within and between the images and words juxtaposed on these pages. The user decides whether architecture is immaterial. But the architect creates conditions in which that decision can be made. Both are creative.

60. Richard S. Wurman, *What Will Be Has Always Been: The Words of Louis I. Kahn* (New York: Rizzoli, 1986), 152.

61. Matter here is a fragment of information rather than a fragment of paper.

62. Walter Benjamin, "Paris, Capital of the Nineteenth Century," in *Reflections: Essays, Aphorisms, Autobiographical Writings*, trans. Edmund Jephcott (New York: Schocken, 1986), 146–162.

63. Jaques Derrida and Peter Eisenman, *Chora L Works: Jaques Derrida and Peter Eisenman.* (New York: Monacelli, 1997).

64. Roland Barthes, "The Death of the Author," in *Image-Music-Text*, trans. Stephen Heath (New York: Hill and Wang, 1977), 142–148.

65. The montage of gaps is discussed in "Index of Immaterial Architectures Nordic Light."

Writing and Discussion Questions

ANALYSIS

1. What was Alberti arguing for and against? What excerpt/quotation best represents this?
2. What was Pallasmaa arguing for and against? What excerpt/quotation best represents this?
3. What was Hill arguing for and against? What excerpt/quotation best represents this?

SYNTHESIS

1. Regarding concepts of materiality and immateriality, discuss one major difference regarding Alberti's, Pallasmaa's, and Hill's texts.
2. Regarding concepts of materiality and immateriality, discuss one primary commonality regarding Alberti's, Pallasmaa's, and Hill's texts.

SELF-REFLECTION

1. For each of the texts, discuss a major issue with which you most agree and most disagree; reflect upon why you hold these views.
2. Select a recent design project, or a current project on which you are working. Discuss the characteristics of the project in regards to materiality and immateriality, in light of the discussion and texts introduced in this chapter. What attitudes regarding materiality and immateriality does your work illustrate?

PROSPECTION

1. Select one of the texts listed in the bibliography for this chapter; locate and read it. To what degree is that text and the attitudes it represents still relevant to architecture today and in the near future?

2. What is the role of materiality and immateriality in architecture today? Is materiality and immateriality predominantly about the expression of material properties, the transformation of materials, human perception, or value judgments; some combination of these; or something else? In other words, if a fourth text were added to this chapter, what would the argument be?

Other Readings on Material and Immaterial

Bell, Victoria Ballard, and Rand, Patrick. *Materials for Design*. (New York: Princeton Architectural Press, 2006).

Beylerian, George, Dent, Andrew, and Moryadas, Anita. *Material Connexion: The Global Resource of New and Innovative Materials for Architects, Artists, and Designers*. (Hoboken: John Wiley & Sons, 2005).

Brownell, Blaine, ed. *Transmaterial: A Catalog of Materials that Redefine Our Physical Environment*. (New York: Princeton Architectural Press, 2006).

Dubbeldam, Winka. "Thing-shapes." *Architectural Design* 72 (2002): 26–31.

Iwamoto, Lisa. *Digital Fabrications: Architectural and Material Techniques*. (New York: Princeton Architectural Press, 2009).

Kahn, Louis. *Essential Texts*. Robert Twombly, ed. (New York: W. W. Norton & Co., 2003).

Mori, Toshiko. *Immaterial/Ultramaterial: Architecture, Design, and Materials*. (New York: George Braziller, 2002).

Murray, Brendan. "Alberti's Window: A Phenomenological Dilemma." *Architectural Theory Review*, 15 (2010): 138–148.

Pezo, Mauricio. "No Thickness." *REVISTA*, 180 (2010): 2–5.

Pottmann, Helmut. "Geometry and New and Future Spatial Patterns." *Architectural Design*, 79 (2009): 60–65.

Saunders, William S. "Durability and Ephemerality." *Harvard Design Magazine* (Autumn 1997): 2–67.

Zumthor, Peter. *Atmospheres: Architectural Environments—Surrounding Objects*. (Basel: Birkhauser, 2006).

Part 2

DIALECTICAL READINGS in ARCHITECTURE: USE

Chapter 5

FUNCTION and FORM

FIGURE 5.1
Photograph of grain elevators in
Buffalo, New York, United States.
Architect and date unknown.

FIGURE 5.2
Photograph of main entry hall of
the Tate Modern (formerly the
turbine hall of the power plant),
London, England, United
Kingdom (2001: renovation).
Renovation architects: Herzog
& de Meuron.

INTRODUCTORY DISCUSSION

1. Of the two images above, which better represents the concept of "function" in
   architecture today? Why?

2. What are the various definitions and connotations of the term "function" in
   architecture? For example, how is "function" similar or different from terms like "use,"
   "program," etc.?

3. How is/is not "function" an appropriate concept or term in architecture today?

Introduction

Of any phrase born in architecture, the phrase "Form follows function" is maybe the most commonplace. It is a phrase found not only in architecture but also in product design, engineering, urban design, and popular media and culture. "Form follows function" is one of a handful of statements non-designers freely use in the praise or critique of products, buildings, or infrastructure. Few non-designers, however, are aware of the origins of this phrase, and even many designers are not aware that phrase is incomplete. In 1896, Louis Sullivan published a short essay entitled "The Tall Office Building Artistically Considered," where he made the statement, "form ever follows function." The essay was the culmination of five decades of rapid change in the city of Chicago.

In 1850, the population of Chicago totaled less than 30,000. By 1870, the population had grown to nearly 300,000. Despite the Great Chicago Fire of 1871, which devastated an enormous swath of the city, including the entire downtown, the population continued to grow at a staggering rate, surpassing one million residents by 1890. The World's Columbian Exposition of 1893 radically transformed the city and its architecture, and cemented Chicago as a major world city. During this time, population growth and commerce led to high land values, while industrialization and the Great Fire led to new methods of construction. Coupled together, architects and engineers in the late 1800s flocked to Chicago for economic reasons, as well as for the thrill of innovation, as the city grew vertically. Sullivan was among these architects.

Despite the excitement and vibrancy of the time, it was a confusing time for architects. Few architects were experienced in the utilization of steel structural systems and large plate glass in "skyscrapers." The greatest architectural questions, however, were not about material, but resided in issues of use and scale. How could large numbers of people conveniently enter and exit these vertical office towers? What would be the form, expression, and "style" of this new architectural type? The first question was answered in part by the invention and development of the high speed electric elevator. The second was answered most emphatically by Sullivan, who worked with William Le Baron Jenney, father of the American skyscraper, and later with Dankmar Adler, in developing a new architecture of steel, glass, and terra cotta. It was in "The Tall Office Building Artistically Considered," which serves as the *original text* in this chapter, that Sullivan acknowledged, "The architects of this land and generation are now brought face to face with something new under the sun—namely . . . a demand for the erection of tall office buildings." Sullivan subsequently articulated a solution: how the building was to be organized, where various uses would be located, how movement would occur, the ways spaces were to be subdivided, and lastly, but most importantly, how the façade was to be designed. It was all to be summed up with the statement, "form ever follows function, and this is the law." Later shortened, "form follows function" became the slogan of many 20th-century designers.

Nevertheless, the phrase has not gone unquestioned. The concept was inverted— "function follows form"—by the belief that a building's form did not need to represent its use. In fact, form could precede use; use could be determined later. For example, Sullivan viewed the elevator as something that made vertical travel "easy and comfortable" and enabled the skyscraper to exist. In *Architecture and Disjunction*, which serves as the *reflective text* in this chapter, Bernard Tschumi saw the elevator differently:

> If architects could self-consciously use such devices as repetition, distortion, or juxtaposition in the formal elaboration of walls, couldn't they do the same thing in terms of the activities that occurred within those very walls? Pole vaulting in the chapel, bicycling in the Laundromat, sky diving in the elevator shaft?

Tschumi stated further that "the relation between program and building could be either highly sympathetic or contrived and artificial," and that he was "fascinated" more by the latter. The "function follows form" concept gained validity through a variety of examples of adaptive reuse: schools turned into apartments, warehouses turned into retail spaces, and churches turned into pubs. The argument was not that function was irrelevant but that form need not rely on function for its expressive character. Furthermore, "the disjunction between expected form and expected use," as Tschumi put it, might result in a more interesting and satisfying architectural experience.

The issue that remains is one of terminology. Tschumi, for example, recognized the interchanging of the terms "function," "use," "program," "activity," "event," and "action," preferring the latter two terms, as they imply a more individualistic, temporary, and idiosyncratic inhabitation of architectural space. Likewise, in an essay entitled "Function," which serves as the *philosophical text* in this chapter, Adrian Forty articulated several definitions of the term, including "function" as a mathematical term, a biological term, and an architectural term. Forty noted of architecture: "The problem now appears to be to develop a satisfactory concept and appropriate terminology to replace 'function.'" The same might be said of the term "form." As a noun, "form" may refer to shape, structure, or appearance; custom or conduct; a document or outline; linguistics; or fitness or health. There are an equal number of verb definitions. Given such ambiguity, it is not surprising that the debate between "form" and "function" is so protracted and contentious.

Original Text

LOUIS SULLIVAN, "THE TALL OFFICE BUILDING ARTISTICALLY CONSIDERED."

First Published in 1896

The architects of this land and generation are now brought face to face with something new under the sun—namely, that evolution and integration of social conditions, that special grouping of them, that results in a demand for the erection of tall office buildings.

It is not my purpose to discuss the social conditions; I accept them as the fact, and say at once that the design of the tall office building must be recognized and confronted at the outset as a problem to be solved—a vital problem, pressing for a true solution.

Let us state the conditions in the plainest manner. Briefly, they are these: offices are necessary for the transaction of business; the invention and perfection of the high-speed elevators make vertical travel, that was once tedious and painful, now easy and comfortable; development of steel manufacture has shown the way to safe, rigid, economical constructions rising to a great height; continued growth of population in the great cities, consequent congestion of centers and rise in value of ground, stimulate an increase in number of stories; these successfully piled one upon another, react on ground values—and so on, by action and reaction, interaction and inter-reaction. Thus has come about that form of lofty construction called the "modern office building." It has come in answer to a call, for in it a new grouping of social conditions has found a habitation and a name.

Up to this point all in evidence is materialistic, an exhibition of force, of resolution, of brains in the keen sense of the word. It is the joint product of the speculator, the engineer, the builder.

Problem: How shall we impart to this sterile pile, this crude, harsh, brutal agglomeration, this stark, staring exclamation of eternal strife, the graciousness of those higher forms of sensibility and culture that rest on the lower and fiercer passions? How shall we proclaim from the dizzy height of this strange, weird, modern housetop the peaceful evangel of sentiment, of beauty, the cult of a higher life?

This is the problem; and we must seek the solution of it in a process analogous to its own evolution—indeed, a continuation of it—namely, by proceeding step by step from general to special aspects, from coarser to finer considerations.

It is my belief that it is of the very essence of every problem that it contains and suggests its own solution. This I believe to be natural law. Let us examine, then, carefully the elements, let us search out this contained suggestion, this essence of the problem.

The practical conditions are, broadly speaking, these:

Wanted—1st, a story below-ground, containing boilers, engines of various sorts, etc.—in short, the plant for power, heating, lighting, etc. 2nd, a ground floor, so called, devoted to stores, banks, or other establishments requiring large area, ample spacing, ample light, and great freedom of access. 3rd, a second story readily accessible by stairways—this space usually in large subdivisions, with corresponding liberality in structural spacing and expanse of glass and breadth of external openings. 4th, above this an indefinite number of stories of offices piled tier upon tier, one tier just like another tier, one office just like all the other offices—an office being similar to a cell in a honey-comb, merely a compartment, nothing more. 5th, and last, at the top of this pile is placed a space or story that, as related to the life and usefulness of the structure, is purely physiological in its nature—namely, the attic. In this the circulatory system completes itself and makes its grand turn, ascending and descending. The space is filled with tanks, pipes, valves, sheaves, and mechanical etcetera that supplement and complement the force-originating plant hidden below-ground in the cellar. Finally, or at the beginning rather, there must be on the ground floor a main aperture or entrance common to all the occupants or patrons of the building.

This tabulation is, in the main, characteristic of every tall office building in the country. As to the necessary arrangements for light courts, these are not germane to the problem, and as will become soon evident, I trust need not be considered here. These things, and such others as the arrangement of elevators, for example, have to do strictly with the economics of the building, and I assume them to have been fully considered and disposed of to the satisfaction of purely utilitarian and pecuniary demands. Only in rare instances does the plan or floor arrangement of the tall office building take on an aesthetic value, and this usually when the lighting court is external or becomes an internal feature of great importance.

As I am here seeking not for an individual or special solution, but for a true normal type, the attention must be confined to those conditions that, in the main, are constant in all tall office buildings, and every mere incidental and accidental variation eliminated from the consideration, as harmful to the clearness of the main inquiry.

The practical horizontal and vertical division or office unit is naturally based on a room of comfortable area and height, and the size of this standard office room as naturally predetermines the standard structural unit, and, approximately, the size of window openings. In turn, these purely arbitrary units of structure form in an equally natural way the true basis of the artistic development of the exterior. Of course the structural spacings and openings in the first or mercantile story are required to be the largest of all; those in the second or quasi-mercantile story are of a somewhat similar nature. The spacings and openings in the attic are of no importance whatsoever (the windows have no actual value), for light may be taken from the top, and no recognition of a cellular division is necessary in the structural spacing.

Hence it follows inevitably, and in the simplest possible way, that if we follow our natural instincts without thought of books, rules, precedents, or any such educational impedimenta to a spontaneous and "sensible" result, we will in the following manner design the exterior of our tall office building—to wit:

Beginning with the first story, we give this a main entrance that attracts the eye to its location, and the remainder of the story we treat in a more or less liberal, expansive, sumptuous way—a way based exactly on the practical necessities, but expressed with a sentiment of largeness and freedom. The second story we treat in a similar way, but usually with milder pretension. Above this, throughout the indefinite number of typical office tiers, we take our cue from the individual cell, which requires a window with its separating pier, its sill and lintel, and we, without more ado, make them look all alike because they are all alike. This brings us to the attic, which, having no division into office-cells, and no special requirement for lighting, gives us the power to show by means of its broad expanse of wall, and its dominating weight and character, that which is the fact—namely, that the series of office tiers has come definitely to an end.

This may perhaps seem a bald result and a heartless, pessimistic way of stating it, but even so we certainly have advanced a most characteristic stage beyond the imagined sinister building of the speculator–engineer–builder combination. For the hand of the architect is now definitely felt in the decisive position at once taken, and the suggestion of a thoroughly sound, logical, coherent expression of the conditions is becoming apparent.

When I say the hand of the architect, I do not mean necessarily the accomplished and trained architect. I mean only a man with a strong, natural liking for buildings, and a disposition to shape them in what seems to his unaffected nature a direct and simple way. He will probably tread an innocent path from his problem to its solution, and therein he will show an enviable gift of logic. If he has some gift for form in detail, some feeling for form purely and simply as form, some love for that, his result in addition to its simple straightforward naturalness and completeness in general statement, will have something of the charm of sentiment.

However, thus far the results are only partial and tentative at best; relatively true, they are but superficial. We are doubtless right in our instinct but we must seek a fuller justification, a finer sanction, for it.

I assume now that in the study of our problem we have passed through the various stages of inquiry, as follows: 1st, the social basis of the demand for tall office buildings; 2nd, its literal material satisfaction; 3rd, the elevation of the question from considerations of literal planning, construction, and equipment, to the plane of elementary architecture as a direct outgrowth of sound, sensible building; 4th, the question again elevated from an elementary architecture to the beginnings of true architectural expression, through the addition of a certain quality and quantity of sentiment. But our building may have all these in a considerable degree and yet be far from that adequate solution of the problem I am attempting to define. We must now heed the imperative voice of emotion.

It demands of us, what is the chief characteristic of the tall office building? And at once we answer, it is lofty. This loftiness is to the artist-nature its thrilling aspect. It is the very open organ-tone in its appeal. It must be in turn the dominant chord in his expression of it, the true excitant of his imagination. It must be tall, every inch of it tall. The force and power of altitude must be in it, the glory and pride of exaltation must be in it. It must be every inch a proud and soaring thing, rising in sheer exultation that from bottom to top it is a unit without a single dissenting line—that it is the new, the unexpected, the eloquent peroration of most bald, most sinister, most forbidding conditions.

The man who designs in this spirit and with the sense of responsibility to the generation he lives in must be no coward, no denier, no bookworm, no dilettante. He must live of his life and for his life in the fullest, most consummate sense. He must realize at once and with the grasp of inspiration that the problem of the tall office building is one of the most stupendous, one of the most magnificent opportunities that the Lord of Nature in His beneficence has ever offered to the proud spirit of man. That this has not been perceived—indeed, has been flatly denied—is an exhibition of human perversity that must give us pause.

One more consideration. Let us now lift this question into the region of calm, philosophic observation. Let us seek a comprehensive, a final solution: let the problem indeed dissolve.

Certain critics, and very thoughtful ones, have advanced the theory that the true prototype of the tall office building is the classical column, consisting of base, shaft and capital—the moulded base of the column typical of the lower stories of our building, the plain or fluted shaft suggesting the monotonous, uninterrupted series of office-tiers, and the capital the completing power and luxuriance of the attic. Other theorizers, assuming a mystical symbolism as a guide, quote the many trinities in nature and art, and the beauty and conclusiveness of such trinity in unity. They aver the beauty of prime numbers, the mysticism of the number three, the beauty of all things that are in three parts—to wit, the day, subdividing into morning, noon, and night; the limbs, the thorax, and the head, constituting the body. So they say, should the building be in three parts vertically, substantially as before, but for different motives. Others, of purely intellectual temperament, hold that such a design should be in the nature of a logical statement; it should have a beginning, a middle, and an ending, each clearly defined—therefore again a building, as above, in three parts vertically.

Others, seeking their examples and justification in the vegetable kingdom, urge that such a design shall above all things be organic. They quote the suitable flower with its bunch of leaves at the earth, its long graceful stem, carrying the gorgeous single flower. They point to the pine-tree, its massy roots, its lithe, uninterrupted trunk, its tuft of green high in the air. Thus, they say, should be the design of the tall office building: again in three parts vertically.

Others still, more susceptible to the power of a unit than to the grace of a trinity, say that such a design should be struck out at a blow, as though by a blacksmith or by mighty Jove, or should be thought-born, as was Minerva, full grown. They accept the notion of a triple division as permissible and welcome, but non-essential. With them it is a subdivision of their unit: the unit does not come from the alliance of the three; they accept it without murmur, provided the subdivision does not disturb the sense of singleness and repose.

All of these critics and theorists agree, however, positively, unequivocally, in this, that the tall office building should not, must not, be made a field for the display of architectural knowledge in the encyclopedic sense; that too much learning in this instance is fully as dangerous, as obnoxious, as too little learning; that miscellany is abhorrent to their sense; that the sixteen-story building must not consist of sixteen separate, distinct and unrelated buildings piled one upon the other until the top of the pile is reached.

To this latter folly I would not refer were it not the fact that nine out of every ten tall office buildings are designed in precisely this way in effect, not by the ignorant, but by the educated. It would seem indeed, as though the "trained" architect, when facing this problem, were beset at every story, or at most, every third or fourth story, by the hysterical dread lest he be in "bad form"; lest he be not bedecking his building with sufficiency of quotation from this, that, or the other "correct" building in some other land and some other time; lest he be not copious enough in the display of his wares; lest he betray, in short, a lack of resource. To loosen up the touch of this cramped and fidgety hand, to allow the nerves to calm, the brain to cool, to reflect equably, to reason naturally, seems beyond him; he lives, as it were, in a waking nightmare filled with the *disjecta membra* of architecture. The spectacle is not inspiriting.

As to the former and serious views held by discerning and thoughtful critics, I shall, with however much of regret, dissent from them for the purpose of this demonstration, for I regard them as secondary only, non-essential, and as touching not at all upon the vital spot, upon the quick of the entire matter, upon the true, the immovable philosophy of the architectural art.

This view let me now state, for it brings to the solution of the problem a final, comprehensive formula.

All things in nature have a shape, that is to say, a form, an outward semblance, that tells us what they are, that distinguishes them from ourselves and from each other.

Unfailingly in nature these shapes express the inner life, the native quality, of the animal, tree, bird, fish, that they present to us; they are so characteristic, so recognizable, that we say, simply, it is "natural" it should be so. Yet the moment we peer beneath this surface of things, the moment we look through the tranquil reflection of ourselves and the clouds above us, down into the clear, fluent, unfathomable depth of nature, how startling is the silence of it, how amazing the flow of life, how absorbing the mystery.

Unceasingly the essence of things is taking shape in the matter of things, and this unspeakable process we call birth and growth. Awhile the spirit and the matter fade away together, and it is this that we call decadence, death. These two happenings seem jointed and interdependent, blended into one like a bubble and its iridescence, and they seem borne along upon a slowly moving air. This air is wonderful past all understanding.

Yet to the steadfast eye of one standing upon the shore of things, looking chiefly in, and most lovingly upon that side on which the sun shines and that we feel joyously to be life, the heart is ever gladdened by the beauty, the exquisite spontaneity, with which life seeks and takes on its forms in an accord perfectly responsive to its needs. It seems ever as though the life and the form were absolutely one and inseparable, so adequate is the sense of fulfillment.

Whether it be the sweeping eagle in his flight or the open apple-blossom, the toiling work-horse, the blithe swan, the branching oak, the winding stream at its base, the drifting clouds, over all the coursing sun, form ever follows function, and this is the law. Where function does not change form does not change. The granite rocks, the ever-brooding hills, remain for ages; the lightning lives, comes into shape, and dies in a twinkling.

It is the pervading law of all things organic, and inorganic, of all things physical and metaphysical, of all things human and all things superhuman, of all true manifestations of the head, of the heart, of the soul, that the life is recognizable in its expression, that form ever follows function. This is the law.

Shall we, then, daily violate this law in our art? Are we so decadent, so imbecile, so utterly weak of eyesight, that we cannot perceive this truth so simple, so very simple? Is it indeed a truth so transparent that we see through it but do not see it? Is it really then, a very marvelous thing, or is it rather so commonplace, so everyday, so near a thing to us, that we cannot perceive that the shape, form, outward expression, design or whatever we may choose, of the tall office building should in the very nature of things follow the functions of the building, and that where the function does not change, the form is not to change?

Does this not readily, clearly, and conclusively show that the lower one or two stories will take on a special character suited to the special needs, that the tiers of typical offices, having the same unchanging function, shall continue in the same unchanging form, and that as to the attic, specific and conclusive as it is in its very nature, its function shall equally be so in force, in significance, in continuity, in conclusiveness of outward expression? From this results, naturally, spontaneously, unwittingly, a three-part division, not from any theory, symbol, or fancied logic.

And thus the design of the tall office building takes its place with all other architectural types made when architecture, as has happened once in many years, was a living art. Witness the Greek temple, the Gothic cathedral, the medieval fortress.

And thus, when native instinct and sensibility shall govern the exercise of our beloved art; when the known law, the respected law, shall be that form ever follows function; when our architects shall cease struggling and prattling handcuffed and vainglorious in the asylum of a foreign school; when it is truly felt, cheerfully accepted, that this law opens up the airy sunshine of green fields, and gives to us a freedom that the very beauty and sumptuousness of the outworking of the law itself as exhibited in nature will deter any sane, any sensitive man from changing into license, when it becomes evident that we are merely speaking a foreign language with a noticeable American accent, whereas each and every architect in the land might, under the benign influence of this law, express in the simplest, most modest, most natural way that which it is in him to say; that he might really and would surely develop his own characteristic individuality, and that the architectural art with him would certainly become a living form of speech, a natural form of utterance, giving surcease to him and adding treasures small and great to the growing art of his land; when we know and feel that Nature is our friend, not our implacable enemy—that an afternoon in the country, an hour by the sea, a full open view of one single day, through dawn, high noon, and twilight, will suggest to us so much that is rhythmical, deep, and eternal in the vast art of architecture, something so deep, so true, that all the narrow formalities, hard-and-fast rules, and strangling bonds of the schools cannot stifle it in us—then it may be proclaimed that we are on the high-road to a natural and satisfying art, an architecture that will soon become a fine art in the true, the best sense of the word, an art that will live because it will be of the people, for the people, and by the people.

Reflective Text

BERNARD TSCHUMI, EXCERPTS FROM *ARCHITECTURE AND DISJUNCTION*

First Published in 1983

VIOLENCE OF ARCHITECTURE

1.   *There is no architecture without action, no architecture without events, no architecture without program.*

2.   *By extension, there is no architecture without violence.*

The first of these statements runs against the mainstream of architectural thought by refusing to favor space at the expense of action. The second statement argues that although the logic of objects and the logic of man are independent in their relations to the world, they inevitably face one another in an intense confrontation. Any relationship between a building and its users is one of violence, for any use means the intrusion of a human body into a given space, the intrusion of one order into another. This intrusion is inherent in the idea of architecture; any reduction of architecture to its spaces at the expense of its events is as simplistic as the reduction of architecture to its façades.

By "violence," I do not mean the brutality that destroys physical or emotional integrity but a metaphor for the intensity of a relationship between individuals and their surrounding spaces. The argument is not a matter of style: modem architecture is neither more nor less violent than classical architecture, or than fascist, socialist, or vernacular variations. Architecture's violence is fundamental and unavoidable, for architecture is linked to events in the same way that the guard is linked to the prisoner, the police to the criminal, the doctor to the patient, order to chaos. This also suggests that actions qualify spaces as much as spaces qualify actions; that space and action are inseparable and that no proper interpretation of architecture, drawing, or notation can refuse to consider this fact.

What must first be determined is whether this relation between action and space is symmetrical—opposing two camps (people versus spaces) that affect one another in a comparable way—or asymmetrical, a relation in which one camp, whether space or people, clearly dominates the other.

BODIES VIOLATING SPACE

First, there is the violence that all individuals inflict on spaces by their very presence, by their intrusion into the controlled order of architecture. Entering a building may be a delicate act, but it violates the balance of a precisely ordered geometry (do architectural photographs ever include runners, fighters, lovers?). Bodies carve all sorts of new and unexpected spaces, through fluid or erratic motions. Architecture, then, is only an organism engaged in constant intercourse with users, whose bodies rush against the carefully established rules of architectural thought. No wonder the human body has always been suspect in architecture: it has always set limits to the most extreme architectural ambitions. The body disturbs the purity of architectural order. It is equivalent to a dangerous prohibition.

Violence is not always present. Just as riots, brawls, insurrections, and revolutions are of limited duration, so is the violence a body commits against space. Yet it is always implicit. Each door implies the movement of someone crossing its frame. Each corridor implies the progression of movement that blocks it. Each architectural space implies (and desires) the intruding presence that will inhabit it.

SPACE VIOLATING BODIES

But if bodies violate the purity of architectural spaces, one might rightly wonder about the reverse: the violence inflicted by narrow corridors on large crowds, the symbolic or physical violence of buildings on users. A word of warning: I do not wish to resurrect recent behaviorist architectural approaches. Instead, I wish simply to underline the mere existence of a physical presence and the fact that it begins quite innocently, in an *imaginary* sort of way.

The place your body inhabits is inscribed in your imagination, your unconscious, as a space of possible bliss. Or menace. What if you are forced to abandon your imaginary spatial markings? A torturer wants you, the victim, to regress, because he wants to demean his prey, to make you lose your identity as a subject. Suddenly you have no choice; running away is impossible. The rooms are too small or too big, the ceilings too low or too high. Violence exercised by and through space is spatial torture.

Take Palladio's Villa Rotonda. You walk through one of its axes, and as you cross the central space and reach its other side you find, instead of the hillside landscape, the steps of another Villa Rotonda, and another, and another, and another. The incessant repetition at first stimulates some strange desire, but soon becomes sadistic, impossible, violent.

Such discomforting spatial devices can take any form: the white anechoic chambers of sensory deprivation, the formless spaces leading to psychological destructuring. Steep and dangerous staircases, those corridors consciously made too narrow for crowds, introduce a radical shift from architecture as an object of contemplation to architecture as a perverse instrument of use. At the same time it must be stressed that the receiving subject—you or I—may wish to be subjected to such spatial aggression, just as you may go to a rock concert and stand close enough to the loudspeakers to sustain painful—but pleasurable—physical or psychic trauma. Places aimed at the cult of excessive sound only suggest places aimed at the cult of excessive space. The love of violence, after all, is an ancient pleasure.

Why has architectural theory regularly refused to acknowledge such pleasures and always claimed (at least officially) that architecture should be pleasing to the eye, as well as comfortable to the body? This presupposition seems curious when the pleasure of violence can be experienced in every other human activity, from the violence of discordant sounds in music to the clash of bodies in sports, from gangster movies to the Marquis de Sade.

VIOLENCE RITUALIZED

Who will mastermind these exquisite spatial delights, these disturbing architectural tortures, the tortuous paths of promenades through delirious landscapes, theatrical events where actor complements decor? Who . . .? The architect? By the seventeenth century, Bernini had staged whole spectacles, followed by Mansart's fêtes for Louis XIV and Albert Speer's sinister and beautiful rallies. After all, the original action, the original act of violence—this unspeakable copulating of live body and dead stone—is unique and unrehearsed, though perhaps infinitely repeatable, for you may enter the building again and again. The architect will always dream of purifying this uncontrolled violence, channeling obedient bodies along predictable paths and occasionally along ramps that provide striking vistas, ritualizing the transgression of bodies in space. Le Corbusier's Carpenter Center, with its ramp that violates the building, is a genuine movement of bodies made into an architectural solid. Or the reverse: it is a solid that forcibly channels the movement of bodies.

The original, spontaneous interaction of the body with a space is often purified by ritual. Sixteenth-century pageants and Nathan Altman's reenactment of the storming of the Winter Palace in St. Petersburg, for example, are ritualistic imitations of spontaneous violence. Endlessly repeated, these rituals curb all aspects of the original act that have escaped control: the choice of time and place, the selection of the victim . . .

A ritual implies a near-frozen relationship between action and space. It institutes a new order after the disorder of the original event. When it becomes necessary to mediate tension and fix it by custom, then no single fragment must escape attention. Nothing strange and unexpected must happen. Control must be absolute.

PROGRAMS: RECIPROCITY AND CONFLICT

Such control is, of course, not likely to be achieved. Few regimes would survive if architects were to program every single movement of individual and society in a kind of ballet mécanique of architecture, a permanent Nuremberg Rally of everyday life, a puppet theater of spatial intimacy. Nor would they survive if every spontaneous movement were immediately frozen into a solid corridor. The relationship is more subtle and moves beyond the question of power, beyond the question of whether architecture dominates events or vice versa. The relationship, then, is as symmetrical as the ineluctable one between guard and prisoner, hunter and hunted. But both the hunter and the hunted also have basic needs to consider, which may not relate to the hunt: sustenance, food, shelter, and so forth. Hunter and hunted enjoy these needs independent of the fact that they are engaged in a deadly game. They are respectively self-sufficient. Only when they confront each other's reality are their strategies so totally interdependent that it becomes impossible to determine which one initiates and which one responds. The same happens with architecture and the way buildings relate to their users, or spaces relate to events or programs. For any organized repetition of events, once announced in advance, becomes a program, a descriptive notice of a formal series of proceedings.

When spaces and programs are largely independent of one another, one observes a strategy of indifference in which architectural considerations do not depend on utilitarian ones, in which space has one logic and events another. Such were the Crystal Palace and the neutral sheds of the nineteenth-century's Great Exhibitions, which accommodated anything from displays of elephants draped in rare colonial silks to international boxing matches. Such, too—but in a very different manner—was Gerrit Rietveld's house in Utrecht, a remarkable exercise in architectural language, and a not unpleasant house to live in, despite, or perhaps because of the fortuitous juxtaposition of space and use.

At other times, architectural spaces and programs can become totally inter-dependent and fully condition each other's existence. In these cases, the architect's view of the user's needs determines every architectural decision (which may, in turn, determine the user's attitude). The architect designs the set, writes the script, and directs the actors. Such were the ideal kitchen installations of the twenties' Werkbund, each step of a near-biochemical housewife carefully monitored by the design's constant attention. Such were Meyerhold's biomechanics, acting through Popova's stage sets, where the characters' logic played with and against the logic of their dynamic surroundings. Such also is Frank Lloyd Wright's Guggenheim Museum. It is not a question of knowing which comes first, movement or space, which molds the other, for ultimately a deep bond is involved. After all, they are caught in the same set of relationships; only the arrow of power changes direction.

(If I outline these two relations of independence and Interdependence, it is to insist on the fact that they exist regardless of the prescriptive ideologies—modernism versus humanism, formalism versus functionalism, and so on—which architects and critics are usually keen to promote.)

Most relations, of course, stand somewhere in between. You can sleep in your kitchen. And fight and love. These shifts are not without meaning. When the typology of an eighteenth-century prison is turned into a twentieth-century city hall, the shift inevitably suggests a critical statement about institutions. When an industrial loft in Manhattan is turned into a residence, a similar shift occurs, a shift that is undoubtedly less dramatic. Spaces are qualified by actions just as actions are qualified by spaces. One does not trigger the other; they exist independently. Only when they intersect do they affect one another. Remember Kuleshov's experiment where the same shot of the actor's impassive face is introduced into a variety of situations, and the audience reads different expressions into each successive juxtaposition. The same occurs in architecture: the event is altered by each new space. And vice versa: by ascribing to a given, supposedly "autonomous" space a contradictory program, the space attains new levels of meaning. Event and space do not merge but affect one another. Similarly if the Sistine Chapel were used for pole-vaulting events, architecture would then cease to yield to its customary good intentions. For a while the transgression would be real and all powerful. Yet the transgression of cultural expectations soon becomes accepted. Just as violent surrealist collages inspire advertising rhetoric, the broken rule is integrated into everyday life, whether through symbolic or technological motivations.

If violence is the key metaphor for the intensity of a relationship, then the very physicality of architecture transcends the metaphor. There is a deep sensuality, an unremittent eroticism in architecture. Its underlying violence varies according to the forces that are put into play—rational forces, irrational forces. They can be deficient or excessive. Little activity—hypoactivity—in a house can be as disturbing as hyperactivity. Asceticism and orgiastic excesses are closer than architectural theorists have admitted, and the asceticism of Gerrit Rietveld's or Ludwig Wittgenstein's house inevitably implies the most extreme bacchanals. (Cultural expectations merely affect the perception of violence, but do not alter its nature: slapping your lover's face is perceived differently from culture to culture.)

Architecture and events constantly transgress each other's rules, whether explicitly or implicitly. These rules, these organized compositions, may be questioned, but they always remain points of reference. A building is a point of reference for the activities set to negate it. A theory of architecture is a theory of order threatened by the very use it permits. And vice versa.

The integration of the concept of violence into the architectural mechanism—the purpose of my argument—is ultimately aimed at a new pleasure of architecture. Like any form of violence, the violence of architecture also contains the possibility of change, of renewal. Like any violence, the violence of architecture is deeply Dionysian. It should be understood, and its contradictions maintained in a dynamic manner, with their conflicts and complementarity.

In passing, two types of partial violence should be distinguished, types which are *not* specifically architectural. The first is *formal violence*, which deals with the conflicts between objects. Such is the violence of form versus form, the violence of Giovanni Battista Piranesi's juxtapositions, Kurt Schwitters' Merzbau collages, and other architectural collisions. Distortions, ruptures, compressions, fragmentations, and disjunctions are inherent in the manipulation of form. This is also the disruption inflicted by any new construction on its surroundings, for it not only destroys what it replaces but also violates the territory it occupies. It is the violence of Adolf Loos's House for Tristan Tzara in the context of vernacular nineteenth-century suburban Paris or, alternatively, the disruptive effect of an historical allusion in a curtain-wall avenue. This contextual violence is nothing but the polemical violence of difference. To discuss it is the task of sociology, psychology, and esthetics.

A door flanked by broken Corinthian columns supporting a twisted neon pediment, however, suggests farce rather than violence. Yet James Joyce's "doorlumn" was both a pun and a comment on the cultural crisis of language. *Finnegans Wake* implied that particular transgressions could attack the constituent elements of architectural language—its columns, stairs, windows, and their various combinations—as they are defined by any cultural period, whether beaux arts or Bauhaus. This formal disobedience is ultimately harmless and may even initiate a new style as it slowly loses the excessive character of a violated prohibition. It then announces a new pleasure and the elaboration of a new norm, which is in turn violated.

The second type of partial violence is not a metaphor. *Programmatic violence* encompasses those uses, actions, events, and programs that, by accident or by design, are specifically evil and destructive. Among them are killing, internment, and torture, which become slaughterhouses, concentration camps, or torture chambers.

SPACES AND EVENTS

Can one attempt to make a contribution to architectural discourse by relentlessly stating that there is no space without event, no architecture without program? This seems to be our mandate at a time that has witnessed the revival of historicism or, alternatively, of formalism in almost every architectural circle. Our work argues that architecture—its social relevance and formal invention—cannot be dissociated from the events that "happen" in it. Recent projects insist constantly on issues of program and notation. They stress a critical attitude that observes, analyzes, and interprets some of the most controversial positions of past and present architectural ideologies.

Yet this work often took place against the mainstream of the prevalent architectural discourse. For throughout the 1970s there was an exacerbation of stylistic concerns at the expense of programmatic ones and a reduction of architecture as a form of knowledge to architecture as knowledge of form. From modernism to postmodernism, the history of architecture was surreptitiously turned into a history of styles. This perverted form of history borrowed from semiotics the ability to "read" layers of interpretation but reduced architecture to a system of surface signs at the expense of the reciprocal, indifferent, or even conflictive relationship of spaces and events.

This is not the place for an extensive analysis of the situation that engulfed the critical establishment. However, it should be stressed that it is no accident that this emphasis on stylistic issues corresponded to a double and wider phenomenon: on the one hand, the increasing role of the developer in planning large buildings, encouraging many architects to become mere decorators, and on the other, the tendency of many architectural critics to concentrate on surface readings, signs, metaphors, and other modes of presentation, often to the exclusion of spatial or programmatic concerns. These are two faces of a single coin, typical of an increasing desertion by the architectural profession of its responsibilities vis-à-vis the events and activities that take place in the spaces it designs.

At the start of the 1980s, the notion of program was still forbidden territory. Programmatic concerns were rejected as leftovers from obsolete functionalist doctrines by those polemicists who saw programs as mere pretexts for stylistic experimentation. Few dared to explore the relation between the formal elaboration of spaces and the invention of programs, between the abstraction of architectural thought and the representation of events. The popular dissemination of architectural images through eye-catching reproductions in magazines often turned architecture into a passive object of contemplation instead of the *place* that confronts spaces and actions. Most exhibitions of architecture in art galleries and museums encouraged "surface" practice and presented the architect's work as a form of decorative painting. Walls and bodies, abstract planes and figures were rarely seen as part of a single signifying system. History may one day look upon this period as the moment of the loss of innocence in twentieth-century architecture: the moment when it became clear that neither supertechnology, expressionist functionalism, nor neo-Corbusianism could solve society's ills and that architecture was not ideologically neutral. A strong political upheaval, a rebirth of critical thought in architecture, and new developments in history and theory all triggered a phenomenon whose consequences are still unmeasured. This general loss of innocence resulted in a variety of moves by architects according to their political or ideological leanings. In the early 1970s, some denounced architecture altogether, arguing that its practice, in the current socioeconomic context, could only be reactionary and reinforce the status quo. Others, influenced by structural linguistics, talked of "constants" and the rational autonomy of an architecture that transcended all social forms. Others reintroduced political discourse and advocated a return to preindustrial forms of society. And still others cynically took the analyses of style and ideology by Barthes, Eco, or Baudrillard and diverted them from their critical aims, turning them over like a glove. Instead of using them to question the distorted, mediated nature of architectural practice, these architects injected meaning into their buildings artificially, through a collage of historicist or metaphorical elements. The restricted notion of postmodemism that ensued—a notion diminished by comparison with literature or art—completely and uncritically reinserted architecture into the cycle of consumption.

At the Architectural Association (AA) in London, I devised a program entitled "Theory, Language, Attitudes." Exploiting the structure of the AA, which encouraged autonomous research and independent lecture courses, it played on an opposition between political and theoretical concerns about the city (those of Baudrillard, Lefèbvre, Adorno, Lukács, and Benjamin, for example) and an art sensibility informed by photography, conceptual art, and performance. This opposition between a verbal critical discourse and a visual one suggested that the two were complementary. Students' projects explored that overlapping sensibility, often in a manner sufficiently obscure to generate initial hostility through the school. Of course the codes used in the students' work differed sharply from those seen in schools and architectural offices at the time. At the end-of-year exhibition texts, tapes, films, manifestos, rows of storyboards, and photographs of ghostlike figures, each with their own specific conventions, intruded in a space arranged according to codes disparate from those of the profession.

Photography was used obsessively: as "live" insert, as artificial documentation, as a hint of reality interposed in architectural drawing—a reality nevertheless distanced and often manipulated, filled with skillful staging, with characters and sets in their complementary relations. Students enacted fictitious programs inside carefully selected "real" spaces and then shot entire photographic sequences as evidence of their architectural endeavors. Any new attitude to architecture *had* to question its mode of representation.

Other works dealing with a critical analysis of urban life were generally in written form. They were turned into a book, edited, designed, printed, and published by the unit; hence, "the words of architecture became the work of architecture," as we said. Entitled *A Chronicle of Urban Politics*, the book attempted to analyze what distinguished our period from the preceding one. Texts on fragmentation, cultural dequalification, and the "intermediate city" analyzed consumerism, totems, and representationalism. Some of the texts announced, several years in advance, preoccupations now common to the cultural sphere: dislocated imagery, artificiality, representational reality versus experienced reality.

The mixing of genres and disciplines in this work was widely attacked by the academic establishment, still obsessed with concepts of disciplinary autonomy and self-referentiality. But the significance of such events is not a matter of historical precedence or provocation. In superimposing ideas and perceptions, words and spaces, these events underlined the importance of a certain kind of relationship between abstraction and narrative—a complex juxtaposition of abstract concepts and immediate experiences, contradictions, superimpositions of mutually exclusive sensibilities. This dialectic between the verbal and the visual culminated in 1974 in a series of "literary" projects organized in the studio, in which texts provided programs or events on which students were to develop architectural works. The role of the text was fundamental in that it underlined some aspect of the complementing (or, occasionally, lack of complementing) of events and spaces. Some texts, like Italo Calvino's metaphorical descriptions of "Invisible Cities," were so "architectural" as to require going far beyond the mere illustration of the author's already powerful descriptions; Franz Kafka's *Burrow* challenged conventional architectural perceptions and modes of representation; Edgar Allan Poe's *Masque of the Red Death* (done during my term as Visiting Critic at Princeton University) suggested parallels between narrative and spatial sequences. Such explorations of the intricacies of language and space naturally had to touch on James Joyce's discoveries. During one of my trips from the United States I gave extracts from *Finnegans Wake* as the program. The site was London's Covent Garden and the architecture was derived, by analogy or opposition, from Joyce's text. The effect of such research was invaluable in providing a framework for the analysis of the relations between events and spaces, beyond functionalist notions.

The unfolding of events in a literary context inevitably suggested parallels to the unfolding of events in architecture.

SPACE VERSUS PROGRAM

To what extent could the literary narrative shed light on the organization of events in buildings, whether called "use," "functions," "activities," or "programs"? If writers could manipulate the structure of stories in the same way as they twist vocabulary and grammar, couldn't architects do the same, organizing the program in a similarly objective, detached, or imaginative way? For if architects could self-consciously use such devices as repetition, distortion, or juxtaposition in the formal elaboration of walls, couldn't they do the same thing in terms of the activities that occurred within those very walls? Pole vaulting in the chapel, bicycling in the laundromat, sky diving in the elevator shaft? Raising these questions proved increasingly stimulating: conventional organizations of spaces could be matched to the most surrealistically absurd sets of activities. Or vice versa: the most intricate and perverse organization of spaces could accommodate the everyday life of an average suburban family.

Such research was obviously not aimed at providing immediate answers, whether ideological or practical. Far more important was the understanding that the relation between program and building could be either highly sympathetic or contrived and artificial. The latter, of course, fascinated us more, as it rejected all functionalist leanings. It was a time when most architects were questioning, attacking, or outright rejecting modem movement orthodoxy. We simply refused to enter these polemics, viewing them as stylistic or semantic battles. Moreover, if this orthodoxy was often attacked for its reduction to minimalist formal manipulations, we refused to enrich it with witty metaphors. Issues of intertextuality, multiple readings and dual codings had to integrate the notion of program. To use a Palladian arch for an athletic club alters both Palladio and the nature of the athletic event.

As an exploration of the disjunction between expected form and expected use, we began a series of projects opposing specific programs with particular, often conflicting spaces. Programatic context versus urban typology, urban typology versus spatial experience, spatial experience versus procedure, and so on, provided a dialectical framework for research. We consciously suggested programs that were impossible on the sites that were to house them: a stadium in Soho, a prison near Wardour Street, a ballroom in a churchyard. At the same time, issues of *notation* became fundamental: if the reading of architecture was to include the events that took place in it, it would be necessary to devise modes of notating such activities. Several modes of notation were invented to supplement the limitations of plans, sections, or axonometrics. Movement notation derived from choreography, and simultaneous scores derived from music notation were elaborated for architectural purposes.

If movement notation usually proceeded from our desire to map the actual movement of bodies in spaces, it increasingly became a sign that did not necessarily refer to these movements but rather to the *idea* of movement—a form of notation that was there to *recall* that architecture was also about the movement of bodies in space, that their language and the language of walls were ultimately complementary. Using movement notation as a means of recalling issues was an attempt to include new and stereotypical codes in architectural drawing and, by extension, in its perception, layerings, juxtaposition, and superimposition of images purposefully blurred the conventional relationship between plan, graphic conventions and their meaning in the built realm. Increasingly the drawings became both the notation of a complex architectural reality and drawings (art works) in their own right, with their own frame of reference, deliberately set apart from the conventions of architectural plans and sections.

The fascination with the dramatic, either in the program (murder, sexuality, violence) or in the mode of representation (strongly outlined images, distorted angles of vision—as if seen from a diving airforce bomber), is there to force a response. Architecture ceases to be a backdrop for actions, becoming the action itself.

All this suggests that "shock" must be manufactured by the architect if architecture is to communicate. Influence from the mass media, from fashion and popular magazines, informed the choice of programs: the lunatic asylum, the fashion institute, the Falklands war. It also influenced the graphic techniques, from the straight black and white photography for the early days to the overcharged grease-pencil illustration of later years, stressing the inevitable "mediatization" of architectural activity. With the dramatic sense that pervades much of the work, cinematic devices replace conventional description. Architecture becomes the discourse of events as much as the discourse of spaces.

From our work in the early days, when event, movement, and spaces were analytically juxtaposed in mutual tension, the work moved toward an increasingly synthetic attitude. We had begun with a critique of the city, had gone back to basics: to simple and pure spaces, to barren landscapes, a room; to simple body movements, walking in a straight line, dancing; to short scenarios. And we gradually increased the complexity by introducing literary parallels and sequences of events, placing these programs within existing urban contexts. Within the worldwide megalopolis, new programs are placed in new urban situations. The process has gone full circle: it started by deconstructing the city, today it explores new codes of *assemblage*.

Philosophical Text

ADRIAN FORTY, "FUNCTION."

First Published in 2000

"Function" (and in this category we shall include also "Functional" and "Functionalism") was without question an important concept in modern architecture, but it has above all been in the *critique* of modernism that it has come into its own. To a considerable extent, its definition, its meaning, even its naming, has come about through the activities of critics of architectural modernism since about 1960. As Bill Hillier has remarked, "One scours the architectural manifestos of the twentieth century in vain for a thoroughgoing statement of the determinism from spatial form to function or its inverse."[1] In so far as we have a "theory" or theories of function, they are of recent making, and not of the period when "functionalism" is alleged to have dominated modern architecture. Our immediate task, then, is to identify what "function" meant *before* it was given its present coherence and intensity.

A "function" describes the result of the action of one quantity upon another; relative to architecture, the question is what is acting upon what? From the first use of "function" in the eighteenth century until the end of the nineteenth century, the quantity acted upon was almost always taken as the building's tectonic elements, its "structure,"[2] a term with which "function" has been closely associated; the quantities performing the action were principally the building's own mechanical forces. In other words, until the beginning of the twentieth century—with a few rare exceptions that will be discussed below—"function" was a term primarily relating to the tectonics of building. During the twentieth century, a new use of "function" became more widespread, one in which buildings themselves were described as acting upon people, or social material. It is this second meaning—and its converse, the action of society in determining the forms of buildings—that have attracted so much attention, but which are the more difficult to trace historically.

Considered historically, we can identify at least five different uses of "function" prior to about 1930. What makes the concept complicated is that it is a metaphor, and a metaphor that borrows from at least two, and perhaps three different fields: from

1. Bill Hillier, *Space is the Machine* (Cambridge: Cambridge University Press, 1996), 377–378.
2. Ibid., 276–285.

164

mathematics, from biology, and maybe from sociology. A further complication is that the English word "function" as applied to architecture is a translation of terms originating in Italian, French and German. . . .

AS A MATHEMATICAL METAPHOR—A CRITIQUE OF THE CLASSICAL SYSTEM OF ORNAMENT

The first use of "function" relative to architecture was by the Venetian friar Carlo Lodolí in the 1740s.[3] Lodolí's motto, "*Devonsi unire e fabrica e ragione e sia funzion la rappresentazione*"—"Unite building with reason and let function be the representation"— summarized an argument against the conventions of the classical system of ornament. Lodolí's main objection was to the imitation in stone of forms developed originally for timber construction; Francesco Algarotti, the author of one of the two surviving accounts of Lodolí's ideas, reported "nothing, he insisted, should be represented which is not also true in function."[4] What Lodolí meant by "function" is inferred from the other, more accurate, source of Lodolí's ideas, by Andrea Memmo. Memmo indicated that Lodolí wanted to develop forms of stone construction and decoration that derived from the mechanical forces acting upon the material. Evidence of the application of this idea is to be found in the surprising lintels and window-sills of the pilgrim hospice attached to S. Francesco della Vigna in Venice, apparently executed to Lodolí's instructions. According to Joseph Rykwert, Lodolí borrowed the term "function" from mathematics, to which it had been introduced in the 1690s by Leibniz, to describe the compound of variables; Lodolí's notion of function is the compound of mechanical force and material within any specific component of architecture. Lodolí's thinking was popularized by the late eighteenth-century Italian architectural writer Francesco Milizia, who misleadingly presented it simply as an argument against superfluous decoration: "whatever is seen should always have a function";[5] but Lodolí had not argued against decoration as such, but for a different system of decoration, based upon the inherent properties of materials. Since Milizia's books were translated into French from the 1790s, they may have provided a source for the term in French architectural circles; however, by this time the precision of Lodolí's mathematical metaphor was entirely lost, first of all misrepresented by Milizia, and now displaced by the arrival of a new analogue for "function", drawn from the developing science of biology.

AS A BIOLOGICAL METAPHOR, DESCRIPTIVE OF THE PURPOSES OF THE PARTS OF THE CONSTRUCTION RELATIVE TO EACH OTHER AND TO THE WHOLE

In biology, a science created in France out of the work of Lamarck and Cuvier in particular, "function" was a key concept. Whereas earlier natural historians had classified specimens according to the visual appearance of their organs, and their position in the body, in the new science of biology developed at the end of the eighteenth century, organs were analysed according to the functions they performed within the organism as a whole, and their hierarchical relationship to other organs. "Function" in this sense was closely related

3. On Lodolí, see Joseph Rykwert, "Lodoli on Function and Representation," *Architectural Review*, 160 (1976): 35; and Joseph Rykwert, *The First Moderns: The Architects of the Eighteenth Century* (Cambridge: MIT Press, 1980), Chapter 8.

4. Francesco Algarotti, "Saggio Sopra l'Architettura," in *Saggi* (Bari: Laterza e Figli, 1963), 35. First published in 1756.

5. Francesco Milizia, *Memorie Degli Architetti Antichi e Moderni* (Parma: Stamperia Reale, 1781), vol. 1, xv.

to "structure,"[6] for it was the identification of "functions"—of individual limbs and organs—which made it possible to deduce the structure.

Although developed by biologists in the 1790s, the term appears to have been little used by architects until rather later. "The genius of modern times, which loves to assign every individual product or object of a distinct function" was manifested most comprehensively in architectural discourse after the 1850s through the writings of Viollet-le-Duc, whose phrase this was.[7] For Viollet, "function" was an important concept, fundamental to his whole theory of rational construction: for example, writing about walls, he says:

> In every specimen of mason-work each piece taken separately in the case of dressed stone, or each section in concrete works, should clearly indicate its function. We ought to be able to analyse a building, as we take a puzzle to pieces, so that the place and function of each of the parts cannot be mistaken.[8]

And Viollet was—repeatedly—explicit about the biological origins of the metaphor.

It is in this sense, of the role played by each part within the structure, that "function" was principally understood in the English-speaking world from the mid-nineteenth century; this may be to do with a familiarity with the careful analyses of the constructive systems of Gothic architecture by the English archeologists William Whewell and Robert Willis in the 1830s and 1840s, or to the influence of Viollet's books. To take a single example of the characteristic English-language use of "function," we may cite the American critic Montgomery Schuyler's recollection of visiting the New York State Capitol at Albany around 1880 with Leopold Eidlitz, the architect of the alterations:

> Standing in the rotunda of the Court House one day, when his own vari-colored brick arches and columns had been inserted between the cast-iron panels of the older work, he said "Is it possible for anybody to fail to see that this," pointing to the new work, "performs a function, and that that," pointing to the old, "does not?"[9]

AS A BIOLOGICAL METAPHOR WITHIN THE "ORGANIC" THEORY OF FORM

A second, but quite different biological metaphor of "function" derives from the organic notion of form developed by the German Romantics. This is the context of Louis Sullivan's famous remarks about form and function. Within German Romanticism, "form" was either "mechanical" or "organic." The distinction, first made by A. W. Schlegel was paraphrased in English by Coleridge in 1818:

> The form is mechanic, when on any given material we impress a pre-determined form, not necessarily arising out of the properties of the material; as when to a mass of wet clay we give whatever shape we wish it to retain when hardened. The organic form, on the other hand, is innate; it shapes, as it develops itself from within,

6. Georges Cuvier, "Discours Préliminaire," in *Recherches sur les Ossemens Fossiles*, trans. Robert Kerr as *Essay on the Theory of the Earth* (Cambridge: Cambridge University Press, 2009), vol. 1, 281–282. First published in 1812.

7. Eugene Emmanuel Viollet-le-Duc, *Lectures on Architecture*, trans. Benjamin Bucknall (New York: Dover Publications, 1987), vol. 1, 449. First published in 1863.

8. Ibid., vol. 2, 33.

9. Montgomery Schuyler, "A Great American Architect: Leopold Eidlitz" in *American Architecture and Other Writings* (Cambridge: Belknap Press, 1961), vol. 1, 181. First published in 1908.

and the fullness of its development is one and the same with the perfection of its outward form, such as the life is, such is the form.[10]

What constitutes the prime-mover within the organic theory of form—a question first posed by Aristotle—was left unanswered: but there is no doubt about the influence the theory had upon a wide variety of architects and writers amongst them the American sculptor and art theorist Horatio Greenough, usually credited as the first English speaker to apply "function" to architecture. Greenough's essays on art and architecture, written in the 1840s, are all essentially to do with the development of organic form in the visual arts. "Function" played a key part in this, but Greenough was never very exact about what it meant—his use of it shifted between the straightforward expression of the building's utilitarian purpose, and a much more transcendental notion of the outward expression of organic form, as, for example, when he writes as follows: "Instead of forcing the functions of every sort of building into one general form, adopting an outward shape for the sake of the eye or of association, without reference to the inner distribution, let us begin from the heart as the nucleus, and work outward."[11] But in whatever sense he used it, Greenough's choice of the term "function" was explicitly biological—"as the first step in our search after the great principles of construction . . . observe the skeletons and skins of animals."[12] And it is from these observations that he concludes "If there be any principle of structure more plainly inculcated in the works of the Creator than all others, it is the principle of unflinching adaptation of forms to functions."[13] Twentieth-century commentators have tended to exaggerate the modernity of Greenough's ideas. We should remember that not only was Greenough's "function" based upon the earlier Romantic notion of organic form, but it is also clear that Greenough was interested in "function" less in terms of the satisfaction of human needs (about which he had no theory, and little to say), and more as a way of achieving that very eighteenth-century architectural aim, the expression of appropriate character: "The unflinching adaptation of a building to its position and use gives, as a sure product of that adaptation, character and expression."[14] Greenough's originality was not to have anticipated twentieth-century functionalism (which he did not do, for he had no sense of the reciprocal action of society upon buildings and of buildings upon society), but rather in putting new life into the old concept of "character" by linking it to use through the idea of "function"—to present, as he put it, "Character as the record of Function."[15]

If Greenough's conception of function was derived in part from the Romantics' organic theory of form, this was wholly true of the doctrine of "suppressed functions" with which the mysterious John Edelmann so captivated the young Louis Sullivan.[16] Exactly where Sullivan—generally agreed to have coined the aphorism *"form follows function"*[17]—acquired his ideas about function is uncertain, but his reliance upon German thought is indisputable.[18] At no point did Sullivan's "function" have anything to do with utility or the satisfaction of user needs; it was instead entirely based in metaphysics, the expression of organic essence. "The Germ is the real thing: the seat of identity. Within its delicate

10. Samuel Taylor Coleridge, *Biographia Literaria*, ed. J. Shawcross, (Oxford: Clarendon Press, 1907), 229. First published in 1817.
11. Horatio Greenough *Form and Function: Remarks on Art, Design, and Architecture*, ed. Harold A. Small (Berkeley: University of California Press, 1958), 62.
12. Ibid., 58.
13. Ibid., 118.
14. Ibid., 62.
15. Ibid., 71.
16. Louis H. Sullivan, *The Autobiography of an Idea* (New York: Dover Publications, 1956), 207. First published in 1924.
17. Ibid., 258.
18. David S. Andrew, *Louis Sullivan and the Polemics of Modern Architecture: The Present against the Past* (Urbana: University of Illinois Press, 1985), 198, 32–34, 62–67.

mechanism lies the will to power: the function which is to seek and eventually to find its full expression in form."[19] When Sullivan talks about "function," one could satisfactorily paraphrase his meaning as "destiny." This is clear from the long and famous discussion in *Kindergarten Chats* 12 and 13 that begins, "generally speaking outer appearances resemble inner purposes. For instances, the form, oak tree, resembles and expresses the function or purpose, oak."[20] Further proof of what Sullivan meant by "function" comes from a remark of his partner, Dankmar Adler: "Function and environment determine form"—implying that "function" was not the same as "environment." "Function," as far as Sullivan was concerned, was the inner spiritual force that determined "organic" form; "environment" is an external agency, a determinate of "mechanical" form, in the terminology of the Romantics. During the twentieth century this distinction has been lost: the organic theory of form, with all its epistemological difficulties, has been largely forgotten, and "function," to which it was once exclusively attached, has been transferred to the action of external agencies—"environment"—upon form.

Sullivan was certainly also aware of the other biological sense of "function" from Viollet-le-Duc, and, inevitably, Sullivan and others allowed the two to be confused. Interesting in this connection is the book by the American architect Leopold Eidlitz, *The Nature and Function of Art* (1881). Eidlitz had studied in Vienna, so was familiar with German thought, but moved to the United States in 1843 and became an enthusiastic disciple of Viollet-le-Duc. In his book, he attempted to reconcile Viollet's strictly mechanical, tectonic sense of "function" with a German, idealist notion of function. Thus he writes:

> All natural organisms are possessed of the mechanical ability to perform certain functions. This ability we find more or less clearly expressed in their forms as a whole or in their crystallization. In this way they convey to the mind an expression of these functions, and thus they tell the story of their being. The architect, in imitation of this natural condition of matter, so models his forms that they also tell the story of their functions; and these functions are always mechanical conditions of strength, elegance and repose, in combinations of various quantities of these properties. The fundamental principle of the modeling of architectural forms is therefore mechanical.[21]

For Eidlitz, the expression of mechanical function provides the means to represent the building's innate function, "the story of its being."

"FUNCTION" MEANING "USE"

By the mid-nineteenth century, in both English and French, "function" had a limited currency as meaning the activities designated for a particular building or part of a building. Two of the writers already discussed, Greenough and Viollet-le-Duc, both used "function" in this sense. For example, Greenough wrote, "to apportion the spaces for convenience, decide their size, and model their shapes for their functions—these acts organize a

19. Louis H. Sullivan, *A System of Architectural Ornament according with a Philosophy of Man's Powers*, (New York: AIA Press, 1924), 299.

20. Louis H. Sullivan, "Kindergarten Chats," in *Kindergarten Chats and Other Writings* (New York: Wittenborn Art Books, 1976), 43. First published in 1901.

21. Leopold Eidlitz, *The Nature and Function of Art, More Especially of Architecture* (London: Sampson Low, 1881), 223–224.

building."[22] Viollet-le-Duc says of domestic architecture—in an overtly biological analogy, discussed in another context [. . .]—"There is in every building . . . one principal organ . . . and certain secondary organs or members, and the necessary appliances for supplying all these parts by a system of circulation. Each of these organs has its own function."[23] And George Gilbert Scott, in 1857, on the design of factories, advised "making the parts which have the same functions uniform and alike."[24] As a description of the activities specific to a particular building or part of a building, "function" occurs more rarely than one might expect before the twentieth century, although this has become a ubiquitous modern meaning. . . .

THE FORM–FUNCTION PARADIGM

Implicit in the polemic about "functional" modernism was the assumption of a relationship between buildings and the members of society inhabiting them. As the issue has come to be understood since the 1960s, the problem was one of describing either the action of the social environment upon the form of the building, or conversely, of the action of the buildings upon society. The difficulty in giving a historical account of this issue is that while such ideas certainly existed, and indeed were crucial to modernism, they were but poorly articulated, and rarely, if ever, referred to as "functionalism" before the late 1920s. The historical question that we have to try and account for is the turning of "function" from a description of the action of a building's own mechanical forces upon its form, into a description of the action of the social environment upon buildings, and of the action of buildings upon society. Crucial to this transformation is the introduction of the concept of "environment," which, it will be noticed, we have not been able to avoid even in describing the phenomenon we are seeking to understand.

As a first step, we might ask how far modern "functionalism" differs from earlier, classical theories about the relationship of people to buildings. There is no doubt that the suitability of buildings to their uses was important in the classical theory of architecture—it is part of what is covered by the Vitruvian term "commodity." This category underwent considerable refinement in eighteenth-century France, and the specific term developed to describe a satisfactory relationship between buildings and their occupants was "*convenance.*" J. F. Blondel writing in 1752 made *convenance* the first principle of architecture, explaining what he meant by it as follows: "For the spirit of *convenance* to reign in a plan, each room must placed according to its use and to the nature of the building, and must have a form and a proportion relative to its purpose."[25] In English *convenance* was usually translated as "fitness": for example J. C. Loudon, a prolific English architectural writer and publisher of the 1830s, followed Blondel's classification fairly closely, rendering *convenance* as "fitness for the end in view," and *bienséance* as "expression of the end in view":

An edifice may be useful, strong and durable, both in reality and in expression, without having any other beauties but those of use and truth; that is of fitness for

22. Greenough, *Form and Function*, 21.

23. Viollet-le-Duc, *Lectures on Architecture*, vol. 2, 277.

24. Sir George Gilbert Scott, *Remarks on Secular and Domestic Architecture: Present and Future* (London: John Murray, 1857), 212.

25. Jacques-Francois Blondel, *Architecture Francoise ou Receuil des Plans, Elévations, Coupes et Profiles* (Paris: Charles-Antoine Jombert, 1752), vol. 1, 26.

the end in view, and of expression of the end in view; or, in familiar language, of being suitable to the use for which it was designed, and of appearing to be what it is.[26]

The vagueness of both Blondel and Loudon as to what constitutes *convenance* or fitness is entirely characteristic of architectural theorists within the classical tradition who, while they considered a building's suitedness to its use as necessary, had nothing that could be called a theory about it. Moreover what Blondel, Loudon and every other writer in the classical tradition lacked was any account of the *relationship* between building and use—there was no suggestion that either one was in any way the outcome of the other; all that was required of the architect was to match the two together within an "appropriate character." *Convenance* became an increasingly undynamic concept that gradually collapsed into "comfort." (The significance of Horatio Greenough, it was suggested earlier, was his attempt to rescue *convenance,* or what he called "adaptation to use," from stasis by linking it, through the German Romantic idea of "function," to "character.") However, what all these classical categories lacked—and it is this lack that distinguishes them from subsequent modernist notions of "function"—was any sense that the building fulfilled, in a mechanical sense, the requirements of the society within which it was produced. To argue this, it was necessary to have both a theory of society, and a theory of social causes and effects, and it is precisely the presence of such theories in modern functionalism that sets it apart from classical *convenance.*

The source of the theory of society that altered the understanding of the relation of buildings to use was, of course, biology. What biology gave to the study of society was, in addition to the notions of "function" and of "hierarchy," the concept of *milieu*, or "environment." What classical *convenance* lacked, and what modern functionalism contains, is this notion that human society exists through its interaction with the physical and social surroundings. Indeed, it cannot be stressed too strongly that without "environment" modern functionalism would not exist (and conversely, whenever one meets the words "environment," or the other coefficient in the functionalist equation, "the user," one can be sure that functionalism is not far away). However, what is peculiarly difficult to establish is when, where and how this paradigm entered the discourse of architecture: we can confirm its absence in the eighteenth century, and we can be sure of its presence in the second half of the twentieth century, but what happened in between? This territory was explored by Michel Foucault in *The Order of Things*, and again more recently by Paul Rabinow in *French Modern*, but we are still very far from understanding how this ubiquitous concept, "environment," became established within modern thought. The best we can do is to summarize some of the better-known points on the way.

Milieu or environment was a concept basic to the understanding of changes in plants and animals from Aristotle's time, but where Aristotle and his successors saw the relationship between the organism and its surroundings as harmonious and balanced, a decisive change was made in the late eighteenth century by Lamarck, who saw the

26. John Claudius Loudon, *Encyclopaedia of Cottage, Farm, and Villa Architecture* (London: Longman, 1833), 1114.

relationship as basically unstable: an active organism seeks endlessly to attach itself to its *milieu,* which is indifferent to its survival, causing the organism to adapt. Adopted by social theorists such as Saint-Simon in the early nineteenth century, Lamarck's theory of the relationship of organisms to their environment became a highly popular model for the understanding of social process. It constitutes, for example, the theme of Honoré de Balzac's cycle of novels written in the 1830s and 1840s, *La Comédie humaine;* in the first, *Le Père Goriot* (1835), dedicated significantly to the Lamarckian naturalist Geoffroy Saint-Hilaire, the fortunes of the occupants of a Paris lodging house are described through their adaptation to their surroundings. But in the identification of its application to architecture and urbanism, we have to be more circumspect. While a writer like Viollet-le-Duc recognized the significance of social conditions (indeed, in Lecture X it was an important part of his argument in explaining why the same principles of construction, when applied in different times and places, produced different results) it was presented only in general terms and there was no reciprocal theory of the action of buildings upon society. Likewise, Leopold Eidlitz in 1881 insisted that "what should be impressed on the mind of the architect is that architectural forms, like all art organisms, and like the organisms of nature, are the result of environments"; but again, we have here no more than a one-way process.[27] On the other hand, by the end of the nineteenth century, in the English model villages built by reformist manufacturers for their employees, and in the early productions of the garden city movement, there was a clear implication of the converse process, of buildings acting upon inhabitants. And in Tony Garnier's imaginary *Cité Industrielle* of 1901–4, there was a definite assumption about the relationship between the layout and buildings of the city and the way of life of the residents, consistent with the thinking of the *Musée Social* group. Rabinow, who discusses this era of French social and spatial thinking in some detail, comments that the rise of the "social question" corresponds with the collapse of the liberal laissez-faire political economy, and the assumption by the state of responsibility for the welfare of its citizens; interest in *milieu,* and faith in "functionalism" (even if it is not known as such), were part of this process, and came to the fore in the social democratic regimes of Weimar Germany, and then of post-war western Europe.[28]

Another, rather different line of argument traces the influence of the eighteenth-century French Physiocrats, and of Scottish Political Economy. The early nineteenth-century Utilitarians, coming out of these traditions, believed in the need for the adjustment of the parts of the society for the greater good of the whole. Buildings had a part in this by bounding particular parts of the world—Bentham's Panopticon is the most famous example, but the same principle underlay the building of not only prisons, but also other institutional buildings, schools, hospitals and asylums. It was particularly in factories that the ideal of the harmonious action of many social units to the good of all was most comprehensively applied. But we should be careful not to assume, as there has been a tendency to do recently, that these institutions manifested an incipient modern func-tionalism. When the French architect L. P. Baltard commented in 1829 of English prisons

27. Eidlitz, *The Nature and Function of Art*, 467.

28. Rabinow, P., *French Modern: Norms and Forms of the Social Environment* (Chicago: University of Chicago Press, 1989), 169.

that they "function like a machine subject to the action of a single motor," he was referring to the harmony of routine within the prison, not to its action upon the inmates; and similarly it was "the idea of a vast automaton, composed of mechanical and intellectual organs acting in uninterrupted concert" that so excited Andrew Ure in 1835 about the cotton-mills of Manchester.[29] In so far as either prisons or factories affected the moral state of those within them, early nineteenth-century contemporaries attributed this to the regimen operated in them, not to the buildings themselves; contrary to the implication of some recent historical writing, it is very hard indeed to find any evidence in the first half of the nineteenth century of a belief that behaviour could be modified by the form of a building. But this distinction is admittedly a fine one, and by the late nineteenth century, when progressive manufacturers started to extend the principle of organization within the factory to the lives of their employees outside the factory, by building model housing for them, the distinction had become imperceptible. At Bournville, for example, Cadbury's model village outside Birmingham, the expectation that the houses and their layout would of themselves bring about a change in the life and social development of the inhabitants was clear.

However, at no point did contemporaries refer to any of these developments as "functional," nor is there a "theory" known by any other name that can be attached to these practices. The invention of a historical narrative descriptive of the development of a practice of functionalism through these and other nineteenth-century examples has been the work of historians in the last thirty years. Similarly, the creation of anything like a theory of "functionalism," synthesized from the disparate range of ideas and historical examples that we have discussed, only emerged in the 1960s when architects and critics started to react against modernism; modernist architects whose approach one might be tempted to describe as "functionalist," like Sir Leslie Martin, were in general extremely careful to distance themselves from any implication of determinist thinking.

One of the first and most famous works to take issue with orthodox modernism was Aldo Rossi's highly influential book *The Architecture of the City*, first published in Italian in 1966. Rossi's critique of "naïve functionalism" is an important part of his argument that the architecture of a city consists of generic types in which its social memory is preserved; European cities consist of buildings that have largely outlasted their original purposes without any loss of meaning, making function an irrelevance for their continued existence. "Naïve functionalist classifications . . . presuppose that all urban artifacts are created to serve particular functions in a static way and that their structure precisely coincides with the function they perform at a certain moment."[30] He continues:

> function alone is insufficient to explain the continuity of urban artifacts; if the origin of the typology of urban artifacts is simply function, this hardly accounts for the phenomenon of survival . . . In reality, we frequently continue to appreciate elements whose function has been lost over time; the value of these artifacts often resides solely in their form, which is integral to the general form of the city.[31]

29. Louis-Pierre Baltard, *Architectonographie des Prisons*, (Paris: Louis-Pierre Baltard, 1829), 18, 13.

30. Aldo Rossi, *The Architecture of the City*, trans. Diane Ghirardo and Joan Ockman (Cambridge: MIT Press, 1982), 55. First published in 1966.

31. Ibid., 60.

In fact, though, Rossi's own conception of "functionalism" was vague: it gathers substance only in so far as it provided him with an antithesis for his notion of "type," and thus enabled him to argue for the primacy of form.

Writing not long after Rossi, the French philosophers Henri Lefebvre and Jean Baudrillard both display a similar impulse to define "functionalism," not so much from any interest in it for its own sake, but because it helped them to develop their arguments about modernity. For Lefebvre, in *The Production of Space*, "functionalism" was one of the features of "abstract space," that flattened, homogenized, asphyxiating form of space characteristic of modern capitalist societies.[32] At one point, says Lefebvre, "The science of space should . . . be viewed as a *science of use*," but, he warns, "It would be inexact and reductionist to define use solely in terms of function, as functionalism recommends." "Functionalism," he continues, "stresses function to the point where, because each function has a specially assigned place within dominated space, the very possibility of multi-functionality is eliminated."[33] In place of the limitations imposed by a functional approach to use, Lefebvre was interested in the co-option of space (he gives the example of early Christianity's co-option of the Roman basilica), for it is through such processes that subjects themselves directly achieve the production of a lived, "social space." For Lefebvre (and he has this in common with Rossi), "functionalism" impoverishes because it fixes use.

To Baudrillard, concerned with the tendency of capitalism to displace commodities by their sign, "functionality is nothing other than a *system of interpretation*": it is a wholly arbitrary (though seemingly rational) attempt to fix the meaning of objects according to their use and so protect them against the effects of fashion.[34] "When one ponders it, there is something unreal and almost surreal in the fact of reducing an object to its function: and it suffices to push this principle of functionality to the limit to make its absurdity emerge."[35] Baudrillard saw functionalism and surrealism as necessary opposites; functionalism pretended that form signified use, while "surrealism plays upon the *distance* instituted by the functionalist calculus between the object and itself . . . Fusion of the skin of breasts and the folds of a dress, of toes and the leather of a shoe: surrealist imagery plays with this split by denying it."[36]

These examples will suffice to show that not just in architecture, but in a variety of disciplines, to give functionalism specific attributes was a necessary part of developing a critique of modernism, and of modernity in general. Historical study took a corresponding course. The extensive investigation of the histories of particular building types, schools, hospitals, prisons, town halls etc., from the late 1960s may be seen as part of a general attempt to find some basis for the form–function paradigm. But there are two books in particular from this period, Peter Collins's *Changing Ideals in Modern Architecture* (1965) and Philip Steadman's *The Evolution of Designs* (1979), that set out to find a pedigree for functionalist thinking in architecture, and in particular to identify the origin of the notion that environment acts upon form: both Collins and Steadman located this in Lamarck's theory of evolution. Yet although it may be perfectly true that some twentieth-century notions of function do correspond to Lamarckian ideas, there is disconcertingly

32. Henri Lefebvre, *The Production of Space*, trans. D. Nicholson-Smith, (Oxford: Blackwell, 1991), 274. First published in 1974.

33. Ibid., 368–369.

34. Jean Baudrillard, *For a Critique of the Political Economy of the Sign*, trans. Charles Levin (St. Louis: Telos Press, 1981), 196–197. First published in 1972.

35. Ibid., 192–193.

36. Ibid., 193.

little evidence, as we have already seen, that any nineteenth-century architect or architectural theorist (with the possible exceptions of Horatio Greenough and James Fergusson) ever understood "function" to mean this, nor had any but the vaguest interest in architecture as part of the interaction between mankind and its environment. Though architectural writers were fond of the biological analogy in relation to theories of construction, there is only the most fragmentary evidence to suggest that they might have seen it as a means to develop an account of architecture as a social phenomenon. If Lamarck's theory of organism-environment is indeed the origin of the modern notion of functionalism, it seems more likely to have reached architecture via sociology than from any direct analogy with biology.

While in the period from the 1960s to the 1980s we see the assembly from the scattered fragments of earlier thinking of a more or less coherent account of functionalism—largely so as to denigrate it—in the period since there have been various attempts to recuperate "function." These have come from people acting with widely different intentions. On the one hand, we have the architect Bernard Tschumi, who, introducing an anthology of his articles from the 1970s and 1980s, explained their general theme as follows: "Opposing an over-rated notion of architectural form, they aim to reinstate the term *function* and, more particularly, to reinscribe the movement of bodies in space, together with the actions and events that take place within the social and political realm of architecture."[37] That Tschumi chose, in 1996, to present his earlier views in this manner was a not-so-oblique lunge at Peter Eisenman, who, for the previous twenty years, had been broadcasting pro-form, anti-function views. In fact, an examination of Tschumi's own earlier views shows him to have been a good deal more critical of "function" than the 1996 remarks suggest. While he had consistently been interested in the realization of event, activity, movement and conflict, earlier he had regarded "function" as inadequate to describe these. In 1983, he had written:

> By going beyond the conventional definition of "function" the [Manhattan] Transcripts use their combined levels of investigation to address the notion of the program . . . To discuss the idea of program today by no means implies a return to notions of function versus form, to cause and effect relationships between program and type or some new version of utopian positivism. On the contrary, it opens a field of research where spaces are finally confronted with what happens in them.[38]

Clearly in the thirteen years between these two texts, the connotations of "function" had changed sufficiently for Tschumi to want to endorse its use.

Another apologist for "function" is Bill Hillier, who has provided by far the most lucid investigation of the "form–function paradigm" (the phrase is his) and its problems in *Space Is the Machine*. Hillier, though, is emphatic that it is not his purpose to dispose of "functionalism," rather to understand what was wrong with the theory, in order to replace it

37. Bernard Tschumi, *Manhattan Transcripts* (London: Academy Editions, 1981), 3–4.
38. Bernard Tschumi, "Illustrated Index: Themes from the Manhattan Manuscripts," *AA Files*, 4 (1983): 71–72.

with a better one. The popular perception of the failure of modern architecture quite correctly interpreted this in terms of failures of "function." "The proper inference from this," writes Hillier:

> would seem to be that the functionalist theories used by the designers were wrong, but that functional failure had confirmed the central importance of the form–function relation. There could, after all, be no functional failure if the relation between form and function were not powerful. The call should then follow for a new theory of function. Instead, there was an abandonment of functional theory in general, and an intellectual abandonment of the form–function problem at exactly the moment when functional failure had brought it dramatically to public attention. To understand this apparently perverse reaction—and also see that it was in a certain sense justified—we must understand exactly what it was that was rejected.[39]

Then, like all previous adventurers on this ground, Hillier has first to create speculatively, out of the few available scraps of evidence, the "theory" that never was, but whose existence is necessary to know modernism. Some of the features of Hillier's account of "form–function" theory I have already made use of in this entry, but it is worth summarizing his argument as a whole.

Hillier says that the error implicit in the form–function paradigm was the fallacious assumption that buildings can act mechanically upon the behaviour of individuals. "How can a material object like a building impinge directly on human behaviour?"[40] Such a claim violates common sense—and it is worth recalling that no utilitarian or early nineteenth-century political economist ever claimed this. Yet nonetheless, also at a common sense level, there is a relationship of some sort between what goes on in buildings and their form. Hillier resolves this conundrum by the hypothesis that "the relation between form and function at all levels of the built environment, from the dwelling to the city, passes through the variable of spatial configurations."[41] However, the modernist formulation of the paradigm, lacking any conception of spatial configuration, was—rightly—rejected as worthless.

The question of how such a fundamentally unsatisfactory theory of the relationship between people and buildings could ever have been given credence, Hillier attributes, as others had before, to the pervasiveness and persistence outside natural science of Lamarck's theory of evolution. Whereas in biology, Lamarck's theory of the interaction of organisms with their environments was quickly superseded by Darwin's theory of the evolution of organisms through a process of random mutations, in architecture and urbanism Lamarckianism survived. The inertia of environmental determinism, remarkable enough given its inability either to explain or to predict anything, was, Hillier stresses, all the more remarkable in that it was founded upon a misleading and fallacious metaphor, in which the artificial environment is treated as if it were a natural environment.

39. Hillier, *Space is the Machine*, 376.
40. Ibid., 379.
41. Ibid., 378,

This blinds the enquirer to the most significant single fact about the built environment: that it is not simply a background to social behavior—it is itself a social behaviour. Prior to being experienced by subjects, it is already imbued with patterns which reflect its origin in the behaviours through which it is created.[42]

It is, according to Hillier, the legacy of this particularly inapt metaphor in modern architecture that caused not only the form–function paradigm to be rejected, but temporarily at least caused the suspension of all interest in the relationship between buildings and their use in avant-garde architectural circles.

Looking back over the history of the concept "function," it is clear that a practical need to talk about the relationship between buildings and the life within and around them has always existed. However, the manner of conceiving this relationship was one of the most distinctive differences between the classical tradition of architectural thought and the modernist one. If the means which modernism found to discuss this relationship was founded upon an inappropriate metaphor, which appears to be in the course of being discontinued, that does not mean that the need to discuss the relationship will also be terminated. The problem now appears to be to develop a satisfactory concept and appropriate terminology to replace "function," or else to purge "function" of its biological and environmental determinist connotations.

42. Ibid., 388–389.

Writing and Discussion Questions

ANALYSIS

1. What is Sullivan arguing for and against? What excerpt/quotation best represents this?
2. What is Tschumi arguing for and against? What excerpt/quotation best represents this?
3. What is Forty arguing for and against? What excerpt/quotation best represents this?

SYNTHESIS

1. Regarding concepts of form and function, discuss one major difference regarding Sullivan's, Tschumi's, and Forty's texts.
2. Regarding concepts of form and function, discuss one primary commonality regarding Sullivan's, Tschumi's, and Forty's texts.

SELF-REFLECTION

1. For each of the texts, discuss a major issue with which you most agree and most disagree; reflect upon why you hold these views.
2. Select a recent design project, or a current project on which you are working. Discuss the characteristics of the project in regards to the relationship between form and function, in light of the discussion and texts introduced in this chapter. What attitudes regarding the relationship between form and function does your work illustrate?

PROSPECTION

1. Select one of the texts listed in the bibliography for this chapter; locate and read it. To what degree is that text and the attitudes it represents still relevant to architecture today and in the near future?

2. What is the relationship between form and function in architecture today? How are new uses, technologies, and materials changing the relationship between them? In other words, if a fourth text were added to this chapter, what would the argument be?

Other Readings on Function and Form

Arnheim, Rudolf. *The Dynamics of Architectural Form* (Berkeley: University of California Press, 1977).

Bill, Max. *Form, Function, Beauty = Gestalt* (London: Architectural Association, 2010).

Blake, Peter. *Form Follows Fiasco: Why Modern Architecture Hasn't Worked* (Boston: Little, Brown, & Co., 1977).

Greenough, Horatio. *Form and Function: Remarks on Art, Design and Architecture* (Berkeley: University of California Press, 1966).

Grillo, Paul Jacques. *Form, Function, and Design* (Mineola: Dover, 1975).

Heschong, Lisa. "Necessity," in *Thermal Delight in Architecture* (Cambridge: MIT Press, 1979).

Hillenbrand, Robert. *Islamic Architecture: Form, Function, and Meaning* (New York: Columbia University Press, 2004).

Moussavi, Farshid. *The Function of Form* (Barcelona: Actar and the Harvard Graduate School of Design, 2009).

Saarinen, Eliel. *The Search for Form in Art and Architecture* (New York: Reinhold Publishing Corp., 1948).

Tanizaki, Junichiro. *In Praise of Shadows* (New Haven: Leete's Island Books, 1977). First published in 1933.

Chapter 6

FUNCTION and FORM (PART 2)

INTRODUCTORY DISCUSSION

1. Of the two images above, which "form" is most appropriate to its "function" in contemporary architecture? Why?

2. How has the concept of "function" in architecture changed in recent years?

3. How important or unimportant is "function" relative to other issues—tectonics, context, etc.—in architecture today?

FIGURE 6.1
Photograph of the exterior of London City Hall, London, England, United Kingdom (1998–2002). Architect: Norman Foster.

FIGURE 6.2
Photograph of the courtyard and exterior façade of the Open-air School for the Healthy Child, Amsterdam, Netherlands (1928–1930). Architect: Johannes Duiker.

Introduction

The form vs. function debate is so central to architecture that it necessitates further exploration. What is the difference between "function" and "use"? Is "function" as essential to architecture as some architects have contended? This chapter extends the discourse of the previous chapter, as new terms and concepts are introduced, such as "continuity," "post-functionalism," "purpose," and "use."

Wright is popularly cited for his promotion of "organic architecture" and the intertwining of architecture and nature. An apprentice to Louis Sullivan, Wright also extended the "form follows function" slogan. In actuality, however, these concepts existed within a larger set of ideas about materials, construction, and space making—the concept of "continuity." To Wright, continuity encompassed both form and function, both material and space. In *An American Architecture*, the *original text* for this chapter, Wright contended that continuity applied to "the concept of the building as a whole." By eliminating post-and-beam construction, Wright asserted that ceiling, wall, and floor could merge, "their surfaces flowing into each other," becoming "not only party to each other but *part of each other*." For Wright, this new formal and structural attitude might enable new spaces, forms, and uses to take place. The exemplar was the Wright-designed Guggenheim Museum in New York, completed in 1959, with a continuous interior spiraling ramp and continuous exterior concrete ribbon.

Eight years later, a group of up-and-coming New York architects, led by Peter Eisenman, founded the Institute for Architecture and Urban Studies, seeking alternative forms of architectural education and practice. The group was critical of the status quo, especially Modernist theories that had become conventions, such as functionalism. In "Post-Functionalism," the *reflective text* for this chapter, Eisenman asserted that a new paradigm in architectural theory and practice had emerged. According to Eisenman, the Modernist notion of functionalism replaced the humanist paradigm in architecture, and, in turn, functionalism was replaced by "post-functionalism." Humanism drew its aesthetic and organizational principles metaphorically from the parts, proportions, and systems of the human body. Functionalism, on the other hand, stemmed from technological and mechanistic metaphors, and from human activities. Modernists saw functionalism as a formula: function → form. Post-functionalism, as stated by Eisenman, pulled form and function apart, where they could be dealt with independently. Eisenman argued that "functionalism" was a cultural construct, an invented way of thinking, not a universal, pre-human principle of nature, as purported by many Modernists. Post-functionalism, in essence, was the recognition of the "reductivist attitude" and over-simplification that resulted from Modernist ideals, as well as the realization that a resulting architectural form "is a state of simplification" of multiple, fragmented concepts, not a single concept.

This multiplicity was also noted by Forty in the previous chapter. It re-emerges in Richard Hill's "Purpose, Function, Use," the *philosophical text* for this chapter, where the relationships among these terms are discussed. Hill defined a hierarchical relationship, where "purpose" is the overarching reason a building exists, "function" is the intended outcome of a building, and "use" involves the constituent parts and activities of a building. According to Hill, the *purpose* of an elementary school, for example, is to accommodate the interaction of teachers and students "in an artificial climate, protected from the weather and intruders." The *function* is "to educate children," and involves the "program-matic whole" of classrooms, storage, circulation, etc. The *use*, on the other hand, is more multifaceted and elusive. It operates at both the micro-scale—individual activities, such as reading, eating, etc.—and the macro-scale—the "ensemble" of the whole. This ensemble includes: (1) a "pattern of human activity," (2) the architectural configuration and form, and (3) the "arrangement of furniture or equipment." According to Hill, purpose, function, and use undoubtedly have aesthetic consequences, affecting both the typo-logical forms of buildings and the lived experiences of the individuals who occupy them.

The dialectical relationship between aesthetics and use is complex, especially due to the variety of concepts and terms associated with "form" and "function." This dialectic is made more complex by changing philosophies in architecture. During the latter 19th century and early 20th century, Modernists viewed form as an outcome of function. Several decades later, architects like Bernard Tschumi (previous chapter) and Peter Eisenman (current chapter) reversed this construct, suggesting that form is given priority and that function is applied later. The current paradigm regarding form and function is not yet clear. Nor is it clear how future architectural philosophies will reshape the form–function dialectic. It is likely, however, that, despite emerging environmental, economic, and technological concerns, "form vs. function" will remain a significant architectural discourse.

Original Text

FRANK L. WRIGHT, EXCERPTS FROM *AN AMERICAN ARCHITECTURE*.

First Published in 1955

CONTINUITY

Classic architecture was all fixation-of-the-fixture. Yes, entirely so. Now why not let walls, ceilings, floors become seen as component parts of each other, their surfaces flowing into each other. . . .

Continuity in this aesthetic sense appeared to me as the natural means to achieve truly organic architecture by machine technique or by any other natural technique. Here was direct means, the only means I could then see or can now see to express, objectify and again bring natural form to architecture. Here by instinct at first (all ideas germinate) principle had entered into building as the new aesthetic, *continuity*.

Gradually proceeding from generals to particulars in the field of work with materials and machines continuity began to grip me and work its own will in architecture. I would watch sequences fascinated, seeing other sequences in those consequences already in evidence. I occasionally look through such early studies as I made at this period (a number of them still remain), fascinated by implications. They seem, even now, generic.

Visions of simplicities so broad and far-reaching would open to me and such building harmonies appear, that I was tireless in search of new ones. In various [forms of research], with all my energy I concentrated upon the principle of plasticity working as continuity. Soon a practical working technique evolved and a new scale within the buildings I was building, in the endeavor to accomplish more sensibly and sensitively this thing we call architecture. Here at work was something that would change and deepen the thinking and culture of the modern world. So I believed. . . .

Rising to greater dignity as idea, the ideal of plasticity was now to be developed and emphasized in the treatment of the building as a whole. Plasticity was a familiar term but something I had seen in no buildings whatsoever. I had seen it in Lieber Meister's

184

(Louis Sullivan) ornament only; it had not found its way into his buildings otherwise. It might now be seen gradually coming into the expressive lines and surfaces of the buildings I was building. You may see the appearance of the thing in the surface of your hand contrasted with the articulation of the bony skeleton itself. This ideal, profound in its architectural implications, soon took another conscious stride forward in the form of a new aesthetic. I called it *continuity*. It is easy to see it in the folded plane.

I promoted plasticity as conceived by Lieber Meister to *continuity* in the concept of the building as a whole. If the dictum, form follows function, had any at all on building it could take form in architecture only by means plasticity when seen at work as complete *continuity*. So why not throw away entirely all implications of post and beam construction? Have no posts, no columns, no pilasters, cornices or moldings or ornament; no divisions of the sort nor allow any fixtures whatever to enter as something added to the structure. Any building should be complete, including all within itself. Instead of many things, *one* thing.

The folded plane enters here emphasized by lines merging wall and ceiling into one. Let walls, ceilings, floors now become not only party to each other but *part of each other,* reacting upon and within one another; continuity in all, eliminating any merely constructed features, fixtures or appliances whatsoever as such.

When Louis Sullivan had eliminated background in his system of ornament in favor of an integral sense of the whole, he had implied this larger sense of the thing. I now began to achieve it.

Conceive that here came a new sense of building on American soil that could *grow* building forms not only true to function but expressive far beyond mere function in the realm of the human spirit. Our new country might now have a true architecture hitherto unknown. Yes, architectural forms by this interior means might now grow up to express a deeper sense of human life-values than any existing before. Architecture might extend the bounds of human individuality indefinitely by way of safe interior discipline. Not only had space come upon a new technique of its own but every material and every method might now speak for itself in objective terms of human life. Architects were no longer tied to Greek space but were free to enter into the space of Einstein.

But later on I found that in the effort to actually eliminate the post and beam in favor of structural continuity, that is to say, make two things one instead of separate, I could get no help at all from regular engineers. By habit, the engineer reduced everything in the field of calculation to the post and the beam resting upon it before he could calculate and tell you where and just how much for either He had no other data. Walls made one with floors and ceilings, merging together yet reacting upon each other, the engineer had never met. And the engineer has not yet enough scientific formulae to enable him to calculate for continuity. Floor slabs stiffened and extended as cantilevers over centered supports, as a waiter's tray rests upon his upturned fingers, such as I now began to use in order to get planes parallel to the earth to emphasize the third dimension, were new, as I used them, especially in the Imperial Hotel. But the engineer soon mastered the element of continuity in floor slabs, with such formulae as he had. The cantilever thus became a new feature of design in architecture. As used in the Imperial Hotel at Tokyo it was the most important of the features of construction that insured the life of that building in the terrific temblor of 1922. So, here came not only a new aesthetic, but, the aesthetic now proven scientifically sound, a great new economic stability derived from steel in tension was able to enter building construction.

Where the beam leaves off and the post begins is no longer important, nor need it be seen at all because it no longer actually is. Steel in tension enables the support to slide into the supported, or the supported to grow into the support, somewhat as a tree branch glides out of its tree trunk. There from arises the new series of interior physical reactions I call continuity. As natural consequence, the new aesthetic is no longer a mere appearance: plasticity actually becomes the normal countenance, the true aesthetic of genuine structural reality. Interwoven steel strands may lie in so many directions in any member that all extensions may be economical of material, much lighter, yet safer in construction than ever before. There as in the branch of the tree you may see the cantilever. The cantilever is the simplest of the important phases of this new structural resource, now demanding new significance. It has yet had little attention in architecture. It can do remarkable things to liberate space.

In the form of the cantilever, as horizontal continuity, this new economy saved the Imperial Hotel from destruction.

Later, in the new design for St. Mark's Tower, New York City, this new working principle promised to economize material, labor, and liberate space. It gave the structure significant outlines of remarkable stability instead of false masonry-mass. The abstract pattern of the structure as an integrity of form and idea may be seen fused, as in any tree, but with nothing imitating a tree.

I am convinced that the pattern made by a cross section of honeycomb has more fertility and flexibility where human movement is concerned than the square. The obtuse angle is more suited to human to and fro than the right angle. Flow and movement is, in this design, a characteristic lending itself admirably to life, as life is to be lived in it. In the Hanna house the hexagon has been conservatively treated, however. It is allowed to appear in plan only and in the furniture which literally rises from and befits the floor pattern of the concrete slab upon which the whole stands.

The proposed new building for the Guggenheim Museum is the latest sense of organic architecture. Here we are not building a cellular composition of compartments, but one where all is one great space on a single continuous floor.

The eye encounters no abrupt change, but is gently led and treated as if at the edge of the shore watching an unbreaking wave—or is that too fancy a phrase?

Here for the first time architecture appears plastic, one floor flowing into another instead of the usual superimposition of stratified layers cutting and butting into each other by post and beam construction.

The whole is cast in concrete more an eggshell in form than a crisscross stick structure. The concrete is rendered strong enough everywhere to do its work by filaments of steel, separate or in mesh. Structural calculations are thus those of cantilever and continuity rather than the conventional post and beam formula. The net result of such construction is greater repose, an atmosphere of the unbroken wave—no meeting of the eye with angular or abrupt changes of form. All is as one and as near indestructible as it is possible to make a building.

INTERIOR SPACE COMES THROUGH

The interior space itself is the reality of the building. The room itself must come through or architecture has not arrived in the modern sense.

Architecture now becomes integral, the expression of a new-old reality: the livable interior space of the room itself. In integral architecture the room-space itself must come through. The room must be seen as architecture, or we have no architecture. We have no longer an outside as outside. We have no longer an outside and an inside as two separate things. Now the outside may come inside, and the inside may and does go outside. They are of each other. Form and function thus become one in design and execution if the nature of materials and method and purpose are all in unison. . . .

Now came clear *an entirely new sense of architecture*, a higher conception of architecture: architecture not alone as form following function, but conceived as space enclosed. The enclosed space itself might now be seen as the reality of the building. This sense of the within, or the room itself, or the rooms themselves, I now saw as the great thing to be expressed as *architecture*. This sense of interior space made exterior as architecture transcended all that had gone before, made all the previous ideas only useful now as means to the realization of a far greater ideal. Hitherto all classical or ancient buildings had been great masses or blocks of building material, sculptured into shape outside and hollowed out to live in. At least that was the sense of it all. But here coming to light was a sense of building as an organism that had new release for the opportunities of the machine age. This interior conception took architecture entirely away from sculpture, away from painting and entirely away from architecture as it had been known in the antique. The building now became a creation of interior space in light. And as the sense of the interior space as the reality of the building began to work, walls as walls fell away. The vanishing wall joined the disappearing cave. Enclosing screens and protecting features of architectural character took the place of the solid wall.

Let us go back, here, to the first self-conscious assertion of the third dimension in building, as it came to be called. The reality of the building is not in the four walls and roof but in the space enclosed by them to be lived in. Earlier than this I had been trying to bring the room through. But in Unity Temple (1904–1905) to bring the room through was consciously a main objective. So Unity Temple has no actual walls as walls. Utilitarian features, the stair-enclosures at the corners; low masonry screens carrying roof supports; the upper part of the structure on four sides a continuous window beneath the ceiling of the big room, the ceiling extending out over them to shelter them; the opening of this slab where it passed over the big room to let sunlight fall where deep shadow had been deemed "religious"; these were to a great extent the means employed to achieve the purpose. Since then the "new" concept of building (expressed by Laotze, 500 B.C.) has never slept. You will find it working in many different ways in all the structures shown in this collection, often seeming contradictory.

This sense of the within, the room itself (or the rooms themselves) I see as the great thing to be realized, that make take the new forms we need as architecture. Such a source would never stultify itself as a mere style.

Reflective Text

PETER EISENMAN, "POST-FUNCTIONALISM."

First Published in 1976

The critical establishment within architecture has told us that we have entered the era of "post-modernism." The tone with which this news is delivered is invariably one of relief, similar to that which accompanies the advice that one is no longer an adolescent. Two indices of this supposed change are the quite different manifestations of the "Architettura Razionale" exhibition at the Milan Triennale of 1973, and the "Ecole Des Beaux Arts" exhibition at The Museum of Modern Art in 1975. The former, going on the assumption that modern architecture was an outmoded functionalism, declared that architecture can be generated only through a return to itself as an autonomous or pure discipline. The latter, seeing modern architecture as an obsessional formalism, made itself into an implicit statement that the future lies paradoxically in the past, within the peculiar response to function that characterized the nineteenth century's eclectic command of historical styles.

What is interesting is not the mutually exclusive character of these two diagnoses and hence of their solutions, but rather the fact that *both* of these views enclose the very project of architecture within the *same* definition: one by which the terms continue to be function (or program) and form (or type). In so doing, an attitude toward architecture is maintained that differs in no significant way from the 500-year-old tradition of humanism.

The various theories of architecture which properly can be called "humanist" are characterized by a dialectical opposition: an oscillation between a concern for internal accommodation—the program and the way it is materialized— and a concern for articulation of ideal themes in form—for example, as manifested in the configurational significance of the plan. These concerns were understood as two poles of a single, continuous experience. Within pre-industrial, humanist practice, a balance between them could be maintained because both type and function were invested with idealist views of man's relationship to his object world. In a comparison first suggested by Colin Rowe, of a French Parisian *hôtel* and an English country house, both buildings from the early

189

nineteenth century, one sees this opposition manifested in the interplay between a concern for expression of an ideal type and a concern for programmatic statement, although the concerns in each case are differently weighted. The French *hôtel* displays rooms of an elaborate sequence and a spatial variety born of internal necessity, masked by a rigorous, well-proportioned external façade. The English country house has a formal internal arrangement of rooms which gives way to a picturesque external massing of elements. The former bows to program on the interior and type on the façade; the latter reverses these considerations.

With the rise of industrialization, this balance seems to have been fundamentally disrupted. In that it had of necessity to come to terms with problems of a more complex functional nature, particularly with respect to the accommodation of a mass client, architecture became increasingly a social or programmatic art. And as the functions became more complex, the ability to manifest the pure type-form eroded. One has only to compare William Kent's competition entry for the Houses of Parliament, where the form of a Palladian Villa does not sustain the intricate program, with Charles Barry's solution where the type-form defers to program and where one sees an early example of what was to become known as the *promenade architecturale*. Thus, in the nineteenth century, and continuing on into the twentieth, as the program grew in complexity, the type-form became diminished as a realizable concern, and the balance thought to be fundamental to all theory was weakened. (Perhaps only Le Corbusier in recent history has successfully combined an ideal grid with the architectural promenade as an embodiment of the original interaction.)

This shift in balance has produced a situation whereby, for the past fifty years, architects have understood design as the product of some oversimplified form-follows-function formula. This situation even persisted during the years immediately following World War II, when one might have expected it would be radically altered. And as late as the end of the 1960s, it was still thought that the polemics and theories of the early Modern Movement could sustain architecture. The major thesis of this attitude was articulated in what could be called the English Revisionist Functionalism of Reyner Banham, Cedric Price, and Archigram. This neo-functionalist attitude, with its idealization of technology, was invested with the same ethical positivism and aesthetic neutrality of the prewar polemic. However, the continued substitution of moral criteria for those of a more formal nature produced a situation which now can be seen to have created a functionalist predicament, precisely because the primary theoretical justification given to formal arrangements was a *moral* imperative that is no longer operative within contemporary experience. This sense of displaced positivism characterizes certain current perceptions of the failure of humanism within a broader cultural context.

There is also another, more complex, aspect to this predicament. Not only can functionalism indeed be recognized as a species of positivism, but like positivism, it now can be seen to issue from within the terms of an idealist view of reality. For functionalism, no matter what its pretense, continued the idealist ambition of creating architecture as a kind of ethically constituted form-giving. But because it clothed this idealist ambition in the radically stripped forms of technological production, it has seemed to represent a break with the pre-industrial past. But, in fact, functionalism is really no more than a late phase of humanism, rather than an alternative to it. And in this sense, it cannot continue to be taken as a direct manifestation of that which has been called "the modernist sensibility."

Both the Triennale and the Beaux Arts exhibitions suggest, however, that the problem is thought to be somewhere else—not so much with functionalism *per se*, as with the nature of this so-called modernist sensibility. Hence, the implied revival of neo-classicism and Beaux Arts academicism as replacements for a continuing, if poorly understood, modernism. It is true that sometime in the nineteenth century, there was indeed a crucial shift within Western consciousness: one which can be characterized as a shift from humanism to modernism. But, for the most part, architecture, in its dogged adherence to the principles of function, did not participate in or understand the fundamental aspects of that change. It is the potential difference in the nature of modernist and humanist theory that seems to have gone unnoticed by those people who today speak of eclecticism, post-modernism, or neo-functionalism. And they have failed to notice it precisely because they conceive of modernism as merely a stylistic manifestation of functionalism, and functionalism itself as a basic theoretical proposition in architecture. In fact, the idea of modernism has driven a wedge into these attitudes. It has revealed that the dialectic form and function is culturally based.

In brief, the modernist sensibility has to do with a changed mental attitude toward the artifacts of the physical world. This change has not only been manifested aesthetically, but also socially, philosophically, and technologically—in sum, it has been manifested in a new cultural attitude. This shift away from the dominant attitudes of humanism, that were pervasive in Western societies for some four hundred years, took place at various times in the nineteenth century in such disparate disciplines as mathematics, music, painting, literature, film, and photography. It is displayed in the non-objective abstract painting of Malevich and Mondrian; in the non-narrative, atemporal writing of Joyce and Apollinaire; the atonal and polytonal compositions of Schönberg and Webern; in the non-narrative films of Richter and Eggeling.

Abstraction, atonality, and atemporality, however, are merely stylistic manifestations of modernism, not its essential nature. Although this is not the place to elaborate a theory of modernism, or indeed to represent those aspects of such a theory which have already found their way into the literature of the other humanist disciplines, it can simply be said that the symptoms to which one has just pointed suggest a displacement of man away from the center of his world. He is no longer viewed as an *originating agent*. Objects are seen as ideas independent of man. In this context, man is a discursive function among complex and already-formed systems of language, which he witnesses but does not constitute. As Levi-Strauss has said, "Language, an unreflecting totalization, is human reason which has its reason and of which man knows nothing." It is this condition of displacement which gives rise to design in which authorship can no longer either account for a linear development which has a 'beginning' and an 'end'—hence the rise of the atemporal—or account for the invention of form—hence the abstract as a mediation between pre-existent sign systems.

Modernism, as a sensibility based on the fundamental displacement of man, represents what Michel Foucault would specify as a new *épistème*. Deriving from a non-humanistic attitude toward the relationship of an individual to his physical environment, it breaks with the historical past, both with the ways of viewing man as subject and, as we have said, with the ethical positivism of form and function. Thus, it cannot be related to functionalism. It is probably for this reason that modernism has not up to now been elaborated in architecture.

But there is clearly a present need for a theoretical investigation of the basic implications of modernism (as opposed to modern style) in architecture. In his editorial "Neo-Functionalism," in *Oppositions* 5, Mario Gandelsonas acknowledges such a need. However, he says merely that the "complex contradictions" inherent in functionalism—such as neo-realism and neo-rationalism—make a form of neo-functionalism necessary to any new theoretical dialectic. This proposition continues to refuse to recognize that the form–function opposition is not necessarily inherent to any architectural theory and so fails to recognize the crucial difference between modernism and humanism. In contrast, what is being called post-functionalism begins as an attitude which recognizes modernism as a new and distinct sensibility. It can best be understood in architecture in terms of a theoretical base that is concerned with what might be called a modernist *dialectic*, as opposed to the old humanist (i.e., functionalist) opposition of form and function.

This new theoretical base changes the humanist balance of form–function to a dialectical relationship within the evolution of form itself. The dialectic can best be described as the potential co-existence within any form of two non-corroborating and non-sequential tendencies. One tendency is to presume architectural form to be a recognizable transformation from some pre-existent geometric or platonic solid. In this case, form is usually understood through a series of registrations designed to recall a more simple geometric condition. This tendency is certainly a relic of humanist theory. However, to this is added a second tendency that sees architectural form in an atemporal, decompositional mode, as something simplified from some pre-existent set of non-specific spatial entities. Here, form is understood as a series of fragments—signs without meaning dependent upon, and without reference to, a more basic condition. The former tendency, when taken by itself, is a reductivist attitude and assumes some primary unity as both an ethical and an aesthetic basis for all creation. The latter, by itself, assumes a basic condition of fragmentation and multiplicity from which the resultant form is a state of simplification. Both tendencies, however, when taken together, constitute the essence of this new, modern dialectic. They begin to define the inherent nature of the object in and of itself and its capacity to be represented. They begin to suggest that the theoretical assumptions of functionalism are in fact cultural rather than universal.

Post-functionalism, thus, is a term of absence. In its negation of functionalism it suggests certain positive theoretical alternatives—existing fragments of thought which, when examined, might serve as a framework for the development of a larger theoretical structure—but it does not, in and of itself, propose to supply a label for such a new consciousness in architecture which I believe is potentially upon us.

Philosophical Text

RICHARD HILL, "PURPOSE, FUNCTION, USE."

First Published in 1999

Architecture is aesthetically distinctive because it is an art of design. . . . Architecture's individuality comes from the fact that it is a useful art, and that the aesthetics of architecture should be based on recognising its usefulness. . . .

It is possible that a distinctive kind of architectural experience is involved in using buildings, one that is not involved in contemplating them. [Previously], I discussed the question of architectural experience but in doing so I avoided making any distinction between the way that users on one hand and enthusiasts and tourists on the other might experience buildings. If it turns out that the use of building does involve a special kind of experience, it might then provide the basis for understanding the relationship between usefulness and aesthetics.

Using buildings does indeed involve a different mode of experience from that involved in contemplating them. However, I suggest that the difference lies in the modes of attention that are employed in each case. Using buildings leads us to engage kinds of attention—for example, "distracted" and repetitive kinds—that are part of our common repertoire in daily life and in our other cultural pursuits. The experience of contemplating and using architecture do have different characteristics but the latter are not unique to architecture, or distinctive of it. This means that the connection between usefulness and the experience of architecture is a loose one, and it is not likely to provide the basis for a clear conceptual link between usefulness and aesthetics.

In the next section . . . I turn away from experience towards the idea that usefulness can be given symbolic or representational significance in the design of buildings. Perhaps this will provide a firmer link between usefulness and aesthetics: that this kind of meaningfulness is constitutive of architecture as a distinctive kind of art. . . .

Note that the assumption has been made that usefulness does have a nature, that there is something complex in it which invites a rich aesthetic response. This assumption needs some discussion and I set this in motion with a fairly grueling trek through definitions and clarifications of the terms "use," "purpose" and "function." I believe this unpromising dissection of terms has an important outcome. It points to the impossibility of the notion that use or function or purpose can be defined separately from a design, with the expectation that a design can then be made to fit that use, function or purpose. In fact, usefulness and design are not related in a problem-solution manner: the real relationship is one where design and usefulness constitute each other. . . .

It may be that we should consider designing with usefulness in mind as a process of finding rather than making. The shift would recognise the fact that we shall always see usefulness and design cohabiting, and that we cannot invent one partner simply as a solution to the other. It also moves the focus of architectural aesthetics away from the modification of traditional forms towards the way that buildings are designed—away from prescriptions about products towards the design process. The aspiration to forge compelling links between usefulness and design via the medium of the design process is, very broadly conceived, the grand theme of modern architecture, considered in a historical perspective that extends from the early part of the nineteenth century to almost the present day. We lack a word for what is involved here: I call it the sustaining outlook of modernism in architecture. . . .

USE

The first proposition that I wish to examine in detail is that use—actual use—involves a distinctive kind of architectural experience, a kind that is different from the experience of simply being a spectator of buildings. The aesthetic experience of architecture, properly considered, is therefore only open to users of buildings. This obviously implies that the pleasures of looking at buildings, as a tourist or as enthusiast of architecture, are now deemed strictly un-aesthetic. We could accommodate the fan or the tourist by saying that their pleasure in architecture derives from seeing its forms, spaces, textures and so on, as if it were a complex large-scale kind of sculpture; but we would have to tell them that they are not experiencing architecture in its aesthetic distinctiveness. We could soothe the fan's pique at being excluded from architecture proper by suggesting that they can participate imaginatively in the experience of users, incidentally suggesting that this would be the appropriate way in which to "experience" historic buildings.

If we were considering the great workroom at the Johnson Wax headquarters, designed by Frank Lloyd Wright, we would assert that an aesthetic experience of the building could only truly be had by a person working there. The tourist or the architecture fan visiting the building could aim to imagine what it would be like to work there, and might thereby get some access to the aesthetic experience of architecture. But it would always be limited by the distance between experience and imagined experience.

The architecture fan might reply by objecting that the argument is overblown. All the Johnson Wax Company needs to do is set aside one desk and chair at which visitors can sit if they wish. They will then have precisely the architectural experience that the office workers have. They will see the mushroom columns, the even glow of the light, the soft red of the brickwork, the lift gliding up and down in its glinting metal cage. The visitor will not be processing invoices, it is true, but how can that be constitutive of architectural experience?

The architecture fan and the user may indeed experience just the same things, seeing, hearing and touching the building in very similar ways. However, the argument could still be made that the user's experience is quite different in texture from that of the architecture fan. We could point to two features, the first of which depends on the idea of "divided attention." The office worker differs from the tourist by paying attention to the invoices, the phone calls from anxious creditors and the manager's enquiries, while at the same time having a greater or lesser awareness of the building and its pace, colours, forms, textures. There is a stream of consciousness[1] in which the building varies in significance moment by moment, rising to conscious attention and then falling away. The second feature is that the office worker does this every day so that an essential aspect of the aesthetics of use is its sheer repetition. Obviously, the architecture fan cannot experience this, though he or she can try to imagine it. In essence these are aspects of a phenomenology which is open to the users of buildings, but not to tourists and visitors.

This could be the starting point of an account of what is specific to the aesthetics of architecture, by virtue of its usefulness. However, if by specific we meant unique, implying that divided attention and repetition are unique to architectural experience, then we would be heading for problems. A remark of Walter Benjamin's alerts us to the difficulty. In "The Work of Art in the Age of Mechanical Reproduction" he discusses changes in modes of perception in the modern world and in particular the ways in which modern culture has created new modes of aesthetic attention.[2] He suggests that one of the characteristics of watching movies (by the masses at any rate) is that it involves a "distracted" attention, in contrast to the conventional idea of concentrated aesthetic attention. The significance of "distracted" attention goes beyond the experience of movies and of art generally: it provides a cover under which the masses will take on new attitudes and learn new skills. Benjamin views the process with considerable anxiety and argues instead for cultural forms where politics is made explicit, rather than communicated during the audience's state of distraction.

Benjamin's model for "distracted" attention is none other than architectural experience. He takes a view broadly similar to the one that I am testing here: that we properly experience architecture by a process of repetition and habitual use. The experience of "the attentive concentration of the tourist before a famous building"[3] should not be taken as the paradigm of architectural experience. We should take distracted experience as the paradigm. Benjamin's view fits the daily experience of the accounts clerk: distraction, not attentive contemplation, characterises his or her daily practical relation to architecture. But the interesting point is not that architecture is unique in all this, that we could take this particular phenomenology as constitutive of it as an art, but precisely that it is a generalised feature of cultural experience. . . .

1. The phrase comes from William James, "The Stream of Consciousness," in *Psychology: Briefer Course* (1892), reprinted in *Modern Philosophy of Mind*, ed. William Lyons (London: Dent, 1995), 3–23.

2. Walter Benjamin, *Illuminations*, ed. Hannah Arendt (London: Fontana/Collins, 1977), 219–253.

3. Ibid., 242.

Now consider a further issue, pointing in the opposite direction. Distracted experience is important but it is unlikely that, in itself, it exhausts the aesthetic experience of architecture by users of buildings. Indeed, it can create its opposite and suddenly deliver moments of concentrated aesthetic attention of a quite conventional kind. So the accounts clerk, taking a break from the invoices, sees undistractedly for a moment that the light in the great workroom is just such a light, that the space is just such a space, that the columns are just such columns and the sense of finality—the Kantian finality that we shall shortly discuss—reigns. . . .

A user experiences buildings differently from the way that a fan or a tourist does but not because they experience different things, or because the nature of their experience as a user is unique to being a user. Rather, their use of the building inserts them into a different pattern of responses, but responses which nevertheless exist generally in the culture. So the user of building has a different range of kinds of experience, a different collection of types of attention, from the visiting spectator. Users are caught in a distinctive web of experiences, but that web is spun out of patterns of attention that are common in other areas of culture and daily life. Experience does not provide us with a distinctive route by which usefulness in itself can become constitutive of architecture as an art.

USE AND AESTHETICS

Let us now turn to an alternative view of the way that usefulness and aesthetics can be related. This centres on the idea that the designs of buildings can incorporate symbolic or representational reference to usefulness. The emphasis moves away from a general type of experience towards the detailed visual configuration of buildings. Kant's account of the place of architecture among the fine arts provides a good example of how such an argument can be structured.

We can take up Kant's argument at the point where he develops an overall classification of the fine arts.[4] Architecture belongs to the sub-group of "formative arts." This comprises the visual arts—painting, sculpture and architecture—as we would nowadays understand them, although it differs in including landscape gardening, on the grounds that it is a kind of painting. The distinctiveness of the formative arts is that they communicate "aesthetic ideas" via "figures in space." In the case of architecture and sculpture "figures in space" can be thought of as the detailed forms that the objects take; and in the case of paintings the relevant "figures" are depictions of objects. By contrast, rhetoric and poetry—"the arts of speech"—give access to aesthetic ideas via the interplay of the understanding and the imagination; in the third group of arts, which comprises music together with Kant's proposal for an art of colour, aesthetic ideas have their basis in the play of the sensations of hearing and sight in themselves. "Figures in space" are aspects of physical buildings, but we should note that for the spectator their significance lies not in their physicality but in the fact that they represent forms which are of aesthetic interest.

4. The discussion of architecture can be found in Section 51 of Kant's *The Critique of Judgement* (1790), trans. James Creed Meredith (Oxford: Clarendon Press, 1928). On the general question of how Kant's division of the fine arts relates to his larger aesthetic theory see Michael Podro, *The Manifold in Perception: Theories of Art from Kant to Hildebrand* (Oxford: Clarendon Press, 1972), 7–35.

Kant's argument depends on the interplay between these "aesthetic ideas" and the "concept" of a building. He means by the latter term the kind of use of purpose to which the building is put. His examples are "temples, splendid buildings for public concourse, or even dwelling-houses, triumphal arches, columns, mausoleums etc., erected as monuments," and in fact he extends the range to include household furniture. Architectural concepts refer to artefacts made for human use and can be distinguished from sculptural concepts which refer to works of nature—"men, gods, animals etc."[5] The architectural concepts that Kant cites are of the kind that would enable us to identify certain kinds of objects in the world: that is a dwelling-house, that a triumphal arch, that a mausoleum. The criterion for differentiating one object from another is its use—as dwelling-house, triumphal arch and so on. We have to assume that Kant has in mind that each of these types of buildings will be recognisable from their general appearance. . . .

Kant suggests three ways in which we can imagine aesthetic ideas being profitably coupled with concepts. They could help us towards a more complete and grounded understanding of notions which are outside our actual experience. So, for example, they could help us to grasp notions of "invisible beings, the kingdom of the blessed, hell, eternity, creation, etc.," the objects of which are strictly inaccessible to us. The second use for aesthetic ideas is in bringing completeness to our grasp of aspects of experience such as "death, envy, and all vices, as also love, fame and the like." In such cases they can bring multiplicities of thoughts to bear which extend our grasp of these concepts beyond immediate experience. Thirdly, and this is the area which is most relevant to architecture, aesthetic ideas can extend the scope of concepts that we are able to understand, "giving aesthetically an unbounded expansion to the concept itself." Aesthetic ideas bring concepts to life, make abstract ideas concrete, make our partial experiences fuller, and surround the core of a concept with a wealth of associations and meanings. That is the general case across all the arts.

The uses of buildings are also concepts, and so in this sense temples and dwelling-houses stand in elevated company, alongside death, envy, love and fame, hell, eternity and so on. They share a density of meaning and significance that cannot be exhausted in words and to which only the multiplicities of imaginative form can do justice. In architecture "aesthetic ideas" flesh out and give a wealth of meaning to the concept of a building's use. . . .

PURPOSE, FUNCTION, AND USE

My [next] point is to allocate more precise meanings to the terms "use," "purpose" and "function," which have been employed more or less interchangeably so far. At first this will seem narrowly prescriptive, because in ordinary life no great harm comes from overlapping the meanings of such terms. But I believe that in order to understand the complexity of usefulness we need to pull apart its various conceptual aspects, and one way of doing so is to give more particular meanings to terms which are in current

5. Kant, *Critique of Judgement*, 186.

use. In everyday life we may say that the use of a particular room is as a lecture theatre, its purpose is to be a lecture theatre, its function is to be a lecture theatre, and mean the same thing in each case. The ambiguity is helpful and quite benign in practice, but underneath it distinct ideas can be identified. My suggestion for distinguishing them is as follows. Purpose denotes a human intention in relation to an object, and function denotes the object's execution of that purpose. For example, my purpose in putting up an umbrella is to prevent myself getting wet; the function of the umbrella is to keep the rain off. To take the more common example of a knife, my stipulation is that we use the term "purpose" for the intention or goal that I entertain of cutting something, and that we reserve the term "function" for the knife, the function of which is to cut.[6] The core of the third term in the group, "use" considered as a noun, refers to what goes on in buildings. As we shall see, "use" is a highly elusive concept and for the moment I simply wish to stress that a notion of human activity is central to it.

Some initial observations on these definitions can he made. First, it is a practical matter to devise an artefact in such a way that it successfully discharges its function. This is where our interest in design enters. A knife can be designed in such a way that it succeeds in its function of cutting. Obviously, there is no necessary connection between a human purpose and the function of an artefact: the latter may fail to carry out the function expected of it, or carry it out partially or badly. The knife might not cut, my umbrella might turn inside out in the slightest wind and rats might get in and eat the grain in the silo that had the function of storing grain. For the present purposes I shall say that the success of a silo in storing grain is a tribute to its design and its failure is an indication of a design fault. If a building does successfully discharge its function it has thereby fulfilled the purpose that was intended. Purpose and function are related, but only in such successful cases.

Then, three aspects of "use" should be noted. First, human subjects must be involved: the concept of use has no relevance to the stones on the beach. Many interesting things could be said about where they came from and what they are made of, but to try to account for or describe them in terms of use would be futile. However, people do not need to be present in a building in order to be involved in its use. Many kinds of storage and industrial buildings such as silos and electricity sub-stations may have no continuous human presence yet still serve a human use.

Secondly, use must involve the physical world. True, I can imagine uses, but I will always be imagining a physical world. Use has no conceptual structure beyond its instances in the world and it and it has no inner logic. Thirdly, in making distinctions between purpose, function and use, I am not suggesting that use merely comprises a series of bodily movements, changes of location and so on, and that these are set in motion by "functions." It is tempting to identify me merely as a series of traces: recall the tracks of cars in the snow that delighted photographers in the 1930s, the tracks of housewives as they moved around their kitchens, or the imagined traces of activity that came out of Bernard

6. This usage is as proposed in Andrew Woodfield, *Teleology* (Cambridge: Cambridge University Press, 1976), 27.

Tschumi's murder mystery in *The Manhattan Transcripts.*[7] In contrast, my notion of use incorporates the intention that goes along with the actions, as well as the actions themselves.

TESTING THE DEFINITIONS

We can test how these terms "purpose," "function" and "use," each wearing their crisp new meanings, actually relate together in a building or a building type. Take the example of a school and imagine someone saying, "The function of this building is to be a school." This is a straightforward descriptive remark, bearing none of the weight of the purpose–function relationship that I have just outlined. It is simply the case that this building is a certain kind of thing, namely a school. . . .

If we wish to explore the purpose–function relationship we shall need to specify a purpose that can be identified separately from the function. So imagine someone expressing the purpose that "children should be educated" and then saying that "the function of a school is to educate children." A school may fail to perform that function, so the statement is not necessarily circular. Suppress for the moment any scepticism about the truth or profundity of this view of a school's purpose: we are only interested in the general character of the argument.

It is unlikely that what is meant is that the school, considered as a building and hence as a physical object, does the educating. A knife can perform the function of cutting, perhaps a silo can perform the function of storing, but a building cannot perform the function of "educating." Evidently, the person has some other notion in mind of what a school is. They might say that it is teachers that educate children and therefore it is teachers that make a school. We might then pursue the point that books, paper, pens, blackboards, computers, science equipment, musical instruments and so on are also needed if children are to be educated. We would then conceive of a school as a distinctive kind of system that has many aspects. There is a purpose, namely that children should be educated, and the function of a school is to fill that purpose. However, what is meant here by "school" is not a building but that complex system—let us call it a "pedagogic system"—of human activity and practical resources.

All this might be interesting but unfortunately it has the effect of pushing the building out of the discussion altogether. We have stated a purpose and discovered that the building is irrelevant to its fulfillment. One way of getting the building—the building as physical object—back into the argument is to suggest that phrases like "the function of this building is to be a school" are contracted version of a phrase such as "the function of this building is to accommodate a pedagogic system." The purpose that corresponds to this function would then be along the lines that "the pedagogic system be accommodated in an artificial climate, protected from the weather and intruders." The underlying point is that whereas a building, considered as a physical object of a certain design, cannot educate a child, it can modify the local climate and it can be a barrier against intruders.

7. Bernard Tschumi, *The Manhattan Transcripts, 2nd Ed.* (London: Academy Editions, 1994).

The building, as a physical object, might then be considered as neutral in relation to the process that takes place within it. This is plausible in some circumstances. Consider the pumping station designed by John Outram in East London. The purpose of the building was to accommodate and protect from the weather and intruders a series of pumps that regulate the surface water level in a low-lying part of the city. Describing its function as "a pumping station" does appear to be a contraction of a phrase such as "the accommodation, etc. of an array of pumps and other equipment."

This kind of approach is not adequate for school buildings, however. They are not neutral in relation to the process that takes place in them. School buildings do not just throw a roof over a group of teachers and their equipment. They are divided into rooms of different shapes and sizes, with defined relationships one to another. Separate rooms may be provided for different age groups and for teaching certain subjects, and there may be a room which is large enough for the whole school to assemble and identify itself as a single community. These arrangements are essential aspects of certain kinds of educational practice. The design of schools is part of the "pedagogic system" and changes in educational practice typically involve some change in the design of school buildings. A notable example occurred in the 1950s, when open-plan design combined with "home bases" replaced an array of separate classrooms. This new architectural arrangement was constitutive of a new approach to education.[8]

It remains true that important aspects of school buildings are climate modifying and security devices. However, these roofs and walls are not just thrown over a group of teachers, children and furniture, but over an internal organisation that brings together a way of teaching, a mode of administration and an architectural setting. I propose that we call such an internal organisation a "programmatic whole." The key point is that the programmatic whole of a school is conceptually separate from its component parts. Only the system as a whole has the function in question. The component parts make possible on a practical, empirical level the execution of that function, but they are not part of the function itself. This logical point enables us to make sense of the fact that buildings cannot, as mute physical objects, do something like educating but that they can, as a practical, empirical matter, contribute to that process. In other words, buildings do not have functions by virtue of their being physical objects but by virtue of what goes on in them; and the building is instrumental in what goes on in them. Strictly speaking, then, school buildings do not have functions. Their significance lies in the way that they contribute to a systematic arrangement which also comprises human activities, practical resources, furniture and so on, and which, when properly mobilised, does fulfil a function.

By contrast, those parts of buildings that are engaged in controlling internal climate and providing security can be in a direct purpose–function relationship, along the lines of our umbrella example. Buildings, considered as physical objects, are the kinds of objects that can logically be involved in changing climate, creating barriers; but objects of that kind cannot educate children. It is the latter case that interests us for the moment, not

8. For a discussion of the relationship between changes in educational ideas and school design see Andrew Saint, *Towards a Social Architecture: The Role of School-building in Post-war England* (New Haven: Yale University Press, 1987).

because climate control and security are unimportant but because the aim is to understand the relationship between use and design.[9]

PURPOSE AND FUNCTION RECONSIDERED

At this point I suggest that we return to the original hypothetical purpose and function— "that children should be educated" and "that the function of a school is to educate children"—and regard them with some of the scepticism that we have so far held in check. Statements of this kind are of limited value and interest. Perhaps the purpose in question is that children should be socialised, or trained, or civilised, or prepared for work; there are numerous possibilities. The interesting point is that it is hardly necessary for there to be any clear answer to questions of purpose and function in order for schools to continue to exist and develop as pedagogic systems.

This is not just a matter of the difficulty of pinning down the functions of social institutions like schools. It is an example of the common situation that building types generally do not have plausible statements of purpose or function associated with them. The term "function" simply operates as the identifier of a building type and the functions that such building types discharge can only be expressed by reference to the kind of buildings that they are. Thus the function of an office block is to enable the carrying-out of those activities appropriate to an office block; the function of a hospital is to provide the kinds of services that a hospital provides; the function of a prison is to effect the kind of incarceration that takes place in a prison; the function of a court-house is to administer those elements of the system of justice that take place in a court-house; the function of a house is to provide that kind of setting and amenities that a house provides; the function of a church is to carry out those liturgical and other activities which are appropriate to a church, and so on.[10]

In none of these cases can I see any virtue in trying to formulate a statement of purpose to which the building would be a functional response. Nor, of course, are such institutions founded, adapted and developed by reference to such functional statements, but rather by a constant process of revision of the relationship between the configurations of the building and its inner system. These processes of revision might take place in unexpected ways. For example, Adrian Forty has suggested that the development of the hospital as a building type in the nineteenth century owed as much to the growing professionalisation of medicine, and the needs of medical training, as to the improvement of the hospital as a "machine for healing." So blanket purpose–function statements might be quite unhelpful in understanding the historical development of building types.[11] These building types comprise "programmatic wholes" in the same sense that I have outlined in relation to a school, but it is neither necessary nor possible to make overall purpose–function statements for them.

The counter-argument to this train of thought is to say that of course buildings are responses to purposes, since their design and construction is not a matter of accident: it is simply that we are looking in the wrong place for the purposes. An office building can

9. When William J. Mitchell, *The Logic of Architecture* (Cambridge: MIT Press, 1990), 183–239, embarks on the formal functional analysis of building designs it is significant that his examples deal with climate control, specifically the pitches of roofs that are desirable in order to shed water. However the attempt at systematic functional analysis is effectively abandoned when issues about the internal use of buildings are discussed.

10. For an example of the kind of discussion that is entailed see Nigel Yates, *Buildings, Faith and Worship: The Liturgical Arrangement of Anglican Churches 1600–1900* (Oxford: Clarendon Press, 1991).

11. Adrian Forty, "The Modern Hospital in England and France: The Social and Medical Uses of Architecture," in *Buildings and Society: Essays on the Social Development of the Built Environment*, ed. Anthony D. King (London: Routledge and Kegan Paul, 1980), 61–93. For discussion of these topics in other contexts see Thomas A. Markus, *Buildings and Power: Freedom and Control in the Origin of Modern Building Types* (London: Routledge, 1993).

be a response to the purpose of making money, a school can be a response to the purpose of providing school places in a new neighbourhood, and so on. Buildings can fulfil innumerable institutional and commercial purposes. The purposes are fulfilled by the operation of these "programmatic wholes," the inner functions of which are so obscure. However, if we ransack that outer purpose for an explanation of the more systemic nature of a building type, we will not find it. Outer purposes simply assume that such and such a systemic character will be present, and will be profitable or institutionally appropriate. Compare the situation with that of farmers. They can put crops and animals to profitable use: those are their purposes and the land and the animals obligingly become functions. But in another sense the farmers' purposes shed no light on the function of a cow or a blade of wheat: indeed, it is doubtful whether cows or wheat, considered as species, have functions at all.

I want to explore the consequences of this scepticism about the explanatory value of ideas of function in trying to understand the relationship between the designs of buildings and their usefulness. But let us hold onto the idea that building types are systemic, programmatic wholes, and bearing that in mind, consider in more detail what is entailed in "use."

ENSEMBLES OF USE

The central difficulty is that in many cases it is hard to define what "use" really means. We could start with a straightforward example. Imagine a sports hall designed to accommodate a basketball pitch. Basketball is an activity, and there is little difficulty in calling it a use so far as the building is concerned. The building has a similar relationship to the use as did John Outram's pumping station. In the one case the building provides accommodation for a set of pumps and in the other for a basketball pitch. Both uses could take place without a building were it not for requirement of climate control and security. The building in both cases is neutral in the way that the use is carried out. In both cases there would be a convincing formula that linked purpose and function: the purpose is that the internal use be protected from weather and intruders and the function of the buildings is to accomplish this.

Now consider the case of the auditorium in a theatre, or rather the combination of the visible stage and the auditorium where the audience sits. This combination I will clumsily call a "use" for the moment. Elsewhere in the theatre are other "uses": the bars, dressing rooms, backstage area, foyer and so on. Theatres as "programmatic wholes" contain such a constellation of "uses." The architecture of the auditorium differs from that of the sports hall in the obvious but important respect that it is not neutral in the way that the "use" is carried out. The design of an auditorium and the visible stage is constitutive of the kind of theatrical use which takes place.

In fact, the "use" now becomes quite elusive. Is it what happens on the stage, or is it the audience's experience? If it is some composite of the two then we would certainly have to accept that the design of the auditorium, from practical matters of sight lines and acoustics, to more intangible ones such as atmosphere, immediacy of impact, was constitutive of the kind of use that takes place. Furthermore, of the two cases—the sports hall and the theatre—it is the latter that we consider to be the paradigm for architecture, the one that brings the greater difficulty to the architect but also the larger gratification to both architect and user.

A number of issues begin to emerge. Although activity, as I have said, is central to use, it would be inadequate to say that the use simply is a certain activity. The use of a theatre auditorium is not just the activity of the actors, no matter how energetically they stride around the stage. Secondly, given that the perimeter of "use" now seems to be obscure, it would be misleading to suggest that the architecture is simply a response to it. Since we cannot clearly say where the conceptual separation is between the originating activity and the architectural response, it seems truer to suggest that use is what happens in dialogue with the building.

In response to the difficulty of pinning down elusive "uses," I shall coin another piece of terminology—"ensembles of use." The term will not solve the difficulty but it will draw attention to the point that, in cases which we find architecturally interesting and challenging, uses are partly constituted by the configuration and detail of the building and by the furniture and equipment within it. These do not simply serve or respond to a pre-existing "use."

I suggest that an ensemble has three components—a certain pattern of human activity, a certain configuration and detail of architectural form, and a certain arrangement of furniture or equipment. The first two aspects are indispensable: there cannot be an ensemble of use without a specific part of a building a particular human activity being involved. Some distinctive furniture or equipment is nearly always involved. An empty office block does not yet contain its intended ensemble of use because the associated human activities are absent. The Hill House, designed by Charles Rennie Mackintosh for the Blackie family, no longer contains the ensembles of use that it once did, because the family left long ago, although in many of its rooms the beautiful combinations of space, architectural detail and furniture designed by Mackintosh have been kept.

An ensemble of use need not necessarily have its own walls. A workstation in an open office, consisting of a definable space, a desk, a chair, a computer and so on, combines with a set of human activities to make an ensemble of use. A priest celebrating mass at an altar, surrounded by the altar plate and furniture that the liturgy demands, all set in a larger space, participates in an ensemble of use. The nature of the surrounding space and of adjacent ensembles also constitute the nature of the use-ensemble, just as do the enclosing walls of a theatre auditorium.

The point to stress is that an ensemble of use is not an arrangement of furniture and architecture in which a piece of use takes place, for the reason that the pattern of activity cannot be specified separately from the architecture or furniture. The activity of working at a desk both requires and is constituted by a desk and chair; the activity of celebrating communion both requires the altar, the chalice and other requisites, the surrounding space and is constituted by them. Someone might say that a certain design of desk and chair determines the way in which "the office activity" operates. This could be just a label for what goes on, but it would have no explanatory power. "The office activity" is precisely what the desk and chair ensemble constitutes, in all its historical development. It is not the determinant of a use-ensemble, but an abstract description of it.

There are similarities with my suggestions about the nature of the "programmatic whole." We can state a function for an ensemble of use, but it will really be no more than an identifier—the dining room, the parlour of the working-class English house, an operating theatre. These are not function responses to external purposes. A dining room, for example, is constituted by its nature as a certain kind of room, not as a response to the purpose of dining.[12] The general point is illustrated by a story about Gerrit Rietveld. When he started work on the design for Mrs. Schröder's house, he is said to have asked her "How do you want to live?," to which she replied "upstairs."[13] Rietveld was asking an unanswerable question: tell me your style of life in abstract so that I can make a building for it. Mrs. Schröder refused to talk in abstractions: she wanted to live the way that happens when the living rooms are upstairs.

The issue is also revealed more clearly when it is turned on its head, as in Christopher Alexander's "pattern language." The "patterns" are recommendations for small-scale elements of design, mostly for houses. They bring together activity, furniture and architectural arrangement into a defined setting. Alexander's recommendations create an extraordinarily vivid image of a way of life, his answer to the question "how do you want to live?" The way of life is partly constituted by the bringing together of a number of architectural traditions: the Arts and Crafts interior, the houses of better-off European peasants, the flexibility of American timber-frame construction, the nookiness of the Edwardian suburban house and so on. However, Alexander is keen to present the patterns as solutions to problems. For example, "in rooms lit from one side, the glare which surrounds people's faces prevents people from understanding one another," a problem which is solved by the proposal that there should be light on two sides of every room.[14] This seems like inventing a problem in order to justify a "pattern" that has quite enough charm and justification in its own right.

Buildings considered as programmatic wholes gather up and embrace a number of ensembles of use. Conversely, ensembles of use are at the end point of analysis in trying to understand the relationship between design and usefulness. There is nothing to be gained by analysing separately the activity, the furniture, the architectural configuration. Usefulness inheres in them as ensembles, not in their constituent elements, and no amount of shaking them will make the use fall out on its own.

CONCLUSION

There is a difficulty with the argument. My case is that there is a certain combination of architecture, furniture and so on, and that it not only responds to a certain use but also

12. For the development of the design and use of the interiors of British houses see Alison Ravetz with Richard Turkington, *The Place of Home: English Domestic Environments 1914–2000* (London: Spon, 1995).

13. Lenneke Büller and Frank den Oudsten, "Interview with Truus Schröder," in *The Rietveld Schröder House*, Paul Overy (London: Butterworth Architecture, 1988), 56.

14. Christopher Alexander, Sara Ishikawa, and Murray Silverstein, *A Pattern Language: Towns, Buildings, Construction* (New York: Oxford University Press, 1977), 159. Part of the interest of this book lies in its differences and continuities with Alexander's earlier work, *Notes on the Synthesis of Form* (Cambridge: Harvard University Press, 1964), in which the idea of the separation of problems and forms was given more abstract treatment. The consensus, with which I agree, is that *Notes on the Synthesis of Form* failed to demonstrate that architectural forms, in any recognisable sense, can be derived from systematically stating problems. However, I believe that the problem carries through into the later work. See also Stephen Grabow, *Christopher Alexander: The Search for a New Paradigm in Architecture* (Stocksfield: Oriel Press, 1983).

helps to make it possible, since the use could not be conceived in isolation from some kind of physical setting. How then do we deal with the case of someone who uses a building in a way that doesn't conform to that ensemble? It would be foolish to suggest that certain arrangements of architecture, furniture, equipment necessarily force people to act in a certain way. A school hall or a dining room can be used for purposes other than those central ones intended by the architect and building owner. There may be innumerable possible ensembles of use which can take advantage of a given physical arrangement of architecture and furniture.

It is true that there is a question of precedence. The unorthodox use of a building is only possible because an owner and architect have developed an intention to provide for a certain ensemble of use in the first place. They decide not only the physical arrangement but they are also the source of authority for the use-ensemble which will take place. We could then call that the central case, recognising that it is not the only possibility and that other kinds of uses, unexpected and unwanted, can cluster around it. For example, a school hall might temporarily be used as a polling station. This poses no problems for the building owner, and we could say that it is merely parasitic on the original intended ensemble. On the other hand, a student who walks straight into the head-teacher's room has devised their own ensemble of use, transgressing the central case in which children are only invited into staff areas. But these uses are, on the face of it, straightforward instances of putting a building to a certain kind of use. They therefore involve exactly the conceptual separation of use and physical setting that I have argued against at such length.

The underlying issue has been pursued by Bernard Tschumi in several essays.[15] He suggests that uses other than the central case should be taken as the paradigm for the relation between usefulness and design in architecture. On his account, my treatment of the central case is both cosy and oppressive. It is not simply that he re-casts the hierarchy which links the uses that owners intend and those that are unapproved. He suggests that there are three sorts of uses: possible ones intended by the owner, possible ones not intended by the owner, and impossible ones. The latter two kinds exist as a challenge and a reproach to the owner's intended uses. Tschumi's point is part of a broader project of re-defining the relationships between authority, order and pleasure in architecture— another aspect of which I noted in the discussion of order and architectural meaning.

But what can be meant by impossible uses? The idea rests on Tschumi's overall view of how uses arise in buildings. He suggests that sequences of events and sequences of space can be considered as operating on separate but overlaid levels. Each level has its own pattern and rhythm. Uses are defined by selecting any point where a moment of activity overlays a particular spatial arrangement. Uses are fundamentally the result of a combinatory process: some will be impossible but interesting, some will be possible and out of these some will gain approval as central cases sanctioned by the building owner. Uses in total are outside the scope of human intention and purpose: they are the sum of all the possible points of overlay between the two levels.

15. Bernard Tschumi, *Architecture and Disjunction* (Cambridge: MIT Press, 1994) and *Manhattan Transcripts*. For discussion of projects in which these ideas are elaborated see Tschumi, *Event-Cities: (Praxis)* (Cambridge: MIT Press, 1994).

The argument assumes a world of structured events, which continue along their way unchanged by the spaces which they intersect; and a world of ordered spaces which are unchanged by the events that take place in them. This is the basis of Tschumi's exploration of the nature of use in architecture. However, as I have tried to show, it is difficult to envisage this kind of abstract separation. It is hard to conceive of what a space-less world of events would mean, and what an event-less world of space would mean. Space and events are founded in each other, and uses arise when space, activity and equipment mutually constitute one another, not when they merely intersect. . . .

An architect designing with usefulness in mind designs an object which has feature relevant to certain kinds of usefulness. He or she may imagine such an object in detail, but it is not at all clear to us how an appropriate object is arrived at. In most cases, architects adjust and modify their first attempt at a design in order to improve its usefulness. At one extreme, an architect might produce a sculptural object and gradually adjust it to make it more useful. For example, Ledoux designed a collective house for the coopers who would work in the ideal city of Chaux, made it resemble the hoops and circles of a barrel, and then squeezed into it an arrangement of useful spaces—living quarters, bedrooms and workshops. At the other extreme, the initial design may need only the merest tinkering to make it appropriately useful.

By contrast, the arguments of this [article] rule out the possibility of a design process in which the architect states certain kinds of purposes and then works according to some logical procedure in order to make an appropriate design. The point is striking because we are accustomed to the idea that it is just that logical progression from use to design that is characteristic of modern architecture. It seems to expose a contradiction very near to the surface of modernism: that it claims to operate with a logical progression from purpose to design but, if the arguments of this chapter are on the right lines, such a claim would be a delusion, would involve a quite mistaken understanding of the real relations of design and usefulness.

I do not believe that modernism, as a general rule, did operate on the assumption that there can be a simple logical progression from stating purposes or uses to deriving a design. In the next chapter I shall begin by sketching out the ideas on which modern architects did base their view of the relationship between usefulness and designs. These developed over a long period, forming a "sustaining outlook" which enabled architects to avoid that stark, logical difficulty. In its place they were able to make an underlying perplexity manageable and fruitful. But the perplexity still remained at the core of modernism's "sustaining outlook." Put in the broadest terms, I shall ask how it is possible to arrive at projects which have that interdependence of usefulness and design, if not by a logical process. The examples that I shall cite add nothing to the standard accounts of the development of modernism. However, my interest is in employing them to further our understanding of the possible way in which usefulness can become thematic to architecture, thematic to the art of architecture perhaps, and so I intend to move through a historical sketch towards an ahistorical outline of that conceptual issue.

Writing and Discussion Questions

ANALYSIS

1. What was Wright arguing for and against? What excerpt/quotation best represents this?
2. What was Eisenman arguing for and against? What excerpt/quotation best represents this?
3. What was Hill arguing for and against? What excerpt/quotation best represents this?

SYNTHESIS

1. Regarding concepts of form and function, discuss one major difference regarding Wright's, Eisenman's, and Hill's texts.
2. Regarding concepts of form and function, discuss one primary commonality regarding Wright's, Eisenman's, and Hill's texts.

SELF-REFLECTION

1. For each of the texts, discuss a major issue with which you most agree and most disagree; reflect upon why you hold these views.
2. Select a recent design project, or a current project on which you are working. Discuss the characteristics of the project in regards to the relationship between form and function, in light of the discussion and texts introduced in this chapter. What attitudes regarding the relationship between form and function does your work illustrate?

PROSPECTION

1. Select one of the texts listed in the bibliography for this chapter; locate and read it. To what degree is that text and the attitudes it represents still relevant to architecture today and in the near future?

2. What is the relationship between form and function over the lifespan of an architectural work? I.e., how does renovation, adaptive reuse, etc. affect how buildings are both designed initially and transformed later? In other words, if a fourth text were added to this chapter, what would the argument be?

Other Readings on Function and Form

Adorno, Theodor. "Functionalism Today," trans. Jane Newman and John Smith, *Oppositions*, 17 (1979): 31–41.

Alexander, Christopher. *Notes on the Synthesis of Form* (Cambridge: Harvard University Press, 1967).

Benton, Tim, Charlotte Benton, and Dennis Sharp. *Form and Function: A Source Book for the History of Architecture and Design 1890–1939* (London: Crosby Lockwood Staples, 1975).

Benton, Tim. "The Myth of Function," in *Modernism in Design*, ed. Paul Greenhalgh (London: Reaktion Books, 1990), 41–52.

Eco, U. "Function and Sign: The Semiotics of Architecture," *Publications of the Graduate School of Fine Arts*, 2 (1973): 131–153.

Hill, Jonathan. *Actions of Architecture: Architects and Creative Users* (New York: Routledge, 2003).

Hill, Jonathan. *Occupying Architecture: Between the Architect and the User* (New York: Routledge, 1998).

Langer, Susanne K. *Feeling and Form* (New York: Prentice Hall, 1953).

Ligo, Larry. *The Concept of Function in Twentieth-Century Architectural Criticism* (Ann Arbor: UMI Research Press, 1984).

Rasmussen, Steen Eiler. *Experiencing Architecture* (Cambridge: MIT Press, 1964).

Chapter 7

BODY and BUILDING

FIGURE 7.1
Photograph of a caryatid and
column in Parc Guell, Barcelona,
Spain (1900–1914). Architect:
Antoni Gaudí.

FIGURE 7.2
Photograph of the entry to the
Museum of Roman Art, Merida,
Spain (1980–1985). Architect:
Raphael Moneo.

INTRODUCTORY DISCUSSION

1. Of the two images above, which is a clearer manifestation of architecture designed
    for the human body? Why?

2. What aspects of the human body are most important to consider when designing
    architecture?

3. What is the responsibility of architects today in regards to the differences between
    human bodies regarding size, age, gender, race, and ability?

Introduction

During the late 1400s, famed Renaissance artist and inventor Leonardo da Vinci created one of his most famed drawings: *Vitruvian Man*. The drawing is so well regarded that Italians selected the *Vitruvian Man* to adorn their national one Euro coin starting in 2002. Developed from the writings of Vitruvius's *Ten Books on Architecture*, the drawing depicted a male figure inscribed within a circle and square. The drawing became highly influential, as, in the late 1400s, new editions of Vitruvius' Classical text were being published, but the majority possessed no illustrations. For the discipline of architecture, da Vinci's drawing provided an important image for one of Vitruvius' most foundational concepts. According to Peter Eisenman, *Vitruvian Man* was seen as the "ideal origin" of architecture.[1] Derived from the human body, or, more accurately, a "well-shaped man," Vitruvius' text and da Vinci's drawing provided principles regarding hierarchy, proportion, order, geometry, organization, symmetry, and part-to-whole relationships, which, at the time, were the most important aspects of architectural design.

As stated by Vitruvius in *The Ten Books on Architecture*, which serves as the *original text* in this chapter:

> Since nature has designed the human body so that its members are duly proportioned to the frame as a whole, it appears that the ancients had good reason for their rule, that in perfect buildings the different members must be in exact . . . relations to the whole general scheme. Hence, while transmitting to us the proper arrangements for buildings of all kinds, they were particularly careful to do so in the case of temples of the gods. . . . Further, it was from the members of the body that they derived the fundamental ideas of the measures which are obviously necessary in all works.

Vitruvius focused not so much on the absolute measurements of parts of the body but the proportional relationships among the parts, for example the human face as one tenth of the height. Vitruvius was not advocating the use of parts of the body—the face, the

1. Peter Eisenman, "The End of the Classical: The End of the Beginning, The End of the End," *Perspecta*, 21 (1984): 159.

foot, the hand—as units of measurement. Instead, he was promoting a concept, that the design of buildings, like that of the human body, strive for a "correspondence among the measures of the members of an entire work, and of the whole to a certain part."

While Vitruvius saw the human body as a proportional analogue to building, Le Corbusier saw the human body as a direct unit of measurement. In *Le Modulor*, the *reflective text* for this chapter, Le Corbusier outlined a system of proportion and measurement to be used in fabrication and construction. Le Corbusier sought to develop a system that would supersede both the English system of feet and inches and the European metric system, and would govern all forms of mass production. For Vitruvius, the human body provided an organizational concept, whereas, for Le Corbusier, the human body provided a system of measurement.

Lance Hosey, however, criticized both precepts. In "Hidden Lines: Gender, Race, and the Body," the *philosophical text* of this chapter, Hosey noted that Vitruvius' and Le Corbusier's theories of the human body were particularly narrow. According to Hosey, this was also the case in architectural books like *Graphic Standards*, where the human figure is highly idealized.[2] Representations depicted full-grown white males of a particular height and weight, and did not address the diversity of human bodies in regards to age, race, gender, and body size. As stated by Hosey, "architecture traditionally has been a restricted profession, its standards of practice have been written by and for a narrow demographic . . . white and male. . . . *Graphic Standards* may be read as a guide for white men to create buildings for themselves in their own image" at the exclusion of the others.

Architecture is built for human inhabitation. In other words, architecture is built to be occupied by the human body (human bodies). As such, it makes sense that architects— Classical, Renaissance, Modern, or contemporary—would use the human body as an inspiration or principle of design. However, given the ever-growing diversity of religious, cultural, political, racial, age-related, gender-related, and physical aspects of human bodies, designers and students of architecture must ask a question previously posed by Diana Agrest: "What body?"[3]

2. *Architectural Graphic Standards* was first published in 1932. Authored by the American Institute of Architects, the 11th edition was published by Wiley & Sons in 2007. According to the publisher, *Graphic Standards* has exceeded one million copies sold. Due to popularity, the 1932 edition was reissued in 1998.

3. Diana Agrest, "Architecture From Without: Body, Logic, and Sex," *Assemblage*, 7 (1988): 30.

Original Text

MARCUS VITRUVIUS, EXCERPTS FROM *THE TEN BOOKS ON ARCHITECTURE*.

First Published ca. 25 B.C.E.

ON SYMMETRY: IN TEMPLES AND IN THE HUMAN BODY

The design of a temple depends on symmetry, the principles of which must be most carefully observed by the architect. They are due to proportion, in Greek ἀναλογία. Proportion is a correspondence among the measures of the members of an entire work, and of the whole to a certain part selected as standard. From this result the principles of symmetry. Without symmetry and proportion there can be no principles in the design of any temple; that is, if there is no precise relation between its members, as in the case of those of a well-shaped man.

For the human body is so designed by nature that the face, from the chin to the top of the forehead and the lowest roots of the hair, is a tenth part of the whole height; the open hand from the wrist to the tip of the middle finger is just the same; the head from the chin to the crown is an eighth, and with the neck and shoulder from the top of the breast to the lowest roots of the hair is a sixth; from the middle of the breast to the summit of the crown is a fourth. If we take the height of the face itself, the distance from the bottom of the chin to the underside of the nostrils is one third of it; the nose from the underside of the nostrils to a line between the eyebrows is the same; from there to the lowest roots of the hair is also a third, comprising the forehead. The length of the foot is one sixth of the height of the body; of the forearm, one fourth; and the breadth of the breast is also one fourth. The other members, too, have their own symmetrical proportions, and it was by employing them that the famous painters and sculptors of antiquity attained to great and endless renown.

Similarly, in the members of a temple there ought to be the greatest harmony in the symmetrical relations of the different parts to the general magnitude of the whole. Then again, in the human body the central point is naturally the navel. For if a man be placed flat on his back, with his hands and feet extended, and a pair of compasses centred at his navel, the fingers and toes of his two hands and feet will touch the circumference of a circle described therefrom. And just as the human body yields a circular outline, so too a square figure may be found from it. For if we measure the distance from the soles of the feet to the top of the head, and then apply that measure to the outstretched arms, the breadth will be found to be the same as the height, as in the case of plane surfaces which are perfectly square.

Therefore, since nature has designed the human body so that its members are duly proportioned to the frame as a whole, it appears that the ancients had good reason for their rule, that in perfect buildings the different members must be in exact symmetrical relations to the whole general scheme. Hence, while transmitting to us the proper arrangements for buildings of all kinds, they were particularly careful to do so in the case of temples of the gods, buildings in which merits and faults usually last forever.

Further, it was from the members of the body that they derived the fundamental ideas of the measures which are obviously necessary in all works, as the finger, palm, foot, and cubit. These they apportioned so as to form the "perfect number," called in Greek τέλειον, and as the perfect number the ancients fixed upon ten. For it is from the number of the fingers of the hand that the palm is found, and the foot from the palm. Again, while ten is naturally perfect, as being made up by the fingers of the two palms, Plato also held that this number was perfect because ten is composed of the individual units, called by the Greeks μονάδες. But as soon as eleven or twelve is reached, the numbers, being excessive, cannot be perfect until they come to ten for the second time; for the component parts of that number are the individual units.

The mathematicians, however, maintaining a different view, have said that the perfect number is six, because this number is composed of integral parts which are suited numerically to their method of reckoning: thus, one is one sixth; two is one third; three is one half; four is two thirds, or δίμοιρος as they call it; five is five sixths, called πεντάμοιρος and six is the perfect number. As the number goes on growing larger, the addition of a unit above six is the ἐφεκτος eight, formed by the addition of a third part of six, is the integer and a third, called ἐπίτριτος; the addition of one half makes nine, the integer and a half, termed ἡμιόλιος; the addition of two thirds, making the number ten, is the integer and two thirds, which they call ἐπιδίμοιρος; in the number eleven, where five are added, we have the five sixths, called ἐπίπεμπτος; finally, twelve, being composed of the two simple integers, is called διπλάσιος.

And further, as the foot is one sixth of a man's height, the height of the body as expressed in number of feet being limited to six, they held that this was the perfect number, and observed that the cubit consisted of six palms or of twenty-four fingers. This principle seems to have been followed by the states of Greece. As the cubit consisted of six palms, they made the drachma, which they used as their unit, consist in the same way of six bronze coins like our *asses*, which they call obols; and, to correspond to the fingers, divided the drachma into twenty-four quarter-obols, which some call dichalca others trichalca.

But our countrymen at first fixed upon the ancient number and made ten bronze pieces go to the denarius, and this is the origin of the name which is applied to the denarius to this day. And the fourth part of it, consisting of two asses and half of a third, they called "sesterce." But later, observing that six and ten were both of them perfect numbers, they combined the two, and thus made the most perfect number, sixteen. They found their authority for this in the foot. For if we take two palms from the cubit, there remains the foot of four palms; but the palm contains four fingers. Hence the foot contains sixteen fingers, and the denarius the same number of bronze *asses*.

Therefore, if it is agreed that number was found out from the human fingers, and that there is a symmetrical correspondence between the members separately and the entire form of the body, in accordance with a certain part selected as standard, we can have nothing but respect for those who, in constructing temples of the immortal gods, have so arranged the members of the works that both the separate parts and the whole design may harmonize in their proportions and symmetry. . . .

In araeostyle temples, the columns should be constructed so that their thickness is one eighth part of their height. In the diastyle, the height of a column should be measured off into eight and a half parts, and the thickness of the column fixed at one of these parts. In the systyle, let the height be divided into nine and a half parts, and one of these given to the thickness of the column. In the pycnostyle, the height should, be divided into ten parts, and one of these used for the thickness of the column. In the eustyle temple, let the height of a column be divided, as in the systyle, into nine and a half parts, and let one part be taken for the thickness at the bottom of the shaft. With these dimensions we shall be taking into account the proportions of the intercolumniations.

For the thickness of the shafts must be enlarged in proportion to the increase of the distance between the columns. In the araeostyle, for instance, if only a ninth or tenth part is given to the thickness, the column will look thin and mean, because the width of the intercolumniations is such that the air seems to eat away and diminish the thickness of such shafts. On the other hand, in pycnostyles, if an eighth part is given to the thickness, it will make the shaft look swollen and ungraceful, because the intercolumniations are so close to each other and so narrow. We must therefore follow the rules of symmetry required by each kind of building. Then, too, the columns at the corners should be made thicker than the others by a fiftieth of their own diameter, because they are sharply outlined by the unobstructed air round them, and seem to the beholder more slender than they are. Hence, we must counteract the ocular deception by an adjustment of proportions.

Moreover, the diminution in the top of a column at the necking seems to be regulated on the following principles: if a column is fifteen feet or under, let the thickness at the bottom be divided into six parts, and let five of those parts form the thickness at the top. If it is from fifteen feet to twenty feet, let the bottom of the shaft be divided into six and a half parts, and let five and a half of those parts be the upper thickness of the column. In a column of from twenty feet to thirty feet, let the bottom of the shaft be divided into seven parts, and let the diminished top measure six of these. A column of from thirty to forty feet should be divided at the bottom into seven and a half parts, and, on the principle of diminution, have six and a half of these at the top. Columns of from forty feet to fifty should be divided into eight parts, and diminish to seven of these at the top of the shaft under the capital. In the case of higher columns, let the diminution be determined proportionally, on the same principles.

These proportionate enlargements are made in the thickness of columns on account of the different heights to which the eye has to climb. For the eye is always in search of beauty, and if we do not gratify its desire for pleasure by a proportionate enlargement in these measures, and thus make compensation for ocular deception, a clumsy and awkward appearance will be presented to the beholder. With regard to the enlargement made at the middle of columns, which among the Greeks is called ἔντασις at the end of the book a figure and calculation will be subjoined, showing how an agreeable and appropriate effect may be produced by it.

Reflective Text

LE CORBUSIER, EXCERPTS FROM *LE MODULOR*.

First Published in 1948

Building should be the concern of heavy industry, and the component parts of
houses should be mass-produced.
A mass-production mentality must be created:
a frame of mind for building mass-produced houses,
a frame of mind for living in mass-produced houses,
a frame of mind for imagining mass-produced houses.'

"Maisons en serie" L'*Esprit Nouveau*, 1921

And, in order to do that, it is necessary to *standardize.* . . .

To set down in concrete form . . . ideas on the subject of a harmonious measure
to the human scale, universally applicable to architecture and mechanics. . . .

My dream is to set up, on the building sites which will spring up all over our country
one day, a "grid of proportions", drawn on the wall or made of strip iron, which will serve
as a rule for the whole project, a norm offering an endless series of different combinations
and proportions; the mason, the carpenter, the joiner will consult it whenever they have
to choose the measures for their work; and all the things they make, different and varied
as they are, will be united in harmony. That is my dream. . . .

I am going to talk to you about a Proportioning Grid, . . . which is expressed in
numbers, figures and diagrams. . . .

I felt that the Proportioning Grid, if it was destined one day to serve as a basis for
prefabrication, should be set above both the system of the foot-and-inch and the metric
system. . . .

The necessities of language demanded that the [Proportioning Grid] should be
given a name. Of several possible words, the "MODULOR" was chosen. . . .

The "Modulor" is a measuring tool based on the human body and on mathematics.
A man-with-arm-upraised provides, at the determining points of his occupation of space—

FIGURE 7.3

Drawing of the proportioning
system of Le Modulor
(1943–1946). Architect:
Le Corbusier.

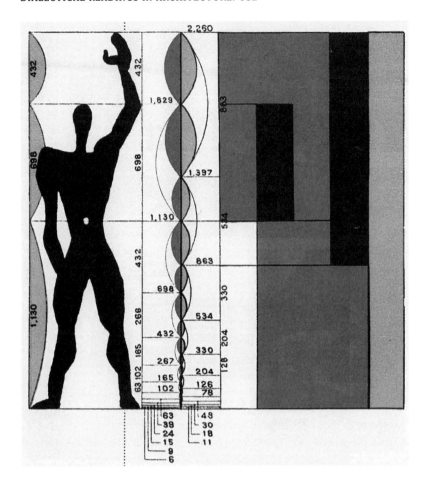

foot, solar plexus, head, tips of fingers of the upraised arm—three intervals which give rise
to a series of golden sections, called the Fibonacci series. On the other hand, mathematics
offers the simplest and also the most powerful variation of a value: the single unit, the
double unit and the three golden sections.

The combinations obtained by the use of the "Modulor'" have proved themselves
to be infinite. . . . The splendid result was the natural gift of numbers—the implacable
and magnificent play of mathematics.

Next, we were asked to round off our figures so as to bring them closer to certain
others in current use. The criticism addressed . . . was, in substance, this: the figures appearing on the first strip . . . and in the first numerical table were based on the metric system,
e.g. 1,080 mm. for the solar plexus. Ill luck so had it that almost all these metric values
were practically untranslatable into feet and inches. Yet the "Modulor" would, one day,
claim to be the means of unification for manufactured articles in all countries. It was
therefore necessary to find *whole values* in feet and inches.

I had never anticipated having to round off certain figures of our two series. . . . One day when we were working together, absorbed in the search for a solution, one of us—Py—said: "The values of the 'Modulor' in its present form are determined by the body of a man 1·75 m. in height. But isn't that rather a *French* height? Have you never noticed that in English detective novels, the good-looking men, such as the policemen, are always six feet tall?"

We tried to apply this standard: six feet = 6 × 30.48 = 182.88 cm. To our delight, the graduations of a new "Modulor," based on a man six feet tall, translated themselves before our eyes into round figures in feet and inches!

It has been proved, particularly during the Renaissance, that the human body follows the golden rule. When the Anglo-Saxons adopted their linear measures, a correlation was established between the value for a foot and that for an inch; this correlation applies, by implication, to the corresponding values in the body. . . .

Overcoming this obstacle brought us unhoped-for encouragement: we felt that the Modulor had automatically resolved the most disturbing difference separating the users of the metre from those of the foot-and-inch. This difference is so serious in its practical effects that it creates a wide gulf between the technicians and manufacturers who use the foot-and-inch system and those who work on the basis of the metre. The conversion of calculations from one system into the other is a paralysing and wasteful operation, so delicate that it makes strangers of the adherents of the two camps even more than the barrier of language.

The 'Modulor' converts metres into feet and inches automatically. In fact, it makes allies—not of the metre, which is nothing but a length of metal at the bottom of a well at the Pavilion du Breteuil near Paris—but of the decimal and the foot-and-inch, and liberates the foot-and-inch system, *by a decimal process*, from the necessity for complicated and stultifying juggling with numbers—addition, subtraction, multiplication and division. . . .

On May 1st, 1946, I took the plane for New York, having been appointed by the French Government to represent the cause of modern architecture at the United Nations on the occasion of the building of the U.N. Headquarters in the United States.

I had the pleasure of discussing the "Modulor" at some length with Professor Albert Einstein at Princeton. I was then passing through a period of great uncertainty and stress; I expressed myself badly, I explained the "Modulor" badly, I got bogged down in the morass of "cause and effect" . . . At one point, Einstein took a pencil and began to calculate. Stupidly, I interrupted him, the conversation turned to other things, the calculation remained unfinished. The friend who had brought me was in the depths of despair. In a letter written to me the same evening, Einstein had the kindness to say this of the "Modulor": "It is a scale of proportions which makes the bad difficult and the good easy." There are some who think this judgment is unscientific. For my part, I think it is extraordinarily clear-sighted. It is a gesture of friendship made by a great scientist towards us who are not scientists but soldiers on the field of battle. The scientist tells us: "This weapon shoots straight: in the matter of dimensioning, i.e. of proportions, it makes your task more certain." . . .

The "Modulor" is a measure based on mathematics and the human scale: it is constituted of a double series of numbers, the red series and the blue. But, if that is all it is, wouldn't a numerical table do the trick just as well?—No. That is where I have to explain again and again the set of ideas which I place at the very root of the invention. The metre is a mere number without concrete being: centimetre, decimetre, metre are only the designations of the decimal system. Later on I will say a few words about the millimetre. The numbers of the "Modulor" are *measures.* That means that they are facts in themselves, they have a concrete body; they are the effect of a choice made from an infinity of values. These measures, what is more, are related to numbers, and possess the properties of numbers. But the manufactured objects whose dimensions these numbers are to determine are either *containers* of man or *extensions* of man. In order to choose the best measures, it is better to see them and appreciate them by the feel of the hands than merely to think them (this applies to measures very close to the human stature). In consequence, the strip of the "Modulor" must be found on the drawing table side by side with the compasses, a strip that can be unrolled with two hands, and that offers to its user a *direct view* of measures, thus enabling him to make a concrete choice. Architecture (and under this term, as I have already said, I understand practically all constructed objects) must be a thing of the body, a thing of substance as well as of the spirit and of the brain.

Having discovered the law of the "Modulor," we had to think of its possible uses and therefore also of its material form. . . . What material form would be given to the "Modulor" and to what industry would it be applied?

The form: (1) a strip, 2·26 m. (89 inches) long, made of metal or plastic; (2) a numerical table giving the appropriate series of values. The word 'appropriate' is meant to indicate that the measures will be kept within a practical range, the limits of which are decreed by actual perception, both visual and sensory. We thought that beyond 400 metres, the measures could no longer be grasped. . . . (3) a booklet containing the explanation of the "Modulor" and various combinations resulting from it.

A delicate and interesting piece of work, a pretty object to put side by side with the technician's precision tools. . . .

The "Modulor," if it has any right to existence, will only be worth something if it is applied on a mass scale in the dimensioning of manufactured articles. . . .

In the minutely detailed work involved in the projects of Marseilles, Saint-Dié, Bally, etc., the "Modulor" was used by constructors and designers, so that I had every opportunity to appreciate its worth. And my reaction was so positive that I feel I am entitled to put the whole mechanism of the "Modulor" before the reader, in order that each man may judge for himself.

One more word needs to be said on the subject of the second version of the "Modulor" established on the basis of a man six feet in height. The reasoning is simple: the objects manufactured on a world-wide scale with the aid of the "Modulor" are to travel all over the globe, becoming the property of users of all races and all heights. Therefore it is right, and indeed imperative, to adopt the height of the tallest man (six feet), so that the manufactured articles should be capable of being employed by him. This involves the largest architectural dimensions; but it is better that a measure should be too large than too small, so that the article made on the basis of that measure should be suitable for use by all.

4. "Foreword," *Architectural Graphic Standards, 4th Ed.* (New York: John Wiley and Sons, 1951), vii.
5. "A Tribute to Architectural Graphic Standards," *10t^h Ed.* (2000), xv.
6. "Preface," *8th Ed.*, 1988. See also "Timeline," *10th Ed.* (2000), xiv. *Graphic Standards* "has mirrored the extraordinary accomplishments of architecture in the 20th century."
7. For example, the second edition (1936) notes that the repeal of Prohibition required the inclusion of data pertaining to the design of bars.
8. In 1964, the American Institute of Architects took on the editorial duties of *Graphic Standards* and has collected royalties from all subsequent editions. However, it and all institutions involved in the publication disclaim responsibility: "The drawings, tables, data, and other information in this book have been obtained from many sources, including government organizations, trade associations, suppliers of building materials, and professional architects or architectural firms. The American Institute of Architects (AIA), the Architectural Graphic Standards Task Force of the AIA, and the publisher have made every reasonable effort to make this reference work accurate and authoritative, but do not warrant, and assume no liability for, the accuracy or completeness of the text *or its fitness for any particular purpose*" (emphasis mine). Verso, *8th Ed.* (1988).
9. "A View of Architectural Graphic Standards at the Beginning of the Twenty-First Century," *10th Ed.* (2000), xiii.

Philosophical Text

LANCE HOSEY, "HIDDEN LINES: GENDER, RACE, AND THE BODY."

First Published in 2001

INTRODUCTION

Next year marks the seventieth anniversary of *Architectural Graphic Standards*. Since 1932, it has become the most common single reference source for design professionals. In 1951, Ralph Walker proclaimed in the foreword to the fourth edition that "every architect—embryonic and established—should have a copy, and should have it close at hand."[4] Philip Johnson reiterates this thought in the most recent edition, published in 2000: "No architect can be without *Graphic Standards*, and with it every architect is empowered and equipped to practice architecture."[5] The book is ubiquitous in American architectural offices, and its widespread use arguably makes it one of the clearest reflections of conventional methodology.

Over the decades, *Graphic Standards* has become a self-professed "chronicle of 20th-century architectural practice."[6] Its ten editions trace the developments and preoccupations of the profession and, moreover, indicate the cultural changes responsible: the decline of classical and craft-oriented detailing, the simultaneous rise of mass-produced systems and prefabricated parts, the birth of historic preservation, the growth of energy conservation techniques, and so on.[7] The book, then, is not simply a technical document: the selection, content, and presentation of the material all suggest discernible values. But the publishers deflect responsibility for the material to the industry at large.[8] This is justifiable, for any work that shapes its subject according to popular habits implicates the culture that produces it. Such a book does not necessarily recommend how to do things; it simply records how they are done. As Robert Ivy writes in the preface to the 2000 edition, *Graphic Standards* serves as "social history."[9]

Graphic Standards reflects the implicit beliefs of architecture and the larger community. Nowhere in the book is this more evident than in the first section, originally titled "Dimensions of the Human Figure." For most of its history, the portrayal of the body in *Graphic Standards* has revealed at once the selection of certain demographic segments as representative of the entire population, as well as the restrictive conception of a preferred or model inhabitant of buildings. The different methods used to represent the body reveal the "human figure" to be gender- and race-specific: male and white. This article examines these different methods, first by reviewing pertinent historical representations of and cultural attitudes toward the body, and second by analyzing the unique representational techniques of *Graphic Standards*.

SETTING STANDARDS

Visual and verbal representations of the body are persistent mechanisms for sustaining the sociopolitical relationships between men and women, and such representations have been integral to architectural discourse. The use of the male body as a model for buildings occurs in various canons of architecture, and the influence of two of these, classicism and modernism, may be seen in *Graphic Standards*.

The table entitled "Dimensions of the Human Figure" first appeared in the third edition (1941), although the drawings themselves, attributed to Ernest Irving Freese, had been published elsewhere in 1934.[10] The table recurred in subsequent editions, virtually unchanged, for forty years. The illustrations dimension the body in a variety of positions, but only one body type is shown. Historically, when a single body is proposed to represent all people, the body is male, and comparison with certain traditions confirms that this is the case here. The figures are abstract silhouettes with few apparent anatomical features, and, as such, they signify the body through the simplest pictorial means, profiling human proportions and symmetry, not physiology. This emblematic quality resembles many Renaissance drawings that glorify the body as a mandala or icon. Some of these, particularly sketches by Leonardo and Dürer, have become so prevalent and universally appropriated that they are signatures of Western culture. These renderings illustrate the Neo-Platonic belief that the natural perfection of man could be seen through the body's relationship to primary geometry. The depiction in *Graphic Standards* of arms tracing arcs in the air is especially reminiscent of this pictorial tradition.

The similarities are not coincidental. In their original publication, the drawings were titled "The Geometry of the Human Figure," so clearly Freese was preoccupied with the body's aesthetic proportions and not just its statistical dimensions.[11] Furthermore, Dürer's book on human proportions was a precursor to the modern field of anthropometry and would have influenced any subsequent pictorial study of the body. But, in architectural history, the body itself is not the primary concern of this tradition. The Renaissance sketches elaborated on the Vitruvian proposition of the "wellshaped man" as a model of architectural harmony: "since nature has designed the human body so that its members are duly proportioned to the frame as a whole . . . in perfect buildings the different members must be in exact symmetrical relations to the whole general scheme."[12] The indivisibility of part and whole, observed in the body, is a fundamental tenet of classical aesthetics.

The table of human dimensions first appeared in *Graphic Standards* during a time when historians such as Rudolf Wittkower and Erwin Panofsky were writing extensively of

10. Freese originally published his drawings in an article titled, "The Geometry of the Human Figure," from *American Architect and Architecture* (July 1934): 57–60. This magazine was absorbed by *Architectural Record* in March 1938.

11. An architect of Freese's generation was likely to have received classical training, and his other published articles confirm his interest. He wrote several articles in the 1930s that betray a fascination with classical geometry. In one publication, for instance, he applies the ancient geometric theory of Apollonius to the dimensioning of modern stairs. See "Correct Proportioning of Stair Treads and Risers," *American Architect and Architecture* (July 1933): 47; also "A Word on the Involute Arch," *Pencil Points* (March 1935): 141. Furthermore, Freese's training is evident from the traditional moldings and profiles in the cabinetry and furniture of the *Graphic Standards* drawings. In the 1970 edition, these details have been edited out.

12. Vitruvius, *The Ten Books on Architecture*, Morris Hicky Morgan, trans. (New York: Dover, 1960), III, I: 3, 4, 72–73. The rule of compositional unity actually began with Aristotle's theory of drama: "the various incidents must be so constructed that, if any part is displaced or deleted, the whole plot is disturbed and dislocated." See *The Poetics*, VII–VIII. From *Aristotle On Poetry and Style*, trans. G. M. A. Grube, (Indianapolis: Bobbs-Merrill, 1958), 17.

13. The connection to Vitruvius in particular is clear when Ivy ascribes "firmness, commodity and delight" to the book's organization ("A View of Architectural Graphic Standards at the Beginning of the Twenty-First Century"). Eero Saarinen made a similar comparison, noting that *Graphic Standards* offers a vocabulary for the future, just as Vitruvius had spelled out the classical language for Renaissance architects. Foreword, *5th Ed.* (1956).

14. The table of human dimensions originally appeared in the back of *Graphic Standards*, under the heading "Miscellaneous Data." With the sixth edition (1970), the table became the first section of the book. The chapters that follow it are organized according to the Uniform System for Construction Specifications.

15. Diana Agrest, "Architecture from Without: Body, Logic, and Sex," *Assemblage*, 7 (1988): 29, 33.

16. Alexander Tzonis and Liane Lefaivre, "The Mechanical Body Versus the Divine Body: The Rise of Modern Design Theory," *Journal of Architectural Education*, 29/1 (1975): 4–5. Tzonis and Lefaivre recount that the revision of the body paradigm coincided with a transition from the guild system to the academy, which sought new objective rules to replace archaic standards. The standardization of practice that *Graphic Standards* is meant to aid began in this period's restructuring of architectural training with new methods of instruction. The purpose of *Graphic Standards*,

Vitruvius' impact on Renaissance thought, so the body metaphor was pervasive. *Graphic Standards* relates to this tradition in more ways than one. Robert Ivy recognizes harmonic unity in the book's conception and structure, although he mistakenly identifies the origins of the idea: "*Graphic Standards* presupposes the interrelationship of parts to whole projects, a nineteenth-century notion articulated by Wright when he said, 'The part is to the whole as the whole is to the part.'"[13] Hence, the organic structure of the book itself relates it to the body paradigm. The introduction displays the dimensions of an actual human body, and what follows is a dissection of the body of a building, its various systems laid out in seemingly anatomical order.[14]

The social prejudice of the Vitruvian model is blatant, the equation of "perfect buildings" with the "well shaped man" being inherently sexist. Men are offered as the image of perfection, which suggests the imperfection of women. Diana Agrest writes that this gendered construct "remains at the very base of Western architectural thought." "This system is defined not only by what it includes, but also by what it excludes, inclusion and exclusion being parts of the same construct. Yet that which is excluded, left out, is not really excluded but rather repressed. . . . The repressed, the interior representation in the system of architecture that determines an outside (of repression) is woman and woman's body." Traditionally in architecture, Agrest states, "the human figure is synonymous with the male figure."[15] "The Human Figure" of *Graphic Standards* echoes this statement in its allusion to the classical paradigm.

The presentation of the body in *Graphic Standards* relates to a larger cultural context that includes not only the classical precedent, but also modern architecture and, more generally, modernity's attempts to standardize the body. Alexander Tzonis and Liane Lefaivre recount that a revision to the classical conception of the body occurred during the French Enlightenment. The shifts in thought from nature to science and faith to reason were represented by a shift in metaphor from the "divine body," an abstract, sacred vessel, to the "mechanical body," a real organism operating in an environment. Scale, a preoccupation with number and proportion in order to maximize aesthetic pleasure, was replaced by size, a concern for exact dimensions in order to increase efficiency. One is a model of form, the other of function.[16]

Quatremère de Quincy refers to a "mechanical analogy" in his discussion of typology, explaining that the body should fit a building the way it fits a chair: "Who does not believe that the form of a man's back ought to be the type of the back of a chair?" Quatremère cites the Greek word *typos*, meaning "to impress" or "to mark," so there is the suggestion of the body inscribing itself on the building for an optimal fit.[17] The *Graphic Standards* diagrams illustrate this functionalist model, picturing the body molded to its environment through the immediate scale of furniture.[18] Nearly half of the chart depicts bodies in actual chairs, a literal realization of Quatremère's model. Like Vitruvius' metaphor of "a well shaped man," Quatremère's description substitutes the specific designation "a man" for the more general "man," so the sex of his model user cannot be mistaken. The rhetoric used to construct the standards of the body is characteristically sexist, and the canonical texts of modern architectural theory are rife with such language.[19]

Graphic Standards appeared at a time when systematic documentation of the body was critical in many disciplines, particularly industry.[20] The science of anthropometry had developed in the late-nineteenth century in order to address the growing desire for a precise understanding of human mechanics. From the start, however, this effort favored men, partly because for many years most studies were conducted by the military.[21] The lack of statistics for women also related to the perceived impropriety of viewing and measuring the female body, as physical examinations were often thought to violate women's natural modesty and "delicacy."[22] Moreover, many scientists did not view women as an important subject for study. Ales Hrdlicka, an eminent Smithsonian anthropologist, pronounced in 1918, "The paramount objective of physical anthropology is the gradual completion . . . of the study of the normal white man under ordinary circumstances."[23] The modern practice of measuring bodies began in large part to reinforce existing social

with its emphasis on classification systems, assembly methods, and fabrication techniques, belongs to the heritage of Quatremère, Durand, and Diderot. The analytical layout of the body in figure/ground poses even resembles the plates from Durand's *Précis* (1809) illustrating generic plan types in their various permutations. The normative views of the body in *Graphic Standards* relate to early modern ideas about normative building types. Buildings are conceived as universal forms, much as the male body is conceived as universal. For discussions of eighteenth-century French theory and typology, see Anthony Vidler, *The Writing of the Walls: Architectural Theory in the Late Enlightenment* (Princeton: Princeton Architectural Press, 1987), and Rafael Moneo, "On Typology," *Oppositions,* 13 (Summer 1978): 22–45.

17. Anthony Vidler, *The Writing of the Walls,* pp. 153–155.

18. In the original publication of the drawings, Freese notes that the diagrams are "particularly to be consulted" for the use of furniture ("The Geometry of the Human Figure," 57). The chair, of course, was a particular fascination of modern architects, and some of the most important modernist chairs, including Mies' Barcelona chair (1929), Le Corbusier's Armchair (1929), and Breuer's Wassily Chair (1925), were designed around the time that the Freese drawings appeared.

19. David Cabianca points out similar language in Le Corbusier, who in the *Modulor* describes architecture as "a symphony of volumes and space meant for men." Cabianca explains, "Although the statement can be made that Le Corbusier was using a variation of a term which only recently has come under attack for its hidden gender bias, his choice of the plural 'men' precludes any such interpretation that includes women. 'Men' is specific in its plurality—although the French 'hommes' would be only slightly more ambiguous in this context and ultimately forms its own mode of silence." See "Notes on James Stirling's Hysterics: Ronchamp, Le Corbusier's Chapel and the Crisis of Modernism," *openspace: Journal of Architecture and Criticism,* on-line journal of the University of Cincinnati, 1997.

20. As industrialization rose through the turn of the century, the mechanical conception of the body evolved to an extreme. F.W. Taylor's theory of scientific management, which employed time and motion studies to increase efficiency, conceived of bodies literally as machines, dictating workers' every move with detailed precision. This theory became increasingly popular between the wars, and with the unparalleled production of World War II, the *Graphic Standards* charts would have appealed to the demand for thorough documentation of human mechanics. Feminist critiques of scientific management highlight not just its dehumanizing effects but its tendency to strengthen sexual boundaries in the workplace. Taylorism gave greater control to managers, mostly men, and tended to increase the division of labor based on generalizations about sex, further limiting women to certain roles. Furthermore, because anthropometric statistics were predominantly male, the "standard" of body mechanics was inevitably gender biased. This often created unequal working conditions that affected women's performance and therefore seemed to give further evidence to the argument that women did not belong in the workforce. See Anson Rabinbach, *The Human Motor: Energy, Fatigue, and the Origins of Modernity* (Berkeley: University of California Press, 1990), 238 ff.; and Alice Kessler-Harris, *Out to Work: A History of Wage-Earning Women in the United States* (New York: Oxford University Press, 1982), 145–147.

21. See, for instance, Niels Diffrient, Alvin R. Tilley, and Joan C. Bardagjy, *Humanscale 1/2/3* (Cambridge: MIT Press, 1974), 4: "Large samplings are taken by the armed forces to make the man-machine relationship successful in a fighting environment, but although these measurements are accurate and comprehensive they are limited to select groups. Civilian surveys have not been extensive in terms of samples and measurements. . . ."

22. See, for example, the *American Medical Association Code of Ethics* (Philadelphia: TK and PG Collins, Printers, 1848), 11–12.

23. Quoted in Jacqueline Urla and Alan C. Swedlund, "The Anthropometry of Barbie," in Jennifer Terry and Jacqueline Urla, eds., *Deviant Bodies: Critical Perspectives on Difference in Science and Popular Culture* (Bloomington: Indiana University Press, 1995), 286. Gustave Le Bon, a founder of social psychology, felt that women "represent the most inferior forms of human evolution and that they are closer to children and savages than to an adult, civilized man." Of course, minorities were seen in the same light. See Stephen Jay Gould's classic study of scientific racism, *The Mismeasure of Man* (New York: W. W. Norton and Company,1981), 104–105.

24. Marquis de Condorcet, quoted in Gould. Ibid., 21.

25. Henry Russell-Hitchcock and Philip Johnson, *The International Style* (New York: W. W. Norton and Company, 1966), 59–62.

26. Tzonis and Lefaivre identify the human body as the most common "epiphoric object" of design theory. An epiphore (literally, from the Greek, that which "bears upon") is an everyday object that presents in a "stenographic" way the conceptual framework in use. It condenses the complex set of logical rules in a simple form, and to use the form is to embrace the logic it represents. "By accepting an epiphoric object in an argumentation, one accepts a conceptual framework in its entirety, which means not only an idea of the work as it is, but also as it can be and should be. . . . References to the human body relate

strata by supporting stereotypes about sex, race, and class. Physiological difference reflected political difference, and supposedly empirical data made "nature herself an accomplice in the crime of political inequality."[24] When *Graphic Standards* was published, any compilation of the body's dimensions would have inherited incomplete and biased data.

The distinction between archaic and modern conceptions of the body provides a convenient contrast, but it is not an absolute split, for much of the canonical discourse of modernism reveals an emphasis on both sacred harmony and mechanical efficiency. In *The International Style*, which appeared the same year as the first edition of *Graphic Standards* (1932), Henry Russell-Hitchcock and Philip Johnson declare that the best modern design rejects extreme functionalism in favor of aesthetic harmony, stating that "a scheme of proportions integrates and informs a thoroughly designed modern building, [which] composes the diverse parts and harmonizes the various elements in to a single whole."[25] This passage simply inserts the word *modern* into a distinctly Vitruvian argument, and similar sentiments have been expressed by Sullivan, Wright, Le Corbusier, and Kahn. As Tzonis and Lefaivre write, "sacred harmony" and the body paradigm are inextricably bound in architectural theory. To invoke one is to invoke the other, as well as the underlying conceptual principles and implications.[26]

The most obvious modernist heir to the classical body paradigm is the *Modulor*, which Le Corbusier proposed to aid both aesthetics and efficiency, referring to the human figure as "divine proportion" and as a "machine."[27] *Graphic Standards*, which first offered its body charts during the period when Le Corbusier was developing and publishing the *Modulor*, similarly combines the two conceptions of the body. The table of figures is divided evenly between images of repose and images of activity, the body in isolation and the body applied to tasks—sitting, reaching, kneeling, and crawling—and Freese acknowledges this balance of aesthetics and mechanics as intended.[28] Pictorial references to classical geometry combine with modernist functionalism in the detailed dimensioning.

Sexism is apparent in both paradigms. Le Corbusier writes, "Architecture . . . must be a thing of the body."[29] But whose body? Vitruvius and Le Corbusier both extol the ancient practice of using the body for units of measurement—the foot, the cubit, the inch, and so on—but historically this habit has been sexually exclusive, whether the source of measurement is the body of the builder, typically male, or, in the imperial system, that of the king. Le Corbusier's choice of bodies is explicit. He refers to "man as measure" and proposes a singular "human figure," as does *Graphic Standards*.[30] With characteristically gender-specific language, he writes that man through his body imposes order "on his own scale, to his own proportion, comfortable for him, *to his measure*. It is on the human *scale*. It is in harmony with him: that is the main point."[31] In this passage, the similarities to the classical paradigm are clear: man as the standard of measure, man as the universal human, the harmony of bodies and buildings, and so forth.

Here, Le Corbusier sounds much like Geoffrey Scott, the early twentieth-century champion of classicism, who defines architecture as "the transcription of the body's states into forms of building," a process that humanizes the world through the "universal metaphor of the body, a language profoundly felt and universally understood."[32] But the supposed universality of the body (or of experience in general) is a prejudiced myth. In their study of cultural views of the body, Jennifer Terry and Jacqueline Urla write that humanism "relied upon ideas of a single, generic human body to generate hypocritical fictions of unity, identity, truth and authenticity. . . . [T]he ideal human body has been cast implicitly in the image of the robust, European, heterosexual gentleman . . ."[33] The humanist projection of a universal individual may be found in both ancient and modern symbols. Modern attempts to systematize the body are similar to previous idealizations to the extent that bodies are constructed as abstractions; idiosyncrasies are ignored in favor of generalizations. *Graphic Standards*, like these exemplars, proposes a solitary "human figure" as the definitive image of the body and, in doing so, succumbs to prevailing patriarchal habits.

simultaneously to all levels of the framework of archaic design. The building *is* a human body: to accept such a concept is to commit oneself to the overall framework of archaic methodology, i.e. sacred harmony as an ultimate warrant" "The Mechanical Body Versus the Divine Body," 4–5.

27. Le Corbusier, *The Modulor*, 5; *Modulor 2*, 296. Both Peter de Francia and Anna Bostock, trans. (Basel, Switzerland: Birkhäuser, 2000). Le Corbusier acknowledges a connection to Renaissance exemplars, listing the work of Dürer, Leonardo, and Francesco di Giorgio, among others, as precursors.

28. Freese notes that he has divided the diagrams into two categories: those illustrating the geometry of the body, which he calls "'working drawings' of the human figure," and those explaining common "applications." ("The Geometry of the Human Figure," 57.) The combination of aesthetics and mechanics parallels the state of American architecture in the early 1930s, for the few major examples of American modernism at the time still showed a distinct affinity for classical principles. Although in 1951 the second edition of *The International Style* would declare that "traditional architecture, which bulked so large in 1932, is all but dead by now" (p. 255), the original edition features only seven projects in the United States, some of which were designed by Europeans and all of which were built circa 1930. Of these, most were obscure houses, and only two—Raymond Hood's McGraw-Hill Building and George Howe's PSFS—were of a large urban scale. Both Hood and Howe were Beaux Arts trained architects, and these two buildings have been shown to blend modern and Beaux Arts sensibilities. See William H. Jordy, *American Buildings and Their Architects: The Impact of European Modernism in the Mid-Twentieth Century* (New York: Oxford University Press, 1972), pp. 87–117; and Robert A. M. Stern, "PSFS: Beaux-Arts Theory and Rational Expressionism," *JSAH* (May 1962): 84–95. The concurrence of the classical and the modern in American architecture of the 1930s is also illustrated by the issue of *American Architect and Architecture* in which Freese's drawings are printed (July 1934). It features articles on the Acropolis (referred to as "masterpieces of perfect building") and Cass Gilbert, as well as on Rockefeller Center and Albert Kahn.

29. *The Modulor*, 60–61.

30. Ibid., 56, 63. Interestingly, Le Corbusier cites Gustave Le Bon, whose misogynistic attitude toward female anatomy is mentioned above. The *Modulor* includes two drawings (Plates 77 and 90) reproduced from Le Bon's *The First Civilizations* that illustrate a sculptural relief from the Egyptian temple of Seti I, in which the pharaoh is depicted with attendant women, and the mathematical proportions of the sovereign figure are delineated. Le Corbusier intends the drawings to convey the universality of the proportioning system, but the images also overtly illustrate patriarchal privilege and the male-centered practice of body measurement. This attitude is prevalent in the *Modulor*. While working in the United States, Le Corbusier devised a second version of the system, in which the original height of 1.75 meters (approximately 5 feet, 8 inches) became six feet. The height seemed to have epic connotations: "Have you never noticed that in English detective novels, the good-looking men, such as the policemen, are always six feet tall?" Hence, the American standard is the heroic male, the "good-looking" man being the modern equivalent of Vitruvius' "well shaped" man. Elsewhere, Le Corbusier recoils at his colleagues' attempt to include women in the *Modulor*. Plate 15 of *Modulor 2* superimposes the male body and the female body, and Le Corbusier merely scoffs at his colleagues who drew the image: "Here is the drawing prepared by Serralta and Maisonnier: you take the square of the 'Modulor Man' of 1.83 m. (but, since Serralta has a soft spot for the ladies, his man is a woman 1.83 metres tall: brrrh!)." *Modulor 2*, 52–53.

31. Le Corbusier, *Towards a New Architecture*, trans. Frederick Etchells (New York: Holt, Rinehart and Winston, 1984), 7–68.

32. Geoffrey Scott, *The Architecture of Humanism* (New York: W. W. Norton and Company, 1974), 161.

33. See Jennifer Terry and Jacqueline Urla, introduction to *Deviant Bodies*, 4.

READING GRAPHICS

To implicate *Graphic Standards* in this way is to view its portrayal of the body as a product of its historical and cultural context, which includes the visual and verbal languages of classicism and modernism, as well as the political agendas and procedural methods of anthropometry. However, a restrictive portrayal of the body may be read more directly in the charts, separately from other precedents.

In the 1941 chart, the body is described graphically and numerically, and both methods are problematic. Just as there is only one type of graphic figure, there is only one set of dimensions. Body sizes and shapes vary according to physical and cultural differences, including sex, race, age, nationality, occupation, and socioeconomic conditions, and the use of a single dimensional set ignores human diversity. The caption note reads, "These dimensions are based on the average or normal adult," and the ambiguity of this phrase is telling. Anthropometrists have long agreed that an average is a misleading shorthand that causes dangerous errors.[34] The designation "average" is less common in science than it is in popular language as an expression of social and cultural judgment.

Similarly, the description "normal" is questionable. The word may be quantitative, referring to a statistical distribution, and the above conclusions hold. Alternatively, it may be qualitative, implying a politically charged standard of evaluation.[35] In general, "normal" necessarily posits the existence of its opposite, and dictionary definitions reinforce this conclusion: "free from physical or emotional disorder."[36] If one type is presented as "normal," any deviation must be taken as abnormal. Extensive critical theory over the last few decades has exposed the idea of normalcy as an elitist fiction. Norms and ideals are routinely confused, and identifying one type as "normal" constructs a distinction between Self and Other, between the privileged subject and the marginalized object.[37] By positioning one type of body to stand for all, *Graphic Standards* supports this dichotomy.

The gender bias of *Graphic Standards* is most overt in its visual representations of the body. In the original Freese drawings, the abstract silhouette might suggest that the "human figure" of the table's title is intended as a generic, genderless state of the body. However, the figure conforms to generalized descriptions of the male body. Frontally, the figure's torso and hips are of a continuous width, as are the chest and stomach in profile. Although the differences in appearance between male and female may not always be self-evident, textbooks list the following among the physiological distinctions: "The male shoulders are much broader, thicker and heavier than those of the female, a difference exaggerated by the females' wider hips. The typical male body shape tapers inwards as it descends, while the typical female shape broadens out."[38]

Speculation is not necessary, because further scrutiny reveals the figure's sex. A diagram primarily demonstrating arm radius and shoulder height also lists the length of the foot or shoe as 11¾". Adjacent to this is another leg, strangely disembodied, with a sole measuring 9¼". Although the image is not labeled, the high-heel shoe and the slight curve of the calf announce this to be a feminine foot. In the entire chart, this fragment by itself is to signify women. If the identity of the primary figure was previously uncertain,

34. "Average" presumably refers to an arithmetical mean, a mathematical figure resulting from the sum of all dimensions compiled divided by the number of people measured, but this approach has many problems. Even if an average were agreed to be useful, the pools of people measured have tended to be relatively small and concentrated within certain demographic groups, so the results are exclusive. Scientists believe that, if all the available data were assembled in one place, it would not constitute a representative sample of humanity. As seen, studies of the body historically have excluded women through the small samples taken, the large percentages of men sampled, the various rationales behind the methods of sampling, and politically motivated interpretations of statistics. Whatever the explanation, it is clear that the idea of a dimensional "average" is restrictive. John Croney writes, "Very few persons in a population are average in a large number of definitive measurements of bodily dimensions or capacities that could be examined in an anthropometric study. . . . If we pursue the average in terms of more and more definitive characteristics we find that as the total number of definitive characteristics increases as the percentage of the "average" person who can represent them all decreases." John Croney, *Anthropometrics for Designers* (New York: Van Nostrand Reinhold Company,

the introduction of the second draws unmistakable lines of gender. The male body is pictured in its entirety in two dozen poses, whereas the female body is only hinted at in one partial detail. The diagram of the dismembered foot literally objectifies women by reducing the female body to the leg alone, apparently intended as a highly iconographic aspect of the feminine profile.

Many feminist critics maintain that disfiguring images of the body is a form of control that sublimates more violent acts.[39] More generally, the fragmented body is often used in the construction of ideal images that reaffirm the cultural emphasis on women's appearance. Advertisements display isolated eyes, hands, and legs in the commercial production of standards of beauty that are often unnatural and unattainable. The fashion designer Donna Karan has remarked that women "are vulnerable when it comes to their legs. We feel they're never long enough, never thin enough, never toned enough."[40] Unlike the ideal male body, which typically is perceived as natural, the ideal female body is often attained only through deformation. The high-heel shoe has been compared to foot-binding and neck- or lip-stretching.[41] Ironically, while the purpose of the *Graphic Standards* chart is to illustrate body sizes, it shows the partial woman in footwear that alters bodily dimensions and proportions.

Architecturally, the dismemberment of the body violates established principles of composition. Using the leg to signify the female body separates the part from the whole and disrupts Vitruvian harmony. Man is complete; woman is not. If the human body provides the basic grammar of architecture, the severed leg breaks syntax. The implication is that men are the creators and subjects of architectural discourse, and women lie outside its established language. "Perfect buildings" follow the perfect male body, and the disintegration of the female body suggests its unsuitability as a model, its irrelevance to the canonical standards of building.

1971), 81. See also Frederick J. Gravetter and Larry B. Wallnau, *Statistics for the Behavioral Sciences* (New York: West Publishing Company, 1992), p. 87.

35. The Americans with Disabilities Act includes *normal* in its list of so-called "No-No Words," "socially incorrect phrases and words associated with . . . minorities." According to the A.D.A., *normal* refers to "people without disabilities but suggests that anybody who has a disability is sub-normal or abnormal." See Evan Terry Associates, *Americans with Disabilities Act Facilities Compliance Workbook* (New York: John Wiley and Sons Inc., 1992), 9–10.

36. *The American Heritage Dictionary of the English Language, 3rd Ed.* (New York: Houghton Mifflin Company, 1996).

37. For summaries of theories on the body as the site of difference, see the introductions to Jennifer Terry and Jacqueline Urla, *Deviant Bodies*; and Mike Featherstone, Mike Hepworth, Bryan S. Turner, eds., *The Body: Social Process and Cultural Theory* (London: Sage Publications, 1995); and Londa Schiebinger, ed., *Feminism and the Body* (New York: Oxford University Press, 2000). Also, for a discussion of the designation "normal," see Georges Canguilhem, *The Normal and the Pathological* (New York: Zone Books, 1989).

38. Desmond Morris, *Bodywatching: A Field Guide to the Human Species* (New York: Crown Publishers, Inc., 1985), 129.

39. Tammy Shefer, "Feminist Theories of the Role of the Body Within Women's Oppression," *Critical Arts 5/2* (1990); and Andrea Dworkin, *Pornography: Men Possessing Women* (New York: Dutton, 1989).

40. Donna Karan, foreword to Donna Karan, Diana Edkins, and Betsy Jablow, eds., *Leg* (Los Angeles: General Publishing Group, 1997), 3.

41. See Shefer, "Feminist Theories," and Rosemarie Garland Thomson, introduction to *Freakery: Cultural Spectacles of the Extraordinary Body* (New York: New York University Press, 1996), 1–19. A feminist poster from 1970, the year *Graphic Standards* eliminated its image of the high-heel-clad foot, features a virtually identical image, with the captions, "AMERICAN FOOT BINDING" and "STAMP OUT HIGH HEELS." See Christine Stansell, "Girlie, Interrupted," *New Republic* (Jan. 15, 2001): 23–30.

42. *The Ten Books on Architecture*, IV, I: 6, 7; 103–104.

43. This line of thinking began with Simone de Beauvoir. See Shefer, "Feminist Theories," and Naomi Wolf, *The Beauty Myth: How Images of Beauty Are Used Against Women* (New York: Anchor Books, 1992).

44. Dr. Robert Stoller, quoted in Marjorie Garber, *Vested Interests: Cross-Dressing and Cultural Anxiety* (New York: Routledge, 1997), 45.

45. Differences between the measurements given in 1944 and 1970 may be attributed both to the rising level of accuracy in survey methods and to physiological variations over the course of thirty years. For example, the difference between the respective male heights of the two editions is one inch, and the rate of growth of the average height is about three-tenths of an inch per decade. See *Humanscale 1/2/3*, 4.

46. Paul Emmons, "The Means and Meanings of Dashed Lines," unpublished manuscript presented at the ACSA Conference, "The Paradoxes of Progress" (March 2001), Baltimore, Maryland. George Hersey also discusses the *linee occulte* as "graphic metaphors for invisible affinities," especially hierarchical relationships. See *Pythagorean Palaces: Magic and Architecture in the Italian Renaissance* (Ithaca: Cornell University Press, 1976), 64–87.

47. Phallic forms, such as the obelisk or the totem, are commonly interpreted as masculine, and womb-like or vulval forms, such as the cave or the shell, are often seen as

The female body is not altogether excluded from the tenets of Vitruvius, who notes that the Corinthian Order originated through mimicry of the female body. However, whereas the Doric Order had been based on "manly beauty, naked and unadorned," the Corinthian emulated feminine "delicacy" and "adornment." The base was added to suggest shoes, the ornamental volutes to imply curly ringlets of hair, and the fluting to imitate the folds of a robe.[42] Again, the distinction between the ideal image of man as natural and that for women as artificial or clothed is a prevalent subject in feminist criticism. The objectification of women commonly occurs in the realm of fashion, as a woman's style of dress often is thought to affect her intrinsic value.[43] Clothing both conceals and augments the body, adding to the perception of women as objects of display, particularly sexual. The high-heel shoe image repeats the cultural tendency to see the female body not as a natural organism but as a cultural construct. While "men's clothes have no erotic value whatsoever," women's attire and particularly the high heel are incessantly fetishized, independently of the body itself.[44]

The suppression of the female from *Graphic Standards* occurs with more subtlety in the sixth edition (1970). Here, the "Dimensions of the Human Figure" table has been revised and rearranged with new numerical dimensions, but the drawings are almost exactly the same, with one significant exception. The female leg has disappeared, replaced by a new and novel form of communicating female statistics. According to the chart's key, the dimensions shown are twofold: above the stringer, a first dimension applies to men, and underneath this, contained in parentheses, a second number represents women. Information regarding women is provided as an aside, literally a parenthetical gesture, as if these statistics are subordinate to the numbers for men. The graphic device of the parenthesis suggests that women are a parallel yet secondary construction. Defined as a qualifying remark, an interruption of continuity, or a digression, the parenthesis in this case renders women not as subjects in their own right but as background information. The feminine is only tentatively present, both there and not there. In the struggle to include women in its representation of the body, *Graphic Standards* reveals a reluctance to disturb the iconic solitary male. Women appear only numerically.[45]

The sixth edition introduces a second table, titled "Human Dimensions at Varying Ages." The silhouette from the older tables is transferred here as a line drawing, but the shape is the same, so its sexual identity remains intact. The figure appears next to graphs measuring height and width from childhood to adulthood. The age chart consists of two separate groups of information, which according to the chart's legend pertain to male versus female. On the graphs, a solid, continuous line traces the growth of the male body. Alongside, a dashed or "hidden" line tracks the corresponding female measurements. This graphic convention aptly portrays the position of women being described here. Next to the figure of the male body, the material for women is only dimly, faintly suggested. A solid line is a demarcation, a declaratory gesture. A hidden line is transparent, used to indicate what is behind a surface, or something out of view. It is a graphic of invisibility. These different techniques recall Quatremère's understanding of the Greek *typos*, the body imprinting itself on buildings. The distinction here suggests that the male body properly shapes and sizes buildings, whereas the female body does not fully mark space.

Paul Emmons has shown that the dashed line is not an insignificant technical convention; its long history of use in architectural drawings reveals particular symbolic meanings. Sebastiano Serlio first defined dashed lines (*linee occulte*) during the Renaissance, using them to refer to the "hidden" or "secret" portions of geometric solids. As Emmons explains, the process of making a dashed line, in which the pen alternates between touching and not touching the surface of the paper, suggests the simultaneous occupation of two separate planes, both on and off the field of representation. Similarly, in grammatical punctuation, a dash is "an unvocalized physical presence indicating an omission or break in thought. Its denotative presence connotes an absence." The architectural dashed line indicates an in-between state, "something invisible but present."[46] This interpretation applies to the use of the line type in *Graphic Standards*. As Agrest writes of architecture in general, the female body is not fully excluded but repressed, defining the mode of representation through its absence. The repressed female body is an invisible presence in the sense Emmons uses to describe the dashed line.

The distinction between the solid line (*linea evidenta)* and the dashed line (*linea occulta*) here is not arbitrary, for the contrast between the exposed exterior and the concealed interior is consistent with common historical and popular representations of the masculine and the feminine.[47] Architectural discourse follows this tendency. Serlio identified the perpendicular line, or *cathetus*, as the essence of architecture, defined by the builder's tools of the set square, the plumb line, and the rod, all obvious phallic images.[48] Le Corbusier echoed this sentiment, calling the perpendicular line and the set square the bases for "strong objectivity of forms . . . *male* architecture."[49] The significance of this idea for the conception of architecture is apparent in the word *normal*, the roots of which mean "carpenter's square."[50]

Similarly, a dashed line graphically approximates a braid, a chain, or a ladder, all of which are archaic symbols of women.[51] According to Emmons, in Renaissance theory, the *linea occulta* was a trope for sewing, in which a needle and thread puncture a fabric to produce the image of a dashed line.[52] Freud saw plaiting or weaving as a metaphor for the female genitalia. Weaving is the one tool of civilization he credited to women, claiming the "unconscious motivation" for this invention to have been matted female pubic hair, which provides "concealment of genital deficiency" (lack of a penis) and therefore the bodily expression of shame, the defining feminine characteristic.[53] Through the trope of weaving, the connection between the dashed line, concealment, and women reappears. The various associations of the two line types support the sociopolitical construction of gender.

Emmons recounts that, in some Renaissance paintings, the dashed line is used as a key symbol, appearing oddly diagrammatic in otherwise realistically representational pictures. In Fra Fillippo Lippi's *Annunciation*, for instance, the *linea occulta* signifies a spiritual in-between, the line from the angel Gabriel to Mary.[54] This single example has myriad sexual

feminine. As crude sexual symbols, the continuous line suggests a rigid boundary, and the dashed line implies penetrability (as with the solid versus broken stripe in the middle of a road). The linguistic representation of anatomy coincides with the sexual associations of the *linee evidente* and the *linee occulte* here. For example, the word *testis* (the singular of *testes*) comes from the Latin for "witness," hence the word *testify*, "to give evidence," and the term *clitoris* contains roots suggesting concealment (*The American Heritage Dictionary*). Thomas Laqueur has shown that, until circa 1800, Western society perceived women as "interiorized" versions of men; the female sexual organs were seen as identical to the male but internal. See *Making Sex: Body and Gender from the Greeks to Freud* (Cambridge: Harvard University Press, 1990).

48. Sebastiano Serlio, *On Architecture*, Vaughan Hart and Peter Hicks, trans. (New Haven: Yale University Press, 1996), 7, 430.

49. *The Modulor*, 223.

50. From the Latin *norma* or Greek *gnomon*; carpenter's square, rule. *The American Heritage Dictionary*.

51. George Hersey notes the similarity between the *linee occulte* and ladders or *scalae* (*Pythagorean Palaces*, 87). Both the chain and the ladder have been symbols of the Virgin Mary, and the braid is associated with many pagan goddesses. See Hans Biedermann, *Dictionary of Symbolism* (Hertfordshire: Wordsworth Reference, 1992).

and political implications. As drawn, the symbol indicates in part a line of sight, and the use of the dashed line to represent vision is prevalent in many contexts. In innumerable drawings and diagrams, Renaissance perspectivists employed the *linee occulte* to trace paths from the eye through the viewing field. Robin Evans has described perspective science's "hegemony over vision," the construction of the world centered on a privileged viewer, as a form of sociopolitical control. Lacan, according to Evans, "extended the accusation beyond perspective, beyond geometry, to vision as a whole, which for most of us, most of the time, must remain irredeemably bound up with the process of domination."[55]

That the privileged viewer in this system of domination is male is evident from many rhetorical and diagrammatic instructions on perspective drawing. Dürer's famous woodcut, "Man Drawing a Reclining Woman," illustrates the use of a perspective machine. A nude woman lies in repose on one end of a tabletop, while the fully clothed male artist sits upright at the other, viewing her body through a gridded transparent screen, the picture plane. For the drawing process to work, the viewer's eye must remain fixed at a particular point, which here is marked by an obelisk-shaped stiletto presumably rising from the table but obscured by the man's arm so as to appear to rise from his lap. Hubert Damisch has remarked that this mechanism reduces the viewer to "a kind of cyclops."[56] In similar machines illustrated by Dürer, the viewed object is traced by a series of puncture points in a sheet of vellum, an act which itself is sexually suggestive. Emmons points out that some translations of Serlio define the geometric point as "a *pricke* made with a Pen or Compass," and the Spanish *puntos* ("point") is also *puntada* ("sewing" or "stitching"), so

Furthermore, there is a linguistic connection between *clitoris* and *ladder*, which share the Indo-European root *klei*. *The American Heritage Dictionary*.

52. "The Means and Meanings of Dashed Lines."

53. In his essay "Femininity," Freud argues that feminine identity evolves around the lack of a penis. Shame, the "feminine characteristic *par excellence*," arose from the need to conceal the genitalia, and pubic hair, the inspiration for plaiting or weaving, provides this function. Anatomy is used to justify the subordination of women. Cited in Ann Bergren, "Female Fetish Urban Form," in Diana Agrest, Patricia Conway, Leslie Kanes Weisman, eds., *The Sex of Architecture* (New York: Abrams, 1996), 94. Bergren also points out the connections between Freud's remarks on textiles, Göttfried Semper's theory of the screen wall enclosures in early dwellings, and feminine-defined images of domesticity. (There is a linguistic relationship between TEXtiles, archiTECT, TECtonic, TECHnology, and TEXt, all from the root *teks*, which can mean "weaving." *The American Heritage Dictionary*.) These ideas also relate to clothing, which in this context may be understood as another woven symbol of the feminine persona. (See above comments on fashion and attire.) Although the Freudian argument may be simplistic and sexist in its own right, it is consistent with other cultural constructions of the feminine discussed here. All of this suggests a feminine influence on the conception of architecture (and, more generally, the making of things) that has been suppressed or supplanted by the assertion of the male body and other masculine images.

54. "The Means and Meanings of Dashed Lines." Of course, in Christian theology, the Annunciation is the paramount moment of representation—through sight, language, creation, and so on.

55. Evans also cites Foucault's account of panopticism, in which "the gathering of lines of sight into a point, like the gathering of reins by a charioteer, is a symbol of control." Architecture expresses social tyranny by conforming to the sight lines of a single man, in this case the governor or watchman. See Robin Evans, *The Projective Cast: Architecture and Its Three Geometries* (Cambridge, MA: The MIT Press, 1995), 123–125.

56. Hubert Damisch, *The Origin of Perspective*, John Goodman, trans. (Cambridge, MA: The MIT Press, 1994), 35–36. The cyclops, a mythological one-eyed cannibalistic giant, seems an overt phallic symbol. On the psychosexual implications of vision, Ann Bergren has studied the mythological character of Baubo, who exposes herself, as a representation of the male fear of the female genitalia, the "irreparable wound." Exposed feminine sexuality, which explodes the normal concealment of women, shocks and threatens the male viewer's control. See "Female Fetish Urban Form," as well as "Baubo and Helen: Gender in the Irreparable Wound," in Andrea Kahn, ed., *Drawing Building Text* (Princeton: Princeton Architectural Press, 1991), 107–126.

the association with weaving recurs.[57] In Dürer's construction, the dotted tracings, or *punte occulte,* mark the male act of controlling the female body through vision. The hidden line reproduces the sexual gaze.

The specific example of visual rays relates to a more general use of the line type in philosophy, theology, astronomy, and other sciences to represent other kinds of emanations. Emmons cites Descartes' use to illustrate "materialistic spirits as bits of matter flowing through the body." The sexual connotations of this description are clearer when applied to Lippi's depiction of the Annunciation, which Emmons calls "a miraculous penetration of the virgin's body without any physical evidence."[58] Here the dotted line, a stream of "bits of matter," depicts insemination, in this case divine. To apply Quatremère's theory of the *typos,* the male body may be understood here to mark not only architectural space, but also the female body, in an act of territorial control. The sexual connotation of the dashed line is also conveyed by the word *dash,* which can imply a violent thrust or splash.[59] Returning to *Graphic Standards,* this simple technique portrays the female body not as independent but as dominated by the male body, through both the sexual gaze and the sexual act itself.

As shown, in successive editions of *Graphic Standards,* various techniques allude to but never fully unveil the female body. In the earlier charts, statistics for women seem irrelevant, with the exception of shoe size. By 1970, the sixth edition's methods imply that statistics for women are relevant enough to include, although secondary to the statistics for men. In the seventh edition (1981), the previous tables have been replaced by charts taken from the ergonomics research of Henry Dreyfuss Associates. The new charts, which remain in the most recent editions, divide the information for men, women, and children into separate, anatomically explicit figures, so the abstracted Everyman is gone. The dimensions given are extremely detailed, listed in both millimeters and inches, and subdivided according to three percentile ranges of statistics, which are noted to be accurate for "95 % U.S. adults." The information is documented in a lucid, thorough manner, and the limits of the statistical range are clear.

In the Dreyfuss charts, the attempt to be comprehensive is evident to a degree, but one aspect of the former charts' exclusivity remains. Although sex has been treated more equitably in the later editions, race has not been treated at all and still continues as a problem. In *Humanscale,* the original document from which the Dreyfuss charts are taken, the first illustration is titled, "Proportional Differences in Races." This diagram shows three superimposed figures representing the "Average U.S. Black male," the "Average U.S. White Male," and the "Average Japanese Male."[60] Distinctions between these three numbers are listed for lengths of the leg, the torso, and the arm, and are graphically and dimensionally obvious. The difference between the leg length of the Japanese male and the black male, for instance, is more than five inches. This chart, however, is not reproduced in *Graphic Standards.* A decision has been made that race is not an important factor in the documentation of body sizes. Every edition classifies all people according to only sex and age.

57. "The Means and Meanings of Dashed Lines."

58. Ibid. Emmons never offers any feminist interpretations of his topic, but they seem abundant. To suggest the *linea occulta* as both a symbol of insemination and an invisible axis (as Emmons does) is to provide a means of resolving long-standing arguments about the Vitruvian man's dual centers. The circle, a symbol of perfection, centers on the navel, whereas the square, a symbol for the earth, centers on the penis, and this misalignment has been much debated. (See, for instance, Giancarlo Maiorino, "The *Vitruvian Man*: At the Navel of Life's Compass," chap. 8 of his *Leonardo da Vinci: The Daedalian Mythmaker* (University Park, PA: Pennsylvania State University Press, 1992), 177–201). If the dashed line may be understood as a third-dimension axis emanating from the penis to penetrate the female body, it returns to the male body as an umbilicus to the navel. The hidden line is the invisible in-between connecting the sexual center to the birth center via the concealed female body. Again, although the female body is integral to this representation, it is removed from view. In a separate analogy, Serlio compares the difference between the *linee evidente* and the *linee occulte* to that between the living human body and the skeleton of a dead body: "the flesh covers the skeleton, but the skeleton is nevertheless there, hidden inside" (*On Architecture,* 48). An important difference between the skeletal and the

fleshed body is the absence of genitalia. The *linee occulte* compare to the sexless body, the body stripped of difference and power.

59. *Dash*: to strike of thrust violently; to splash, bespatter. *The American Heritage Dictionary*.

60. In this diagram, the averages are used to illustrate an argument rather than a range of applicability. See *Humanscale 1/2/3*, 5.

61. Sarah Turner, the current AIA Archivist and Records Manager, recounts that there were six female American architects in 1900. Interview with author, Dec. 12, 2000.

62. "As It Looks to the Editors," *American Architect and Architecture* (July 1934): 36.

63. "Employed persons by detailed occupation, sex, and race, 1972–1981," Bureau of Labor Statistics.

64. Sarah Turner, interview with author, Dec. 12, 2000.

65. "Employed persons by detailed occupation and sex, 1983–99 annual averages," Bureau of Labor Statistics.

66. Dennis Alan Mann, Professor of Architecture, University of Cincinnati, interview with author, Dec. 11, 2000.

Race is never in any way alluded to in the *Graphic Standards* charts, but, again, the system of representation is defined as much by what it excludes as what it includes. If the text may be seen as sympathetic to classical paradigms, the attitude regarding race is implicit. The "human figure" is specifically the Western white male, and the restrictions of the classical model may be extended not only to women, but to all minorities. *Graphic Standards*, as the bible of modern architectural practice, carried this legacy into the twentieth century. If Robert Ivy's introductory comments are correct, and *Graphic Standards* may be read as social history, the repression implied by its representation of the body is perfectly in keeping with society's slow progress in the treatment of gender and race.

CONCLUSION

Graphic Standards demonstrates the repression of women through its historical predecessors, through the biased procedures of statistics, and through its unique graphic methods. The culturally ingrained conception of the human body as a singular entity, an emblem of unity, seems to have weighed heavily on these diagrams for decades. The desire to picture the body as solitary inevitably forces problems of representation. How may diversity be expressed in a single image? If human bodies are to be used as paradigms, the Dreyfuss diagram of superimposed racial types suggests a possible alternative.

The *Graphic Standards* diagrams are restrictive whether they are interpreted as aesthetic exemplars or as dimensions to accommodate the anticipated occupants of buildings. The implicit sexism of architecture's standards of practice should not be surprising, given that the profession has always been male dominated. At the beginning of the twentieth century, only a handful of women in the United States were architects.[61] In 1934, the same issue of *American Architect and Architecture* in which the Freese drawings originally appeared includes an editorial titled, "Architect: Professional or Business Man?" The presumed sex of architects was understood.[62] In 1970, when *Graphic Standards* began to include separate statistics for women, approximately 3 percent of architects in this country were female, compared to 40 percent of other professionals and of all workers.[63]

The numbers are still very low. The AIA estimated its female membership in 1999 to be below ten percent.[64] In the same year, women comprised 15 percent of all licensed and non-licensed architects, although they comprised approximately half of the general workforce.[65] Minorities fare much worse. The number of licensed African-American architects, for instance, is thought to be between 1 and 2 percent.[66] Because architecture traditionally has been a restricted profession, its standards of practice have been written by and for a narrow demographic. The authors, advocates, and audience of *Graphic Standards* typically have been white and male. And, because anthropometric statistics historically have been limited to men, it becomes clear that both the presumed designers and users of buildings have been male. In this sense, *Graphic Standards* may be read as a guide for white men to create buildings for themselves in their own image.

Writing and Discussion Questions

ANALYSIS

1.   What was Vitruvius arguing for and against? What excerpt/quotation best represents this?
2.   What was Le Corbusier arguing for and against? What excerpt/quotation best represents this?
3.   What was Hosey arguing for and against? What excerpt/quotation best represents this?

SYNTHESIS

1.   Regarding concepts of the human body in architecture, discuss one major difference regarding Vitruvius', Le Corbusier's, and Hosey's texts.
2.   Regarding concepts of the human body in architecture, discuss one primary commonality regarding Vitruvius', Le Corbusier's, and Hosey's texts.

SELF-REFLECTION

1.   For each of the texts, discuss a major issue with which you most agree and most disagree; reflect upon why you hold these views.
2.   Select a recent design project, or a current project on which you are working. Discuss the characteristics of the project in regards to the human body, in light of the discussion and texts introduced in this chapter. What attitudes regarding the human body in architecture does your work illustrate?

PROSPECTION

1. Select one of the texts listed in the bibliography for this chapter; locate and read it. To what degree is that text and the attitudes it represents still relevant to architecture today and in the near future?
2. What is the relationship between "building" and "body" today? Are buildings metaphors of the body; abstractions of the body; direct responses to the body; some combination of these; or something else? In other words, if a fourth text were added to this chapter, what would the argument be?

Other Readings on Body and Building

Agrest, Diana. "Architecture From Without: Body, Logic, and Sex," *Assemblage,* 7 (1988): 28–41.

Agrest, Diana. *The Sex of Architecture* (New York: Abrams, 1996).

Ahluwalia, J. J. S. "Human Proportions in Buildings." *Build International,* 3 (November 1970): 339–344.

Bloomer, Kent C., and Charles W. Moore, *Body, Memory and Architecture* (New Haven: Yale University Press, 1977).

Dodds, George, and Robert Tavernor, eds. *Body and Building: Essays on the Changing Relation of Body and Architecture* (Cambridge: MIT Press, 2005).

Frascari, Marco. *Monsters of Architecture: Anthropomorphism in Architectural Theory* (Lanham: Rowman & Littlefield, 1991).

Freese, Ernest I. "The Geometry of the Human Figure," *American Architect and Architecture,* 144/145 (July 1934).

Hight, Christopher. *Architectural Principles in the Age of Cybernetics* (New York: Routledge, 2007).

Rykwert, Joseph. *The Dancing Column: On Order in Architecture* (Cambridge: MIT Press, 1996).

Tzonis, Alexander, and Liane Lefaivre. "The Mechanical Body Versus the Divine Body: The Rise of Modern Design Theory," *Journal of Architectural Education,* 29 (1975): 4–7.

Wittkower, Rudolf. *Architectural Principles in the Age of Humanism* (London: Academy Editions, 1998).

Chapter 8

PROPORTION and ORGANIZATION

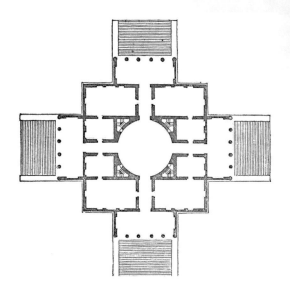

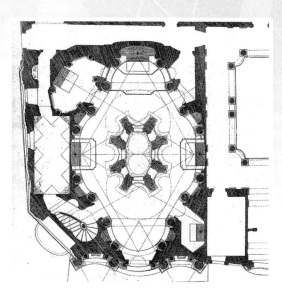

INTRODUCTORY DISCUSSION

1. Of the two images above, which better represents the use of geometry in architecture? Which better represents the use of proportion? Which better represents the use of organization? Why?

2. In architecture, what are the various definitions and connotations of the terms "proportion" and "organization"? How are these concepts related? How do they differ?

3. Which is more important in architecture today, spatial proportion (dimensions) or spatial organization (arrangement)?

FIGURE 8.1
Plan drawing of the Villa Rotunda, Vicenza, Italy (ca. 1567–1591). Architects: Andrea Palladio and Vincenzo Scamozzi.

FIGURE 8.2
Plan drawing of San Carlo alle Quattro Fontane, Rome, Italy (ca. 1638-1667). Architect: Franceso Borromini.

Introduction

On one hand, architecture is about assembling materials. On the other, architecture is about assembling spaces. When we are first introduced to the term "space," it is often in the context of astronomy: outer space. In this case, "space" is boundless, infinite. It is an area of nothingness between planetary objects and solar systems. In architecture, however, the concept of "space" is quite the opposite. Architects define and enclose space, creating bounded areas for human inhabitation, each with a particular geometry, proportion, and organization (relationship to other spaces). Spatial geometry, proportion, and organization have been central discourse in architecture for centuries, but their hierarchical relationships among them have varied.

Spatial geometry affects acoustics and views, as well as one's sense of enclosure or openness. *Spatial proportion* may be used to imply different uses—a long, low, narrow space, for example, suggests movement, while a space that is more cubic, more equal in length, height, and width, insinuates repose—or to provoke certain human affects—a sense of bigness or smallness, for example. *Spatial organization* determines separation or connection between similar or dissimilar uses, helps to clarify aspects of use, such as public vs. private, and establishes similarity or contrast between spaces, e.g., light qualities, scale, material, etc. In contrast to previously discussed dialectics, the dialectic of proportion and organization, therefore, is not so much a choice—this or that—but a negotiation between the two.

Vitruvius, concerned primarily with the "whole," emphasized organization, or the arrangement of the different parts, spaces, or functions of a building. Palladio, on the other hand, stressed the value of proportioning individual spaces, especially the relationships between the plan and the section of a single space. In the mid-16th century, Palladio, not unlike Vitruvius and Alberti before him, developed an architectural treatise entitled *The Four Books on Architecture*, the *original text* for this chapter. Among other things, Palladio outlined how rooms should be arranged (especially in housing), how individual spaces should be proportioned, and how doors and windows should be dimensioned. Palladio advocated square and rectangular volumes (and, in rare cases, circular volumes), and asserted that the height of a room be "calculated" based on proportional relationships between the breadth and length.

While Palladio's recommendations were built around certain Classical and Renaissance principles of architecture, Le Corbusier sought new principles, many of which refuted traditional tenets. Le Corbusier believed that new systems of construction, e.g., steel and reinforced concrete, as well as changes in lifestyle, allowed for and necessitated, in his words, an "architectural revolution." This was clearly manifest in Le Corbusier's built work; it was also evident in a number of his texts, including "The Plan of the Modern House," the *reflective text* for this chapter. Similar to Palladio, Le Corbusier noted the importance "to plan a dwelling in accordance with the logic of reasonable functions." In contrast, however, Le Corbusier not only discussed how to arrange spaces but introduced a new architectural concept: circulation. Whereas Palladio and other Renaissance architects utilized a cellular arrangement of rooms and *enfilade*, direct axial connections from room to room, Le Corbusier saw circulation as independent of the primary rooms, a separate function and separate space. Le Corbusier also differed from Palladio in regards to window size and placement. While Palladio advocated verticality, symmetry, and centrality in window (and door) placement, Le Corbusier promoted horizontality, asymmetry, and continuity in the placement of windows.

Numerous architectural historians and critics dubbed both Palladio's Villa Rotunda and Le Corbusier's Villa Savoye as canonical, but for very different reasons. Colin Rowe labeled them "ideal." In "The Mathematics of the Ideal Villa," the *philosophical text* of this chapter Rowe, instead, compared Palladio's Villa Foscari (La Malcontenta) and Le Corbusier's Villa Stein (Garches). Rowe identified both similarities and differences between the works. For example, both projects possessed archetypal cubic qualities. Likewise, regarding the dialectical relationship between proportion and organization, Rowe noted that Le Corbusier and Palladio held "equal reverence for mathematics" and the use of historical precedents in the organization and arrangement of the plan. However, according to Rowe, Palladio maintained a singular devotion to Roman archetypes, while Le Corbusier utilized "dissipated," eclectic, and abstract cultural references. Moreover, it is in the design of the elevation that the differences between the two architects are most notable. Palladio emphasized centrality, while Le Corbusier sought "dispersal." Moreover, Rowe asserted that *plans* were "the ultimate proof" of Palladio's theories, whereas, *façades* were the "primary demonstrations" of Le Corbusier's theories.

Nevertheless, the most striking differences between Palladio's stance and Le Corbusier's stance on proportion and organization may be more fundamental than this. One was the emphasis on centrality, symmetry, and the plan. The second was an emphasis on dispersion, asymmetry, and the elevation. These were the differences not only between Palladio's and Le Corbusier's theories but also the differences between two generations of architects, between two paradigms of architecture. Whether or not these two paradigms can be combined, or even co-exist, remains a central question in architecture.

Original Text

ANDREA PALLADIO, EXCERPTS FROM *THE FOUR BOOKS ON ARCHITECTURE*.

First Published in 1570

ON LOGGIAS, ENTRANCES, HALLS, AND ROOMS, AND THEIR SHAPES

Loggias are usually built on the front and the back of the house and, if they are built in the middle, then there is only one, or, if at the sides, two. These loggias have many uses, such as for walking in, eating in, and other pastimes, and they are made larger or smaller depending on the size and function of the building; but for the most part they are not made less than ten nor more than twenty feet broad. Besides these, all well-designed houses have places in the middle and in the most beautiful parts which all the others correspond to and can be reached from. These places in the lower story are popularly called entrances and those in the upper story, halls. The entrances are, as it were, public spaces and serve as a place where those waiting for the master to come out of his lodgings can stand to greet him and do business with him, and they are the first part (beyond the loggias) which anyone entering the house is presented with. Halls are designed for parties, banquets, as the sets for acting out comedies, weddings, and similar entertainments, and so these spaces must be much larger than the others and must have a shape that will be as capacious as possible so that many people can gather in them comfortably and observe what is going on. Usually I do not make halls longer than two squares, which are derived from the breadth, but the closer they are to being square, the more praiseworthy and practical they will be.

Rooms must be distributed at either side of the entrance and the hall, and one must ensure that those on the right correspond and are equal to those on the left so that the building will be the same on one side as on the other and the walls will take the weight of the roof equally; the reason is that if the rooms on one side are made large and those on the other side small, the former will be more capable of resisting the load because of the thickness of their walls, while the latter will be weaker, causing grave problems that will in time ruin the whole building. There are seven types of room that are the most beautiful and well proportioned and turn out better: they can be made circular, though these are rare; or square; or their length will equal the diagonal of the square of the breadth; or a square and a third; or a square and a half; or a square and two-thirds; or two squares. . . .

ON THE HEIGHTS OF ROOMS

Rooms are built with either a vault or a ceiling; if with a ceiling, the height from the pavement to the joists will be the same as the breadth and the rooms above will be a sixth less in height than those below. If they are vaulted (as is customary for rooms on the ground floor, because that way they turn out to be more beautiful and less susceptible to fire), the heights of the vaults in square rooms will be a third greater than their breadth. But with those that are longer than they are broad it is essential to derive the height from the breadth and length, so that they are in proportion to each other. One will establish this height by adding the breadth to the length and dividing the product into two equal parts so that one of these halves will be the height of the vault. . . .

Using numbers the height will be calculated like this: if you know the breadth and length of the room in feet, let us find a number that has the same proportion to the breadth as the length has to it, and let us identify it by multiplying the lesser extreme with the greater, because the square root of the result of the multiplication will be the height that we are looking for. So, for example, if the place that we want to vault is nine feet long and four broad, the height of the vault will be six feet, and in terms of proportions, nine is to six as six is to four, that is, the sesquialtera. But one should take note that it will not always be possible to calculate this height with whole numbers. . . .

There are other heights for vaults which do not come under any rule, and the architect will make use of these according to his judgment and practical circumstances. . . .

ON THE DIMENSIONS OF DOORS AND WINDOWS

One cannot give a certain and predetermined rule covering the heights and breadths of the main doors of buildings or the doors and windows of rooms; so the architect must build the principal doors to match the size of the building, the type of patron, and the things that must be brought in and out. It seems to me a good idea to divide the space between the level or floor and the surface of the wooden ceiling into three and a half parts (as Vitruvius says in Book IV, chapter 6) and make two of these the clear height and one of them the breadth, minus a twelfth of the height. The ancients used to make their doors narrower above than below, as one sees in a temple at Tivoli; and Vitruvius advises this, perhaps for greater strength. One must choose a position for the principal doors to which one can go from all parts of the house. The doors of rooms must not be made more than three feet wide or six and a half feet high, nor less than two feet wide and five high. Make sure when making windows that they do not let in too much or too little light and that they are not more spread out or closer together than necessary. One should, therefore, take great care over the size of the rooms which will receive light from them, because it is obvious that a larger room needs much more light to make it luminous and bright than a small one; and if the windows are made smaller and less numerous than necessary, they will be made gloomy; and if they are made too large the rooms are practically uninhabitable because, since cold and hot air can get in, they will be extremely hot or cold depending on the seasons of the year, at least if the region of the sky to which they are oriented does not afford some relief. For this reason windows must not be made broader than a quarter of the length of the rooms nor narrower than a fifth and their height should be made two squares and a sixth of their breadth. Because rooms in houses are made large, medium, and small, the windows must still remain the same size in a given order or story; when calculating the dimensions of these windows I like very much those rooms which are two-thirds longer than their breadth; that is, if the breadth is eighteen feet then the length should be thirty. I divide the breadth into four and a half parts; and with one part I establish the clear breadth of the windows and with the other two, adding a sixth of the breadth, I make all the windows of the other rooms the same size as these windows. The windows above, that is those of the second story, should be a sixth less than the clear height of those below, and if more windows are built above, they should similarly diminish by a sixth. The windows at the right must correspond to those on the left and those in the upper story must be vertically above those below; similarly all the doors must be vertically above one another so that there will be void above void and solid above solid; they should also face each other so that someone standing in one part of the house is able to see across to the other, which brings beauty and fresh air in the summer and other advantages. For greater strength it is usual to incorporate some arches so that the lintels or heads of doors and windows are not overburdened by the weight; these are popularly called *remenati* and contribute greatly to the durability of the building. The windows must be set away from the angles or corners of the building, as I have explained above, because that part of the building which must keep all the rest aligned and held together must not be open and weak. The little pilasters or jambs of the doors and windows should not be narrower than a sixth nor broader than a fifth of their clear breadth. It remains for us to look at their ornaments. . . .

ON THE DECORUM OR SUITABILITY THAT MUST BE MAINTAINED IN PRIVATE BUILDINGS . . .

One must describe as suitable a house which will be appropriate to the status of the person who will have to live in it and of which the parts will correspond to the whole and to each other. But above all the architect must observe that (as Vitruvius says in Books I and VI), for great men and especially those in public office, houses with loggias and spacious, ornate halls will be required, so that those waiting to greet the master of the house or to ask him for some help or a favor can spend their time pleasantly in such spaces; similarly, smaller buildings of lesser expense and ornament will be appropriate for men of lower status. One must build in the same way for judges and lawyers so that in their houses there are beautiful and ornate areas to walk about in and their clients can pass the time without tedium. Merchants' houses should have places for storing their goods which face north and are so arranged that the owners have no fear of burglars. A building will also have decorum if the parts correspond to the whole, so that in large buildings there will be large members, and in small ones, small, and in medium-sized ones, medium; it would certainly be displeasing and inappropriate if the halls and rooms in a very large building were small and, conversely, if two or three rooms in a small building were to occupy all of it. Therefore, as far as possible one must (as I have said) pay particular attention to those who want to build, not so much for what they can afford as for the type of building that would suit them; then, when the choice has been made, the parts should be so arranged that they match the whole and each other, and the appropriate decoration applied; but the architect is frequently obliged to accommodate himself to the wishes of those who are paying rather than attending to what he should.

ON THE PLANNING OF ROOMS AND OTHER PLACES

In order that houses may be suitable for family use—for, if they are not suitable their chances of praise would be very slight and they would deserve the harshest criticism—one must take great care not only with the most important elements, such as loggias, halls, courtyards, magnificent rooms, and large staircases, which should be well lit and easy to ascend, but also so that the smallest and ugliest parts will be in places that are subordinate to those which are larger and more prestigious. The reason is that since there are some noble and beautiful parts of the human body and some that are less pleasant and agreeable than otherwise, we can nevertheless see that the former have an absolute dependence on the latter and cannot exist without them; similarly too in buildings there must be some parts that are admirable and praiseworthy and others which are less elegant, without which, however, the former could not remain independent and thus would, in part, lose their dignity and beauty. But, just as our blessed God has arranged our own members so that the most beautiful are in positions most exposed to view and the more unpleasant are hidden, we too when building should place the most important and prestigious parts in full view and the less beautiful in locations concealed as far from our eyes as possible, because all the unpleasant things of the house are placed in them as well as all those that could be a nuisance and tend to make the most beautiful parts ugly. So I am in favor of putting the cellars, the wood stores, the pantries, the kitchens, the smaller dining rooms, the laundries, the ovens, and the other things essential for daily life in the lowest part of the building, which I put partly underground: two advantages arise from this; one is that the upper part of the house remains entirely unencumbered and the other, which is no less important, is that the story above becomes healthy to live in since its floor is distanced from the dampness of the earth; moreover, raising the upper part up has the added charm that it can be seen from a distance and one has views from it. Then one will note that in the rest of the building there should be large, medium-sized, and small rooms, one side by side with the next, so that they can be mutually useful. The small ones should be divided up to create even smaller rooms where studies or libraries could be located, as well as riding equipment and other tackle which we need every day and which would be awkward to put in the rooms where one sleeps, eats, or receives guests. It would also contribute to comfort if the summer rooms were large and spacious and oriented to the north, and those for the winter to the south and west and were small rather than otherwise, because in the summer we seek the shade and breezes, and in the winter, the sun, and smaller rooms get warmer more readily than large ones. But those we would want to use in the spring and autumn will be oriented to the east and look out over gardens and greenery. Studies and libraries should be in the same part of the house because they are used in the morning more than at any other time. But the large rooms should be distributed with the medium-sized, and the latter with the small rooms in such a way that (as I have said elsewhere) one part of the building corresponds to the other so that the whole body of the building would have an inherently suitable distribution of its members, making the whole beautiful and graceful. But because in cities neighbors' walls, the streets, or public squares nearly always predetermine certain boundaries over which the architect cannot trespass, he must abide by the constraints of the sites.

Reflective Text

LE CORBUSIER, "THE PLAN OF THE MODERN HOUSE."

First Published in 1930

We are now tooled to find solutions for the plan of the modern house, if we want to look for them.

Let me remind you of the "paralyzed plan" of the masonry house and what we arrived at with the steel or concrete one:

- the free plan
- the free façade
- the independent structure
- ribbon windows or window walls
- pilotis
- roof gardens
- and the interior furnished with cabinets and rid of the congestion of furniture.

. . .

How to take advantage of these new freedoms? In favor of *economy*,

- of *efficiency*,
- of resolving *numerous modern functions*,
- of *beauty*.

The *architectural revolution*—for it is a real revolution   implies different acts:

1. *to classify*
2. *to dimension*
3. *to circulate*
4. *to compose*
5. *to proportion.*

I. TO CLASSIFY

Two independent factors are present, simultaneous, synchronous, inseparable, indissoluble:

a. a biological phenomenon
b. an aesthetic phenomenon.

The biological is the end proposed, the problem stated, the fundamental function of the undertaking.

The aesthetic is the physiological sensation, an "impression," a pressure by the senses, a compulsion.

The biological affects our common sense.

The aesthetic affects our sensitivity and our reason.

The two united in simultaneous perceptions produce the architectural *emotion—good* or bad. One must therefore recognize the *organs* of the house, list them, classify them; one must determine the useful contiguities, unfold successive operations in their normal order. And for each purpose, say to oneself:

- heating: what is it?
- ventilation or airing: what is it?
- daylighting: what is it?
- artificial lighting: what is it?
- vertical connections, elevators, ramps, stairways, ladders; horizontal connections (circulation): what are they?

A cold-blooded examination of these questions can give solutions that will make a revolution in the building industry.

A revolution? Yes, for in current practice, successive inventions have produced innumerable new objects, and no thought has been given to the subject, everything has accumulated in disorder, in confusion, and this confusion *has led us simply to wastefulness.* (An example among hundreds: if I discovered the possibility of living with three-fortieths of a servant, do I not also have the right to want to heat myself with a tenth or a hundredth of a furnace?)

II. TO DIMENSION

I am speaking of the dimensions of rooms in dwellings.

Until now the question has been taken up superficially, since masonry construction, depending on the superposing of rooms from floor to floor, prevented all innovation, contradicted that effort of research into economizing of which we have made a fundamental basis.

Today we can, as we like, introduce the greatest variety of rooms in a house without concern for superposing floors; I have demonstrated it.

Now then, let us analyze these dimensions, let us calculate them in detail. An operation of rationalization similar to dealing out space in modern factories. A toilet would not have more than 8 square meters and a bedroom would no longer have the same form and surface as a dining room for the simple reason—quite unreasonable—that it is just above it.

With my charcoal and my chalks I describe the series of reasoned actions that presided at the construction of a tiny little house on the edge of Lake Leman.

I knew that the region where we wanted to build included 10 to 15 kilometers of hills along the lake. A fixed point: the lake; another, the magnificent view facing it; another, the south, also facing it.

Should one first have searched for the site and made the plan in accordance with it? That is the usual practice.

I thought it was better to make an exact plan, corresponding ideally to the use one hoped from it and determined by the three factors above. This done, to go out with the plan in hand to look for a suitable site.

Notice, in this apparently contradictory procedure, the key to the problem of modern living. To plan a dwelling in accordance with the logic of reasonable functions. Then to place one's building; I showed you before that the new elements of modern architecture made it possible to adapt to a site whatever the circumstances. . . .

III. TO CIRCULATE

It is an important modern word. In architecture and city planning, circulation is everything.

What is a house for?

- One enters,
- one carries on methodical functions.

Workers' houses, villas, townhouses, the League of Nations building, the Centrosoyuz of Moscow, the World City, the plan of Paris, *circulation is everything*.

One can line up the functional elements of a house in a circuit, these being dimensioned and the indispensable contiguities determined.

I draw:

- An entrance; it opens on the left onto the reception area, on the right onto the services.
- The dining room and living room are combined; nevertheless a sideboard (in concrete) forms a spine to separate them.
- The small sitting room, transformable immediately into a guest room with beds coming out of the floor, a closet hidden by a sliding panel, and a washbowl built frankly outside the volume of the house.

- A circulation is created between the entrance and the garden to the left, which is surrounded by walls and used as a summer living room.
- To the right of the dining area, the sleeping space is near the bath and the toilet.
- One single window 11 meters long unites and lights all the elements, making the majesty of the magnificent site enter into the house: the lake with its movement, the Alps with their miraculous light.
- To the right of the entrance the kitchen and the laundry, the stairs to the cellar and the service door to the paved courtyard; then, on the other hand, the connection with the bedroom through the dressing room, a second "service" circulation.
- The doors are either 75 or 55 centimeters wide. The house is 4 meters deep. Inside, this house of 57 square meters offers a perspective of 14 meters! The 11-meter-long window introduces the immensity of the outdoors, the unfalsifiable unity of a lakeside landscape with its storms or radiant calms.

There is really not a square centimeter lost here; and that's not a small job!

Beauty? But this is the very characteristic of the intention that determined all these operations.

The plan in my pocket, I went off to look for a site. I discovered a little ribbon of shore so small that I should never have thought of buying it, if I had not had in my pocket the certitude that its dimensions were adequate.

Let us go on now to another example of modern circulation inside a house. This scheme corresponds to a particular way of life: I draw only the plan of the bedroom floor.

Monsieur will have his *cell*, Madame also, Mademoiselle also. Each of these cells has floors and ceilings carried by freestanding independent columns. Each cell opens by a door on a walkway along the three apartments. Once through each door one is in a complete unit made up of an entrance, a dressing room (storage of underwear, linens, and clothing), an exercise room, a boudoir or office, a bathroom, and finally the bed. Low or ceiling-height partitions, built from cabinets or not, subdivide the space, letting the ceilings through. Everyone lives as if in his own small house. . . .

It would be easy to multiply these examples, which are prompted by daily problems if one acquires the habit of strolling with one's pencil, step by step, thinking out well the functions by which our occupant will find pleasure in living in his house.

IV. TO COMPOSE

Let us take into consideration the personal qualities of the architect.

It is good to persuade oneself of the existence of certain things, among others this one that is of capital importance and of which I have already spoken:

I draw a personage. I have him enter a house; he discovers a certain dimension, a certain shape of room, or a certain arrival of light through a window or window wall. He goes on: another volume, another entrance of light. Further on, another source of light; still further, a flood of light and half-shade just beside it, etc.

These successive volumes lit differently, *one breathes them in*: breathing is activated by them. . . .

As you can imagine, I use light freely; light for me is the fundamental basis of architecture. *I compose with light.* . . .

You will let light in wherever you like. Your window wall will be made of transparent glass, or special glass . . . that will have the insulating value of a thick wall and will stop the sun's rays; or finally, wire-reinforced glass, translucent glass, or glass bricks. Window walls, diaphragms, are new terms in the language of architecture.

V. TO PROPORTION

Everything is geometrical to our eyes (biology exists only as organization, and this is something that the mind understands only after study). *Architectural composition is geometric*, an event primarily of a *visual* nature; an event implying judgments of quantities, of relationships; the appreciation of *proportions*. Proportions provoke sensations; a series of sensations is like the melody in music. Erik Satie used to say: the melody is the idea, harmony (in music) is the means, the tool, the presentation of the idea.

The architectural *idea* is strictly an individual phenomenon, inalienable. It is good to push an idea to a state of purity; I have explained the reason for the regulating diagrams. I have also said that simplicity is derived from richness, from abundance, by choice, by selection, by concentration.

Each of us gives a personal expression to an idea: individual poetry. Each one has the right to observe himself, to judge himself, to know himself, and to act with clear-sightedness. We, Pierre Jeanneret and I, have built quite a lot of houses. Studying our own production, I manage to discern the general intention that determined the tendency of our work. With similar methods of *classification*, of *dimensioning*, of *circulation*, of *composition*, of *proportioning*, up to now we have worked on four distinct types of plans, each expressing characteristic intellectual preoccupations.

The first type shows each organ rising up next to its neighbor, in accordance with an organic reasoning: "the inside takes its ease, and pushes out to form diverse projections." This principle leads to a "pyramidal" composition, which can become busy if one doesn't watch out (Auteuil).

The second type shows the compression of organs within a rigid envelope, absolutely pure. A difficult problem, perhaps a spiritual delight; spending spiritual energy within self-imposed limitations (Garches).

The third types furnishes, with a visible framework (skeleton structure), a simple envelope, clear, transparent as a network; it allows the creation of useful volumes of rooms different on each floor in form and quantity. An ingenious type appropriate to certain climates; such compositions are easy, full of possibilities (Tunis).

The fourth type attains, on the outside, the pure form of the second type; inside, it has the advantages, the characteristics of the first and the third. A very pure type, very ample, also full of possibilities (Poissy).

It is not useless, I repeat, to read constantly in one's own work. The consciousness of events is the springboard of progress.

CONCLUSION

To conclude, let us analyze that construction going up in Poissy, near Paris.

The visitors, till now, turn round and round inside, asking themselves what is happening, understanding with difficulty the reasons for what they see and feel; they don't find anything of what is called a "house." They feel themselves within something entirely new. And . . . they are not bored, I believe!

The site: a big lawn, slightly convex. The main view is to the north, therefore opposite to the sun; the front of the house would usually be inverted.

The house is a box raised above the ground, perforated all around, without interruption, by a long horizontal window. No more hesitation about architectural plays of voids and solids. The box is in the center of fields, overlooking orchards.

Under the box, going through the pilotis, a carriageway arrives turning in a hairpin whose curve encloses, exactly under the pilotis, the door to the house, the entrance, the garage, the services (laundry, linen room, servants' quarters). Automobiles drive up under the house, park or drive off.

From inside the entrance, a ramp leads easily, hardly noticed, up to the first floor, where the life of the inhabitants goes on: reception, bedrooms, etc. Receiving views and light from around the periphery of the box, the different rooms center on a hanging garden that is there like a distributor of adequate light and sunshine.

It is on the hanging garden that the sliding plate glass walls of the salon and other rooms of the house open freely: thus the sun is everywhere, in the very heart of the house.

From the hanging garden, the ramp, now on the outside, leads to the solarium on the roof.

This is connected by a spiral staircase three stories high down to the cellar dug out in the earth under the pilotis. This spiral, a pure vertical organ, is inserted freely into the horizontal composition.

To finish, look at the section: air circulates everywhere, there is light at every point, it penetrates everywhere. Circulation furnishes architectural impressions of such diversity that they disconcert visitors ignorant of the architectural liberties brought by modern techniques. The simple columns of the ground floor, by their suitable plan, frame the landscape with a regularity that suppresses all notions of "front" or "back" or "side" of the house. The plan is pure, made exactly in accordance with needs. It is in its right place in the rural landscape of Poissy. . . .

This same house, I should set it down in a corner of the beautiful Argentine countryside; we shall have twenty houses rising from the high grass of an orchard where cows continue to graze. Instead of laying them out along the customary detestable garden-city streets, which result in destroying a site, we have a handsome traffic system, poured in concrete, into the grass self, in full nature. Grass will grow along the edge of the roads, nothing will be disturbed, neither trees nor flowers nor herds. The inhabitants, who came here because this countryside with its *rural life* was beautiful, will contemplate it, maintained intact, from their hanging gardens, or through the four sides of the long windows. Their home life will be set in a Virgilian dream.

You won't hold it against me, I hope, that I have gone at length before your eyes into this example of *liberties taken.* They have been taken because they were *acquired,* torn out of the live resources of modern materials. Poetry, lyricism, brought by techniques.

Philosophical Text

COLIN ROWE, "THE MATHEMATICS OF THE IDEAL VILLA."

First Published in 1947

> There are two causes of beauty—natural and customary. Natural is from geometry consisting in uniformity, that is equality and proportion. Customary beauty is begotten by the use, as familiarity breeds a love for things not in themselves lovely. Here lies the great occasion of errors, but always the true test is natural or geometrical beauty. Geometrical figures are naturally more beautiful than irregular ones: the square, the circle are the most beautiful, next the parallelogram and the oval. There are only two beautiful positions of straight lines, perpendicular and horizontal; this is from Nature and consequently necessity, no other than upright being firm.
>
> Sir Christopher Wren, *Parentalia*

As the ideal type of centralized building Palladio's Villa Capra-Rotonda has, perhaps more than any other house, imposed itself upon the imagination. Mathematical, abstract, four square, without apparent function and totally memorable, its derivatives have enjoyed universal distribution; and, when he writes of it, Palladio is lyrical.

> The site is as pleasant and delightful as can be found, because it is on a small of very easy access, and is watered on one side by the Bacchiglione, a navigable river; and on the other it is encompassed about with most pleasant risings look like a very great theatre and are all cultivated about with most excellent fruits and most exquisite vines; and therefore as it enjoys from every part most beautiful views, some of which are limited, some more extended, and others which terminate with the horizon, there are loggias made in all four fronts.[1]

When the mind is prepared for the one by the other, a passage from Le Corbusier's *Précisions* may be unavoidably reminiscent of this. No less lyrical but rather more explosive, Le Corbusier is describing the site of his Savoye House at Poissy.

1. Isaac Ware, *The Four Books of Palladio's Architecture* (London, 1738), 41.

Le site: une vaste pelouse bombée en dôme aplati. . . . La maison est une boîte en l'air . . . au milieu des prairies dominant le verger. . . . Le plan est pur. . . . Il à sa juste place dans l'agreste paysage de Poissy. . . . Les habitants, venus ici parce que cette campagne agreste était belle avec *sa vie de campagne,* ils la contempleront, maintenue intacte, du haut de leur jardin suspendu ou des quatre faces de leurs fenêtres en longueur. Leur vie domestique sera inserée dans un rêve virgilien.[2]

The Savoye House has been given a number of interpretations. It may indeed be a machine for living in, an arrangement of interpenetrating volumes and spaces, an emanation of space-time; but the suggestive reference to the dreams of Virgil may put one in mind of the passage in which Palladio describes the Rotonda. Palladio's landscape is more agrarian and bucolic, he evokes less of the untamed pastoral, his scale is larger; but the effect of the two passages is somehow the same.

Palladio, writing elsewhere, amplifies the ideal life of the villa. Its owner, from within a fragment of created order, will watch the maturing of his possessions and savor the piquancy of contrast between his fields and his gardens; reflecting on contemplate throughout the years the antique virtues of a simpler race, and the harmonious ordering of his life and his estate will be an analogy of paradise.

The ancient sages commonly used to retire to such places, where being oftentimes visited by their virtuous friends and relations, having houses, gardens, fountains and such like pleasant places, and above all their virtue, they could easily attain to as much happiness as can be attained here below.[3]

Perhaps these were the dreams of Virgil; and, freely interpreted, they have gathered around themselves in the course of time all those ideas of Roman virtue, excellence, Imperial splendor, and decay which make up the imaginative reconstruction of the ancient world. It would have been, perhaps, in the landscapes of Poussin—with their portentous apparitions of the antique—that Palladio would have felt at home; and it is possibly the fundamentals of this landscape, the poignancy of contrast between the disengaged cube and its setting in the *paysage agreste*, between geometrical volume and the appearance of unimpaired nature, which lie behind Le Corbusier's Roman allusion. If architecture at the Rotonda forms the setting for the good life, at Poissy it is certainly the background for the lyrically efficient one; and, if the contemporary pastoral is not yet sanctioned by conventional usage, apparently the Virgilian nostalgia is still present. From the hygienically-equipped boudoirs, pausing while ascending the ramps, the memory of the Georgics no doubt interposes itself; and, perhaps, the historical reference may even add a stimulus as the car pulls out for Paris.

However, a more specific comparison which presents itself is that between Palladio's Villa Foscari, the Malcontenta of *c.* 1550–60, and the house which in 1927 Le Corbusier built for Mr. and Mrs. Michael Stein at Garches.

These are two buildings which, in their forms and evocations, are superficially so entirely unlike that to bring them together would seem to be facetious; but, if the obsessive

2. Le Corbusier, *Précisions sur un état Présent de l'Architecture et de l'Urbanisme* (Paris, 1930), 136–138.

3. Ware, *The Four Books,* 46.

psychological and physical gravity of the Malcontenta receives no parallel in a house which sometimes wishes to be a ship, sometimes a gymnasium, this difference of mood should not be allowed to inhibit scrutiny.

For, in the first case, both Garches and the Malcontenta are conceived of as single blocks; and, allowing for variations in roof treatment, it might be noticed that both are blocks of corresponding volume, each measuring 8 units in length, by 5½ in breadth, by 5 in height. Then, further to this, there is a comparable bay structure to be observed. Each house exhibits (and conceals) an alternating rhythm of double and single spatial intervals; and each house, read from front to back, displays a comparable tripartite distribution of lines of support.

But, at this stage, it might be better to introduce an *almost*. Because, if the distribution of basic horizontal coordinates is, in both cases, much the same, there are still some slight and significant differences relating to the distribution of those lines of support which parallel the façades; and thus at Garches, reading from front to back, the fundamental spatial interval proceeds in the ratio of ½ : 1½ : 1½ : 1½ : ½ , while at the Malcontenta we are presented with the sequence 2 : 2 : 1½ . In other words, by the use of a cantilevered half unit Le Corbusier obtains a compression for his central bay and thereby transfers interest elsewhere; while Palladio secures a dominance for his central division with a progression towards his portico which absolutely focuses attention in these two areas. The one scheme is, therefore, potentially dispersed and possibly equalitarian and the other is concentric and certainly hierarchical; but, with this difference observed, it might simply be added that, in both cases, a projecting element—extruded terrace or attached portico—occupies 1½ units in depth.

Structures, of course, are not to be compared; and, to some extent, both architects look to structure as a justification for their dispositions. Thus Palladio employs a solid bearing wall; and of this system he writes:

> It is to be observed, that those (rooms) on the right correspond with those on the left, that so the fabric may be the same in one place as in the other, and that the walls may equally bear the burden of the roof; because if the walls are made large in one part and small in the other, the latter will be more firm to resist the weight, by reason of the nearness of the walls, and the former more weak, which will produce in time very great inconveniences and ruin the whole work.[4]

Palladio is concerned with the logical disposition of motifs dogmatically accepted, but he attempts to discover a structural reason for his planning symmetries; while Le Corbusier, who is proving a case for structure as a basis for the formal elements of design, contrasts the new system with the old and is a little more comprehensive.

> Je vous rappelle ce "plan paralyse" de la maison de pierre et ceci à quoi nous sommes arrivés avec la maison de fer ou de ciment armé.

4. Ibid., 27.

plan libre

façade libre

ossature indépendante

fenêtres en longueur ou pan de verre

pilotis

toit-jardin

et l'intérieur muni de "casiers" et débarrassé de l'encombrement des meubles.[5]

Palladio's structural system makes it almost necessary to repeat the same plan every level of the building, while point support allows Le Corbusier a flexible arrangement; but both architects make a claim which is somewhat in excess of the reasons they advance. Solid wall structures, Palladio declares, demand absolute symmetry; a frame building, Le Corbusier announces, requires a free arrangement: but these must be, at least partly, the personal exigencies of high style—for asymmetrical buildings of traditional structure remain standing and even frame buildings of conventional plan continue to give satisfaction.

In both houses there is a *piano nobile* one floor up, which is linked to the garden by a terrace or portico and a flight (or flights) of steps. At the Malcontenta this main floor shows a cruciform hall with, symmetrically disposed about it, two suites of three rooms each and two staircases; but at Garches there is nothing so readily describable. At Garches there is a central hall and there are two staircases; but while one of the staircases occupies a similar position to those of the Malcontenta, the other has been turned through an angle of ninety degrees. Further, the entrance hall has been revealed from this level by an asymmetrical cutting open of floor; and the terrace (which corresponds to the Malcontenta's portico) has become partly a reentrant volume obliterating a line of support, placed in distinctly less perceptible relationship to the principal room. Thus, at Garches, the cruciform shape survives only vestigially (perhaps it may be thought to be registered by the apse of the dining room?); and therefore, instead of the centrality of Palladio's major space, a Z-shaped balance is achieved which is assisted by throwing the small library into the main apartment. Finally, while at the Malcontenta there is a highly evident cross axis, at Garches this transverse movement which is intimated by the central voids of the end walls is only allowed to develop implicitly and by fragments.

The wall at the Malcontenta comprises the traditional solid pierced by vertical openings with a central emphasis in the portico and subsidiary accents in the outer windows placed toward the extremities of the façade. The double bay in the center of the building which carries the upper pediments of the roof is expressed on the one front by a single door, on the other by a "Roman baths" motif; and, horizontally, the wall also falls into three primary divisions: base; *piano nobile*, corresponding to the Ionic order of the portico; and superimposed attic. The base plays the part of a projecting, consistently supporting solid upon which the house rests; but, while the *piano nobile* and attic are rusticated, the base is treated as a plain surface and a feeling of even greater weight carried here is achieved by this highly emotive inversion of the usual order.

5. Le Corbusier, *Précisions*, 123.

259

Again the situation at Garches is more complex; and there the exploitation of the structural system has led to a conception of the wall as a series of horizontal strips—a strategy which places equal interest in both center and extremity of the façade and which is then maintained by Le Corbusier's tendency to suppress the wider spans of the double bays. By these means any system of central vertical accent and inflection of the wall leading up to it is profoundly modified; and the immediate result in the garden elevation of Garches shows itself in the displacing of the elements which may be considered equivalent to the Malcontenta's portico and superimposed pediment. These become separate; and, transposed as terrace and roof pavilion, the one occupies the two (or three) bays to the left of the façade, the other a central position in the solid but an asymmetrical one in the whole elevation.

On the other hand, the entrance front at Garches retains what could be regarded as the analogue of Palladio's upper pediment. This is the central element of the upper story; but then it is also noticeable, in spite of its symmetrical position, that the further development of this element within itself is not symmetrical. Nor does it promote symmetry in the façade as a whole; and, though it is responded to by the large central window of the entrance hall, since the horizontal gashes of the windows act to prohibit any explicit linking of these two manifestations, there ensues in the elevation something very like that simultaneous affirmation and denial of centrality which is displayed in the plan. Thus a central focus is stipulated; its development is inhibited; and there then occurs a displacement and a breaking up of exactly what Palladio would have presumed to be a normative emphasis.

Another chief point of difference lies in the interpretation of the roof. At the Malcontenta this forms a pyramidal superstructure which amplifies the volume of the house; while at Garches it is constituted by a flat surface, serving as the floor of an enclosure, cut out from—and thereby diminishing—the house's volume. Thus, in the one building the behavior of the roof might be described as additive and in the other as subtractive; but, this important distinction apart, both roofs are then furnished with a variety of incident, regular or random, pediment or pavilion, which alike enter into important—though very different—relationships with the vertical surfaces of the walls below.

That mathematics and musical concord were the basis of ideal proportion was a common belief of the circles in which Palladio moved. Here there was felt to be a correspondence between the perfect numbers, the proportions of the human figure and the elements of musical harmony;[6] and Sir Henry Wotton, as British ambassador to Venice at a slightly later date, reflects some part he writes:

> The two principal Consonances that most ravish the Ear are, by the consent of all Nature, the *Fifth* and the *Octave*; whereof the first riseth radically, from the Proportion between two and three. The other from the double Interval, between one and two, or between two and four, etc. Now if we shall transport these

6. For these particular observations I am highly indebted to Rudolf Wittkower, *Architectural Principles in the Age of Humanism* (Warburg Institute: London, 1949).

Proportions, from audible to visible Objects, and apply them as shall fall fittest . . ., there will indubitably result from either, a graceful and harmonious Contentment to the Eye.[7]

It was not, in fact, suggested that architectural proportions were derived from musical harmonies, but rather that the laws of proportion were established mathematically and everywhere diffused. The universe of Platonic and Pythagorean speculation was compounded of the simpler relationships of numbers, and such a cosmos was formed within the triangle made by the square and the cube of the numbers 1, 2, 3. Also, its qualities, rhythms, and relationships were established within this framework of numbers up to 27; and if such numbers governed works of God, it was considered fitting that the works of man should be similarly constructed, that a building should be a representative, in microcosm, of the process exhibited at a larger scale in the workings of the world. In Alberti's words: "Nature is sure to act consistently and with a constant analogy in all her operations";[8] and, therefore, what is patent in music must also be so in architecture. Thus, with proportion as a projection of the harmony of the universe, its basis—both scientific and religious—was quite unassailable; and a Palladio could enjoy the satisfactions of an aesthetic believed to be entirely objective.

Le Corbusier has expressed similar convictions about proportion. Mathematics bring "des vérité réconfortantes," and "on ne quitte pas son ouvrage qu'avec la certitude d'être arrivé à la chose exacte";[9] but if it is indeed exactness which Le Corbusier seeks, within his buildings it is not the unchallengeable clarity of Palladio's volumes which one finds. It is, instead, a type of planned obscurity; and, consequently, while in the Malcontenta geometry is diffused throughout the internal volumes of the entire building, at Garches it seems only to reside in the block as a whole and in the disposition of its supports.

The theoretical position upon which Palladio's position rested broke down in the eighteenth century when proportion became a matter of individual sensibility and private inspiration;[10] and Le Corbusier, in spite of the comforts which mathematics afford him, simply in terms of his location in history can occupy no such unassailable position. Functionalism was, perhaps, a highly Positivistic attempt to reassert a scientific aesthetic which might possess the objective value of the old, and the ultimately Platonic-Aristotelian critique. But its interpretation was crude. Results may be measured in terms of process, proportions are apparently accidental and gratuitous; and it is in contradiction to this theory that Le Corbusier imposes mathematical patterns upon his buildings. These are the universal "vérités réconfortantes."

Thus, either because of or in spite of theory both architects share a common standard, a mathematical one, defined by Wren as "natural" beauty; and, within limitations of a particular program, it should therefore not be surprising that the two blocks should be of corresponding volume or that both architects should choose to make didactic advertisement of their adherence to mathematical formulae. Of the two—and, perhaps, characteristically—Le Corbusier is the more aggressive; and at Garches he carefully

7. Sir Henry Wotton, "The Elements of Architecture," in *Parallel of the Ancient Architecture with the Modern*, 3rd Ed., ed. John Evelyn (London, 1723), xv.

8. Giacomo Leoni, *Ten Books on Modern Architecture by Leon Battista Alberti, 3rd Ed.* (London, 1755), 196.

9. Le Corbusier and Pierre Jeanneret, *Oeuvre Complète 1910–1929, 3rd Ed.* (Zurich: Girsberger, 1943), 144. These remarks refer to Garches.

10. "The break away from the laws of harmonic proportion in architecture" is extensively discussed in Wittkower (see note 6), but the parallel disintegration of the Platonic-Aristotelian critical tradition is somewhat more laconically observed by Logan Pearsall Smith: "There are great youths too whose achievements one may envy; the boy David who slew Goliath and Bishop Berkeley who annihilated, at the age of twenty five, in 1710, the external world in an octavo volume; and the young David Hume, who, in 1739, by sweeping away all the props of the human understanding, destroyed for ever and ever all possibility of knowledge." Logan Pearsall Smith, *All Trivia* (London: Constable & Co., 1947), 159.

indicates his relationships by an apparatus of regulating lines and figures and by placing on the drawings of his elevations the ratio of the golden section, A : B = B : (A + B).

But, if Le Corbusier's façades are for him the primary demonstrations of the virtues of a mathematical discipline, with Palladio it would seem that the ultimate proof of his theory lies in his plan. Throughout his *Quattro libri*, Palladio consistently equips both his plans and elevations with their numerical apologetic; but the cryptic little figures which he appends to his drawings seem always to be more convincing, or at least more comprehensible, when they relate to the plan. And this is, possibly, to be understood, for in a house such as the Malcontenta the plan may be seen as an exhibition of "natural" beauty, as the pure thing, abstract and uncomplicated; but the façades are, of necessity, adulterated (though scarcely to their detriment) by an intrusion of "customary" material. The façades become complicated, their strict Platonic rationale may be ultimately vitiated by the traditional presence, in this case, of the Ionic order which possesses its own rationale and which inevitably introduces an alternative system of measurement.

The conflict between the "customary" demands of the order and a series of "natural" relationships might be assumed to be the source from which the façades of the Malcontenta derive. They are suggestive, evocative, but they are not easily or totally susceptible to mathematical regulation; and, therefore, it is again toward Palladio's plan that one reverts. Provided with explanatory two suites comprising three rooms each can be read as a progression from 3 : 4 to a 2 : 3 relationship. They are numbered 12 : 16, 16 : 16 and 16 : 24.

And here, on the part of Corbusier and Palladio, we have to recognize, if not duplicity, at least wishful thinking; but, if the ratio of 3 : 5 = 5 : 8 is only an approximation to that of the golden section, and if the ideal measurement of Palladio's rooms does not concur with what is their actual size,[11] this is to be expected and it should not be considered useful to enlarge upon these inconsistencies. Instead it should be considered much more opportune to examine Palladio's preference for the triple division and Le Corbusier's propensity to divide by four.

At the Malcontenta, as already noticed, the façades are divided vertically into three principal fields, those of the portico and the flanking walls, and horizontally the same situation prevails in the sequence, basement, *piano nobile*, attic; but at Garches, in spite of the comparable structural *parti*, it is always a situation if not of one, at least of two *or*, alternatively, of four fields of interest with which we are presented. Thus in the entrance elevation, it is a business of four and one which prevails; and, in the garden façade, this breakdown becomes a matter of four and two.

But, in both houses, there are elaborations in detail of the dominant schema which becomes complicated by its interplay with a subsidiary system. That is: it is by vertical extension into arch and vault, diagonal of roof line and pediment that Palladio modifies the geometrical asperities of his cube; and this use of the circular and pyramidal elements with the square seems both to conceal and to amplify the intrinsic severity of the volumes. However, the arch, the vault, and the pyramid are among the prerogatives of solid wall

11. For the actual rather than the ideal internal measurements of the Malcontenta see Ottavio Bertotti Scamozzi, *Les batiments et les desseins de andre palladio*, Vicenza, 1776–1783.

construction. They are among the freedoms of the traditional plan, the "*plan paralysé*"; and the introduction of arched forms and pitched roofs is a liberty which at Garches Le Corbusier is unable to allow himself. For in the frame building it is obviously not, as in the solid wall structure, the vertical planes which predominate. Rather it is the planes of floor and roof slabs; and, therefore, the quality of paralysis which Le Corbusier noticed in the plan of the solid wall structure is, to some extent, transferred in the frame building to the section. Perforation of floors, giving a certain vertical movement of space, is possible; but the sculptural quality of the building as carving has disappeared and there can be nothing of Palladio's firm sectional transmutation and modeling of volume. Instead, following the predominant planes of the slabs, in the frame building extension and elaboration must occur horizontally. In other words, free plan is exchanged for free section; but the limitations of the new system are quite as exacting as those of the old; and, as though the solid wall structure has been turned on its side, with the former complexities of section and subtleties of elevation now transposed to plan, there may be here some reason for Palladio's choice of plan and Le Corbusier's choice of elevations as being the documents, in each case, most illustrative of elementary mathematical regulation.

The spatial audacities of the Garches plan continue to thrill; but it may sometimes seem to be an interior which is acceptable to the intellect alone—to the intellect operating from within a stage vacuum. Thus there is at Garches a permanent tension between the organized and the apparently fortuitous. Conceptually, all is clear; but, sensuously, all is deeply perplexing. There are statements of a hierarchical ideal; there are counter statements of an egalitarian one. Both houses may seem to be apprehensible from without; but, from within, in the cruciform hall of the Malcontenta, there is a clue to the whole building; while, at Garches, it is never possible to stand at any point and receive a total impression. For at Garches the necessary equidistance between floor and ceiling conveys an equal importance to all parts of the volume in between; and thus the development of absolute focus becomes an arbitrary, if not an impossible, proceeding. This is the dilemma propounded by the system; and Le Corbusier responds to it. He accepts the principle of horizontal extension; thus, at Garches central focus is consistently broken up, concentration at any one point is disintegrated, and the dismembered fragments of the center become a peripheral dispersion of incident, a serial installation of interest around the extremities of the plan.

But it is now that this system of horizontal extension which is *conceptually* logical comes up against the rigid boundary of the block which, almost certainly, is felt to be *perceptually* requisite;[12] and, consequently, with horizontal extension checked, Le Corbusier is obliged to employ an opposite resource. That is, by gouging out large volumes of the block as terrace and roof garden, he introduces a contrary impulse of energy; and by opposing an explosive moment with an implosive one, by introducing inversive gestures alongside expansive ones, he again makes simultaneous use of conflicting strategies.

By its complexities, the resultant system (or symbiosis of systems) throws into intense relief the elementary, geometrical substructure of the building; and, as a sequel,

12. It is possible to suppose that the rigid boundaries of Garches were considered to be necessary. The house is presented as one of 'the four compositions' in *Oeuvre complète 1910–1929*, 189; and, in *Précisions*, 73, Le Corbusier writes of Garches: "Pour s'imposer à l'attention, pour occuper puissamment l'espace, il fallait d'abord une surface première de forme parfaite, puis une exaltation de la platitude de cette surface par l'apport de quelges saillies ou de trous faisant intervenir un mouvement avant-arrière."

the peripheral incident which substitutes for the Palladian focus can also become compounded with the inversions (of terrace and roof garden) which represent an essentially analogous development to Palladio's strategy of vertical extension.

Finally, a comparable process to that which occurs in plan takes place also in the elevations, where there is the same regular diffusion of value and irregular development of points of concentration; and here, with the horizontal windows conveying an equality to both the center and verge of the façades, a disintegration of focus which is never complete causes a brisk oscillation of attention. Here, as in the plan, there is nothing residual, nothing passive, nothing slow moving; and the extremities of the block, by this means, acquire an energetic clarity and tautness, as though they were trying to restrain the peripheral incident from flying out of the block altogether.

A detailed comparison is less easy to sustain between the two houses which, initially, seemed to invite their linking together: the Savoye House and the Villa Rotonda; and, conceivably, this is because neither of these buildings is so entirely condensed in its structure and its emotional impact as are, respectively, the earlier Garches and the later Malcontenta. The Savoye House and the Rotonda are both more famous; but they are also, in each case, more obviously Platonic and easy to take. Possibly this is because they are both in the round; and that, therefore, what is concentrated in two fronts at Garches and the Malcontenta is here diffused through four, resulting in far greater geniality of external effect. But, if there is a noticeable easiness and lack of tension to be found in these façades, there are analogous developments to those in the other houses. Such are Palladio's concern, both in plan and elevation, with central emphasis and Le Corbusier's determined dispersal of focus. At Poissy, just possibly, the complicated volumes of the upper roof garden replace the Palladian pitched roof and cupola; and again, just possibly, Palladio's four projecting loggias are subsumed within the block as the enclosed terrace which, alternatively, as the dominant element of the *piano nobile*, could also be considered to correspond to the domed salon of the Rotonda.

But, symbolically and in the sphere of "customary" beauty, Palladio's and Le Corbusier's buildings are in different worlds. Palladio sought complete clarity of plan and the most lucid organization of conventional elements based on symmetry as the most memorable form of order, and mathematics as the supreme sanction in the world of forms. In his own mind his work was essentially that of adaptation, the adaptation of the ancient house; and, at the back of his mind were always the great halls of the Imperial thermae and such buildings as Hadrian's villa at Tivoli. He had several schemes of archaeological reconstruction of Greek and Roman domestic buildings, based on Vitruvius and Pliny, incorporating elements which in Greek and Roman practice would have been found only in public buildings, but which he regarded as general. Indeed, Rome for him was still supremely alive; and, if the ancients had adapted the temple from the house, their large scale planning was, no doubt, similarly reflective.

Notoriously, Le Corbusier has an equal reverence for mathematics and he would appear also, sometimes, to be tinged with a comparable historicism. For his plans he seems to find at least one source in those ideals of *convenance* and *commodité* displayed in the ingenious planning of the Rococo hotel, the background of a social life at once more amplified and intimate. The French, until recently, possessed an unbroken tradition of this sort of planning; and, therefore, one may often discover in a Beaux Arts utilization of an irregular site, elements which if they had not preceded Le Corbusier might seem to be curiously reminiscent of his own highly suave vestibules and boudoirs. Le Corbusier admires the Byzantine and the anonymous architecture of the Mediterranean world; and there is also present with him a purely French delight in the more overt aspects of mechanics. The little pavilion on the roof at Garches is, at the same time, a temple of love and the bridge of a ship. The most complex architectural volumes are fitted with running water.

Geometrically, both architects may be said to have approached something of the Platonic archetype of the ideal villa to which the fantasy of the Virgilian dream might be supposed to relate; and the realization of an idea which is represented by the house as a cube could also be presumed to lend itself very readily to the purposes of Virgilian dreaming. For here is set up the conflict between the absolute and the contingent, the abstract and the natural; and the gap between the ideal world and the too human exigencies of realization here receives its most pathetic presentation. The bridging must be as competent and compelling as the construction of a well-executed fugue; and, if it may be charged, as at the Malcontenta with almost religious seriousness, or, as at Garches, imbued with sophisticated and witty allusion, its successful organization is an intellectual feat which reconciles the mind to what may be some fundamental discrepancies in the program.

As a constructor of architectural fugues, Palladio is the convinced classicist with a sixteenth century repertory of well-humanized forms; and he translates this received material with a passion and a high seriousness fitting to the continued validity that he finds it to possess. The reference to the Pantheon in the superimposed pediments of the Malcontenta, to the thermae in its cruciform salon, the ambiguity, profound in both idea and form, in the equivocal conjunction of temple front and domestic block; these are charged with meaning, both for what they are and what they signify; and their impression is poignant. By such apparatus the ancient house is not recreated, but something far more significant is achieved: a creative nostalgia evokes a manifestation of mythical power in which the Roman and the ideal are equated.

By contrast Le Corbusier is, in some ways, the most catholic and ingenious of eclectics. The orders, the Roman references, were the traditional architectural clothing of authority; and, if it is hard for the modern architect to be quite so emphatic about any particular civilization as was Palladio about the Roman, with Le Corbusier there is always an element of wit suggesting that the historical (or contemporary) reference has remained a quotation between inverted commas, possessing always the double value of the quotation, the associations of both old and new context. In spite of his admiration for the Acropolis and Michelangelo, the world of high classical Mediterranean culture on which Palladio drew so expressively is largely closed for Le Corbusier. The ornamental adjuncts of humanism, the emblematic representations of the moral virtues, the loves of the Gods and the lives of the Saints have lost their former monopoly; and as a result, while allusion at the Malcontenta is concentrated and direct, at Garches it is dissipated and inferential. Within the one cube the performance attempts the Roman; but, within the other, no such exclusive cultural ideal is entertained. Instead, as the sponsors of his virtuosity, Le Corbusier largely selects a variety of hitherto undiscriminated phenomena. He selects the casual incidents of Paris, or Istanbul, or wherever it may be; aspects of the fortuitously picturesque, of the mechanical, of objects conceived to be typical, of whatever might seem to represent the present and the usable past; and all those items, while transformed by their new context, retain their original implications which signify maybe Platonic ideality, maybe Rococo intimacy, maybe mechanical precision, maybe a process of natural selection. That is, one is able to seize hold of all these references as something known; but, in spite of the new power with which they become invested, they are only transiently provocative. Unlike Palladio's forms, there is nothing final about any of their possible-relationships; and their rapprochement would seem to be affected by the artificial emptying of the cube in which they find themselves located, when the senses are confounded by what is apparently arbitrary and the intellect is more than convinced by the intuitive knowledge that, despite all to the contrary, here problems have been both recognized and answered and that here there is a reasonable order.

The neo-Palladian villa, at its best, became the picturesque object in the English park and Le Corbusier has become the source of innumerable pastiches and of tediously amusing exhibition techniques; but it is the magnificently realized quality of the originals which one rarely finds in the works of neo-Palladians and exponents of 'le style Corbu.' These distinctions scarcely require insistence; and no doubt it should only be sententiously suggested that, in the case of the derivative works, it is perhaps an adherence to 'rules' which has lapsed.

Though a parallel of Schinkel with late Corbu might not be so rewarding as the comparison of early Corbu and Palladio, much the same arguments as those surfacing in this article might quite well be found developing themselves if, for the Villa Malcontenta, one were to substitute the Berlin Altes Museum and, for Garches, the Palace of the Assembly at Chandigarh. Illustrations might suffice to make the point: a conventional classical *parti* equipped with traditional *poché* and much the same *parti* distorted and made to present a competitive variety of local gestures—perhaps to be understood as compensations for traditional *poché*.

A criticism which begins with approximate configurations and which then proceeds to identify differences, which seeks to establish how the same general motif can be transformed according to the logic (or the compulsion) of specific analytical (or stylistic) strategies, is presumably Wölflinian in origin; and its limitations should be obvious. It cannot seriously deal with questions of iconography and content; it is perhaps over symmetrical; and, because it is so dependent on close analysis, if protracted, it can only impose enormous strain upon both its consumer *and* producer. However, if one would not like to imagine oneself confronted with the results of an intensive critical workout on the *matériel* provided by the Altes Museum and the Palace of the Assembly, this reservation should not be understood as depreciating the limited value of such an exercise. For the two buildings incite comparison and can also, both of them, stimulate further parallel with certain productions of Mies van der Rohe. But, if normal intuition might suggest so much, a Wölflinian style of critical exercise (though painfully belonging to a period *c.* 1900) might still possess the merit of appealing primarily to what is thereby, making the minimum of pretences to erudition and the least possible number of references outside itself. It might, in other words, possess the merits of accessibility—for those who are willing to accept the fatigue.

Writing and Discussion Questions

ANALYSIS

1. What was Palladio arguing for and against? What excerpt/quotation best represents this?
2. What was Le Corbusier arguing for and against? What excerpt/quotation best represents this?
3. What was Rowe arguing for and against? What excerpt/quotation best represents this?

SYNTHESIS

1. Regarding concepts of proportion and organization, discuss one major difference regarding Palladio's, Le Corbusier's, and Rowe's texts.
2. Regarding concepts of proportion and organization, discuss one primary commonality regarding Palladio's, Le Corbusier's, and Rowe's texts.

SELF-REFLECTION

1. For each of the texts, discuss a major issue with which you most agree and most disagree; reflect upon why you hold these views.
2. Select a recent design project, or a current project on which you are working. Discuss the characteristics of the project in regards to proportion, spatial organization, and inhabitation, in light of the discussion and texts introduced in this chapter. What attitudes regarding proportion, spatial organization, and inhabitation does your work illustrate?

PROSPECTION

1. Select one of the texts listed in the bibliography for this chapter; locate and read it. To what degree is that text and the attitudes it represents still relevant to architecture today and in the near future?
2. What is the role of proportion and organization in architecture today? Are proportion and organization necessary for human inhabitation and functioning; are they compositional strategies of drawing and design; some combination of these; or something else? In other words, if a fourth text were added to this chapter, what would the argument be?

Other Readings on Proportion and Organization

Bachelard, Gaston. *The Poetics of Space* (Boston: Beacon Press, 1994). First published in 1958.

Ching, Francis D. K. *Architecture: Form, Space, and Order, 3rd Ed.* (Hoboken: John Wiley & Sons, 2007).

Doczi, Gyorgy. *The Power of Limits: Proportional Harmonies in Nature, Art, and Architecture* (Boston: Shambhala Publications, 1981).

Elam, Kimberly. *Geometry of Design: Studies in Proportion and Composition* (New York: Princeton Architectural Press, 2001).

Ingersoll, Richard, and Cristina Tartari. "Architecture without People," *Lotus International,* 124 (2005): 94–103.

Kraftl, Peter, and Peter Adey. "Architecture/Affect/Inhabitation: Geographies of Being-in Buildings." *Annals of the Association of American Geographers,* 98 (2008): 213–231.

Lefebvre, Henri. *The Production of Space,* trans. Donald Nicholson-Smith (Malden: Blackwell Publishing, 1991). First published in 1974.

Padovan, Richard. *Proportion: Science, Philosophy, Architecture* (New York: Taylor & Francis, 1999).

Seamon, David, and Robert Mugerauer, eds. *Dwelling, Place & Environment: Towards a Phenomenology of Person and World* (New York: Columbia University Press, 1982).

Tavernor, Robert. "Measure, Metre, Irony: Reuniting Pure Mathematics with Architecture," *ARQ: Architectural Research Quarterly,* 6 (2002): 67–[75].

Part 2

DIALECTICAL READINGS in ARCHITECTURE: SITE

Chapter 9

CONTEXT and BUILDING

FIGURE 9.1

Photograph of the steps, entry, street, and façade of the Ara Pacis Museum, Rome, Italy (1996–2006). Architect: Richard Meier.

FIGURE 9.2

Photograph of Piazza Ducale and the façade of the Vigevano Cathedral, Vigevano, Italy (ca. 1532–1612: plan; ca. 1673–1680: façade). Architects: Antonio da Lonate (main cathedral) and Juan Caramuel y Lobkowitz (façade).

INTRODUCTORY DISCUSSION

1. Of the two images above, which better represents the concept of "contextual" architecture? Why?

2. What are the various definitions and connotations of the term "context" in architecture? For example, how is "context" similar or different from terms like "site," "situation," "location," etc.

3. How is or is not "context" an appropriate concept or term in architecture today?

274

Introduction

In 2000, the world's population was slightly more than 6 billion. It is anticipated that by 2025 there will be more than 8 billion people living on Earth. Growth will be highest in less-developed nations. Niger, Yemen, Somalia, Uganda, and Mali, respectively, will experience the fastest rates of growth.[1] This will be coupled with a tremendous growth of urban environments. In 1900, only 13 percent of the world's population lived in urban areas. In 2005, the world's population reached the tipping point, as 49 percent of people lived in urban areas. As of 2010, for the first time in world history, more people lived in urban areas than nonurban areas.[2] Existing cities will be transformed; new cities and towns will emerge. Urban planners, designers, and architects will gain increasing importance, and they will face a wide array of challenges resulting from rapid economic, technological, or population growth. Some challenges and responses will be new, while others will have historical precedents.

During the first half of the twentieth century, for instance, Europe experienced vast social, economic, technological, and political changes as a consequence of the first and second World Wars. Architecture and urban design were not exempt. Many European cities—such as, Rotterdam, Hamburg, Dresden, Warsaw, and London—as well as cities in the Asian Pacific, suffered major destruction during WWII, which resulted in widespread homelessness. In the decades following the War, northern and western European countries experienced major population booms. Coupled together, these circumstances led to pressing questions about urban reconstruction, especially strategies for housing the displaced and growing middle class. A prime example was Le Corbusier's Unité d'Habitation, a multi-unit housing design scheme utilized in both France and Germany in the late 1940s and early 1950s.

The Unité d'Habitation is an extension and transformation of Le Corbusier's earlier writings on urban planning, such as *The Radiant City: Elements of a Doctrine of Urbanism to Be Used as the Basis of Our Machine-age Civilization* of the mid-1930s, the *original text* for this chapter. Le Corbusier viewed architecture and urban design as a means of organizing society. The design for the Radiant City reordered both the infrastructure and

1. United Nations, "World Population Prospects: The 2008 Revision, Highlights," Working Paper No. ESA/P/WP.210 (United Nations: New York, 2009).

2. United Nations, Department of Economic and Social Affairs, Population Division, *Urban Population, Development and the Environment, 2007* (United Nations: New York, 2008).

social hierarchy of traditional cities. It was an attempt to increase economic vitality, worker productivity, convenience, and access to recreation, and to foster, in the words of Le Corbusier, "the liberty of the individual." One primary aspect of the design was the separation of vehicular and pedestrian routes. A second strategy was the use of *pilotis* (columns at the ground floor) and elevated streets to make a park-like "ground surface [that] is left entirely free." Le Corbusier went on further to describe the distribution, size, and interior organization of the apartments and other supporting functions. Le Corbusier's scheme relied heavily on classification and the separation of various functions. This proved to be one of the greatest critiques of Le Corbusier's concepts, in particular, and Modernist city planning, in general.

One of the most notable criticisms came from Jane Jacobs in *The Death and Life of Great American Cities*, the *reflective text* for this chapter, published in 1961. Jacobs contended that Modernist urban planning principles contributed to "delinquency, vandalism and general social hopelessness" in the neighborhoods of many American cities, such as East Harlem in New York City. Jacobs stated further that Le Corbusier's Radiant City "tells . . . nothing but lies." The most notable difference between the principles promoted by Le Corbusier and those advanced by Jacobs is in regards to the distribution of uses. Whereas Le Corbusier sought to separate uses, Jacobs asserted the importance of an "intricate and close-grained diversity of uses"—traffic, housing, employment, leisure, etc.—"that give each other constant mutual support, both economically and socially." In addition, in contrast to Le Corbusier's personal visioning of cities, Jacobs utilized both case studies and scientific data to articulate successful and unsuccessful urban planning and design strategies, including the accommodation of automobiles.

In his 1971 essay "Contextualism: Urban Ideals and Deformations," the *philosophical text* for this chapter, Tom Schumacher identified two different urban strategies: (1) the "city-in-the-park" and (2) the "traditional city." The city-in-the-park, according to Schumacher, is exemplified by Le Corbusier's Radiant City, a series of object-buildings, predominantly towers, set in a park-like landscape, while the traditional city, inversely, is composed of a network of streets and squares. In the former, the building volumes are dominant; in the latter, the public spaces are dominant. Schumacher noted the economic, social, and ideological differences between the two, but proposed a middle ground might be viable and necessary. Schumacher suggested that this might be accomplished by deemphasizing the Modernist assertion that "form follows function" and distorting idealized programmatic building types to better conform to spatial and organizational "pressures" of the surrounding context. Schumacher's concept of "contextualism" was less about what the surrounding buildings look like and more about the hierarchy between buildings and exterior public space, where exterior public space is given priority over building form and interior space.

The debate about city planning principles and strategies remains unresolved, especially in capitalist economies. In addition to the aforementioned debates about public space vs. building form and social health vs. economic vitality, a number of other issues make urban design and planning in existing and emerging capitalist societies enormously complex: public vs. private funding, individual vs. collective interests, single-site vs. urban master-planning projects, etc. Architects of future cities will be required to provide answers to these debates.

Original Text

LE CORBUSIER, EXCERPTS FROM *THE RADIANT CITY*.

First Published in 1935

These studies are based on an unalterable, indisputable, essential foundation, the only true basis for any attempt at social organization: *individual liberty*. Where the planning of collective life threatens to demolish the liberty of the individual, we must respect it; at a time when the consequences of machine-age evolution seem daily more likely to destroy it, we must revive it; it is our aim, in this rich new era, to create an even greater measure of individual liberty now that modern technology is providing us with new and fabulously powerful means of progress.

This present work is not the development of an arbitrary structure, an exposition of some idealistic system, or pure speculation on the part of a brain that has willfully set itself above the struggle of life. The ideas it presents are all derived from that struggle: they are the products of our age. Their spiritual direction is that of our age because they have been developed from the actual, carefully observed, tangible, material conditions of the world we live in. . . .

For the task before us is to satisfy men's hearts.

Every day the anxiety and depression of modern life spring up afresh: the city is swelling, the city is filling up. The city simply builds itself anew on top of itself: the old houses towered in a cliff at the edge of the streets; the new houses still tower in new cliffs along the same streets. All the houses are on streets, the street is the basic organ of the city, and the house is the individual, infinitely repeated mold. The street becomes appalling, noisy, dusty, dangerous; automobiles can scarcely do more than crawl along it; the pedestrians, herded together on the sidewalks, get in each other's way, bump into each other, zigzag from side to side; the whole scene is like a glimpse of purgatory. Some of the buildings are office buildings; but how is it possible to work well with so little light and so much noise? Elsewhere, the buildings are residential; but how is it possible to breathe properly in those torrid canyons of summer heat; how can anyone risk bringing up children in that air tainted with dust and soot, in those streets so full of mortal peril? How can anyone achieve the serenity indispensable to life, how can anyone relax, or ever give a cry of joy, or laugh, or breathe, or feel drunk with sunlight? How can anyone *live*! The houses are cliffs facing one another across the street. Worse still, behind the houses that face the street these are more houses still. They are built around courtyards. Where is the light? What do I see out of my window? Other windows, only six or ten yards away, with people behind them looking back at me. Where is freedom here? There is no freedom for men in this present age, only slavery. A slavery to which they themselves consent, and which is no longer even confined within set limits. To live, to laugh, to be master in one's own home, to open one's eyes to the light of day, to the light of the sun, to look out on green leaves and blue sky. No! Nothing of all that for the man who lives in a city. . . .

More recently, there has been a reaction, one made possible by the railroad. The laborer, the clerk and the shopgirl have been whisked out of the city along steel rails. Like an exploding shell, the city has shot out in all directions, pushing its tentacles out as far as the eye can see. At dawn, then again in the evening, the laborer, the clerk and the shopgirl sit in their railroad cars and are pulled along the rails. Their little house are surrounded by greenery, away in the country. What could be nicer? They can really enjoy themselves—every Sunday. That's only one day out of seven, but never mind. So on Sunday, there they are, all alone in their little green nests: their boy friends, their girl friends, live on the opposite side of town, in another suburb. So on Sundays, the laborer, the clerk and the shopgirl still tick off the hours without living and without laughter. Or rather, there they are back in their railroad cars riding those steel rails again. Suburbs? Suburbs are broken, dislocated limbs! The city has been torn apart and scattered in meaningless fragments across the countryside. What is the point of life in such places? How are people to live in them?

Suburban life is a despicable delusion entertained by a society stricken with blindness!

. . .

A readjustment has become necessary.

. . .

We have to look ahead, at what must be built.

. . .

The architect who is attempting to build a house (a home) for any member of mankind today must be guided by a modern consciousness. That same modern consciousness must also be the basis of all our proposals for the reorganization of the great cities in which we are to live together in our millions. . . .

A solitary man living in his solitary house is nothing; he does not exist. Men in a city are legion; there are millions of them. Architecture, having accomplished its own revolution, can no longer do anything to help modern society; it is doomed to stagnation as long as it has no program (official social status) and no environment (its precise urban function must be formulated). Cities are made by planning, and architecture can do nothing without such plans. For the houses it creates are in cities; they are the cities themselves, as we shall see. . . .

The problem is to create the Radiant City. The Radiant City already exists on paper. And when once a technological product has been designed on paper (calculations and working drawings), *it does exist.* . . . We are only waiting for a "*yes*" from a government with the will and the determination to see it through!

I shall explain the plan for this city, and the explanation will be neither literary nor an approximation. It will be technical and rigorously precise.

The general characteristics of the plan are as follows: the city (a large city, a capital) is much less spread out than the present one; the distances within it are therefore shorter, which means more rest and more energy available for work every day. There are no suburbs or dormitory towns; this means an immediate solution to the transportation crisis that has been forced upon us by the paradox of the city + garden cities.

The garden city is a pre-machine-age utopia.

The population density of the new city will be from three to six times greater than the idealistic, ruinous and inoperative figures recommended by urban authorities stilt imbued with romantic ideology. This new intensification of population density thus becomes the financial justification for our enterprise: *it increases the value of the ground.*

The pedestrian never meets a vehicle inside the city. The mechanical transportation network is an entirely new organ, a separate entity. The ground level (the *earth*) belongs entirely to the pedestrian.

The "street" as we know it now has disappeared. All the various sporting activities, take place directly outside people's homes, in the midst of parks—trees, lawns, lakes. The city is entirely green; *it is a Green City.* Not one inhabitant occupies a room without sunlight; everyone looks out on trees and sky.

The keystone of the theory behind this city is the *liberty of the individual.* Its aim is to create respect for that liberty, to bring it to an authentic fruition, to destroy our present slavery. The restitution of every individual's personal liberty. Waste will also have its throat cut. The cost of living will come down. The new city will break the shackles of poverty in which the old city has been keeping us chained. . . .

The city dweller, as a pedestrian, must have the entire ground surface of the city at his disposal. The ground surface of the city is made up of parks. The city is one uninterrupted park. *No pedestrian ever meets an automobile*; the automobiles are there of course, but in the air, passing by behind screens of foliage. (This will be gone into later.)

The city dweller who owns an automobile will be able to keep it in a garage at the foot of his elevator.

Anyone who wishes to take a taxi, wherever he may be in the residential district, need never walk more than 100 meters to find one. And when he returns home, whatever the hour of the day or night, he will be taken up to his apartment by specially trained elevator operators.

From the door of his elevator, the longest distance that he will have to walk to his own front door will be less than 100 meters, along a corridor that will be *an indoor street*. The outdoor streets of the city (for traffic) will be curtailed to an astonishing degree. As we shall see shortly. Most of the city's streets will now be *inside the buildings*. There will be 12 or 15 of them, one on top of the other, the highest being 47 meters above ground level. The policeman, if he is still needed, will be able to say goodbye forever to his old beat in the heat of the sun or the rain, battered by storms and bustling crowds: he will now be employed on the indoor streets, *streets that actually run inside the houses.*

2,700 people will use one front door. Though in fact, if one looks at it another way, the idea of the house will have lost its present form. People will live in apartment houses with no breaks between the units, a ribbon of housing winding in an unbroken pattern across the city. The interior streets will be inside the ribbons, the roads outside. And wherever it is convenient, the roads will cross the lines of apartment buildings. The houses will not form obstructions at ground level because they are built up on pilotis. The ground surface is left entirely free. And, as I have already mentioned, the longest horizontal distance along an inside street from the door of any elevator to the furthest apartment door is 100 meters. Once over the threshold of his apartment, the city dweller will find himself in a self-contained, *soundproofed* cell. The apartment will be impervious to all outside noise; even a hermit in the depths of a forest could not be more cut off from other men. This is a new architectural fact made possible by the new science of acoustic isolation. . . .

And once inside his home, this same city dweller, through the sheet of glass constitutes one entire wall of the apartment, can look out on a magnificent vista parks, of sky, of space and light and sun, stretching out below him (and I am talking about the average worker, not about millionaires).

Each occupant has 14 square meters of floor space at his disposal. . . .

We shall also be able to build special nurseries for very young children outside the apartment houses, actually in the parks; though they will be *directly* connected to the apartment unit in which the parents live by a corridor sheltered from the elements. These nurseries will be surrounded by greenery. They will be run by qualified nurses and supervised by doctors   security – selection – scientific child-rearing.

The schools too will be outside the apartment houses, set in the midst of the parks. For each pair of apartment units (one on each side of a double elevator shaft, each of which will be used by 2,700 people) there will be a kindergarten for children between the ages of 3 and 6, then a primary school nearby for children between the ages of 7 and 14. The schools will be reached by an avenue running through the park for a distance of from 50 to 100 meters.

The sports grounds will be at the foot of the apartment houses: soccer, basketball, tennis, playgrounds, etc. . . . walks, shady avenues and lawns. Each residential unit of 400 by 400 meters will have a swimming pool from 100 to 150 meters in length.

For rainy days, there are the covered playgrounds extending the whole length of the apartment buildings. Paths and walks everywhere. Limitless opportunities for walking. It will be possible to cross the entire residential area from end to end, in any direction, either entirely in the open air or entirely sheltered from sun and rain. It will be as though the houses have been surrounded by a new Bois de Boulogne.

And that is still not all: on the roof gardens, there will be sandy beaches for the occupants to sunbathe on in magnificently pure air 50 meters above ground level. And not little beaches either; they will be from 18 to 20 meters wide and several kilometers in length. Spaced out along these beaches there will also be pools and open-air hydrotherapy establishments. Beds of flowers and shrubbery too. All made freely available by modern scientific techniques: flowers, trees, shrubs all around the sand and the lawns on the rooftops—(trees, flowers and grass all grow remarkably well on roof gardens)—tennis courts, games of all sorts, etc. . . .

But now we come to the keystone of modern housing methods: directly above the pilotis of the apartment houses, and running all along them for several kilometers, there will be a whole floor devoted to the provision of communal services (Note added in 1963: the communal services have been moved up to the seventh floor—halfway up the height of each block).

What about delivery trucks? Obviously food supplies and consumer goods will have to be brought into the residential areas. So where are the service roads for them? Under the raised highways. How do they reach the buildings? At certain given points where unloading bays are provided for them. These unloading bays occur regularly along the line of buildings, each one under the aegis of a separate catering section. There will be one unloading bay for every 3,000 to 4,000 residents; and a separate catering department for every 3,000 to 4,000 residents likewise. Each catering manager will thus be assured of a very sizeable clientele. And there will be a cooperative organization to see that the profits from this catering business will be used for the benefit of the customers themselves. Each catering section will have at its disposal an area of floorspace 18 meters wide and from 200 to 400 meters in length.

What functions will these catering departments perform? Primarily, they will to the storing of incoming food supplies in storage rooms and deep-freeze rooms. These foodstuffs will arrive directly from processing plants or from the country, from the breeder, the hunter, the fisherman, the market gardener, the winegrower. They will be sold at low retail prices reflecting the elimination of the middleman. . . . What about buyers and representatives? All done away with! And also done away with, at the same time will be the insane chaos of carts and trucks thundering daily into the central markets of today from suburbs or the railroad stations. No more individual delivery trucks plying between the central market and the butcher's shop, or the small dairy, or small grocer's, etc. No more traffic in from the suburbs and out again. No further need for the housewife to trudge out shopping in the rain, then trudge back again with all that heavy shopping. . . . I repeat: new techniques make social reorganization essential. . . .

We must refuse to afford even the slightest consideration to *what is*: to the mess we are in now. There is no solution to be found there. We should simply end up in the same state as our present city authorities, who are just as clever as we are and infinitely better informed. . . . Our city authorities, having been given the task of "keeping things going" from day to day, have been similarly petrified by the effects of this immense and age-old society of ours which is now dying, which is burning, which is crumbling away, which is dragging and will continue to drag with it into disaster all those who persist in clinging to its ruins. We must tear ourselves away. . . . The only thing to do is to take a sheet of clean paper and to begin work on the calculations, the figures, the realities of life as it is today:

1. Classification of speeds. Normal biological speeds must never be forced into contact with the high speeds of modern vehicles.
2. Creation of one-way traffic. No *high-speed* vehicle should ever be subjected to possibility of meeting or crossing the path of other moving objects. "One-way traffic" should become an automatic element of high-speed locomotion put into universal effect (and should not merely imply innumerable quantities of round signs stuck up on posts with white letters against a red background); crossroads (traffic meeting on the same level) should be eliminated.
3. High-speed vehicles must all be employed for specifically designated purposes.
4. The functions of heavy vehicles.
5. The liberation of pedestrians.

Classification according to speed: high-speed vehicles (traveling at 80 km. an hour) should never meet pedestrians traveling at 4 km. an hour: men, women, old men, children, people rushing to work, people out for a stroll, alone, with others, in groups, in processions, watching where they are going, dreaming, etc. . .

The street has become a demon beyond our control. DEADLY DANGER on every side as soon as we step over our thresholds. The newspapers have instituted a new column: TRAFFIC ACCIDENTS—a *daily* list of the injured and the dead.

And all over the world, in the United States (San Francisco, Chicago, New York), in Germany (Berlin, Cologne), in England (London), in France (Paris), solutions are being suggested. And all the solutions come to the same thing: SEPARATION OF TRAFFIC ACCORDING TO SPEED. *The pedestrian, from now on, will be confined to raised walks built up above street level, while the traffic lanes remain at their present ground level.*

Madness!!! . . .

In the plans for the Radiant City, I have proposed that the pedestrian should quite simply be given sole possession of the entire ground surface of the city, the e-n-t-i-r-e ground surface, as though he were living in the heart of the countryside. And I have put the roads up in the air, 5 meters above ground level.

NO PEDESTRIAN WILL EVER AGAIN MEET A HIGH-SPEED VEHICLE.

Creation of one-way traffic. . . .

As I stated, explained and proved in *Précisions:* traffic is a river; traffic can be thought of as obeying the same laws as rivers do.

People will say: "That's easily said! But all your intersections are right angles. What about the infinite variations (excessively acute or obtuse angles, crossroads, multiple intersections) that constitute *the reality of our cities*?" But that's precisely the point: *I eliminate all those things. That is my starting point.* With the high-speed traffic of today we are obliged to take that as our starting point, otherwise we shall never get anywhere. *. . . I insist on right-angled intersections. . . .*

Assignation of specific aims to high-speed vehicles.

a) To transport loads quickly from the door of one apartment house to the door another.

b) To be immediately available for use at all points throughout the city.

From one door to another. Are there a great many front doors in the city? In city as it is today, alas, yes. . . . Given such conditions, the automobile problem is quite intractable; the front doors *are all side by side*—a door every 10 or 14 meters. The automobile ought to stop right in front of any given door; it ought to be able to stop *in front of all the doors. Which means that the traffic lane run directly alongside all those doors; which means that it is directly beneath the houses; which means that the houses open out onto the traffic lane.* And that is what we can no longer tolerate. . . . The present idea street must be abolished: DEATH OF THE STREET! DEATH OF THE STREET!

In the Radiant City, one door provides access and egress for 2,700 residents. It is not merely a door, therefore, but also a *port.* A harbor for automobiles to drive into in front of each door. The automobile leaves the main traffic lane (which is a steadily flowing river of vehicles) and enters the appropriate auto-port. Instead of 75 doors opening onto a street, there is *only one door, well away from the street.*

The street has disappeared in fact. It has been replaced by the highway with its unbroken flow of traffic. *No vehicle ever parks on the highway.* A motionless vehicle on the side of the traffic lane would create a bottleneck in the flow, paralyze the rest of the traffic. But what possible cause could a vehicle have to stop in this case? None. *The highway is inaccessible on foot.* Pedestrians cannot leave the natural ground level of the city (the parks) except by means of the elevator that will take them up to the auto-port platforms (a maximum walk of 100 meters) *on which all vehicles are parked.* The pedestrian walks out of the apartment house elevators straight into the automobile parking lot *which is outside his front door. . . .*

In the residential areas, these airborne highways are 12, 16 and 24 meters in width.

Let us take a look at them in cross-section: each highway has two lanes with a thin median wall between the two lanes: jockeying for position, violent and dangerous attempts at overtaking are things of the past. The auto-port, facing the main door used by the 2,700 occupants, is on the same level. Underneath it is the garage for private cars belonging to the residents of the apartment house. Directly beneath the main door into the apartment building there is a similar door opening out onto the parks. This is the entrance for pedestrians into the main hall of the catering section.

Through this lower door for pedestrians only, the occupants of the apartments have access to a direct and yet sinuous network of pedestrian walks criss-crossing diagonally and orthogonally at the same time. Where does this fluid network of paths lead to? *Everywhere* in the city, *by the shortest route*. The pedestrian is able to take the most direct route to any part of the city, on foot. The paths that make up this fluid network are slightly sinuous, but only slightly: in fact, the pedestrians' diagonal and orthogonal networks are direct routes. The sinuosity is there only in order to provide a certain charm, an element of pleasure, a feeling of being out for a stroll. . . .

These enclosures reserved for the pedestrian, all measuring 400 by 400 meters, are linked together by underground passages as wide as you like, pleasant to walk through, bathed in light. These enclosures are the parks. Within the parks are the schools and the sports grounds. We walk along beside a swimming pool 100 meters in length and designed in the shape of a natural lake; on one side it is bordered by a sandy beach; at one point, curving away from the main body of water and forming a tranquil bay, there is a paddling place for the younger children. Then there are the tennis courts, the running tracks, the soccer fields. From time to time we glimpse the graceful silhouette of a highway amongst the foliage of the trees. . . .

In the Radiant City, the streetcar has regained its right to existence (whereas in city as it is today, the streetcar is a critical cause of disturbance). Here, they run on their rails at ground level, to the left and right of the service roads under the highways. There are stops beside every underground passage. At these points, there are breaks on the park fences where shelters for waiting passengers have been provided. The bus no longer be needed in the Radiant City. For though the bus is the most marvelous adaptable form of mass transport for *cities in chaos* (Paris in particular), in an *ordered* city, the streetcar, which is much less costly, will regain its pre-eminence, provided it is subjected to certain improvements. . . .

So the classification of the various vehicles has been accomplished: pedestrians, cars, trucks, streetcars. The street no longer runs alongside the houses; the houses no longer cliffs overlooking a street. Man as he should be has returned to his norm: he lives *on the earth*; when he walks, he walks with his feet on the ground. The life-giving joy of the trees, of the flowers, of lawns, of the sight of a wide-open sky, of birdsong, rustling leaves and a delightful calm, these are the gifts that careful calculations scientific plans can confer on us. . . .

We have ceased being animals hunted down through a desert of stone. Man's own imminent death in the Great City has been replaced by the *death of the street.* An improvement!

Reflective Text

JANE JACOBS, EXCERPTS FROM *THE DEATH AND LIFE OF GREAT AMERICAN CITIES*.

First Published in 1961

This . . . is an attack on current city planning and rebuilding. It is also, and mostly, an attempt to introduce new principles of city planning and rebuilding, different and even opposite from those now taught in everything from schools of architecture and planning to the Sunday supplements and women's magazines. My attack is not based on quibbles about rebuilding methods or hair-splitting about fashions in design. It is an attack, rather, on the principles and aims that have shaped modern, orthodox city planning and rebuilding.

In setting forth different principles, I shall mainly be writing about common, ordinary things: for instance, what kinds of city streets are safe and what kinds are not; why some city parks are marvelous and others are vice traps and death traps; why some slums stay slums and other slums regenerate themselves even against financial and official opposition; what makes downtowns shift their centers; what, if anything, is a city neighborhood, and what jobs, if any, neighborhoods in great cities do. In short, I shall be writing about how cities work in real life, because this is the only way to learn what principles of planning and what practices in rebuilding can promote social and economic vitality in cities, and what practices and principles will deaden these attributes.

There is a wistful myth that if only we had enough money to spend—the figure is usually put at a hundred billion dollars—we could wipe out all our slums in ten years, reverse decay in the great, dull, gray belts that were yesterday's and day-before-yesterday's suburbs, anchor the wandering middle class and its wandering tax money, and perhaps even solve the traffic problem.

But look what we have built with the first several billions: Low-income projects that become worse centers of delinquency, vandalism and general social hopelessness than the slums they were supposed to replace. Middle-income housing projects which are truly marvels of dullness and regimentation, sealed against any buoyancy or vitality of city life. Luxury housing projects that mitigate their inanity, or try to, with a vapid vulgarity. Cultural centers that are unable to support a good bookstore. Civic centers that are avoided by everyone but bums, who have fewer choices of loitering place than others. Commercial centers that are lackluster imitations of standardized suburban chain-store shopping. Promenades that go from no place to nowhere and have no promenaders. Expressways that eviscerate great cities. This is not the rebuilding of cities. This is the sacking of cities.

Under the surface, these accomplishments prove even poorer than their poor pretenses. They seldom aid the city areas around them, as in theory they are supposed to. These amputated areas typically develop galloping gangrene. To house people in this planned fashion, price tags are fastened on the population, and each sorted-out chunk of price-tagged populace lives in growing suspicion and tension against the surrounding city. When two or more such hostile islands are juxtaposed the result is called "a balanced neighborhood." Monopolistic shopping centers and monumental cultural centers cloak, under the public relations hoohaw, the subtraction of commerce, and of culture too, from the intimate and casual life of cities. . . .

Cities are an immense laboratory of trial and error, failure and success, in city building and city design. This is the laboratory in which city planning should have been learning and forming and testing its theories. Instead the practitioners and teachers of this discipline (if such it can be called) have ignored the study of success and failure in real life, have been incurious about the reasons for unexpected success, and are guided instead by principles derived from the behavior and appearance of towns, suburbs, tuberculosis sanatoria, fairs, and imaginary dream cities—from anything but cities themselves.

If it appears that the rebuilt portions of cities and the endless new developments spreading beyond the cities are reducing city and countryside alike to a monotonous, unnourishing gruel, this is not strange. It all comes, first-, second-, third- or fourth-hand, out of the same intellectual dish of mush, a mush in which the qualities, necessities, advantages and behavior of great cities have been utterly confused with the qualities, necessities, advantages and behavior of other and more inert types of settlements.

There is nothing economically or socially inevitable about either the decay of old cities or the fresh-minted decadence of the new unurban urbanization. On the contrary, no other aspect of our economy and society has been more purposefully manipulated for a full quarter of a century to achieve precisely what we are getting. Extraordinary governmental financial incentives have been required to achieve this degree of monotony, sterility, and vulgarity. Decades of preaching, writing and exhorting by experts have gone into convincing us and our legislators that mush like this must be good for us, as long as it comes bedded with grass.

Automobiles are often conveniently tagged as the villains responsible for the ills of cities and the disappointments and futilities of city planning. But the destructive effects of automobiles are much less a cause than a symptom of our incompetence at city building. Of course planners, including the highwaymen with fabulous sums of money and enormous powers at their disposal, are at a loss to make automobiles and cities compatible with one another. They do not know what to do with automobiles in cities because they do not know how to plan for workable and vital cities anyhow—with or without automobiles.

The simple needs of automobiles are more easily understood and satisfied than the complex needs of cities, and a growing number of planners and designers have come to believe that if they can only solve the problems of traffic, they will thereby have solved the major problem of cities. Cities have much more intricate economic and social concerns than automobile traffic. How can you know what to try with traffic until you know how the city itself works, and what else it needs to do with its streets? You can't.

It may be that we have become so feckless as a people that we no longer care how things do work, but only what kind of quick, easy outer impression they give. If so, there is little hope for our cities or probably for much else in our society. But I do not think this is so.

Specifically, in the case of planning for cities, it is clear that a large number of good and earnest people do care deeply about building and renewing. Despite some corruption, and considerable greed for the other man's vineyard, the intentions going into the messes we make are, on the whole, exemplary. Planners, architects of city design, and those they have led along with them in their beliefs are not consciously disdainful of the importance of knowing how things work. On the contrary, they have gone to great pains to learn what the saints and sages of modern orthodox planning have said about how cities *ought* to work and what *ought* to be good for people and businesses in them. They take this with such devotion that when contradictory reality intrudes, threatening to shatter their dearly won learning, they must shrug reality aside. . . .

Bankers, like planners, have theories about cities on which they act. They have gotten their theories from the same intellectual sources as the planners. Bankers and government administrative officials who guarantee mortgages do not invent planning theories nor, surprisingly, even economic doctrine about cities. They are enlightened nowadays, and they pick up their ideas from idealists, a generation late. Since theoretical city planning has embraced no major new ideas for considerably more than a generation, theoretical planners, financers and bureaucrats are all just about even today.

And to put it bluntly, they are all in the same stage of elaborately learned superstition as medical science was early in the last century, when physicians put their faith in bloodletting, to draw out the evil humors which were believed to cause disease. With bloodletting, it took years of learning to know precisely which veins, by what rituals, were to be opened for what symptoms. A superstructure of technical complication was erected in such deadpan detail that the literature still sounds almost plausible. However, because people, even when they are thoroughly enmeshed in descriptions of reality which are at variance with reality, are still seldom devoid of the powers of observation and independent thought, the science of bloodletting, over most of its long sway, appears usually to have been tempered with a certain amount of common sense. Or it was tempered until it reached its highest peaks of technique in, of all places, the young United States. Bloodletting went wild here. It had an enormously influential proponent in Dr. Benjamin Rush, still revered as the greatest statesman–physician of our revolutionary and federal periods, and a genius of medical administration. Dr. Rush Got Things Done. Among the things he got done, some of them good and useful, were to develop, practice, teach and spread the custom of bloodletting in cases where prudence or mercy had heretofore restrained its use. He and his students drained the blood of very young children, of consumptives, of the greatly aged, of almost anyone unfortunate enough to be sick in his realms of influence. His extreme practices aroused the alarm and horror of European bloodletting physicians. And yet as late as 1851, a committee appointed by the State Legislature of New York solemnly defended the thoroughgoing use of bloodletting. It scathingly ridiculed and censured a physician, William Turner, who had the temerity to write a pamphlet criticizing Dr. Rush's doctrines and calling "the practice of taking blood in diseases contrary to common sense, to general experience, to enlightened reason and to the manifest laws of the divine Providence." Sick people needed fortifying, not draining, said Dr. Turner, and he was squelched.

Medical analogies, applied to social organisms, are apt to be farfetched, and there is no point in mistaking mammalian chemistry for what occurs in a city. But analogies as to what goes on in the brains of earnest and learned men, dealing with complex phenomena they do not understand at all and trying to make do with a pseudoscience, do have point. As in the pseudoscience of bloodletting, just so in the pseudoscience of city rebuilding and planning, years of learning and a plethora of subtle and complicated dogma have arisen on a foundation of nonsense. The tools of technique have steadily been perfected. Naturally, in time, forceful and able men, admired administrators, having swallowed the initial fallacies and having been provisioned with tools and with public confidence, go on logically to the greatest destructive excesses, which prudence or mercy might previously have forbade. Bloodletting could heal only by accident or insofar as it broke the rules, until the time when it was abandoned in favor of the hard, complex business of assembling, using and testing, bit by bit, true descriptions of reality drawn not from how it ought to be, but from how it is. The pseudoscience of city planning and its companion, the art of city design, have not yet broken with the specious comfort of wishes, familiar superstitions, oversimplifications, and symbols, and have not yet embarked upon the adventure of probing the real world. . . .

The way to get at what goes on in the seemingly mysterious and perverse behavior of cities is, I think, to look closely, and with as little previous expectation as is possible, at the most ordinary scenes and events, and attempt to see what they mean and whether any threads of principle emerge among them. . . .

One principle emerges so ubiquitously, and in so many and such complex different forms. . . . This ubiquitous principle is the need of cities for a most intricate and close-grained diversity of uses that give each other constant mutual support, both economically and socially. The components of this diversity can differ enormously, but they must supplement each other in certain concrete ways.

I think that unsuccessful city areas are areas which lack this kind of intricate mutual support, and that the science of city planning and the art of city design, in real life for real cities, must become the science and art of catalyzing and nourishing these close-grained working relationships. I think, from the evidence I can find, that there are four primary conditions required for generating useful great city diversity, and that by deliberately inducing these four conditions, planning can induce city vitality (something that the plans of planners alone, and the designs of designers alone, can never achieve). . . .

Cities are fantastically dynamic places, and this is strikingly true of their successful parts, which offer a fertile ground for the plans of thousands of people. . . .

The look of things and the way they work are inextricably bound together, and in no place more so than cities. But people who are interested only in how a city "ought" to look and uninterested in how it works will be disappointed . . . It is futile to plan a city's appearance, or speculate on how to endow it with a pleasing appearance of order, without knowing what sort of innate, functioning order it has. To seek for the look of things as a primary purpose or as the main drama is apt to make nothing but trouble.

In New York's East Harlem there is a housing project with a conspicuous rectangular lawn which became an object of hatred to the project tenants. A social worker frequently at the project was astonished by how often the subject of the lawn came up, usually gratuitously as far as she could see, and how much the tenants despised it and urged that it be done away with. When she asked why, the usual answer was, "What good is it?" or ''Who wants it?" Finally one day a tenant more articulate than the others made this pronouncement: "Nobody cared what we wanted when they built this place. They threw our houses down and pushed us here and pushed our friends somewhere else. We don't have a place around here to get a cup of coffee or a newspaper even, or borrow fifty cents. Nobody cared what we need. But the big men come and look at that grass and say, 'Isn't it wonderful! Now the poor have everything!'"

This tenant was saying what moralists have said for thousands of years: Handsome is as handsome does. All that glitters is not gold.

She was saying more: There is a quality even meaner than outright ugliness or disorder, and this meaner quality is the dishonest mask of pretended order, achieved by ignoring or suppressing the real order that is struggling to exist and to be served. . . .

The point is, we need desperately to learn and to apply as much knowledge that is true and useful about cities as fast as possible.

I have been making unkind remarks about orthodox city planning theory, and shall make more as occasion arises to do so. By now, these orthodox ideas are part of our folklore. They harm us because we take them for granted. To show how we got them, and how little they are to the point, I shall give a quick outline here of the most influential ideas that have contributed to the verities of orthodox modem city planning and city architectural design.[3]

The most important thread of influence starts, more or less, with Ebenezer Howard, an English court reporter for whom planning was an avocation. Howard looked at the living conditions of the poor in late-nineteenth-century London, and justifiably did not like what he smelled or saw or heard. He not only hated the wrongs and mistakes of the city, he hated the city and thought it an outright evil and an affront to nature that so many people should get themselves into an agglomeration. His prescription for saving the people was to do the city in.

The program he proposed, in 1898, was to halt the growth of London and also repopulate the countryside, where villages were declining, by building a new kind of town— the Garden City, where the city poor might again live close to nature. So they might earn their livings, industry was to be set up in the Garden City, for while Howard was not planning cities, he was not planning dormitory suburbs either. His aim was the creation of self-sufficient small towns, really very nice towns if you were docile and had no plans of your own and did not mind spending your life among others with no plans of their own. As in all Utopias, the right to have plans of any significance belonged only to the planners in charge. The Garden City was to be encircled with a belt of agriculture. Industry was to be in its planned preserves; schools, housing and greens in planned living preserves; and in the center were to be commercial, club and cultural places, held in common. The town and green belt, in their totality, were to be permanently controlled by the public authority under which the town was developed, to prevent speculation or supposedly irrational changes in land use and also to do away with temptations to increase its density—in brief, to prevent it from ever becoming a city. The maximum population was to be held to thirty thousand people.

Nathan Glazer has summed up the vision well in *Architectural Forum*: "The image was the English country town—with the manor house and its park replaced by a community center, and with some factories hidden behind a screen of trees, to supply work."

The closest American equivalent would probably be the model company town, with profit-sharing, and with the Parent-Teacher Associations in charge of the routine, custodial political life. For Howard was envisioning not simply a new physical environment and social life, but a paternalistic political and economic society.

Nevertheless, as Glazer has pointed out, the Garden City was "conceived as an alternative to the city, and as a solution to city problems; this was, and is still, the foundation of its immense power as a planning idea." Howard managed to get two garden cities built, Letchworth and Welwyn, and of course England and Sweden have, since the Second World War, built a number of satellite towns based on Garden City principles. In the United States, the suburb of Radburn, N.J., and the depression-built, government-sponsored Green Belt towns (actually suburbs) were all incomplete modifications on the idea. But Howard's

3. Readers who would like a fuller account, and a sympathetic account which mine is not, should go to the sources, which are very interesting, especially: *Garden Cities of Tomorrow*, by Ebenezer Howard; *The Culture of Cities*, by Lewis Mumford; *Cities in Evolution*, by Sir Patrick Geddes; *Modern Housing*, by Catherine Bauer; *Toward New Towns for America*, by Clarence Stein; *Nothing Gained by Overcrowding*, by Sir Raymond Unwin; and *The City of Tomorrow and Its Planning*, by Le Corbusier. The best short survey I know of is the group of excerpts under the title "Assumptions and Goals of City Planning," contained in *Land-Use Planning, A Casebook on the Use, Misuse and Re-use of Urban Land*, by Charles M. Haar.

influence in the literal, or reasonably literal, acceptance of his program was as nothing compared to his influence on conceptions underlying all American city planning today. City planners and designers with no interest in the Garden City, as such, are still thoroughly governed intellectually by its underlying principles.

Howard set spinning powerful and city-destroying ideas: He conceived that the way to deal with the city's functions was to sort and sift out of the whole certain simple uses, and to arrange each of these in relative self-containment. He focused on the provision of wholesome housing as the central problem, to which everything else was subsidiary; furthermore he defined wholesome housing in terms only of suburban physical qualities and small-town social qualities. He conceived of commerce in terms of routine, standardized supply of goods, and as serving a self-limited market. He conceived of good planning as a series of static acts; in each case the plan must anticipate all that is needed and be protected, after it is built, against any but the most minor subsequent changes. He conceived of planning also as essentially paternalistic, if not authoritarian. He was uninterested in the aspects of the city which could not be abstracted to serve his Utopia. In particular, he simply wrote off the intricate, many-faceted, cultural life of the metropolis. He was uninterested in such problems as the way great cities police themselves, or exchange ideas, or operate politically, or invent new economic arrangements, and he was oblivious to devising ways to strengthen these functions because, after all, he was not designing for this kind of life in any case.

Both in his preoccupations and in his omissions, Howard made sense in his own terms but none in terms of city planning. Yet virtually all modem city planning has been adapted from, and embroidered on, this silly substance.

Howard's influence on American city planning converged on the city from two directions: from town and regional planners on the one hand, and from architects on the other. Along the avenue of planning, Sir Patrick Geddes, a Scots biologist and philosopher, saw the Garden City idea not as a fortuitous way to absorb population growth otherwise destined for a great city, but as the starting point of a much grander and more encompassing pattern. He thought of the planning of cities in terms of the planning of whole regions. Under regional planning, garden cities would be rationally distributed throughout large territories, dovetailing into natural resources, balanced against agriculture and woodland, forming one far-flung logical whole.

Howard's and Geddes' ideas were enthusiastically adopted in America during the 1920s, and developed further by a group of extraordinarily effective and dedicated people—among them Lewis Mumford, Clarence Stein, the late Henry Wright, and Catherine Bauer. While they thought of themselves as regional planners, Catherine Bauer has more recently called this group the "Decentrists," and this name is more apt, for the primary result of regional planning, as they saw it, would be to decentralize great cities, thin them out, and disperse their enterprises and populations into smaller, separated cities or, better yet, towns. At the time, it appeared that the American population was both aging and leveling off in numbers, and the problem appeared to be not one of accommodating a rapidly growing population, but simply of redistributing a static population.

As with Howard himself, this group's influence was less in getting literal acceptance of its program—that got nowhere—than in influencing city planning and legislation affecting housing and housing finance. Model housing schemes by Stein and Wright, built mainly in suburban settings or at the fringes of cities together with the writings and the diagrams, sketches and photographs presented by Mumford and Bauer, demonstrated and popularized ideas such as these, which are now taken for granted in orthodox planning: The street is bad as an environment for humans; houses should be turned away from it and faced inward, toward sheltered greens. Frequent streets are wasteful, of advantage only to real estate speculators who measure value by the front foot. The basic unit of city design is not the street, but the block and more particularly the super-block. Commerce should be segregated from residences and greens. A neighborhood's demand for goods should be calculated "scientifically," and this much and no more commercial space allocated. The presence of many other people is, at best, a necessary evil, and good city planning must aim for at least an illusion of isolation and suburbany privacy. The Decentrists also pounded in Howard's premises that the planned community must be islanded off as a self-contained unit, that it must resist future change, and that every significant detail must be controlled by the planners from the start and then stuck to. In short, good planning was project planning.

To reinforce and dramatize the necessity for the new order of things, the Decentrists hammered away at the bad old city. They were incurious about successes in great cities. They were interested only in failures. All was failure. A book like Mumford's *The Culture of Cities* was largely a morbid and biased catalog of ills. The great city was Megalopolis, Tyrannopolis, Nekropolis, a monstrosity, a tyranny, a living death. It must go. New York's midtown was "solidified chaos" (Mumford). The shape and appearance of cities was nothing but "a chaotic accident . . . the summation of the haphazard, antagonistic whims of many self-centered, ill-advised individuals" (Stein). The centers of cities amounted to "a foreground of noise, dirt, beggars, souvenirs and shrill competitive advertising" (Bauer).

How could anything so bad be worth the attempt to understand it? The Decentrists' analyses, the architectural and housing designs which were companions and offshoots of these analyses, the national housing and home financing legislation so directly influenced by the new vision—none of these had anything to do with understanding cities, or fostering successful large cities, nor were they intended to. They were reasons and means for jettisoning cities, and the Decentrists were frank about this.

But in the schools of planning and architecture, and in Congress, state legislatures and city halls too, the Decentrists' ideas were gradually accepted as basic guides for dealing constructively with big cities themselves. This is the most amazing event in the whole sorry tale: that finally people who sincerely wanted to strengthen great cities should adopt recipes frankly devised for undermining their economies and killing them.

The man with the most dramatic idea of how to get all this anti-city planning right into the citadels of iniquity themselves was the European architect Le Corbusier. He devised in the 1920s a dream city which he called the Radiant City, composed not of the low buildings beloved of the Decentrists, but instead mainly of skyscrapers within a park. "Suppose we are entering the city by way of the Great Park," Le Corbusier wrote. "Our fast car takes the special elevated motor track between the majestic skyscrapers: as we approach nearer, there is seen the repetition against the sky of the twenty-four skyscrapers; to our left and right on the outskirts of each particular area are the municipal and administrative buildings; arid enclosing the space are the museums and university buildings. The whole city is a Park." In Le Corbusier's vertical city the common run of mankind was to be housed at 1,200 inhabitants to the acre, a fantastically high city density indeed, but because of building up so high, 95 percent of the ground could remain open. The skyscrapers would occupy only 5 percent of the ground. The high-income people would be in lower, luxury housing around courts, with 85 percent of their ground left open. Here and there would be restaurants and theaters.

Le Corbusier was planning not only a physical environment. He was planning for a social Utopia too. Le Corbusier's Utopia was a condition of what he called maximum individual liberty, by which he seems to have meant not liberty to do anything much, but liberty from ordinary responsibility. In his Radiant City nobody, presumably, was going to have to be his brother's keeper any more. Nobody was going to have to struggle with plans of his own. Nobody was going to be tied down.

The Decentrists and other loyal advocates of the Garden City were aghast, at Le Corbusier's city of towers in the park, and still are. Their reaction to it was, and remains, much like that of progressive nursery school teachers confronting an utterly institutional orphanage. And yet, ironically, the Radiant City comes directly out of the Garden City. Le Corbusier accepted the Garden City's fundamental image, superficially at least, and worked to make it practical for high densities. He described his creation as the Garden City made attainable. "The garden city is a will-o'-the-wisp," he wrote. "Nature melts under the invasion of roads and houses and the promised seclusion becomes a crowded settlement . . . The solution will be found in the vertical garden city."

In another sense too, in its relatively easy public reception, Le Corbusier's Radiant City depended upon the Garden City. The Garden City planners and their ever increasing following among housing reformers, students and architects were indefatigably popularizing the ideas of the super-block, the project neighborhood, the unchangeable plan, and grass, grass, grass; what is more they were successfully establishing such attributes as the hallmarks of humane, socially responsible, functional, high-minded planning. Le Corbusier really did not have to justify his vision in either humane or city-functional terms. If the great object of city planning was that Christopher Robin might go hoppety-hoppety on the grass, what was wrong with Le Corbusier? The Decentrists' cries of institutionalization, mechanization, depersonalization seemed to others foolishly sectarian.

Le Corbusier's dream city has had an immense impact on our cities. It was hailed deliriously by architects, and has gradually been embodied in scores of projects, ranging from low-income public housing to office building projects. Aside from making at least the superficial Garden City principles superficially practicable in dense city, Le Corbusier's dream contained other marvels. He attempted to make planning for the automobile an integral part of his scheme, and this was, in the 1920s and early 1930s, a new, exciting idea. He included great arterial roads for express one-way traffic. He cut the number of streets because "cross-roads are an enemy to traffic." He proposed underground streets for heavy vehicles and deliveries, and of course like the Garden City planners he kept the pedestrians off the streets and in the parks. His city was like a wonderful mechanical toy. Furthermore, his conception, as an architectural work, had a dazzling clarity, simplicity and harmony. It was so orderly, so visible, so easy to understand. It said everything in a flash, like a good advertisement. This vision and its bold symbolism have been all but irresistible to planners, housers, designers, and to developers, lenders and mayors too. It exerts a great pull on "progressive" zoners, who write rules calculated to encourage nonproject builders to reflect, if only a little, the dream. No matter how vulgarized or clumsy the design, how dreary and useless the open space, how dull the close-up view, an imitation of Le Corbusier shouts "Look what I made!" Like a great, visible ego it tells of some achievement. But as to how the city works, it tells, like the Garden City, nothing but lies.

Although the Decentrists, with their devotion to the ideal of a town life, have never made peace with the Le Corbusier vision, most of their disciples have. Virtually all sophisticated city designers today combine the two conceptions in various permutations. The rebuilding technique variously known as "selective removal" or "spot renewal" or "renewal planning" or ''planned conservation"—meaning that total clearance of a run-down area is avoided—is largely the trick of seeing how many old buildings can be left standing and the area still converted into a passable version of Radiant Garden City. Zoners, highway planners, legislators, land-use planners, and parks and playground planners—none of whom live in an ideological vacuum—constantly use, as fixed points of reference, these two powerful visions and the more sophisticated merged vision. They may wander from the visions, they may compromise, they may vulgarize, but these are the points of departure.

We shall look briefly at one other, less important, line of ancestry in orthodox planning. This one begins more or less with the great Columbian Exposition in Chicago in 1893, just about the same time that Howard was formulating his Garden City ideas. The Chicago fair snubbed the exciting modem architecture which had begun to emerge in Chicago and instead dramatized a retrogressive imitation Renaissance style. One heavy, grandiose monument after another was arrayed in the exposition park, like frosted pastries on a tray, in a sort of squat, decorated forecast of Le Corbusier's later repetitive ranks of towers in a park. This, orgiastic assemblage of the rich and monumental captured the imagination of both planners and public. It gave impetus to a movement called the City Beautiful, and indeed the planning of the exposition was dominated by the man who became the leading City Beautiful planner, Daniel Burnham of Chicago.

The aim of the City Beautiful was the City Monumental. Great schemes were drawn up for systems of baroque boulevards, which mainly came to nothing. What did come out of the movement was the Center Monumental, modeled on the fair. City after city built its civic center or its cultural center. These buildings were arranged along a boulevard as at Benjamin Franklin Parkway in Philadelphia, or along a mall like the Government Center in Cleveland, or were bordered by park, like the Civic Center at St. Louis, or were interspersed with park, like the Civic Center at San Francisco. However they were arranged, the important point was that the monuments had been sorted out from the rest of the city, and assembled into the grandest effect thought possible, the whole being treated as a complete unit, in a separate and well-defined way.

People were proud of them, but the centers were not a success. For one thing, invariably the ordinary city around them ran down instead of being uplifted, and they always acquired an incongruous rim of ratty tattoo parlors and second-hand-clothing stores, or else just nondescript, dispirited decay. For another, people stayed away from them to a remarkable degree. Somehow, when the fair became part of the city, it did not work like the fair.

The architecture of the City Beautiful centers went out of style. But the idea behind the centers was not questioned, and it has never had more force than it does today. The idea of sorting out certain cultural or public functions and decontaminating their relationship with the workaday city dovetailed nicely with the Garden City teachings. The conceptions have harmoniously merged, much as the Garden City and the Radiant City merged, into a sort of Radiant Garden City Beautiful, such as the immense Lincoln Square project for New York, in which a monumental City Beautiful cultural center is one among a series of adjoining Radiant City and Radiant Garden City housing, shopping and campus centers.

And by analogy, the principles of sorting out—and of bringing order by repression of all plans but the planners—have been easily extended to all manner of city functions, until today a land-use master plan for a big city is largely a matter of proposed placement, often in relation to transportation, of many series of decontaminated sortings.

From beginning to end, from Howard and Burnham to the latest amendment on urban-renewal law, the entire concoction is to the workings of cities. Unstudied, unrespected, cities served as sacrificial victims.

Philosophical Text

TOM SCHUMACHER, "CONTEXTUALISM: URBAN IDEALS AND DEFORMATIONS."[4]

First Published in 1971

The time is ripe for construction, not foolery.

Le Corbusier, 1922

We can work it out.

The Beatles, 1966

If one momentarily puts aside most of our urban problems (overcrowding, transportation, economics, etc.), if one places himself in the unlikely position of abstracting a small aspect of reality, he can examine the shape of the modern city independent of its many functions. The twentieth century town is physically a combination of two simple concepts: the traditional city of corridor streets, grids, squares, etc., and the city-in-the-park. The traditional city is primarily an experience of spaces defined by continuous walls of building which are arranged in a way that emphasizes the spaces and de-emphasizes the building volumes. It is an experience which can be thought of as resulting from a subtractive process in which spaces have been carved out of solid masses. By contrast, the city-in-the-park (a phenomenon most clearly articulated by Le Corbusier as the "Ville Radieuse"), is compositionally the reverse of the traditional city. Composed of isolated buildings set in a park-like landscape, the city-in-the-park presents an experience which emphasizes the building volumes and not the spaces which the buildings define or imply.

Although the division of urban form into two types is somewhat arbitrary, it approximates reality. Because the twentieth century town is an unhappy combination of the traditional city and various misconceptions of the Ville Radieuse. Contextualism has attempted to resolve this dilemma and made the city as we find it a viable form in a future which promises enormous expansion. Faced with the reality that orgies of construction at economically ripe times have made a mess of our urban life, it seems imperative to stop and reflect.

4. This approach to urban design is the result of collaboration of graduate students at Cornell University under the guidance of Professor Colin Rowe, between 1963 and the present. Professor Rowe is responsible for many of the points made in this paper. The terms "Contextualism" was first used by Stuart Cohen and Steven Hurtt in an unpublished master's thesis titled *Le Corbusier: The Architecture of City Planning*.

So far, modern theories of urbanism and their applications have tended to devalue the traditional city.[5] Yet we have not broken our ties to it. We respect and enjoy the charm and human scale of the picturesque medieval town, while we destroy—in the name of progress—what little traditional urbanism we possess. The criterion of economic obsolescence overrides all others. If a building doesn't keep paying for itself, it goes. "Big ball" renewal projects have created a chasm between the existing and the new preventing either from offering any reasonable amenity.[6] Modern architecture promised a utopia fashioned after the machine. The promise hasn't been kept. One could, at this point, understandably argue for a revisionist philosophy and a return to traditional city ideas. Yet this alone does not solve so many of our real problems. Land values and the economic necessities of grouping people in high concentrations have greatly limited the flexibility of the capitalist city. Economic pressures and design preferences, for example, have led to the typification of housing as packages which can be assembled only as the city-in-the-park, endlessly repetitious and based on profit rather than need. The results are urban configurations which relate neither to the human being nor to the neighborhoods which they interrupt.

Obviously some middle ground is needed. To retreat to a hopelessly artificial past is unrealistic, but to allow a brutalizing system to dominate and destroy traditional urbanism is irresponsible. Contextualism, professing to be a reconciliation of the above ideas, has attempted such a middle ground. But before any specific discussion of these ideas can be made, it is necessary to state a few of the basic assumptions which have formed the groundrules for this approach to solving urban problems. Very briefly, the argument might be stated as follows: because form need not follow function, building programs and uses need not be expressed in the configuration of buildings and towns. This renders out-of-context comparisons feasible. Hence a church plan and a housing block can be rationally compared. The manipulation of forms at large scale relates directly to the organizational patterns of buildings. Such smaller scale works serve as analogue models for larger projects. Thus, urban form is seen as possessing a life of its own, irrespective of use, culture and economic conditions. Formal continuities transcending periods therefore become an important consideration.[7] Moreover, the communicative nature of architecture as a mimetic art is given new importance. This attitude depends upon the proposition that the modern-movement concept of utility and economy of means as expressed in functionalist theory is inadequate to cope with the complexities of modern experience, and that an "overplus" of communication is a necessary constituent of both buildings and cities.[8] Thus, "the various forms of architecture . . . are above all structures or representation; which means in actual terms that architecture, like every other art, is both reality and representation."[9]

The validity of these assumptions cannot be tested. While they do not appear to relate directly to the solution of so many of our urban problems, it can be argued that those problems cannot be solved by architecture (or urban design) as a medium of direct communication but more likely by a social and economic process of which architecture is only a part. One is not arguing against social relevance. One "is" arguing that after a

5. The assumption of the modern movement was that existing western forms had to be completely replaced. Van Doesburg's *Europe Is Lost It* and Le Corbusier's *There Can Be No New Architecture Without New City Planning* are but two examples among many.

6. See Robert A. M. Stern, *New Directions in American Architecture* (New York: George Braziller, 1969).

7. This approaches the theories of Julien Guadet. See Colin Rowe, "Review of Talbot Hamlin's Forms and Functions of 20th Century Architecture," *Art Bulletin* (May 1953). Also see Reyner Banham, *Theory and Design in the First Machine Age* (London: Architectural Press, 1959).

8. See Christian Norberg-Schulz, "Meaning in Architecture," in *Meaning in Architecture*, eds. Charles Jencks and George Baird (New York: George Braziller, 1969).

9. Luigi Moretti, "Form as Structure," *AA Journal Arena* (1967).

certain point in the planning process other criteria surface which allow us to make judgments about the final form of our cities. And although it is just as easy to leave out this phase (indeed, today it is always left out), it is the application of such criteria (either consciously or unconsciously) which give many cities their particular ambiences.

Le Corbusier, in *Towards a New Architecture* (1923), stated, "A building is like a soap bubble. This bubble is perfect and harmonious if the breath has been evenly distributed from the inside. The exterior is the result of an interior." Theo Van Doesburg, in *24 Points of the New Architecture* (1924), stated, "In contrast to frontalism, born out of a static conception of life, the new architecture will reach a great richness by developing an 'all-sided plastic' way in space and time."

The above statements typify an attitude toward architectural form which, while it gave modern architecture and urbanism some of its important peculiarities as a style, also created many of the problems we face today in the siting of buildings and the design of cities. The concept that a building should exist as an object in the round, isolated from its neighbors, multi-sided and without preferential faces, is of course not new.[10] What was new for modern architecture was the insistence that this type of configuration be typical for all building types rather than special to particularly important building uses.

The development of Renaissance architecture is generally described as the historical progression from the Loggia degli Innocenti of Brunelleschi to the Tempietto of Bramante. This progression is presented as the continuing refinement of motifs from inscribed to real forms—from surface to volume—culminating in a cylindrical temple capped by a dome. Independent of context, round and idealized (almost without function) this little pavilion represented an ideal scarcely attainable in buildings with only slightly more complicated programs and site conditions. Allusions to the perfection of the Ternpietto are common in buildings up to the twentieth century. Certainly Santa Maria della Consolazione in Todi approaches this condition. But in most cases architects have been required to soften the ideal and conform to both use and situation.[11] The Villa Badoer of Palladio is an example of the alterations made to an "ideal", multi-sided form in order to accommodate the attendant functions housed in the wings. This building still lacks the site restrictions which promote the elaborate formal disguises that urban buildings so often possess.

By comparison, Van Doesburg's and Van Eesteren's project for a private house, 1922, represents an intent similar to that of the tempietto, and can be contrasted to the Villa Badoer. Van Doesburg's construction is a multi-sided figural building which is dependent upon separation from its context. But aside from being figural (like the Villa Badoer), it is also "non"-frontal. Lacking any plane of reference as face and thereby lacking flanks, this project approaches the state of idealization of the Tempietto. Like the Tempietto this project is a prototype. Such idealization of buildings has been a constant imperative of modern architecture either as a purely formal preference like the de Stijl prospects, or as representing a functional unit or a program, as in the Bauhaus projects and buildings. The image of the building as an object in the round is so much a part of the modern architect's vision that he is prone to see all ages of building in these "sculptural"

10. Alberti discusses the siting of temples separated from their surroundings, as does Palladio.

11. Sitte has shown how, in the 19th century, of 255 churches in Rome, only 6 were free standing. Camillo Sitte, *City Planning According to Artistic Principles* (New York: Random House, 1965), 26.

terms. Hence, the modern architect is often disappointed is appointed in the buildings he visits which do not reflect this pre-conception.

The notion that some ideal forms can exist as fragments, "collage" into an empirical environment, and that other ideal forms can withstand elaborate deformations in the process of being adjusted to a context have largely eluded the modern architect. This attitude was recognized and deplored by Robert Venturi who called for elements which were "hybrid rather than 'pure', distorted rather than 'straightforward,' ambiguous rather than 'articulated.'"[12]

It is precisely the ways in ways idealized forms can be adjusted to a context or used as "collage"[13] that contextualism seeks to explain, and it is the systems of geometric organization which can be abstracted from any given context that contextualism seeks to divine as design tools.

To return to the question of the city as solids "in" voids and voids "in" solids, a comparison of the Uffizi in Florence and the Unité d'habitation in Marseilles, provides a useful analogy. The Unité is a rectangular prism, oblong and solid. The Uffizi is a rectangular prism, oblong and void. Both may be seen as "figures" surrounded by a "ground", and each represents a way of looking at the city. An archetypal void seen as a figure in plan is a conceptual ambiguity since figures are generally thought of as solid. Yet when a void has the properties of a figure it is endowed with certain capabilities which "ground" voids lack. While the Piazza Barberini in Rome, a "ground" void, functions well as a distributor of traffic but not as a collector of people, the Piazza Navona, a figural void, collects pedestrians easily.

In an unpublished masters thesis at Cornell University, Wayne Copper has explored the nature of void as figure and solid as ground.[14] "Once it is recognized that figure and ground are conceptually reversible, it follows quite naturally that their roles are interdependent." To consider a famous urban space without the back-up solid which provides its "ground" is to render an incomplete picture. Obviously the Piazza San Marco in Venice owes much its vitality as a figural space and a collector of people to the densely packed areas around it which feed it people and provide the contrast solid to its void. When seen reversed in an all black and white drawing the ambivalence of solid and void is obvious, and the tension created by the equality of the visual "weight" poses some interesting questions: does a regular space require irregular back-up solids? Can any norm of size relationships between streets and squares be abstracted from examining such spaces? But mainly, is this all simply irrelevant since building heights vary and the actual surfaces which define space "really" give urbanism its particular ambience? (The old idea that the Sistine Chapel is simply a barn without its painted-on architecture comes to mind here). Yet, as Copper argues, "it would be absurd to attempt to analyse midtown Manhattan with only one level of plan . . . although with Rome it would not." Obviously this abstraction does not provide the whole story, and for New York it is almost meaningless. As a tool of analysis, however, the figure ground drawing does involve us immediately with the urban structure of a given context.

12. Robert Venturi, *Complexity and Contradiction in Architecture* (New York: Museum of Modern Art, 1966), 22.

13. Literal urban collage is probably a semantic impossibility, except in an instance like the placing of a Clues Oldenburg lipstick in an urban landscape. For my purposes here, collage is taken to mean the placement of formally disparate elements into a given context.

14. Wayne Copper, *The Figure-Grounds* (Ithaca: Cornell University, 1967).

The abstraction of ideas via the concept of figure-ground and figure-ground reversal (or ambivalence) proceeds to the examination of ideal forms which have become "classic urbanism" as well as to the contexts into which these ideals are placed. The ideal city of the Renaissance, for example, begins as a medieval town containing a collection of idealized buildings and culminates as a geometric abstraction devised to accept all forms of individually idealized structures. Between the two is the reality of the Renaissance city, a medieval town which both deforms and is deformed by the Renaissance buildings it hosts. The "città ideale" of Peruzzi should be contrasted to the siting of the Palazzo Rucellai. The palace is in a narrow street where it is impossible to ever achieve a frontal view of the façade. While this is contrary to renaissance intentions for the city, it is necessary to accept the condition and allow oneself the luxury of his perceptual ability to "lift" the building out of context.

In a constricted environment, the siting of culturally important buildings for which specific deformations are created is important to note. S. Agnese in Piazza Navona is perhaps the quintessential example. The basic parti is that of a centralized cross surmounted by a dome (not unlike S. M. della Consolazione), a basically figural building. The insistently flat façade of the Piazza implied the need for a building which adhered to the existing geometry, contrary to the ideal parti type. S. Agnese is both. The façade of the Piazza is maintained and at the same time warped in such a way that its integrity is not broken while the dome is perceptually thrust forward into the prominence it requires as a symbol. The deformations of a particular building parti which maintain a reading of the building as an ideal form is not solely a function of the pressures exerted by a tight context. The differentiation of the faces of completely figural buildings is also of interest. Colin Rowe has stated that the absolute idealization of any useful building is logically impossible because, if no other pressures influence its design, at least entrance and orientation must act as deforming pressures.

The deforming pressures of an entry sequence may be seen in Le Corbusier's Pavillion Suisse which has been widely misconceived and emulated as a nonhierarchical, two-faced slab. It is in fact a two sided slab, but it has a clearly defined front and back, which are treated as differently as possible within the limits of a flat surface. The entrance façade is prefaced by two curved surfaces, one rough and one smooth, that heighten the flatness of the block itself which is basically solid. The "garden" façade, by contrast, is a transparent flat curtain wall.

If the Pavillion Suisse is an example of a building "distorted" by a relatively loose context, an example of the opposite (an undistorted building within a tight context) is the CBS building of Eero Saarinen. Confined within the tight grid of New York City and placed at the end of a block, the CBS tower takes no account of the fact that its four façades face different conditions. The two streets, the wide avenue and the adjacent buildings have in no way been recognized. Indeed, the site pressures have been so well camouflaged that the entrances to the building are almost impossible to find. The interaction of the idealised parti with its environment may be further seen in a small scale analogy, a detail in the Palazzo Farnese of Antonio da Sangallo the younger. In the entry sequence, the central aisle of a three-aisled entrance, is the width of the typical bays of the courtyard arcade. The side aisles, however, are narrower, thus leaving a discrepancy where they meet the courtyard. This is accomodated by a fanlike forced perspective band at the inner courtyard façade. Here the two conflicting forms are brought together in a resolution that not only solves an otherwise awkward intersection, but also does not completely disguise the existence of the problem. It is a kind of "75% solution" to a compositional problem that, through its incompleteness, enriches the entire composition.

Although this example is not literally a microcosm of problems of urban form (particularly plan problems), the nature of the solution is analogous and contextualism attempts to create a milieu in which abstractions of this kind and great jumps in scale can be useful tools for breaking sets.

At a larger scale, the siting of the Palazzo Borghese and the adjustments made to it in order to accommodate a complex condition explain the urban implication of Sangallo's moves in the Palazzo Farnese. This sort of adjustment differs from that in S. Agnese in the way the configuration and building are more complicated and in the way more responses are made to site pressures. Here the archetypal renaissance cortile is imbedded in an oddly shaped configuration. The geometric inconsistencies are resolved by the addition of new geometries which "collect" and absorb the odd directions.

The above examples, S. Agnese in Piazza Navona and the Palazzo Borghese, represent configurations in which fragmentary responses are made to appear as part of the parti. A second type of urban configuration, where buildings are put together with elements which relate directly to the context and only haphazardly to the building itself, is seen in the complex of S. Giovanni in Laterano. Growing slowly over many centuries and responding to specific pressures, the Lateran complex (an urban "megastructure" of moderate scale) exhibits the characteristics of a collage. The principle façade relates to the Portal S. Giovanni, the benediction loggia relates to the Via Merulana (the Sixtus V axis from Santa Maria Maggiore), and the Palazzo Laterano relates to the Piazza S. Giovanni. All of the elements are tacked on to the body of the church which does "not" respond to their pressures but remains internally the archetypal basilica almost without deformation.

Similar to S. Giovanni in its local accommodation of context is the cathedral of Florence. Here the concept of building is both figure and ground is exploited. The major façade serves as ground to the Baptistry which is totally figural and to the Piazza S. Giovanni. The rear of the Cathedral acts as a figure which intrudes into and activates the Piazza del Duomo. It is this sort of differentiated building which can respond to many pressures created by a context without losing its imageability as a Gestalt. This type of building is rare in modern architecture (Aalto's Pensions Institute in Helsinki is a noticeable exception as are many of Le Corbusier's works). It is different from the typical picturesque modern building which "separates function into interlocking wings or connected pavilions."[15]

If we relate the urban pressures recognized in the aforementioned examples to the concept of idealization through programatic requirements (i.e., if we deform Le Corbusier's

15. Venturi, *Complexity and Contradiction*, 38.

303

soap bubble), we can arrive at a logically balanced "contextual" building. The office building type, although most often idealized as a point block, can assume any number of functioning shapes. A beautiful example of this flexibility is Gunnar Asplund's 1922 competition for the Royal Chancellery in Stockholm. Produced at the same time that Le Corbusier was creating his "Ville Contemporaine", Asplund's project presented an opposite point of view. In the "Ville Contemporaine", the office building was idealized as a cruciform tower—a collection of concepts about the building type—presented in almost cartoon fashion. To Asplund, the specific symbolic impact of the building type was subordinate to the relationship of the building and site. The resulting parti ties the building inextricably to the context in a manner that tends to disguise the limits of the actual building lot. Here the relative symbolic importance of the complex in the town is accomplished locally, by the placement of the entrance portico on the major axis. This portico functions in a manner similar to the benediction loggia of S. Giovanni in Laterano. The chancellery configuration begins to imply a strategy of "progressive substitution" in which successive elements relate directly to the adjacent elements. Although the building complex responds to its site context, it is by no means a simple catalogue of site pressures. On the contrary, Asplund's scheme is in the best tradition of Venturi's idea of "Both-And". It is both responsive and assertive, both figure and ground, both introverted and extroverted, and both idealized and deformed.

A further jump in scale leads to the study of "zones" and "fields" within particular city plans.[16] When abstracted, these are obvious organizing devices for further development as well as conceptually prototypical schemes for building in deformations. The plans of Stuttgart and Munich exhibit the presence of zones generally related to certain periods of development. The figure-ground abstractions show how accident, important buildings, and major spaces tend to section the city into a series of phenomenally transparent fields, the organizations of which are not unlike those of a cubist painting. "Within cubist paintings," Copper asserts, "pictorial space has been shattered into an endless collage of overlapping elements rarely complete in themselves," which "find their organization via reference to larger elements often superimposed over them." In urban groupings, "a field of objects would be seen as a unit when they are defined by some dissimilar means of organization, or when, via some idiosyncrasy of form, polarize themselves into a cogent grouping."

As in the cubist painting, when the organizational geometries do not reside in the objects themselves, the possibilities of combining various buildings within a system of order which attributes to each piece a bit of the organization become almost infinite. To limit the range of possibilities the use of grid systems has been traditional. The interaction of grids with diagonals and curved systems has been explored in the Urban Design Department at Cornell University under the direction of Colin Rowe. In the plan for the Buffalo waterfront prepared by students under Professor Rowe's guidance, the existing city grids of Buffalo have been exploited, and moves have been made to bring the grids into a condition of spatial overlap in order to facilitate movement and "sense of place."[17] The plan represents a careful use of cubist-like order and specific deformations of idealized

16. See Cohen and Hurtt, *Le Corbusier*, 22.

17. Buffalo Waterfront Project: Colin Rowe, Werner Seligmann, Jerry Alan Wells, critics; Richard Baiter, Richard H. Cardwell, David W. K. Chan, Wayne Copper, Harris N. Forusz, Alfred H. Koetter, Makota Miki, Elpidio F. Olimpio, Franz G. Ozwald, student collaborators.

buildings. The system works almost as a straight line process. Fields are identified through the abstraction of the town via figure-ground drawings. Those considered useful in terms of activity and location are reinforced and clarified. The areas of collision are brought into sharp focus as needing resolution. In this case the city hall area was taken as the focus of two major grid systems, one of which relates to the waterfront, and the other of which relates to the existing town. These are brought together through the use of overlapping zones and geometrically multi-functioning buildings.

A further development of this approach, but in a more rigid context, was the Cornell team's Harlem plan, part of an exhibit sponsored by the Museum of Modern Art: *New Cities, Architecture and Urban Renewal.*[18] The scheme dealt with the particularities of the Manhattan Grid. Virtually without hierarchy, the grid offers no inherent possibilities for specific important building sites or centers of activity. Nor are any particular intersections given real prominence over others. This has the opposite effect of that in a medieval town. Because all streets are the same, initial orientation changes and becomes disorientation. No sense of "place" occurs because no place is different from any other place. The medieval town is, of course, the reverse. Initially impossible to fathom, it ultimately offers total orientation with familiarity. In the case of Harlem, the uneven terrain and the diagonal of St. Nicholas avenue provide the only resources for enlivening the grid. Furthermore, the intrusion of vast wastelands of housing, all rather poor examples of concepts abstracted from the Ville Radieuse, provided clues as to how to approach redevelopment of the area. From this viewpoint it appeared obvious that some attempt should be made to make the many housing projects appear as if they were designed to co-exist with each other and with the context. This was accomplished by either "springing loose" the projects into zones of predominant void and defining these zones with hard edges, or by "wrapping up" the projects in order to give them back a context. The areas of great activity, where important new spaces were created, adjusted themselves to the existing context via multi-functioning buildings. The complex of buildings on the major east-west axis of 125 St. adheres on one side to the blocks opposite and on the other side reacts almost violently to various pressures on its "garden" façade which front an immense plaza.

These schemes have assumed a level of abstraction which permits the idealization of buildings either as particular urban symbols or as building programs. There is, therefore, a reliance on certain modern architecture parti-types. Although in many instances in the Urban Design Studio at Cornell buildings have been given functions roughly relating to their form-type, it should be emphasized that the primary intention has been to create a formal "shorthand" which explains site pressures to an imaginary project architect. Thus, when presented with a design problem against which to measure the pre-deformed shapes given as the urban design exercise, the individual architect is in possession of an input which shows him how to start making decisions. The process can function only if the designer is willing to recognize the ultimate flexibility of any program and its ability to imply any number of partis. The process is also aided by the designer's knowledge of parti-types for traditional building programs.

18. *The New City: Architecture and Urban Renewal* (New York: Museum of Modern Art, 1967).

Writing and Discussion Questions

ANALYSIS

1. What was Le Corbusier arguing for and against? What excerpt/quotation best represents this?
2. What was Jacobs arguing for and against? What excerpt/quotation best represents this?
3. What was Schumacher arguing for and against? What excerpt/quotation best represents this?

SYNTHESIS

1. Regarding concepts of context and building, discuss one major difference regarding Le Corbusier's, Jacobs', and Schumacher's texts.
2. Regarding concepts of context and building, discuss one primary commonality regarding Le Corbusier's, Jacobs', and Schumacher's texts.

SELF-REFLECTION

1. For each of the texts, discuss a major issue with which you most agree and most disagree; reflect upon why you hold these views.
2. Select a recent design project, or a current project on which you are working. Discuss the characteristics of the project in regards to context, in light of the discussion and texts introduced in this chapter. What attitudes regarding context does your work illustrate?

PROSPECTION

1. Select one of the texts listed in the bibliography for this chapter; locate and read it. To what degree is that text and the attitudes it represents still relevant to architecture today and in the near future?

2. What is the role of context in architecture today? Is context predominantly a physical, social, economic, or political issue; some combination of these; or something else? In other words, if a fourth text were added to this chapter, what would the argument be?

Other Readings on Context and Building

Bacon, Edmund. *Design of Cities: Revised Edition* (New York: Penguin Classics, 1976).

Fishman, Robert. *Urban Utopias in the Twentieth Century: Ebenezer Howard, Frank Lloyd Wright, Le Corbusier* (Cambridge: MIT Press, 1982).

Geddes, Sir Patrick. *Cities in Evolution: An Introduction to the Town Planning Movement and to the Study of Civics* (London: Williams & Norgate, 1915).

Howard, Sir Ebenezer. *Garden Cities of Tomorrow* (London: S. Sonnenschein & Co., 1902).

Lynch, Kevin. *The Image of the City* (Cambridge: MIT Press, 1960).

Rossi, Aldo. *The Architecture of the City* (Cambridge: MIT Press, 1984).

Rowe, Colin, and Fred Koetter. *Collage City* (Cambridge: MIT Press, 1984).

Whyte, William H. *The Social Life of Small Urban Spaces* (Washington, DC: Conservation Foundation, 1980).

Chapter 10

CONTEXT and BUILDING (PART 2)

FIGURE 10.1
Photograph of canal and waterfront infill housing, Amsterdam, Netherlands. Each building was designed by a different architect.

FIGURE 10.2
Photograph of Chicago River, Trump Tower (left), and skewed façade of the Wrigley Building (right), Chicago, Illinois, United States (1920–1931). Architects: Graham, Anderson, Probst, and White.

INTRODUCTORY DISCUSSION

1. Of the two images above, which better represents the concept of "contextual" architecture? Why?

2. How has the concept of "context" in architecture changed in recent years?

3. How important or unimportant is "context" relative to other issues—tectonics, use, etc.—in architecture today?

Introduction

What is the most important city to architectural history? Carthage, Babylon, or Jericho? Athens or Constantinople? London, Paris, Beijing, Tokyo, or New York? This would be a difficult debate to resolve. Nevertheless, one city worth discussing would be Rome, Italy, which holds a unique and distinguished position in architectural history and theory. It was the physical, political, and ideological center of the Roman Empire, it is home to an unparalleled collection of cultural and architectural artifacts, and it is the exemplar of medieval and Renaissance European urban design and planning. It is a city that has been transformed again and again over centuries. Rome has been transformed by religious rulers, political regimes, and by the media. During the 16th century, Pope Sixtus the Fifth conceived a street plan for Rome that linked prominent nodes of the city. During the 1930s reign of Benito Mussolini, the historic Roman Forum was permanently altered by the insertion of the Via dei Fori Imperiali. The grandeur of Rome was recast in the 2000 film *Gladiator*, starring Russell Crowe. And, with the growing suburbanization of North America and Europe, many urban planners, designers, and architects have returned to Rome for inspiration. While urban sustainability is a primary motive behind neo-traditional town planning, Rome arose and developed for different reasons.

Military strategy was a primary factor in the emergence of Rome, and it was a primary motive behind Vitruvius's recommendations for the design of Roman cities in Book I of *The Ten Books on Architecture*, the *original text* in this chapter. Vitruvius, who served in the Roman military, was primarily concerned with the selection of advantageous sites and the construction of fortifying walls. Issues more common in urban planning today—such as, the planning of streets and the positioning of public buildings and spaces—was secondary. In parallel, Vitruvius placed issues of "healthfulness," determined by the local geography and climate, above aesthetic and spatial matters.

In *Learning from Las Vegas*, the *reflective text* for this chapter, American architects and architectural theorists Robert Venturi, Denise Scott Brown, and Steven Izenour saw Rome differently. To them, aesthetics and space were essential factors. Drawing comparisons to Rome, they utilized Las Vegas, Nevada, as a case study to reveal the emergence of new architectural concepts, spaces, and styles. They compared the relationships between public and private space, as well as exterior public space and interior public space, in both cities—the piazza and church, in the case of Rome, and the strip and casino lobby, in the case of Las Vegas. Likewise, for both cities, chaos appears to dominate, but it is underpinned by ephemeral order—political and religious in Rome, economic in Las Vegas. Venturi, Scott Brown, and Izenour saw these cites as "archetypes" rather than "prototypes." This concept of the archetypal city parallels the late-Modern notion of "context" and the rise of "contextualism."

Citing Italian architectural critic Ernesto Rogers, Adrian Forty described contextualism as an approach that views "architecture as a dialogue with its surroundings, both in the immediate physical sense [and] as a historical continuum." In "Context," the *philosophical text* for this chapter, Forty underscored the diverse meanings that the word held. Some architects and theorists saw context as a relationship between urban solids (buildings) and voids (public spaces), as was the case for Colin Rowe and Fred Koetter in the 1978 book *Collage City*; others viewed context as being historically or stylistically motivated; and yet others, such as Rem Koolhaas, pondered whether or not context was at all important to urban and architectural design.

The texts for this chapter illustrate that urban planning, design, and construction have been influenced by a variety of factors, from military stratagem to visual aesthetics. Changing social, technological, economic, environmental, political, and legal factors transform the way planners and architects shape cities and towns. New cities and towns will arise and existing cities, like Rome, will be further transformed. Urban planners, designers, and architects will continue to debate which issues are relevant and irrelevant to contemporary and future cities and towns. But they will not be making autocratic decisions as has been the case in the past. The public, the inhabitants of cities themselves, will be central participants in the shaping and re-shaping of their cities. Urban planners, designers, and architects will become moderators of the debates among these diverse inhabitants and their diverse ideals.

Original Text

MARCUS VITRUVIUS, EXCERPTS FROM *THE TEN BOOKS ON ARCHITECTURE*.

First Published ca. 25 B.C.E.

THE SITE OF A CITY

For fortified towns the following general principles are to be observed. First comes the choice of a very healthy site. Such a site will be high, neither misty nor frosty, and in a climate neither hot nor cold, but temperate; further, without marshes in the neighbourhood. For when the morning breezes blow toward the town at sunrise, if they bring with them mists from marshes and, mingled with the mist, the poisonous breath of the creatures of the marshes to be wafted into the bodies of the inhabitants, they will make the site unhealthy. Again, if the town is on the coast with a southern or western exposure, it will not be healthy, because in summer the southern sky grows hot at sunrise and is fiery at noon, while a western exposure grows warm after sunrise, is hot at noon, and at evening all aglow.

These variations in heat and the subsequent cooling off are harmful to the people living on such sites. The same conclusion may be reached in the case of inanimate things. For instance, nobody draws the light for covered wine rooms from the south or west, but rather from the north, since that quarter is never subject to change but is always constant and unshifting. So it is with granaries: grain exposed to the sun's course soon loses its good quality, and provisions and fruit, unless stored in a place unexposed to the sun's course, do not keep long.

For heat is a universal solvent, melting out of things their power of resistance, and sucking away and removing their natural strength with its fiery exhalations so that they grow soft, and hence weak, under its glow. We see this in the case of iron which, however hard it may naturally be, yet when heated thoroughly in a furnace fire can be easily worked into any kind of shape, and still, if cooled while it is soft and white hot, it hardens again with a mere dip into cold water and takes on its former quality.

We may also recognize the truth of this from the fact that in summer the heat makes everybody weak, not only in unhealthy but even in healthy places, and that in winter even the most unhealthy districts are much healthier because they are given a solidity by the cooling off. Similarly, persons removed from cold countries to hot cannot endure it but waste away; whereas those who pass from hot places to the cold regions of the north, not only do not suffer in health from the change of residence but even gain by it.

It appears, then, that in founding towns we must beware of districts from which hot winds can spread abroad over the inhabitants. For while all bodies are composed of the four elements, . . . heat, moisture, . . . earth, and air, . . . there are mixtures according to natural temperament which make up the natures of all the different animals of the world. . . .

Therefore, if one of these elements, heat, becomes predominant in any body what-soever, it destroys and dissolves all the others with its violence. . . . Again, if too much moisture enters the channels of a body, and thus introduces disproportion, the other elements, adulterated by the liquid, are impaired, and the virtues of the mixture dissolved. . . . In the same way, increase or diminution of the proportion of air or of the earth which is natural to the body may enfeeble the other elements. . . .

If one wishes a more accurate understanding of all this, he need only consider and observe the natures of birds, fishes, and land animals, and he will thus come to reflect upon distinctions of temperament. One form of mixture is proper to birds, another to fishes, and a far different form to land animals. . . .

Therefore, if all this is as we have explained, our reason showing us that the bodies of animals are made up of the elements, and these bodies, as we believe, giving way and breaking up as a result of excess or deficiency in this or that element, we cannot but believe that we must take great care to select a very temperate climate for the site of our city, since healthfulness is, as we have said, the first requisite.

I cannot too strongly insist upon the need of a return to the method of old times. Our ancestors, when about to build a town or an army post, sacrificed some of the cattle that were wont to feed on the site proposed and examined their livers. If the livers of the first victims were dark-coloured or abnormal, they sacrificed others, to see whether the fault was due to disease or their food. They never began to build defensive works in a place until after they had made many such trials and satisfied themselves that good water and food had made the liver sound and firm. If they continued to find it abnormal, they argued from this that the food and water supply found in such a place would be just as unhealthy for man, and so they moved away and changed to another neighbourhood, healthfulness being their chief object. . . .

THE CITY WALLS

After insuring on these principles the healthfulness of the future city, and selecting a neighbourhood that can supply plenty of food stuffs to maintain the community, with good roads or else convenient rivers or seaports affording easy means of transport to the city, the next thing to do is to lay the foundations for the towers and walls. Dig down to solid bottom, if it can be found, and lay them therein, going as deep as the magnitude of the proposed work seems to require. They should be much thicker than the part of the walls that will appear above ground, and their structure should be as solid as it can possibly be laid.

The towers must be projected beyond the line of wall, so that an enemy wishing to approach the wall to carry it by assault may be exposed to the fire of missiles on his open flank from the towers on his right and left. Special pains should be taken that there be no easy avenue by which to storm the wall. The roads should be encompassed at steep points, and planned so as to approach the gates, not in a straight line, but from the right to the left; for as a result of this, the right hand side of the assailants, unprotected by their shields, will be next the wall. Towns should be laid out not as an exact square nor with salient angles, but in circular form, to give a view of the enemy from many points. Defence is difficult where there are salient angles, because the angle protects the enemy rather than the inhabitants.

The thickness of the wall should, in my opinion, be such that armed men meeting on top of it may pass one another without interference. In the thickness there should be set a very close succession of ties made of charred olive wood, binding the two faces of the wall together like pins, to give it lasting endurance. For that is a material which neither decay, nor the weather, nor time can harm, but even though buried in the earth or set in the water it keeps sound and useful forever. And so not only city walls but substructures in general and all walls that require a thickness like that of a city wall, will be long in falling to decay if tied in this manner.

The towers should be set at intervals of not more than a bowshot apart, so that in case of an assault upon anyone of them, the enemy may be repulsed with scorpiones and other means of hurling missiles from the towers to the right and left. Opposite the inner side of every tower the wall should be interrupted for a space the width of the tower, and have only a wooden flooring across, leading to the interior of the tower but not firmly nailed. This is to be cut away by the defenders in case the enemy gets possession of any portion of the wall; and if the work is quickly done, the enemy will not be able to make his way to the other towers and the rest of the wall unless he is ready to face a fall.

The towers themselves must be either round or polygonal. Square towers are sooner shattered by military engines, for the battering rams pound their angles to pieces; but in the case of round towers they can do no harm, being engaged, as it were, in driving wedges to their centre. The system of fortification by wall and towers may be made safest by the addition of earthen ramparts, for neither rams, nor mining, nor other engineering devices can do them any harm. . . .

With regard to the material of which the actual wall should be constructed or finished, there can be no definite prescription, because we cannot obtain in all places the supplies that we desire. Dimension stone, flint, rubble, burnt or unburnt brick—use them as you find them. For it is not every neighbourhood or particular locality that can have a wall built of burnt brick like that at Babylon, where there was plenty of asphalt to take the place of lime and sand, and yet possibly each may be provided with materials of equal usefulness so that out of them a faultless wall may be built to last forever.

THE DIRECTIONS OF THE STREETS; WITH REMARKS ON THE WINDS

The town being fortified, the next step is the apportionment of house lots within the wall and the laying out of streets and alleys with regard to climatic conditions. They will be properly laid out if foresight is employed to exclude the winds from the alleys. Cold winds are disagreeable, hot winds enervating, moist winds unhealthy. We must, therefore, avoid mistakes in this matter and beware of the common experience of many communities. . . . When the wind is south, the people fall ill; when it is northwest, it sets them coughing; with a north wind they do indeed recover but cannot stand about in the alleys and streets, owing to the severe cold.

Wind is a flowing wave of air, moving hither and thither in definitely. It is produced when heat meets moisture, the rush of heat generating a mighty current of air. . . .

By shutting out the winds from our dwellings, therefore, we shall not only make the place healthful for people who are well, but also in the case of diseases due perhaps to unfavourable situations elsewhere, the patients, who in other healthy places might be cured by a different form of treatment, will here be more quickly cured by the mildness that comes from the shutting out of the winds. The diseases which are hard to cure in neighbourhoods such as those to which I have referred above are catarrh, hoarseness, coughs, pleurisy, consumption, spitting of blood, and all others that are cured not by lowering the system but by building it up. They are hard to cure, first, because they are originally due to chills; secondly, because the patient's system being already exhausted by disease, the air there, which is in constant agitation owing to winds and therefore deteriorated, takes all the sap of life out of their diseased bodies and leaves them more meagre every day. On the other hand, a mild, thick air, without draughts and not constantly blowing back and forth, builds up their frames by its unwavering steadiness, and so strengthens and restores people who are afflicted with these diseases. . . .

These facts being thus determined, to find the directions and quarters of the winds your method of procedure should be as follows.

In the middle of the city place a marble amussium, laying it true by the level, or else let the spot be made so true by means of rule and level that no amussium is necessary. In the very centre of that spot set up a bronze gnomon or "shadow tracker". . . . At about the fifth hour in the morning, take the end of the shadow cast by this gnomon, and mark it with a point. Then, opening your compasses to this point which marks the length of the gnomon's shadow, describe a circle from the centre. In the afternoon watch the shadow of your gnomon as it lengthens, and when it once more touches the circumference of this circle and the shadow in the afternoon is equal in length to that of the morning, mark it with a point.

From these two points describe with your compasses intersecting arcs, and through their intersection and the centre let a line be drawn to the circumference of the circle to give us the quarters of south and north. Then, using a sixteenth part of the entire circumference of the circle as a diameter, describe a circle with its centre on the line to the south, at the point where it crosses the circumference, and put points to the right and left on the circumference on the south side, repeating the process on the north side. From the four points thus obtained draw lines intersecting the centre from one side of the circumference to the other. Thus we shall have an eighth part of the circumference set out for Auster and another for Septentrio. The rest of the entire circumference is then to be divided into three equal parts on each side, and thus we have designed a figure equally apportioned among the eight winds. Then let the directions of your streets and alleys be laid down on the lines of division between the quarters of two winds.

On this principle of arrangement the disagreeable force of the winds will be shut out from dwellings and lines of houses. For if the streets run full in the face of the winds, their constant blasts rushing in from the open country, and then confined by narrow alleys, will sweep through them with great violence. The lines of houses must therefore be directed away from the quarters from which the winds blow, so that as they come in they may strike against the angles of the blocks and their force thus be broken and dispersed. . . .

THE SITES FOR PUBLIC BUILDINGS

Having laid out the alleys and determined the streets, we have next to treat of the choice of building sites for temples, the forum, and all other public places, with a view to general convenience and utility. If the city is on the sea, we should choose ground close to the harbour as the place where the forum is to be built; but if inland, in the middle of the town. For the temples, the sites for those of the gods under whose particular protection the state is thought to rest and for Jupiter, Juno, and Minerva, should be on the very highest point commanding a view of the greater part of the city. Mercury should be in the forum, or, like Isis and Serapis, in the emporium: Apollo and Father Bacchus near the theatre: Hercules at the circus in communities which have no gymnasia nor amphitheatres; Mars outside the city but at the training ground, and so Venus, but at the harbour. It is moreover shown by the Etruscan diviners in treatises on their science that the fanes of Venus, Vulcan, and Mars should be situated outside the walls, in order that the young men and married women may not become habituated in the city to the temptations incident to the worship of Venus, and that buildings may be free from the terror of fires through the religious rites and sacrifices which call the power of Vulcan beyond the walls. As for Mars, when that divinity is enshrined outside the walls, the citizens will never take up arms against each other, and he will defend the city from its enemies and save it from danger in war.

Ceres also should be outside the city in a place to which people need never go except for the purpose of sacrifice. That place should be under the protection of religion, purity, and good morals. Proper sites should be set apart for the precincts of the other gods according to the nature of the sacrifices offered to them.

Reflective Text

ROBERT VENTURI, DENISE SCOTT BROWN, AND STEVEN
IZENOUR, EXCERPTS FROM *LEARNING FROM LAS VEGAS*.

First Published in 1972

FROM ROME TO LAS VEGAS

Las Vegas is the apotheosis of the desert town. Visiting Las Vegas in the mid-1960s was
like visiting Rome in the late 1940s. For young Americans in the 1940s, familiar only with
the auto-scaled, gridiron city and the antiurban theories of the previous architectural
generation, the traditional urban spaces, the pedestrian scale, and the mixtures, yet
continuities, of styles of the Italian piazzas were a significant revelation. They rediscovered
the piazza. Two decades later architects are perhaps ready for similar lessons about large
open space, big scale, and high speed. Las Vegas is to the Strip what Rome is to the
Piazza.

There are other parallels between Rome and Las Vegas: their expansive settings in
the Campagna and in the Mojave Desert, for instance, that tend to focus and clarify their
images. On the other hand, Las Vegas *was* built in a day, or rather, the Strip was developed
in a virgin desert in a short time. It was not superimposed on an older pattern as were
the pilgrim's Rome of the Counter-Reformation and the commercial strips of eastern cities,
and it is therefore easier to study. Each city is an archetype rather than a prototype, an
exaggerated example from which to derive lessons for the typical. Each city vividly
superimposes elements of a supranational scale on the local fabric: churches in the religious
capital, casinos and their signs in the entertainment capital. These cause violent juxtapositions of use and scale in both cities. Rome's churches, off streets and piazzas, are open
to the public; the pilgrim, religious or architectural, can walk from church to church. The
gambler or architect in Las Vegas can similarly take in a variety of casinos along the Strip.
The casinos and lobbies of Las Vegas are ornamental and monumental and open to the
promenading public; a few old banks and railroad stations excepted, they are unique in
American cities. Nolli's map of the mid-eighteenth century reveals the sensitive and
complex connections between public and private space in Rome. Private building is shown

in gray crosshatching that is carved into by the public spaces, exterior *and* interior. These spaces, open or roofed, are shown in minute detail through darker poché. Interiors of churches read like piazzas and courtyards of palaces, yet a variety of qualities and scales is articulated.

MAPS OF LAS VEGAS

A "Nolli" map of the Las Vegas Strip reveals and clarifies what is public and what is private, but here the scale is enlarged by the inclusion of the parking lot, and the solid-to-void ratio is reversed by the open spaces of the desert. Mapping the Nolli components from an aerial photograph provides an intriguing crosscut of Strip systems. These components, separated and redefined, could be undeveloped land, asphalt, autos, buildings, and ceremonial space. Reassembled, they describe the Las Vegas equivalent of the pilgrims' way, although the description, like Nolli's map, misses the iconological dimensions of the experience.

A conventional land-use map of Las Vegas can show the overall structure of commercial use in the city as it relates to other uses but none of the detail of use type or intensity. "Land-use" maps of the insides of casino complexes, however, begin to suggest the systematic planning that all casinos share. Strip "address" and "establishment" maps can depict both intensity and variety of use. Distribution maps show patterns of, for example, churches, and food stores that Las Vegas shares with other cities and those such as wedding chapels and auto rental stations that are Strip-oriented and unique. It is extremely hard to suggest the atmospheric qualities of Las Vegas, because these are primarily dependent on watts, animation, and iconology; however, "message maps," tourist maps, and brochures suggest some of it.

MAIN STREET AND THE STRIP

A street map of Las Vegas reveals two scales of movement within the gridiron plan: that of Main Street and that of the Strip. The main street of Las Vegas is Fremont Street, and the earlier of two concentrations of casinos is located along three of four blocks of this street. The casinos here are bazaarlike in the immediacy to the sidewalk of their clicking and tinkling gambling machines. The Fremont Street casinos and hotels focus on the railroad depot at the head of the street; here the railroad and main street scales of movement connect. The depot building is now gone, replaced by a hotel, and the bus station is now the busier entrance to town, but the axial focus on the railroad depot from Fremont Street was visual, and possibly symbolic. This contrasts with the Strip, where a second and later development of casinos extends southward to the airport, the jet-scale entrance to town.

One's first introduction to Las Vegas architecture is a forebear of Eero Saarinen's TWA Terminal, which is the local airport building. Beyond this piece of architectural image, impressions are scaled to the car rented at the airport. Here is the unraveling of the famous Strip itself, which, as Route 91, connects the airport with the downtown.

SYSTEM AND ORDER ON THE STRIP

The image of the commercial strip is chaos. The order in this landscape is not obvious. The continuous highway itself and its systems for turning are absolutely consistent. The median strip accommodates the U-turns necessary to a vehicular promenade for casino crawlers as well as left turns onto the local street pattern that the Strip intersects. The curbing allows frequent right turns for casinos and other commercial enterprises and eases the difficult transitions from highway to parking. The streetlights function superfluously along many parts of the Strip that are incidentally but abundantly lit by signs, but their consistency of form and position and their arching shapes begin to identify by day a continuous space of the highway, and the constant rhythm contrasts effectively with the uneven rhythms of the signs behind.

This counterpoint reinforces the contrast between two types of order on the Strip: the obvious visual order of street elements and the difficult visual order of buildings and signs. The zone *of* the highway is a shared order. The zone *off* the highway is an individual order. The elements of the highway are civic. The buildings and signs are private. In combination they embrace continuity *and* discontinuity, going *and* stopping, clarity *and* ambiguity, cooperation *and* competition, the community *and* rugged individualism. The system of the highway gives order to the sensitive functions of exit and entrance, as well as to the image of the Strip as a sequential whole. It also generates places for individual enterprises to grow and controls the general direction of that growth. It allows variety and change along its sides and accommodates the contrapuntal, competitive order of the individual enterprises.

There *is* an order along the sides of the highway. Varieties of activities are juxtaposed on the Strip: service stations, minor motels, and multi-million-dollar casinos. Marriage chapels ("credit cards accepted") converted from bungalows with added neon-lined steeples are apt to appear anywhere toward the downtown end. Immediate proximity of related uses, as on Main Street, where you *walk* from one store to another, is not required along the Strip because interaction is by car and highway. You *drive* from one casino to another even when they are adjacent because of the distance between them, and an intervening service station is not disagreeable.

CHANGE AND PERMANENCE ON THE STRIP

The rate of obsolescence of a sign seems to be nearer to that of an automobile than that of a building. The reason is not physical degeneration but what competitors are doing around you. The leasing system operated by the sign companies and the possibility of total tax write-off may have something to do with it. The most unique, most monumental parts of the Strip, the signs and casino façades, are also the most changeable; it is the neutral, systems-motel structures behind that survive a succession of facelifts and a series of themes up front. The Aladdin Hotel and Casino is Moorish in front and Tudor behind.

Las Vegas's greatest growth has been since World War II. There are noticeable changes every year: new hotels and signs as well as neon-embossed parking structures replacing on-lot parking on and behind Fremont Street. Like the agglomeration of chapels in a Roman church and the stylistic sequence of piers in a Gothic cathedral, the Golden Nugget casino has evolved over 30 years from a building with a sign on it to a totally sign-covered building. The Stardust Hotel has engulfed a small restaurant and a second hotel in its expansion and has united the three-piece façade with 600 feet of computer-programmed animated neon.

THE ARCHITECTURE OF THE STRIP

It is hard to think of each flamboyant casino as anything but unique, and this is as it should be, because good advertising technique requires the differentiation of the product. However, these casinos have much in common because they are under the same sun, on the same Strip, and perform similar functions; they differ from other casinos—say, on Fremont Street—and from other hotels that are not casinos.

Philosophical Text

ADRIAN FORTY, "CONTEXT."

First Published in 2000

> The task of the architectural project is to reveal, through the transformation of form, the essence of the surrounding context.
>
> V. Gregotti, 1982 introduction to French
> edition of *Le Territoire de l'Architecture*

Introduced into the architectural vocabulary in the 1960s, "context," "contextual" and "contextualism" were part of the first substantial critique of modernist practice, and might on that account be classed as postmodernist terms. But whether they were the last modernist terms, or the first postmodernist ones matters very little; they are included here partly on chronological grounds, as belonging to the period of late modernism, and partly because they were wholly directed towards the discourse of modernism, but most particularly because illustrate so well the imperialism effected by the act of translation from one language to another.

The story begins in Milan in the 1950s, when in the editorials written by Ernesto Rogers for the magazine *Casabella Continuità* in the middle of the decade there appeared the first serious critique of the work of the first generation of modernist architects. Rogers criticized their tendency to treat every scheme as a unique abstract problem, their indifference to location, and their desire to make of every work a prodigy. Rather, Rogers argued, consider architecture as a dialogue with its surroundings, both in the immediate physical sense, but also as a historical continuum. The terms used by Rogers were "*le preesistenze ambientali*" (surrounding pre-existences), or "*ambiente*," and although both have since been translated into English as "context" this is misleading, for Rogers used neither this word, nor its Italian equivalent *contesto*—which entered general use in Italy in the 1970s as a translation of the English word "context" only after that had become current in the USA. It is worth investigating what Rogers meant by *preesistenze ambientali*, for it differed in several respects from the Anglo-Saxon "context" with which it has subsequently become confused. Compared to previous arguments for the responsiveness of architecture to location—such as the *genius loci* of the English picturesque, or the English critic Trystan Edwards's objections to the "selfish" modern commercial building— what distinguished Rogers's concept was the absolute importance of the historical continuity manifested by the city and existing in the minds of its occupants.[1] As Rogers wrote in one of his editorials, "to consider *l'ambiente* means to consider history."[2] For Rogers, the two concepts of *preesistenze ambientali* and "history"[3] were indissolubly linked: "*to understand history is essential for the formation of the architect,* since he must be able to insert his own work into the *preesistenze ambientali* and to take it, dialectically, into account."[4] Rogers's idea of *ambiente* as a historical process came from a variety of sources, but one in particular which he cited specifically was an essay by the poet T. S. Eliot, "Tradition and the Individual Talent" (1917). It is worth quoting from this essay, for it helps make clear the interconnectedness of continuity, history and *ambiente* in Rogers's mind. Eliot wrote, "the historical sense involves a perception, not only of the pastness of the past, but of its presence"—

> The existing monuments form an ideal order among themselves, which is modified by the introduction of the new (the really new) work of art among them. The existing order is complete before the new work arrives; for order to persist after the super-vention of novelty, the *whole* order must be, if ever so slightly, altered; and so the relations, proportions, values of each work of art towards the whole are readjusted; and this is conformity between the old and the new. Whoever has approved this idea of order, of the form of European, of English literature will not find it pre-posterous that the past should be altered by the present as much as the present is directed by the past.[5]

It is this sense that all work impacts upon present consciousness of the historical past that was so essential to Rogers's notion of "*ambiente*."

Two examples will suffice to show how Rogers used *preesistenze ambientali* in his critique of orthodox modern architecture: "One might accuse of formalism an architect who does not absorb into his work the particular and characteristic contents suggested by the *ambiente*";[6] or,

> Let us resist the affected cosmopolitanism which in the name of a still shallowly felt universal style raises the same architecture in New York, Tokyo, or Rio; identical architecture in both the country and the town. Let us seek rather to blend our works into the *preesistenze ambientali,* both the natural surroundings, and those created historically by human genius.[7]

The scheme which first brought these ideas to international notice—as well as contributing to Rogers's own formulation of them—was the controversy in 1954 over Frank Lloyd

1. Trystan Edwards, *Good and Bad Manners in Architecture* (London: Tiranti, 1924), 2.
2. Ernesto N. Rogers, "Preexisting Conditions and Issues of Contemporary Building Practice," in *Architecture Culture: 1943–1968*, ed. Joan Ockman (New York: Rizzoli, 1993), 203. First published in 1955.
3. Ibid., 196–205.
4. Ernesto N. Rogers, *Gli Elementi del Fenomeno Architettonico* (Naples: Guida Editori, 1961), 96.
5. T. S. Eliot, "Tradition and the Individual Talent," in *Points of View* (London: Faber and Faber, 1941), 26–27.
6. Rogers, "Preexisting Conditions," 201.
7. Ernesto N. Rogers, "L'Architettura Moderna dopo la generazione dei Maestri," *Casabella Continuità,* 211 (June–July 1956), 3.

Wright's Masieri Memorial in Venice. His project, which would have occupied a prominent location on the Grand Canal, provoked passionate argument inside Italy and abroad about the suitedness of modern architecture to historic sites, and about the degree to which Wright's design did or did not take sufficient account of its surroundings. That the scheme was not built had less to do with the merits of the design than with the political objections at the time to an American building in Italy.[8]

Rogers's *ambiente* became a topic of general discussion amongst the circle of Milan architects associated with *Casabella*, and featured significantly in their writings; particularly worth remarking on are Vittorio Gregotti's *Il Territorio dell'Architettura* (1966), and above all Aldo Rossi's *The Architecture of the City* (1966) whose subsequent fame has eclipsed all other Italian architectural criticism of that era, but which can only satisfactorily be understood in relation to it. *The Architecture of the City* is in part an extended disquisition upon the concept of *ambiente*. For readers of the American edition of the book, where the word *ambiente* was translated throughout as "context," this nuance is rendered invisible, and it is made to seem that Rossi was party to the same debate as Colin Rowe and others at Cornell University where, as we shall see, "contextualism" was invented. Nothing could have been further from the truth: the word Rossi used throughout was *ambiente*, never *contesto* or "context," and his objections to "context" were in fact objections to Rogers's *ambiente* (or its perversion by others), and unrelated to any New England conversations. The paradox presented to readers of the English-language edition, of how someone could be so critical of "context" and yet put forward such a persuasive argument for it, is purely an effect of the translation and does not arise in the Italian original. Rossi's objections that "context seems strangely bound up with illusion, with illusionism. As such it has nothing to do with the architecture of the city,"[9] or "As for the term *context*, we find that it is mostly an impediment to research,"[10] were, we must remember, objections to *l'ambiente*, not "context." Rossi's criticism of Rogers's *l'ambiente* was that it was insufficiently concrete: and what Rossi wanted to show was that it could be made concrete if one studied architectural forms themselves, independently of their functions, for in these forms was the only tangible point of contact between the economic processes of cities, on the one hand, documented through the verifiable histories of land development and partition, and on the other hand the vagueness of the "collective historical consciousness" of the city that was Rogers's *preesistenze ambientali*.

If we turn now to the history of the English-language word "context," its first significant appearance within the vocabulary of architecture seems to have been in Christopher Alexander's *Notes on the Synthesis of Form* of 1964, though its presence in this particular text seems to have had little to do with its subsequent usage. Alexander used "context" as a synonym for "environment": introducing the book, he wrote "every design problem begins with an effort to achieve fitness between two entities: the form in question, and its context. The form is the solution to the problem; the context defines the problem."[11] This mechanistic relationship is softened later in the book—the aim of design, he writes, is not to meet the requirements in the best possible way, but "to prevent

8. See Neil Levine, *The Architecture of Frank Lloyd Wright* (New York: Princeton University Press, 1996), 374–383.

9. Aldo Rossi, *The Architecture of the City*, trans. D. Ghirardo and J. Ockman (Cambridge: MIT Press, 1982), 123. First published in 1966.

10. Ibid., 126.

11. Christopher Alexander, *Notes on the Synthesis of Form* (Cambridge: Harvard University Press, 1964), 15.

misfit between the form and the context."[12] Nonetheless, the purpose of the book was to devise a scheme for ordering the variables that constituted "context" so as to develop a method of design free from all the preconceptions that, in Alexander's opinion, had hampered previous efforts to achieve truly functional design. Alexander's choice of "context" instead of the more customary "environment" may have been due to his desire to include cultural variables, but otherwise his strictly functionalist use of the term had little to do with its subsequent history.

The introduction of "contextualism" and "contextualist" into the architectural vocabulary occurred in 1966 in the Urban Design studio that the English critic Colin Rowe had started teaching at Cornell University in 1963.[13] It seems likely that the terms were borrowed from the literary New Criticism movement—even though their sense there was entirely different, and negative, rather than positive, as was the case in architecture. Rowe's Cornell studio developed a critique of modernist architecture that had a good deal in common with Ernesto Rogers's. They shared a distaste for "prodigy" architecture, and for the modernist supposition that the particularity of a building's programme justified in every case a unique solution; and many of the examples they chose to illustrate their ideas were the same. But there were also significant differences. Whereas Rogers was concerned with how the dialectical processes of history were manifested through architecture, Rowe was uninterested in this speculative understanding of the historical environment, and concentrated on the formal properties of works of architecture. And whereas Rogers thought of the environment as formed by objects, "monuments," Rowe was more interested in the relationships between objects and the spaces they occupied. Indicative of Rowe's approach were his preferred exemplars, like Antoine Le Pautre's Hôtel de Beauvais (1652–55) in Paris, where the model French town house was compressed and deformed to fit the irregular site without losing the distinctive features of the type; Rowe compared this to Le Corbusier's Villa Savoie, an isolated primary solid, indifferent to the boundless spatial field it occupies.[14] In the first published statement of the Cornell studio's "contextualism" (which appeared, significantly, in *Casabella*), an ex-student, Thomas Schumacher, wrote: "It is precisely the ways in which idealized forms can be adjusted to a context or used as 'collage' that contextualism seeks to explain, and it is the systems of geometric organization which can be abstracted from any given context that contextualism seeks to divine as design tools."[15] In general, Rogers's and Rossi's interest in *ambiente* was distinguished by "history," whereas the Cornell studio's concern with "context" was formal, marked in particular by its study of figure/ground relationships.[16] And where the Italians were polemical, marked by an underlying commitment to the "modern," Rowe's aim was compromise, between the modernist, and the pre-modernist city. Rowe has since summed up the studio's approach: "If not conservative, its general tone was radical middle of the road. . . . Its ideal was a mediation between the city of Modern architecture—a void with objects—and the historical city—a solid with voids."[17]

In the final testament of Cornell contextualism, Rowe and Koetter's book *Collage City* (1978), the authors made practically no reference to "context" or "contextualism."

12. Ibid., 99.
13. Colin Rowe, *As I was Saying: Recollections and Miscellaneous Essays*, ed. A. Carragone (Cambridge: MIT Press, 1996), vol. 3, 2; Tom Schumacher, "Contextualism: Urban Ideals and Deformations," *Casabella*, 359/60 (1971): 86.
14. Colin Rowe and Fred Koetter, "Collage City," *Architectural Review*, 158 (August 1975): 78; revised and expanded as *Collage City* (Cambridge: MIT Press, 1978).
15. Schumacher, "Contextualism," 84.
16. For a useful comparison of European and American notions of context, see Shane, "Contextualism," *Architectural Design*, 46 (November 1976): 676–679.
17. Rowe, *As I was Saying*, vol. 3, 2.

By this time, though, "context" had become well established in the architectural vocabulary. Kenneth Frampton in 1976 reviewed James Stirling's 1975 competition entry for the Düsseldorf Museum in terms of its "contextual" content, and it was not long before Stirling himself began to talk about his own work, including schemes designed before the word had gained currency, in terms of "context"; for example, commenting in 1984 on the 1971 design for an art gallery at St Andrews University, Stirling wrote "It was both *formal* and *contextual*."[18]

Rowe and Koetter were already avoiding the words "context" and "contextual" by the late 1970s, yet it was around this time, as if to stiffen up the idea and give it broader credibility, that the Italian *ambiente* was taken over and subsumed into the American "context." However, it was not to be long before reservations about the concept itself started to be voiced. Commenting in 1985 on a scheme to extend Frank Lloyd Wright's Guggenheim Museum in New York, the American critic Michael Sorkin wrote, "A consequence of the profession's present preoccupation with 'context' is a kind of collective confidence about the possibility of adding on. There's an implicit argument that architects, duly skilled and sensitized, should be able to intervene anywhere."[19] Sorkin went on to explain why he thought this wrong. By the late 1980s, there was no doubt that many architects were uncomfortable about "context," and were increasingly prepared to say so; in his "diary" of the design for the French national library competition in 1989, Rem Koolhaas wrote in exasperation, "But can such a container still have a relationship with the city? Should it? Is it important? Or is 'fuck context' becoming the theme?"[20]

18. James Stirling, *Writings on Architecture*, ed. R. Maxwell (Milan: Skira, 1998), 153.
19. Michael Sorkin, *Exquisite Corpse: Writings on Buildings* (London: Verso, 1991), 148.
20. Rem Koolhaas and Bruce Mau, *S, M, L, XL*, (Rotterdam; 010 Publishers, 1994), 640.

Writing and Discussion Questions

ANALYSIS

1. What was Vitruvius arguing for and against? What excerpt/quotation best represents this?
2. What were Venturi, Scott Brown, and Izenour arguing for and against? What excerpt/quotation best represents this?
3. What was Forty arguing for and against? What excerpt/quotation best represents this?

SYNTHESIS

1. Regarding concepts of context and building, discuss one major difference regarding Vitruvius', Venturi, Scott Brown, and Izenour's, and Forty's texts.
2. Regarding concepts of context and building, discuss one primary commonality regarding Vitruvius', Venturi, Scott Brown, and Izenour's, and Forty's texts.

SELF-REFLECTION

1. For each of the texts, discuss a major issue with which you most agree and most disagree; reflect upon why you hold these views.
2. Select a recent design project, or a current project on which you are working. Discuss the characteristics of the project in regards to context, in light of the discussion and texts introduced in this chapter. What attitudes regarding context does your work illustrate?

PROSPECTION

1. Select one of the texts listed in the bibliography for this chapter; locate and read it. To what degree is that text and the attitudes it represents still relevant to architecture today and in the near future?

2. What is the role of context in architecture today? Is context more important, less important, or of the same importance as it was a century ago? In other words, if a fourth text were added to this chapter, what would the argument be?

Other Readings on Context and Building

Duany, Andres. *Suburban Nation: The Rise of Sprawl and the Decline of the American Dream* (New York: North Point Press, 2001).

Koolhaas, Rem. *Delirious New York: A Retroactive Manifesto* (New York: Monacelli Press, 1997).

Kostof, Spiro. *The City Shaped: Urban Patterns and Meanings Through History* (Boston: Bulfinch, 1991).

Kunstler, James H. *The Geography of Nowhere: The Rise and Decline of America's Man-Made Landscape* (New York: Simon & Schuster, 1994).

Mumford, Lewis. *The City in History: Its Origins, Its Transformations* (New York: Harcourt, 1961).

Tschumi, Bernard. *The Manhattan Transcripts* (San Francisco: John Wiley & Sons, 1994).

Wheeler, Stephen M., and Timothy Beatley, eds. *The Sustainable Urban Development Reader* (London: Routledge, 2004).

Chapter 11

NATURAL and CONSTRUCTED

FIGURE 11.1
Photograph of the exterior
of Falling Water, Bear Run,
Pennsylvania, United States
(1936–1939). Architect: Frank
Lloyd Wright.

FIGURE 11.2
Photograph of granaries and
meeting hut made of local
thatch, stone, and mud in a
Dogon village in Mali (ca. 2008).

INTRODUCTORY DISCUSSION

1. Of the two images above, which better represents the importance of "nature" in architecture? Why?

2. What are the various definitions and connotations of the term "nature" in architecture? How do the terms "nature" and "natural" differ?

3. How are or are not "nature" and "natural" appropriate concepts or terms in architecture today?

Introduction

The tenuous relationship between humans and nature may be the very reason that architecture came to be. According to Vitruvius, Alberti, Laugier, and others, the need for shelter—from rain, sun, and wind; from predators; and from extreme heat or cold—is the origin of architecture.[1] Nevertheless, the relationship between humans and nature, as conceptualized by humans, has been ever changing. Across histories and cultures, "nature" has been theorized in many ways: as adversary, comrade, deity, resource, inspiration, terror, or sanctuary. As cultural perceptions of the relationship between nature and humans have changed, so too has the debate about the relationship between nature and architecture. At times, architects sought to overcome nature, building bridges, dams, monuments, homes, and high rises in seemingly impossible conditions. At other times, architects sought to "build with nature," using indigenous building materials, carefully considering climate, and utilizing existing topographies. At yet other times, architects used nature as a source for design principles, insights, or aspirations.

In *An Essay on Architecture*, the *original text* for this chapter, Marc-Antoine Laugier asserted that nature offered architectural principles and inspirations. Laugier began, "It is the same in architecture as in all other arts: its principles are founded on simple nature, and nature's process clearly indicates its rules." He further asserted that only three elements were necessary in architecture—column (i.e., vertical structure), entablature (i.e., ceiling or horizontal members spanning between columns), and pediment (i.e., roof). Laugier paid particular focus on the column and how its form and role in architecture was derived from nature. Columns, according to Laugier, had to follow five rules, as dictated by nature: (1) they must be strictly vertical, (2) they must be free-standing, (3) they must be round, (4) they must be tapered, and (5) they must rest directly on the floor.[2]

Rather than imitating nature, Vittorio Gregotti believed that architecture and nature must be differentiated from one another. In "Territory and Architecture," the *reflective text* of this chapter, Gregotti saw nature as a geographical "collection" of visual and material features, and that the purpose of architecture was to call attention to these features by way of modification, transformation, and contrast. In the design for the

1. See: Leon Battista Alberti, *On the Art of Building in Ten Books*, trans. Joseph Rykwert, Neil Leach, and Robert Tavernor (Cambridge: MIT Press, 1988), first published in 1486; Marc-Antoine Laugier, *An Essay on Architecture*, trans. Wolfgang Herrmann and Anni Herrmann (Los Angeles: Hennessey & Ingalls, 1977), first published in 1753; and Marcus Vitruvius, *Ten Books on Architecture* trans. Morris H. Morgan (New York: Cambridge, 1999), first published ca. 25 B.C.E.

2. These "rules" have been broken by any number of architects, for example: Frank Lloyd Wright with the "lily pad" columns of the Johnson's Wax Administrative Building or Mark West's research at the Centre for Architectural Structures and Technology (C.A.S.T.) at the University of Manitoba, Canada.

University of Calabria, Italy, for example, Gregotti utilized a strict linear organization to contrast with the surrounding undulating topography. The architecture serves as a datum—a reference line—for measuring the landscape.

Carol Burns recast these two opposing theories—Laugier's and Gregotti's—in "On Site: Architectural Preoccupations," the *philosophical text* of this chapter. More precisely, Burns compared two attitudes regarding the relationship between nature and architecture: "cleared site" and "constructed site." The "cleared site" mindset sees places (e.g., nature) as void of content—geometric and neutral—and awaiting architectural intervention or human use. The "constructed site" mindset, on the other hand, "emphasizes the visible physicality, morphological qualities, and existing conditions of land and architecture . . . connecting the earth as natural form to the building as constructed form." Though the former was the dominant paradigm throughout much of Western architectural history, Burns noted that the latter concept recognizes that an architectural "site"—natural or constructed—is political and ideological, and is an open-ended or unfinished "product of culture."

In other words, "nature" is a concept defined by culture, and this concept is ever-changing. With contemporary discourses about humans' impact on local ecologies and the global climate, nature has come to be seen as a fragile, limited resource.[3] The dominant paradigm once saw nature as something to be overcome; the paradigm that currently dominates, in contrast, views nature as something to be shepherded, giving rise to the concept of designers as "stewards of the land."[4] Product design, architecture, landscape architecture, and urban design have all been affected by this new paradigm. History, nevertheless, has shown that these contemporary notions of nature and what is "natural" will be transformed or replaced by future paradigms.

3. See, for example: Marilyn A. Brown and Frank Southworth, "Mitigating Climate Change through Green Buildings and Smart Growth," *Environment & Planning A,* 40 (2008): 653–675.

4. See, for example: Wendy Redfield Lathrop, ed. *Modulus 20: The Architectural Review at the University of Virginia: Stewardship of the Land* (New York: Princeton Architectural Press, 1991).

Original Text

MARC-ANTOINE LAUGIER, EXCERPTS FROM *AN ESSAY ON ARCHITECTURE*.

First Published in 1753

It is the same in architecture as in all other arts: its principles are founded on simple nature, and nature's process clearly indicates its rules. Let us look at man in his primitive state without any aid or guidance other than his natural instincts. He is in need of a place to rest. On the banks of a quietly flowing brook he notices a stretch of grass; its fresh greenness is pleasing to his eyes, its tender down invites him; he is drawn there and, stretched out at leisure on this sparkling carpet, he thinks of nothing else but enjoying the gift of nature; he lacks nothing, he does not wish for anything. But soon the scorching heat of the sun forces him to look for shelter. A nearby forest draws him to its cooling shade; he runs to find a refuge in its depth, and there he is content. But suddenly mists are rising, swirling round and growing denser, until thick clouds cover the skies; soon, torrential rain pours down on this delightful forest. The savage, in his leafy shelter, does not know how to protect himself from the uncomfortable damp that penetrates everywhere; he creeps into a nearby cave and, finding it dry, he praises himself for his discovery. But soon the darkness and foul air surrounding him make his stay unbearable again. He leaves and is resolved to make good by his ingenuity the careless neglect of nature. He wants to make himself a dwelling that protects but does not bury him. Some fallen branches in the forest are the right material for his purpose; he chooses four of the strongest, raises them upright and arranges them in a square; across their top he lays four other branches; on these he hoists from two sides yet another row of branches which, inclining towards each other, meet at their highest point. He then covers this kind of roof with leaves so closely packed that neither sun nor rain can penetrate. Thus, man is housed. Admittedly, the cold and heat will make him feel uncomfortable in this house which is open on all sides but soon he will fill in the space between two posts and feel secure.

Such is the course of simple nature; by imitating the natural process, art was born. All the splendors of architecture ever conceived have been modeled on the little rustic hut I have just described. It is by approaching the simplicity of this first model that fundamental mistakes are avoided and true perfection is achieved. The pieces of wood set upright have given us the idea of the column, the pieces placed horizontally on top of them the idea of the entablature, the inclining pieces forming the roof the idea of the pediment. This is what all masters of art have recognized. But take note of this: never has a principle been more fertile in its effect. From now on it is easy to distinguish between the parts which are essential to the composition of an architectural Order and those which have been introduced by necessity or have been added by caprice. The parts that are essential are the cause of beauty, the parts introduced by necessity cause every license, the parts added by caprice cause every fault. This calls for an explanation; I shall try to be as clear as possible.

Let us never lose sight of our little rustic hut. I can only see columns, a ceiling or entablature and a pointed roof forming at both ends what is called a pediment. So far there is no vault, still less an arch, no pedestals, no attic, not even a door or a window. I therefore come to this conclusion: in an architectural Order only the column, the entablature and the pediment may form an essential part of its composition. If each of these parts is suitably placed and suitably formed, nothing else need be added to make the work perfect.

We still have in France a beautiful ancient monument, which in Nîmes is called the *Maison Carrée*. Everybody, connoisseur or not, admires its beauty. Why? Because everything here accords with the true principles of architecture: a rectangle where thirty columns support an entablature and a roof—closed at both ends by a pediment—that is all; the combination is of a simplicity and a nobility which strikes everybody.

. . .

Let us now consider in detail the essential parts of an architectural Order.

ARTICLE I: THE COLUMN

(1) The column must be strictly perpendicular, because, being intended to support the whole load, perfect verticality gives it its greatest strength. (2) The column must be free-standing so that its origin and purpose are expressed in a natural way. (3) The column must be round because nature makes nothing square. (4) The column must be tapered from bottom to top in imitation of nature where this diminution is found in all plants. (5) The column must rest directly on the floor as the posts of the rustic hut rest directly on the ground. All these rules find their justification in our model; all deviations from this model without real necessity must, therefore, be considered as so many faults.

1. Fault: when columns, instead of standing free, are engaged in the wall. The column certainly loses much of its grace when even a small obstacle obscures its outline. I admit that circumstances frequently seem to rule out the use of free-standing columns. People want to live in closed spaces, not in open halls. Therefore, it becomes necessary to fill in the space between the columns and consequently to engage them. In this case,

an engaged column will not be regarded as a fault, but as a license sanctioned by necessity. It should, however, always be remembered that any license points to an imperfection and must be used cautiously and only when it is impossible to find a better way. If, therefore, the columns have to be engaged, the degree of engagement should be as small as possible—a quarter at most or even less so that, even when constrained, they retain some quality of the freedom and ease which gives them so much grace. We must avoid getting into the awkward situation where engaged columns have to be employed. It would be best to reserve the use of columns for peristyles where they can be completely free-standing and to omit them altogether whenever necessity compels us to back them onto a wall. After all, even though we have to submit to *bienséance* why should we not disengage the column so that it can be seen in the round? Would the façade of St. Gervais not be improved if the Doric columns were free-standing like those of the upper Orders? Is there anything impossible in this? . . .

To dare criticize a work which the public commonly takes for a faultless masterpiece suggests that one defers little to public opinion. However, pointing out the defects of this building gives me the right to be unsparing in my criticism of any other building without hurting anybody's pride. That is why I shall speak bluntly. After what I have said, it will be less surprising that the connoisseurs set so little value on the Church of the Jesuits in the rue St. Antoine. Without counting other faults, of which there are many, the effect of the three Orders of engaged columns is most disagreeable. This, as M. de Cordemoy so adroitly says, is no more than architecture in relief to which the eyes of enlightened people will never be reconciled. I have often bemoaned the craze of architects for engaged columns, but I should never have believed that it could occur to the mind of a thinking person to engage one column into the other. No fault is more unbearable, more shocking than this. Even those new to architecture will agree on this, and yet this fault is repeatedly committed on all four sides of the inner courtyard of the Louvre. Such a glaring blunder on such a magnificent work of art ranks among the degradations of the human spirit.

2. Fault: when instead of round columns pilasters are used. Pilasters are only a poor representation of columns. Their corners indicate a constraint of art and deviate noticeably from the simplicity of nature; their sharp and awkward edges hurt the eye, their surfaces, not being rounded, make the whole Order seem flat. They are not adaptable to that diminution which makes columns so attractive. Pilasters are never necessary; wherever they are used, columns could be applied just as advantageously. They must, therefore, be regarded as a bizarre innovation, in no way founded on nature or authorized by any need, which can only have been adopted out of ignorance and is still tolerated only by habit. The fashion for pilasters has triumphed everywhere: alas, where are they not to be found? Yet to realize how distasteful they are, one only needs to think of the grand effect which columns always make, an effect that is unfailingly destroyed by pilasters. Change the coupled columns of the Colonnade of the Louvre into pilasters and you take away all its beauty. Compare the two wings of this superb façade with the pavilions at both corners:

what a difference! Even valets and maidservants want to know why the pavilions are different from the rest. This vexation is aroused by the taste for true beauty, a taste that is natural to everybody. The identical architectural Order extends over the whole façade, but the main part has columns, the pavilions have pilasters; this difference alone is enough to disturb the pleasure that a more unified whole would have given. . . .

On entering the nave of the Chapel of Versailles everybody is struck by the beauty of its columns, by the picturesque vista (*âpreté*) through its intercolumniations; but as soon as one approaches the apse, there is not a person who does not notice with regret the stupid interruption of the beautiful row of columns by a depressing pilaster. One can, therefore, be quite certain that the use of pilasters is one of the great abuses that have found their way into architecture, and since an abuse never comes alone we have been presented with folded pilasters in corners, with curved pilasters in circular buildings, with pilasters lost in the confused interpenetration of one into the other. The pilaster is a frivolous ornament which has been put to all sorts of uses; it has even been married to a column which, it seems, is there as its inseparable companion. Has there ever been a more ridiculous match? What does the engaged column mean behind a free-standing column? Honestly, I do not know and I defy anybody to explain it. Does it make sense to unite two things which are quite incompatible? The column has its diminution, whereas the pilaster could not have any which is the reason that the latter will always look either too narrow at the bottom or too wide at the top. Whenever there is a void to be filled, one fills it with a pilaster; whenever there is a fault to be covered up or a place to be embellished, one cuts out one half or one quarter of a pilaster. The ancients were not more scrupulous about this matter, at times even less particular, than the moderns, since they built colonnades where they mixed columns and pilasters. In short, the pilaster is a thing I cannot bear. This is an inborn aversion. The more I studied architecture, the more I found in its true principles the justification for my own aversion. . . .

It will be said that pilasters are used so as to avoid the excessive cost of columns. To that I answer: if the column is barred only for reasons of economy, all that is needed is a decision to suppress architectural Orders altogether. Beautiful buildings can be created without their help, but if one wants to employ the five Orders I shall never forgive cutting out the column which is their most essential part.

3. Fault: to give a swelling to the shaft at about the third of its height instead of tapering the column in the normal way. I do not believe that nature has ever produced anything that could justify this swelling. Let us do justice to our artists who a long time ago have given up spindle-shaped columns which are not to be found on any recent work. Rusticated columns are no less faulty than spindle-shaped columns. Philibert de l'Orme had a high opinion of rusticated columns and covered the Palais des Tuileries with them. His taste, however, was not sufficiently refined to make them admissible on his authority alone. This great man deserves to be highly praised and will always be counted among the great masters of architecture. We owe to him the rebirth of this beautiful art in our country, yet his work still savors of the depraved taste of the preceding

centuries. Rusticated columns are only a capricious fancy; we do not see a whole column but various drums of a different scale piled up one above the other, producing an effect which is rather mean and infinitely harsh. The beautiful Palais de Luxembourg is quite disfigured by these rusticated columns. Far worse are spiral columns. Whoever thought of them was certainly skillful because it needs much skill to make them well; but had he had judicious taste, he would surely not have taken so much care in carrying out such a foolish invention. Spiral columns are to architecture what the bandy legs of a cripple are to the human body; yet at first their peculiar appearance pleased some people who were enemies of the natural and who believed the work to be beautiful because it was difficult. Others, more eccentric still, have offered us stumps of straight columns on which they had mounted in a most miserable manner two-thirds of a spiral column; others again, prompted by the same taste but defeated by practical difficulties, wanted at least the satisfaction of twisting the flutings of straight columns. These absurdities have been reserved mainly for altars. I admire the baldachins of St. Peter's in Rome, of the Val de Grâce and of the Invalides, but I shall never forgive the great men who designed them for using twisted columns. Do not let us be deceived by false jewels: they only demonstrate the failings of a genius. Let us keep to the simple and natural; it is the only road to beauty.

. . .

4. Fault: when the columns, instead of resting directly on the ground, are raised on pedestals. Since the columns are, if I may say so, the legs of a building, it is absurd to give them another pair of legs. The pedestals I am speaking of have been invented out of misfortune. If columns were found to be too short, it was decided to put them on stilts in order to make up for the lack of height. The same difficulty led to having recourse to double pedestals when a single pedestal was not sufficient. Nothing makes a building look more heavy and clumsy than these huge angular masses which serve as substructures to the columns. The colonnade of the Hôtel Soubise is unbearable because of these hideous pedestals; but if the columns were rising from the ground, it would be a charming building. Columns may rest on a massive, continuous wall, that is to say on a simple socle without base, without cornice and of medium height; and this will be done whenever a colonnade is being built and the level of the inner floor is higher than the surrounding ground. Far from criticizing this practice, I am convinced that it will always be successful. Sometimes too, when the intercolumniations are filled by a balustrade as at the bay of the Chapel of Versailles and of the Colonnade of the Louvre, each column may rest separately on a small socle. This second manner is less perfect and would even be defective if it were not justified by the necessity of having a balustrade on a colonnade which is erected on the first floor; but to place pedestals under columns at ground level is an inexcusable fault. Nearly all the altars in our churches present this ridiculous sight. Columns are needed here but they would cost too much if they were on a scale large enough to make them rest directly on the floor—hence one needs pedestals. This is the reason why the columns at the main altar of the Church of the Jesuits in the rue St. Antoine are set on two pedestals, one above the other. Only this once shall I cite this shocking work. All one can say about

it is that none of the glaring blunders that architects can make has been forgotten here. . . . In short, pedestals are only good for carrying statues and to make them serve any other purpose is essentially bad taste. However much it is said that pedestals have been admitted at all times, that Vitruvius and all his commentators assign to each Order its particular pedestal and that they are to be found on the most beautiful buildings of antiquity, I have my principle which I shall never give up. Any device—even if approved by great men—which is either contrary to nature or cannot be convincingly explained is a bad device and must be proscribed.

Reflective Text

VITTORIO GREGOTTI, "TERRITORY AND ARCHITECTURE."

First Published in 1985

While presenting my project for the University or Calabria, I thought again of some of the theoretical reflections I had made in *The Territory of Architecture* ten years earlier, in 1966, for they seemed relevant to many aspects of the overall layout of the Calabria project.

The theory of the materials of architecture and the pre-eminence of the figure as their organisational structure was central to *The Territory of Architecture*, but it did not resolve the specific organisational problems at Calabria. It concerned itself primarily with questions of theory and history, whether as hypotheses of the organisation of personal and group memory, or as a specific history of the discipline—the vacillations of its margins and the shifts in its centre of interests, its territory and its privileged relations with other disciplines. However, the physical spirit of history is the built environment which surrounds us, the manner of its transformation into visible things, its gathering of depths and meanings which differ not only because of what the environment appears to be, but also because of what it *is* structurally. The environment is rather composed of the traces of its own history. If geography is therefore the way in which the signs of history solidify and are superimposed in a form, the architectural project has the task of drawing attention to the essence of the environmental context through the transformation of form.

From 1963–64 onwards I began to put these problems at the centre of my reflections on architecture: my first opportunity to experiment with their consequences in planning was at the XIIIth Triennale in Milan in 1964. Since then, I have always tried to keep the relationship between my theory and my work open, if not consistent. I have attempted, for instance, to understand what one could conclude from reflecting on the idea of landscape and nature as the sum total of all things and of their of past configurations. Nature, in this sense, is not seen as an indifferent, inscrutable force or a divine cycle of creation, but rather as a collection of material things whose reasons and relations architecture has the task of revealing. We must therefore modify, redouble, measure, situate and utilise the landscape in order to know and meet the environment as a geographical totality of concrete things which are inseparable from their historical organisation.

This can only be done if we abandon the sociological or ecological or administrative notion of the environment as an imprisoned element and think of it instead as material for architecture. It should be made clear that this idea of the environment is not a system in which architecture is dissolved, but is on the contrary a load-bearing material for the architectural project, enabling new planning principles and methods to accommodate the spirit of the specific terrain.

The spirit behind these new methods is *modification*. Modification reveals an awareness of being part of a pre-existing whole, of changing one part of a system to transform the whole. Through its etymological root, *modus*, modification is linked to the concept of measure and the geometrical world of regulated things. It is modification which transforms *place* into *architecture* and establishes the original symbolic act of making contact with the earth, with the physical environment, with the idea of nature as a totality. Such a concept of the project sees architecture as a system of relations and distances, as the measurement of intervals rather than as isolated objects. Thus the specificity of the solution is closely related to differences in situation, context or environment. We do not, therefore, conceive of space as a uniform and infinite extension where no place is privileged: space is not of identical value in all directions, but rather is composed of differences, discontinuities considered as value and as experience. The organization of space, therefore, starts from the idea of *place*: the project transforms *place* into *settlement*.

The origin of architecture does not lie in the hut, in the cave or in the mythical "Adam's house in paradise". Before a support was transformed into a column, a roof into a pediment, and stone heaped upon stone, man put stone on the ground in order to recognise place in the midst of the unknown universe and thereby measure and modify it. Like every aspect of measuring, this required a radical simplicity. From this point of view, there are essentially two ways to place oneself in relation to the context. The instruments of the first way are mimetic imitation, organic assimilation and visible complexity. The second way uses measurement: distance, definition, rotation within complexity.

In the first case the problem is mirroring reality, in the second it is establishing the double. The latter mode is based on restless division: putting up a wall, building an enclosure, defining regions, producing a densely articulated interior which will correspond to the fragmentation and differences of behaviour. A simple exterior will thus appear as a measure of the larger environment's complexity. For this reason a material is not actually a thing of nature: it is more earthly and more abstract, alluding to the form of the place, to things as they are combined, but also to what is beneath, to the stable geological support, to a nature which is historically transformed, to a nature which is the product of thought, and which as a result of being frequented or settled has become a shared memory.

The project, then, must be established upon the regulating tradition of style and métier. But what gives architectural truth and concreteness to this tradition is its meeting with the site, for only by perceiving the site as a specific environment can those exceptions which generate architecture emerge.

My current work explores the implications of developing an architecture of context. This has led me to confront the problem of implementing large-scale works and to examine which principles and methods would stand up to the realities of production. I have been especially concerned with work environments in industry and universities, and was involved with the important competition for the University of Calabria. The project's main proposal was to base the design of the new university on a principle of settlement. This principle is evinced by an irregular alignment and by the connection between it and the sinuous terrain of the countryside. It functions as a way of gauging the landscape and regulating and characterising a large-scale design. Alignment and discontinuity are, moreover, ancient and characteristic methods of regulating settlements in Calabria.

The project also attempts to bring about an interaction between morphological and functional systems. The first system consists of a linear succession of university departments running across the hill system to the plain of the River Crati. The blocks housing the departmental activities accommodate the varying levels of the land and are laid out on a square plan on the axis of a bridge. The second system considers the morphology of the hills, the succession of their slopes and peaks (which carry the local road system) and their relationship to the fabric of the low-tiered houses along the northern slope intended as university residences. Since the southern slopes are cultivated with olive trees, an alternating succession of residential units and natural spaces results. The university services, which are open towards the exterior, are situated at the junctures between the bridge system and the hilltop roads.

The 7m-wide upper lane of the bridge caters for public transport and goods traffic; the lower lane is for pedestrians and internal student traffic. Between the two lanes, the various installations run along a conduit with a triangular section. The tall blocks of the university departments are linked to the bridge by a narrow body of services placed perpendicular or parallel to the bridge depending on the type of cube.

The whole layout of the university is regulated by a grid of 25.20×25.20m extended over two modules to the two sides of the axis, forming a settlement strip 110m wide. The tall blocks vary between two and five storeys to maintain a constant height of 232.40m above sea-level and project onto the line of transverse section of the valley below. They are enclosed by load-bearing reinforced concrete walls measuring 21.60×25.20m at distances of 3.60m on centre. The horizontal structures are supported by metal beams with a span of 19.60m for internal linkage. These control the positioning of the structures of the floors, spaces between floors and intermediate floors. In the second type, the internal structures are also reinforced concrete, and pillars divide the interior into two different articulated spaces: on the one hand, small spaces for studies and offices; on the other, large collective spaces for laboratories, lecture halls, libraries, etc.

343

The natural lighting for the interiors is obtained through large openings in the perimeter wall and the transparent, partially sun-screened roofing. This strategically regulates the view of the natural landscape and external architecture.

The outer modules of the grid are occupied by the extension of the tall blocks on the ground floor to form a support base and house the more cumbersome technical equipment. The 250-seat lecture halls are suspended between the volumes of two lateral blocks in order to leave the continuity of the slope unbroken and form a passageway below the tiered arches. The blocks which house the various departments and a whole range of teaching and research activities form the basic element in the grouping and set up a morphological referent for the university's future growth and change of layout. The final phase of [the] project, providing accommodation for 12,000 students, suggested the doubling of the departmental spaces. In this projection, a rapid link-up service would replace the bridge and would continue both to the new station with parking facilities at the mouth of the Paola tunnel and to additional parking at the Cozenza tunnel. The level part of the northern area would house the buildings and supply areas of the main regional sports centre and the laboratories of the national research centre.

At this stage in its development, the university organism would be making full use of two access systems deriving from the settlement system: the two ends of alignment would be linked by a fast, efficient urban transport system while the hill roads would continue to function as they had in the first phase. The squares would be the meeting point of the two systems.

Philosophical Text

CAROL BURNS, "ON SITE: ARCHITECTURAL PREOCCUPATIONS."

First Published in 1991

In architectural design, the demands of relating a building to a physical location are necessary and inevitable; the site is initially construed and finally achieved in the architectural work. The problems attendant to siting have a pervasive and profound impact on buildings. Nonetheless, architectural theory and criticism have tended to address siting issues with descriptive or analytic references to specific exemplary projects. This approach exclusively reveals through circumstantial strategies the lack of a clear conceptual basis for the notion of site within architecture.[5] Because of its intrinsic importance and generative potential, the conceptual content of site must be made available for study and opened to question as a means to disclose and, ultimately, to challenge the motives and precepts of the discipline.

I suggest a twofold consideration of the site in architecture: in terms of theory or knowledge (what we think site is), and in terms of the impact of theory on action (what we make of a site, or how it informs constructions and is formed through them). This emphasis on thought and action poses fundamental questions: What is a site? How is it constructed? And how can a site inform building and architecture? These obvious but remarkably resistant questions stem from a conviction that architecture is not constituted of buildings or sites but arises from the studied relationship of the two and from an awareness that site is received as an architectural construct, even if unconsciously. Historically the notions of site and architecture have shifted from the sacred to the profane (churches to institutions), from the specific to the general (premodern to modern), and from the unique to the nostalgic (prototype to type). Considering the site in terms of theory and siting in terms of architectural activity outlines the insistent intersections of architecture, site, and construction and also illuminates design thinking in architecture. The topic here is not simply the site; it is equally the architectural understanding of the site. This inquiry is comprised of a survey of the changing status of site, certain applications of the concept, and a reading of the terms by which site is construed. It is meant to be suggestive, not exhaustive.

5. Two noteworthy sources in art theory have potential relevance to architecture. Robert Irwin, in *Being and Circumstance* (San Francisco: The Lapis Press, 1985), delimits four categories of built works in terms of their relation to site: site dominant, site adjusted, site specific, and site conditioned. Rosalind Krauss, in "Sculpture in the Expanded Field," first published in *October* 8 (Spring 1979), locates sculpture in a "logically expanded field" established by the binary pairing of architecture and landscape.

The emergence of "site" as a concern in areas other than architecture underscores its importance to theoretical constructions in economics, politics, and sociocultural conditions. The term's nuance has been expanded by its appropriation in divergent discourses, although, as Desa Philippi has noted, it has not been given definition in these disciplines: "[This] is signalled by the ubiquity of the notion of site across the discourses that constitute the domains of knowledge in the Western World, from sociology to philosophy, from political science to the arts . . . Indeed, 'site' threatens to become a free floating signifier, attaching itself to an astounding number of objects: the artwork has become a site itself rather than existing in relation to one; the body is a site; as are even its organs."[6] The text is called a site, so are discourses. Texts are constructs, and discourses are contexts in which texts are read; site applies to both, indicating its simultaneous and multiple scales of reference.

The present status of site as a shaping force within architecture is a reaction to the mainstream ideology of modern architecture. Called "the International Style" or "functional modernism," the names given to modern architecture betray a concern for universalizing issues unrelated—even opposed—to those arising from the specificity of a given place. Motivated by technological developments, the possibility of producing widely available quality goods, and a social program with utopian aspirations, the modernist program in conjunction with a developing global economy led to standardization of environments and cultures. Reactions against the resulting widespread homogeneity are evident in diverse architectural responses of the last twenty years: attempts by environmental planners to search out and involve local community groups in decision-making processes; the identification of specific practices within defined geographic or cultural locales (for example, the Ticino or Southern California); academic ideologies based on methodological response as the Cornell school); and the theory of regionalism in architecture.[7] Vittorio Gregotti summarizes the arguments this way: "The worst enemy of modern architecture is the idea of space considered solely in terms of its economic and technical exigencies indifferent to the idea of the site."[8] Admittedly, the concern for site is only one of the reactive developments that have become initiatory, contributing to widespread alteration in the perceived hierarchy of forces shaping architecture today. As the awareness of the relationship between cultural production and the local circumstances of material practice has come to the fore, attention to site has begun to frame the problem of making and interpreting architecture.

At present, site is frequently seen as a synchronic phenomenon, irrevocably divorced from other times. The history of a setting is acknowledged only insofar as the forces acting upon it have affected its present visible form. "'Site' has come to mark a particular conjunction where the temporal is eroded by the spatial and where history becomes the isolated image of its residue."[9] However, local circumstances cannot be considered simply in terms of space; they also require a diachronic apprehension of time. As Kurt Forster has said, "No understanding of a site is conceivable without a communal history, or conceivable with a substitution of that history. . . . We may very well suffer from a curious

6. Desa Phillippi, "Invisible Sites," in *Sight Works Volume One: Several Enquiries* (London: Chance Books, 1988).

7. See Kenneth Frampton, "Towards A Critical Regionalism: Six Points for an Architecture of Resistance," *The Anti-Aesthetic*, ed. Hal Foster (Seattle: Bay Press, 1983).

8. Vittorio Gregotti, "Lecture at the Architectural League," *Section A*, 1 (March 1983), 8.

9. Phillipi, "Invisible Sites."

historical impatience. The expectation that meaning can be generated instantaneously seems to have become, partly, a surrogate subject of contemporary projects."[10] Traditionally, the exclusive object of site planning is space; the potential to plan or "plot" time is not pursued. The principle of the (so-called) master plan is to design the space of a terrain over an extended time; there must exist a similar, perhaps paradoxical, potential for plotting the time of a terrain over space, which would differ from an architectural narrative or promenade by specifically accounting for growth and change in time.

ARCHITECTURAL PREOCCUPATIONS: THE CLEARED SITE/
THE CONSTRUCTED SITE

In order to focus on the site within architectural thinking, two opposed conceptions (resulting from the reactive processes outlined above and representing positions that have currency) will be examined: the cleared site and the constructed site.

The idea of the cleared site is based on an assumption that the site as received is unoccupied, lacking any prior constructions and empty of content. It posits space as objective and "pure," a neutral mathematical object. This assumed neutrality fosters the impression that the land and the space of a site are independent of political motive.[11] This attitude prevails most strongly over undeveloped land, which is perceived as void of architectural context even though replete with natural constructions—vegetation, drainage systems, wind patterns, animal habitats, and so forth. Natural constructions are considered secondary to human constructions by architecture and the planning disciplines; only landscape architecture recognizes their status insofar as the disciplinary means and methods are developed around them. The disregard for natural constructions betrays the presumption that they are politically and ideologically immaterial. The cleared site conception, which is apparently nonpolitical and nonideological, implies that the mechanisms adapted by the planning disciplines are equally neutral in ideological terms, equally unengaged with issues of power. As a stratagem, it offers great latitude by fostering an illusion that planning is apolitical.

The cleared site argument depends on the mathematicization of land, a technique fundamental to the basic comprehension of the environment. "In Western societies the first step toward control of an environment usually is the assigning of tracts as grants of property—done by drawing lines on paper, although little may be known about the tract that is to be colonized."[12] To rationalize land is to objectify it profoundly. For example, the so-called Jeffersonian grid—inspired by precedents as old as Ptolemy's map and centuriation, the Roman system of land division—has been applied to 69 percent of the land in 48 American states. Taken for granted and generally accepted as an advantage for settlement, its application was explicitly motivated by economic and governmental control: "Congressional townships of thirty-six miles were created by federal law for the sole purpose of making available easily identifiable and saleable tracts . . . The Land Ordinance Act of 1785 [has divided land] into rectangles of sections and townships by whose lines the settler has been able easily and certainly to locate his farm and the forester

10. Kurt Forster, "Site: The Meaning of Place in Art and Architecture," in *Design Quarterly*, 122, ed. Mildred Friedman (Cambridge: MIT Press, 1983), 27.
11. See Henri LeFebvre, "The Politics of Space," *Antipode*, 8 (May, 1976), 31.
12. Hildegard Binder Johnson, *Order Upon the Land* (New York: Oxford University Press, 1976), 21.

his forty. In the local organization of the Middle West these lines have played an important part."[13] The pervasive presence of the federal rectangular grid has rendered it, for most Americans and Canadians, inevitable or even natural. Nevertheless, the grid has the effect of making real differences in sites invisible; it presumes equal access to all land; and it denies specificity to each parcel. As an embodiment of the human effort to conquer space, surveying has enormous impact on the understanding of land use, the perception of landscape, and the ensuing land development; it shapes the outline and content of any piece of land available as a location for architecture. Far from being objective or neutral, geometry and mathematics are constructions that occupy sites.

When applied to land, the abstract clarity of geometry becomes "invisible."[14] The rationalism that objectifies the site via geometry masks itself by virtue of its uniformity and masks the site's topographical irregularities, flattening the land and the perception of the land. Ernst Cassirer has said:

> Cognition devises symbolic concepts—the concepts of space and time [and geometry]—in order to dominate the world of sensory experience and survey it as a world ordered by law, but nothing in the sensory data themselves immediately corresponds to [the symbolic concepts] . . . The logic of things cannot be separated from the logic of signs. For the sign is no mere accidental cloak of the idea, but its necessary and essential organ . . . No form of cultural activity can develop its appropriate and peculiar type of comprehension and configuration without, as it were, creating a definite sensuous substratum for itself. This substratum is so essential that it sometimes seems to constitute the entire content, the true 'meaning' of these forms.[15]

13. Johnson, *Order Upon the Land*, 116.
14. For a discussion of the relation of geometry, mapping, and landscape representation in land reclamation and the settlement of the Veneto, see Denis Cosgrove, "The Geometry of Landscape: Practical and Speculative Arts in Sixteenth-Century Venetian Land Territories," ed. D. Cosgrove and S. Daniels in *The Iconography of Landscape* (Cambridge: Cambridge University Press, 1988).
15. Ernst Cassirer, *The Philosophy of Symbolic Forms, Vol. 1: Language* (New Haven: Yale University Press, 1955), 86.

Geometry, laid over land, providing it with content, is one such substratum. Invisible and immaterial, it cannot be extracted from land because it emplaces and encloses the land: one cannot divorce the site from the way it is known.

The technique of the cleared site depends on the map and the plan, organizational constructs that help to level the ground, presenting it as a supporting platform or foundation of no important matter. The debased ground plane is abstracted so that ensuing planning operations may introduce content to the cleared site. For the architecture of the cleared site, buildings form that content—visible superstructures imported onto and overriding the demoted terrain.

The most notable designs founded on the cleared site are of a scale massive enough to clear and rebuild the setting literally. Projects conceived on a podium—such as United Nations Plaza, Albany Government Center, or the Acropolis—convey the requisite power to claim, "flatten," and build powerful sites. However, the ensuing architecture need not carry such weight symbolically or literally; residential structures, the most commonplace of architectural commissions, without programmatic "weight," can also use the cleared site to convey monumentality. Mies van der Rohe's large urban complexes on Lake Shore

Drive in Chicago and Westmount Square in Montreal place buildings with ideal plans into contradictory city fabrics, which are rendered ideal by clearing the immediate premises. The Farnsworth House, elevated above the high-water mark in a flood plain periodically cleared by nature, is built on land that might be considered "unbuildable" were it not for the strategy of the cleared site. Such clearing, conveying self-expression and the "heroic" perception of the modern architect as artist, attempts to conquer a territory completely in a single effort, precluding change, development, and all future planning. In aiming to determine definitively the life of the place, the cleared site strategy undertakes to isolate architecture from time. The past is denied and the future is deemed powerless to change the situation, much less improve it. Denying any relationship to existing conditions, the architecture of the cleared site presumes a power to initiate and finalize the site in both spatial and temporal terms.

However, a real site cannot be removed from human time. The space of the site is made by humans and is by necessity political; any piece of land subject to human attention becomes charged with power and its mechanisms. This is the meaning or content that humans bring to nature, that architecture must bring to the site. The cleared site exists only in eternity. It is a fantastic, poetic, or mythical character, a fiction invented by humans for the conquest of space and time. By presuming to arrest time and condemn physicality, the cleared site tries to deny its origin in human construction; it is a veiled attempt to remove itself from the human condition.

Opposed to the idea of the cleared site is that of the constructed site, which emphasizes the visible physicality, morphological qualities, and existing conditions of land and architecture. Connecting the earth as natural form to the building as constructed form, the notion of the constructed site implies that the resulting architecture is meant to be understood in physical terms—building and setting are seen to be shaped through obviously physical processes.

The constructed site argument depends on the visible layers of landscape phenomena: first, the prehuman or prehistoric landforms resulting from chthonic forces; second, that which remains of the efforts and projects of the period when agriculture was dominant, in other words, rural landscapes, districts, and regions; third, a layer of transformations that occurred primarily during the industrial period, including increased settlement densities afforded by the invention of transportation systems such as railroads and canals; and, finally, the present processes, which are more diffuse but of a larger scale of operation and include, for example, highway systems and suburban and exurban development. These natural and human forces have shaped land, and any situation available for building has already been somehow physically constructed by these agencies.

Though these layers are constituted of physical material (in contrast to mathematical abstractions) they are also difficult to see. The layers, accumulated over time, are not seen as distinct strata, nor do their phenomena appear as discrete. They are visually obscure because they are physically and spatially coextensive, which leads to interruption, simultaneity, discontinuity, synchronism, fragmentation, coincidence, and disruption; they cohere only in abrupt juxtapositions. As the abstract overlay of mathematics masks topography by systematizing it, the physical phenomena, in apparently incoherent conjunction, effectively mask the systems—natural and man-made—that determine their present form.

The technique of the constructed site depends on the section as a composite device. Conveying the topographic qualities of both building and setting in the base line, the horizon line, and the profile line, the section also presents the visual character of the vertical surfaces beyond. It shows the visual construction of the setting in phenomenological terms and the conceptual or structural use of the visible setting in design thinking.

The method of the constructed site singles out particular visible phenomena to provide a generative concept, which is then used as a literal basis of construction. Several opportunities are lost in this approach. By valuing visible material, what is not immediately present is not addressed (for example, the history or the poetics of a place). The architecture devised for the spot is conceived as a constructive extension of the conditions of the location itself; it thus provides a further construction of the already constructed site. Though it may mediate between the landscape and the building, such architecture uses the site for its own support and extension. Therefore, though the situation is seen as generative, it is not intentionally shaped or designed by the architect; it is simply appropriated. But because building architecture necessarily entails building a site, even this apparently passive appropriation necessarily changes the situation. Therefore, rather than attempt to maintain a neutral stance, the architect must take responsibility for the site and assume its control for a limited passage of time.

Conceptions of the site—cleared and constructed—can be compared to certain attitudes about designing an addition to an existing work of architecture or construction.[16] One strategy for addition is the extension, which hides the new work by reproducing the forms and materials of the existing structure. As a pure strategy, this is obviously impossible in thinking about architecture as an addition to the (already constructed) site because the physical requirements of architecture are not satisfied by the forms of materials in nature. The other obvious strategy for addition is to design the new without relation to the existing structure as analogous to the model of the cleared site, which brings imported content to a situation conceived as without meaning. Yet another possibility is to investigate the existing situation—building, city, or native land—to discover its latent qualities or potential; inherent conditions can motivate the ensuing construction so that the new participates in the existing. This allows both a criticism and a release from the received conditions and, reciprocally, a reverberation of them so that the boundaries between the conditions as received and as renovated become blurred; both may be productive because both are aggressive with respect to each other.

In arguing that a site, as a result of human action, is always already conceptually and physically constructed prior to building architecture—which is to say, preoccupied by the way it is known and by its history—the apparent opposition of the cleared site and the constructed site are thrown into question. The site as received is never cleared or

16. This discussion of the addition was originally set out with respect to the work of Frank Gehry in my essay, "The Gehry Phenomenon," in *Thinking the Present: Recent American Architecture* (New York: Princeton Architectural Press, 1990), 72–88.

empty; indeed, it is not possible for the architect to clear the site of its own constituent formal content. Therefore, a cleared site model reveals itself to be a strategy for adding over and against the received site. The cleared site and constructed site are thus only ostensibly opposed. By denying or erasing the site, and by reducing its physical and temporal dimensions through a limited appropriation, the cleared site and the constructed site circumscribe the productive potential of the site.

ARCHITECTURAL PREOCCUPATIONS: CONSTRUING COMMON LANGUAGE

> In every series of real terms, not only do the terms themselves and their associations and environments change, but we change, and their meaning for us changes, so that new kinds of sameness and types of causations continually come into view and appeal to our interest.
>
> William James[17]

As commonly used, the word "site" means the local position of a building, town, monument, or similar work; it may also signify a space of ground occupied or to be occupied by a building; more generally, it describes the place or scene of something.[18] The term approaches some architectural characteristics in colloquial use—it is inclusive in scale (encompassing both the building and the town) and is explicitly associated with the position of three-dimensional constructs. Derived from verbs stressing action (*sinere*, meaning to leave, place, or lay; and *serere*, meaning to sow), a site results from human agency.

The architectural site eludes precise definition partly because of the disarming immediacy of its physical setting, which all too easily eclipses apprehension of its constructive and constitutive aspects. The initial approach to understanding site through some models and strategies within architecture is now followed through citation of its own meanings, the diverse denomination by which it is described in common language. Briefly, each term is taken in itself and to derive a suggestion as to how its understanding may illuminate or be brought into architectural thought and practice. This is to try to open to study the conceptual possibilities of the site in its own potential, not as a contingency to architecture but in its own multivalence.

The "lot" is a measured parcel of land with fixed boundaries as designated on a plot or survey. By association, it is simultaneously a fortune and a duty (to "draw lots" is to be subject to an operation of chance). The word also conveys contradictory meanings with respect to amount or measure: a lot is a fraction or a portion of some larger thing, as in a share; yet it is also a quantity significant in itself, as in "a lot of something." In architecture the term "lot" seems neutral. A person may buy a lot on which to build a house, but the location for the house is determined by ascribing values to certain aspects of the lot—orientation, setback, view, etc. The lot exists "prior" to the site and conveys only boundary and measure. However, boundary is a function of both legal and economic

17. William James, "On the Notion of Reality as Changing," in *A Pluralistic Universe* (Cambridge: Harvard University Press, 1977).
18. *Webster's Seventh New Collegiate Dictionary* (Springfield: Merriam Co., 1970).

power, and measure is a function of knowledge. Thus, the apparently neutral term "lot" is situated at the intersection of knowledge and power, potent forces preoccupying the architectural site.

"Plot," like "lot," is an ancient word with consistent precise use and many different accompanying connotations. Most simply, plot is a measured piece of land. It is also a small area of planted ground; a graphic representation, as in a chart; and the outline of a literary work. The act of plotting implies careful foresight and intrigue, as in a devious plan. (Deviousness typically insinuates underhandedness or evil, though its strict derivation simply means "off the main road.") A plot is similar to a scheme in that each is a systematic plan, a representation of some type, and also devious in connotation. Thus, the plot at once demarcates the piece of land for a building, represents the land, and conveys the intended plan of action for change: to plot is to scheme is to design. Architectural design is by definition a "plot," a plan of positive action intending to promote change as a deviation from given reality. Each small area of measured land reveals the constructively deviant character of architectural thought.

A particular building or site is characterized at a scale larger than itself as being within a particular "context," a word widely used in architecture. Context literally means the "connection of words" and is defined as "the parts of a discourse that surround a word or passage and can throw light on its meaning." Local context is a topical concern in current architecture where, in contrast to the literary suggestion, it is implemented as generator, something that provides meaning or content in itself. In architecture context is broadly synonymous with environment. Both exist in relation to scale—a local context may have a specificity at odds with a larger regional context. Both are also subject to change over time—buildings around a site may be erected and demolished; a new building changes its own site and also changes its own larger context. The content of context—its constituent aspects and their ascribed values—is relative: one person may see construction materials as important; another individual may value the relationship of built parts over their material nature; a public agency may be concerned with context only as described by zoning, bulk, or setback rules. In architectural design, context is also subject to changes in representational—and conceptual—means. For example, context as seen in a figure/ground diagram stems from a spatial conception introduced by the Nolli map; the ongoing technological developments in cartography encourage different visual perceptions of context at different scales. Finally, context may not be exclusively visual—cultural context situates human efforts, and for architecture this includes, but is not circumscribed by, physical and spatial constructs.

The concept of the "region" has provided a means of analyzing and promoting tendencies opposed to the homogenizing forces of modernism's "International Style." Ironically, the region is by definition "a broadly homogeneous or indefinite geographical area." The region can only be described indefinitely in dimensional or perceptual terms because geographical boundaries are often physically imprecise (for example, the Shenandoah Valley is topographically inseparable from the surrounding Appalachian

Mountains) even if they limit or circumscribe movement (the mountains have a confining effect). The stabilizing of settlement sponsors the emergence of cultural distinctions from within different geographic regions; therefore, the region can be seen as the product of the interaction between geography and culture. Given the instability of the population today, the ease of transportation across natural boundaries, and a culture fueled by mass media, such interaction between geography and culture does not necessarily occur spontaneously, but depends on intentional effort. The derivation of region stems from the Latin *regere*, meaning "to rule," recalling the precise relationship between the land and the power of the ruler or king. Today, we must choose to be ruled by the region. The architectural implications of this term underline the power of political and ideological control in shaping physical areas.

Perception itself gives rise to the term "landscape," which literally means the portion of land that the eye can comprehend in a single view. A word of relatively recent origin, it stems from eighteenth-century concerns for the visible and the picturesque. The force of viewing is likewise felt in the word "survey," which in etymology means "to look over," and in definition means "to delineate extent and position by measurement." These two terms point out the difference between the "aesthetic" and "mathematic" conceptions of the site, yet each reflects and contributes to a distancing between the individual—or society—and land; this distancing has an economic basis in industrialization. The aesthetic and mathematic conceptions are also analogous to the tension between art and science in contributing to and determining architecture.

Emerson points out that aesthetic and mathematical conceptions are fundamentally different but intimately bound to one another:

> The charming landscape which I saw this morning is indubitably made up of some twenty or thirty farms. Miller owns this field, Locke that, and Manning the woodland beyond. But none of them owns the landscape. There is a property in the horizon which no man has but he whose eye can integrate all the parts, that is, the poet. This is the best part of these men's farms, yet this their warranty deeds give no title.[19]

Landscape and survey inform ways of seeing because they are forms of knowledge. Like architecture, they frame information or content; they control by establishing principles that make the world comprehensible.

The broad notion of placement underlies the terms "location" and "position." Their derivation from the Latin verbs *locare* and *ponere*, meaning "to place," bespeaks their applicability to circumstances including but not limited to buildings or constructs. The force of these general words within architecture is not to be underestimated (even within the maxims of real estate, the three most important criteria of property are reputedly location, location, and location). The local is defined as "not broad or general; characterized by, relating to, or occupying a particular place." Its root word, *locus*, has the nearly

19. As cited by Johnson in *Order Upon the Land*, frontispiece.

mathematical definition of "the set of all points whose location is determined by stated conditions." Without precise technical application to architecture, the Latin source of "local" is in "stall," suggesting some attributes of architectural siting: one sense of "stall" is that of a physical compartment, a space marked off; another is temporal, that of bringing to a standstill or delaying in time. Such stalling is embodied in architecture, most directly in the stela, a commemorative slab or pillar intentionally sustaining a moment in time in an enduring physical form. By extension, to locate or to site any construction is to mark off and delay the architecture and the site both spatially and temporally.

"Position" denotes the point or area occupied by a physical object. In physical terms it implies a site. "Position" derives from "positive," so that it also implies an advocacy, as, for example, in arguing a proposition or making a proposal. Taking a position implicates affirmation: having an idea is fundamentally affirmative; the making of an idea is the making of the place of the idea. Henri LeFebvre goes so far as to insist on the utopian quality of any idea: "Today more than ever, there are no ideas without a utopia . . . There is no idea which neither explores a possibility nor tries to discover a direction . . . The architects, like the town planners, know this perfectly well."[20] Position, as the location of an idea or architectural construction, affirmatively asserts the connection between place and ideology.

CONCLUSION

Reviewing these terms reveals the elastic nature of the breadth and scale of site semantically, experientially, and temporally. The "architectural" character of the site is suggested in the consistent motives of politics and logic, latent ideologies under apparent neutrality, which inform and are imbedded in the architectural site and are revealed when approached from unrelated, even opposing, viewpoints. Each approach to site has its own specificity, and through association each speaks to a particular understanding of architecture. It is the gaps between the terms, the overlaps and inconsistencies among them, that finally betray the nature of the architectural site as both inclusive and evasive. In their multiplicity and disjunction the words associated with the general notion of site bespeak the relative impossibility of defining the specifically architectural site.

The understanding of site is neither self-evident in looking at a particular example nor explicit in theoretical terms.[21] Every site is a unique intersection of land, climate, production, and circulation. Peirce Lewis has stated that "most objects in the landscape—although they convey all kinds of 'messages'—do not convey those messages in any obvious way."[22] The condition of each individual site makes its understanding in relation to the notion of site extremely difficult. Ernst Cassirer describes this as a basic noetic problem: "It is, as it were, the fundamental principle of cognition that the universal can be perceived only in the particular, while the particular can be thought only in reference to the universal."[23] The problematic reciprocity of the universal and particular speaks to architectural thinking and making. Though the architect's practical task is always specific to its circumstances, architecture as a discipline theorizes such tasks in general terms. In

20. LeFebvre, "The Politics of Space," 35.
21. This points to the paradox that it is necessary to approach site, which is a non-discursive construct, through language. In fact, this paradox underlies all writing about architecture.
22. F. Peirce Lewis, "Axioms for Reading the Landscape," The Interpretation of Ordinary Landscapes, ed. D. W. Meinig (New York: Oxford University Press, 1979), 19.
23. Cassirer, The Philosophy of Symbolic Forms, 86.

practical response to the complexity of the whole, designers attempt to reduce the site by seizing its particular aspects. This is exemplified by the constructed site's emphasis on the visible and by the cleared site's preference for the abstract. Architectural reductions of site, these conceptions implicate architectural practice.

Any site is already constructed by its specific circumstances. Adding a new building to a site transforms its use as well as its topography, microclimate, and circulation. The construction of a building defines successive sites for ensuing constructions—that is, any building alters adjoining sites as well as its own. The site is neither pure nor ideal; it is "claimed," which is to say it is preoccupied, by knowledge and power and time. As the embodiment and inscription of these preoccupations, the site is made in the work of architecture and is necessary if the work of architecture is to be made.

The site is a work, a human or social trace. It is comparable to a myth, temple, or city in that it is open to archeological deciphering. The site is a significative system with no singular author. Using nature to convey ideology, the site is a social product. The natural environment, long understood simply as a technical problem to be conquered, is now seen as threatened with destruction. However, like architecture, the environment and the site can also be created, molded, and transformed. The face of the earth, the landscape, and the site are products of human efforts. The site is also an economic product, and sites can be likened to "merchandise" in that there are interrelationships between the production of goods and that of the environment: the former accrues to groups who appropriate sites in order to manage or exploit them. John Locke theorized that land has no value without labor and that its value increases with the progress of settlement.

Settlement patterns are visual statements on the land that can be deciphered. Such a functional reading, however, fails to reveal the genetic aspect that brought the site into being. A complete assessment of the site must exist at several levels: the site can be described formally; critical analysis can define how and according to what methods the site was produced, including the crucial junctures of land use determination; finally, the real site must be analyzed, in other words, one must look at the people using the site, who perhaps are opposed to its physical form and purpose.

The apparent neutrality of the site—linked to the lack of comprehensive assessment—is a mask for issues of control. The discipline of architecture avoids admitting or taking responsibility for control and denies such power in relation to site. To attempt to detach the building from the site, in practice and theory alike, is to deny that any work of architecture is a work of site, to suppress that the work is political, ideological, and temporal, and to forget that it is implicated in the history of architecture.

In closing, it must be acknowledged that these remarks are both generally broad and specifically limited. They do not outline future work but suggest its potential. There are latent assumptions here to be challenged. For example, the persistent consideration of site as existing solely at or above the surface of the earth, the bias toward native rather than urban sites, or the apparent impossibility of a site in "wilderness" all argue for the need to qualify different kinds or types of sites. Because the topic of site initially seemed bounded or finite, it also seemed to be part of the discipline of architecture. However, in concluding that the means of thinking site is a means of thinking architecture, it ends by enveloping the discipline.

Though the site is a product of culture, it is by nature not a finished or closed product. It is an artefact of human work that can neither be completed nor abandoned. Its meaning can never be determinable. The site, like the human condition, is open. This is the surplus of site, its indefinable excess.

No totality can be meaningful in any case, except finished one (a historical humanism, an intellectual object, a book, some other product of écriture), which can only be a part of our present totality and which necessarily has a closed structure, whereas the "structurality" of [the human] situation . . . is open.[24]

24. Caws, Peter, "Structuralism," *The History of Ideas*, ed. Philip P. Weiner, (New York: Charles Scribner's Sons, 1973), 329.

Writing and Discussion Questions

ANALYSIS

1. What was Laugier arguing for and against? What excerpt/quotation best represents this?
2. What was Gregotti arguing for and against? What excerpt/quotation best represents this?
3. What was Burns arguing for and against? What excerpt/quotation best represents this?

SYNTHESIS

1. Regarding concepts of nature, discuss one major difference regarding Laugier's, Gregotti's, and Burns' texts.
2. Regarding concepts of nature, discuss one primary commonality regarding Laugier's, Gregotti's, and Burns' texts.

SELF-REFLECTION

1. For each of the texts, discuss a major issue with which you most agree and most disagree; reflect upon why you hold these views.
2. Select a recent design project, or a current project on which you are working. Discuss the characteristics of the project in regards to nature, in light of the discussion and texts introduced in this chapter. What attitudes regarding nature does your work illustrate?

PROSPECTION

1.   Select one of the texts listed in the bibliography for this chapter; locate and read it. To what degree is that text and the attitudes it represents still relevant to architecture today and in the near future?

2.   What is the role of nature in architecture today? Is nature predominantly a design metaphor, a set of physical factors to emulate, or a set of physical factors to overcome or oppose; some combination of these; or something else? In other words, if a fourth text were added to this chapter, what would the argument be?

Other Readings on Natural and Constructed

Ferrier, Jacques. "The Sensual City: The Artificial Enabling the Natural," *Harvard Design Magazine,* 30 (2009): 42–49.

Lewis, Charles A. *Green Nature/Human Nature* (Champaign: Illini Books, 1996).

Marx, Leo. *The Machine in the Garden: Technology and the Pastoral Ideal in America* (New York: Oxford University Press, 1964).

Mostafavi, Mohsen. *Ecological Urbanism* (Baden: Lars Muller Publishers, 2010).

McHarg, Ian. *Design with Nature* (San Francisco: John Wiley & Sons, 1992). First published in 1969.

Neutra, Richard. *Building with Nature* (New York: Universe Books, 1971).

Redfield Lathrop, Wendy, ed. *Modulus 20: The Architectural Review at the University of Virginia: Stewardship of the Land* (New York: Princeton Architectural Press, 1991).

Scully, Vincent. *Architecture: The Natural and the Man-Made* (New York: St. Martin's Press, 1991).

Steiner, Frederick. *The Living Landscape: An Ecological Approach to Landscape Planning* (New York: McGraw-Hill College, 1990).

Williams, Raymond. *The Country and the City* (Oxford: Oxford University Press, 1973).

Wrede, Stuart, and Adams, William Howard, Eds. *Denatured Visions: Landscape and Culture in the Twentieth Century* (New York: Museum of Modern Art, 1991).

Chapter 12

NATURAL and CONSTRUCTED (PART 2)

INTRODUCTORY DISCUSSION

1. Of the two images above, which better represents the concept of "natural" architecture? Which better represents the concept of "constructed" architecture? Why?

2. How has the concept of "nature" in architecture changed in recent years?

3. How important or unimportant is "nature" to architecture today?

FIGURE 12.1
Photograph of the approach, foliage, low wall, and tree-capped hill of the Woodland Cemetery, Stockholm, Sweden (1017–1940). Architects: Gunar Asplund and Sigurd Lewerentz.

FIGURE 12.2
Photograph of the walkway, trees, and tombs of Igualada Cemetery, Igualada, Spain (1985–). Architects: Enric Miralles and Carme Pinos.

Introduction

While architects design "shelters," it may also be said that architects design "places." While architecture is filled with words and concepts that are foreign to the general public—terms like "tectonics" and "contextualism"—the term "place," not unlike "nature," is familiar to both designers and non-designers. However, such conventional and seemingly simple words like "place" often disguise what is truly a complex and diverse concept.[1] For example, from Vitruvius of the first century B.C.E to Alberti of the Renaissance, architects noted the role that regional differences in climate, topography, and construction materials played in architectural design. Viollet-le-Duc, likewise, in the 19th century, insisted on the importance of creating an architectural style unique and suitable to the time, place, and culture. At the beginning of the 20th century, Modernism and the International Style set out on a radical departure, suggesting that architecture could be less place-based and more universal. During the middle of the 20th century, a new generation of architects caused the pendulum to swing back, arguing that designing according to a specific time and place was central to architecture.

Genius Loci: Towards a Phenomenology of Architecture, the *original text* of this chapter, articulated the worldview of these mid-20th-century designers. *Genius Loci* culminated nearly two decades of work by Norwegian architect, historian, and theorist Christian Norburg-Shulz. In this text, Norburg-Shulz described how natural and constructed environments, together as a set of complex and "concrete phenomena," affect human perceptions, experiences, and emotions. Norburg-Shulz stated that the "character" of a place—*genius loci* or "spirit of place"—stems from several things: organization, spatial geometry, proximity, rhythm, boundaries, materials and construction, and variation. At the same time, the perception of these concrete phenomena, according to Norburg-Shulz, is influenced by cultural and individual identity. In essence, "phenomenology of place" was the relationship between concrete environmental phenomena and intangible human phenomena. As per Norburg-Shulz, the purpose of architecture "is to help man dwell," that "man dwells when he is able to concretize the world in buildings and things," and that buildings (architecture) must understand and, then, "concretize the *genius loci*."

1. This chapter extends the discussion initiated in the previous chapter and possesses parallels to concepts presented in Chapter 4. See the note regarding "phenomenology" in the introduction to Chapter 4. The set of readings in Chapter 12 also clearly demonstrates how a particular theory of architecture emerges, is transformed, is questioned, and is eventually replaced by an alternate theory, a clear illustration of the cyclic nature of architectural theory.

The phenomenological approach to design gained tremendous momentum during the 1970s, and was not limited to architecture. Urban designers, landscape architects, geographers, and social theorists gained interest in place-based design. This included Edward Relph's *Place and Placelessness*, the *reflective text* for this chapter.[2] In that text, Relph, a geographer, sought to add clarity to what many saw as a vague, ephemeral concept. Relph accomplished this by distinguishing the term "place" from other similar terms, such as, "region." In addition, Relph described various aspects of human perception and behavior associated with space and place. For example, Relph saw differences between "instinctive" spatial behavior ("primitive space"), "self-conscious" spatial behavior ("perceptual space"), and "lived" spatial behavior ("existential space"). Like Norburg-Shulz, Relph viewed architecture and planning as substantive mediators of human perception and behavior. Relph asserted that place-based design was being substituted by "placelessness," a devastating result of uniformity, standardization, globalization, destruction, impermanence, and scalelessness.

A new generation of architects, landscape architects, and urban designers of the late 20th and early 21st centuries ascribed to the principles of phenomenological, place-based design set forth by Norburg-Shulz and Relph. Renowned architects Steven Holl, Juhani Pallasmaa, and Peter Zumthor were among them. Others, however, remained skeptical. Landscape architect Kathryn Moore, for example, was among the skeptics. In "Genius Loci: Hidden Truth or Hidden Agenda?," the *philosophical text* for this chapter, Moore asserted that *genius loci* was outdated and especially problematic in design education, further mystifying the design process. In addition, Moore contended that the concept of *genius loci* limited "imaginative and intelligent debate," as designers searched for an "invisible" and unverifiable "fallacy."

Like the various concepts of "nature" put forth in the previous chapter—or the diverse definitions of "complexity" or "honesty" in earlier chapters—"place" is a seemingly modest term. But, like "nature," "place" is among the most volatile terms in the architectural lexicon. While it may be said that architects *design* "places," it may also be said that each architect, in his or her own mind, *defines* "places."

2. It needs to be noted that *Genius Loci* was published after *Place and Placelessness*. However, *Genius Loci* is seen as the *original text* here because it was the culmination of work developed by Norburg-Shulz over multiple years. Norburg-Shulz is often referenced in *Place and Placelessness*, and is, therefore, seen as the *reflective text*.

Original Text

CHRISTIAN NORBURG-SHULZ, EXCERPTS FROM *GENIUS LOCI: TOWARDS A PHENOMENOLOGY OF ARCHITECTURE*.

First Published in 1979

PLACE?

THE PHENOMENON OF PLACE

Our everyday life-world consists of concrete "phenomena." It consists of people, of animals, of flowers, trees and forests, of stone, earth, wood and water, of towns, streets and houses, doors, windows and furniture. And it consists of sun, moon and stars, of drifting clouds, of night and day and changing seasons. But it also comprises more intangible phenomena such as feelings. This is what is "given," this is the "content" of our existence. Thus Rilke asks: "Are we perhaps *here* to say: house, bridge, fountain, gate, jug, fruit tree, window— at best: column, tower."[3] Everything else, such as atoms and molecules, numbers and all kinds of "data," are abstractions or tools which are constructed to serve other purposes than those of everyday life. Today it is common to give more importance to the tools than our life-world.

The concrete things which constitute our given world are interrelated in complex and perhaps contradictory ways. Some of the phenomena may for instance comprise others. The forest consists of trees, and the town is made up of houses. "Landscape" is such a comprehensive phenomenon. In general we may say that some phenomena form an "environment" to others.

A concrete term for environment is *place*. It is common usage to say that acts and occurrences *take place*. In fact it is meaningless to imagine any happening without reference to a locality. Place is evidently an integral part of existence.

What, then, do we mean with the word "place"? Obviously we mean something more than abstract location. We mean a totality made up of concrete things having material substance, shape, texture and colour. Together these things determine an "environmental character," which is the essence of place. In general a place is given as

3. Rainer M. Rilke, *The Duino Elegies*, (New York: IX Elegy, 1972). First German edition 1922.

such a character or "atmosphere." A place is therefore a qualitative, "total" phenomenon, which we cannot reduce to any of its properties, such as spatial relationships, without losing its concrete nature out of sight.

Everyday experience moreover tells us that different actions need different environments to take place in a satisfactory way. As a consequence towns and houses consist of a multitude of particular places. This fact is of course taken into consideration by current theory of planning and architecture, but so far the problem has been treated in a too abstract way. "Taking place" is usually understood in a quantitative, "functional" sense, with implications such as spatial distribution and dimensioning. But are not "functions" inter-human and similar everywhere? Evidently not. "Similar" functions, even the most basic ones such as sleeping and eating, take place in very different ways, and demand places with different properties, in accordance with different cultural traditions and different environmental conditions. The functional approach therefore left out the place as a concrete "here" having its particular identity.

Being qualitative totalities of a complex nature, places cannot be described by means of analytic, "scientific" concepts. As a matter of principle science "abstracts" from the given to arrive at neutral "objective" knowledge.

What is lost, however, is the everyday life-world, which ought to be the real concern of man in general and planners and architects in particular.[4] Fortunately a way out of the impasse exists, that is, the method known as *phenomenology*.

Phenomenology was conceived as a "return to things," as opposed to abstractions and mental constructions. So far phenomenologists have been mainly concerned with ontology, psychology, ethics and to some extent aesthetics, and have given relatively little attention to the phenomenology of the daily environment. A few pioneer works however exist, but they hardly contain any direct reference to architecture.[5] A phenomenology of architecture is therefore urgently needed. . . .

Natural elements are evidently the primary components of the given, and places are in fact usually defined in geographical terms. We must repeat however, that "place" means something more than location.

Various attempts at the description of natural places are offered by current literature on "landscape," but again we find that the usual approach is too abstract, being based on "functional" or perhaps "visual" considerations.[6] Again we must turn to philosophy for help. As a first, fundamental distinction Heidegger introduces the concept of "earth" and "sky," and says: "Earth is the serving bearer, blossoming and fruiting, spreading out in rock and water, rising up into plant and animal." "The sky is the vaulting path of the sun, the course of the changing moon, the glitter of the stars, the year's seasons, the light and dusk of day, the gloom and glow of night, the clemency and inclemency of the weather, the drifting clouds and blue depth of the ether."[7] Like many fundamental insights, the distinction between earth and sky might seem trivial. Its importance however comes out of when we add Heidegger's definition of "dwelling": "The way in which you are and I am, the way in which we humans *are* on the earth, is dwelling." But "on the earth" already

4. The concept "every life-world" was introduced by Husserl in *The Crisis of European Sciences and Transcendental Phenomenology*, 1936
5. Heidegger, *Bauen Wohen Denken*; Bollow, *Mensh und Raum*; Merleau-Ponty, *Phenomenology of Perception*; Bachelard, *Poetics of Space*, also L. Kruse, *Räumliche Umwelt*, Berlin 1974.
6. See for instance Jay Appleton, *The Experience of Landscape* (London: Wiley, 1975).
7. Heidegger, *Bauen Wohen Denken*, 149.

means "under the sky."[8] He also calls what is *between* earth and sky *the world*, and says that "the world is the house where the mortals dwell."[9] In other words, when man is capable of dwelling the world becomes an "inside." In general, nature forms an extended comprehensive totality, a "place," which according to local circumstances has a particular identity. This identity, or "spirit," may be described by means of the kind of concrete, "qualitative" terms Heidegger uses to characterizes earth and sky, and has to take this fundamental distinction as its point of departure. In this way we might arrive at an existentially relevant understanding of *landscape*, which ought to be preserved as the main designation of natural places. Within the landscape, however, there are subordinate places, as well as natural "things" such as Trakl's "tree." In these things the meaning of the natural environment is "condensed."

The man-made parts of the environment are first of all "settlements" of different scale, from houses and farms to villages and towns, and secondly "paths" which connect these settlements as well as various elements which transform nature into a "cultural landscape." If the settlements are organically related to their environment, it implies that the serve as *foci* where the environmental character is condensed and "explained." Thus Heidegger says: "The single houses, the villages, the towns are works of building which within and around themselves gather the multifarious in-between. The building bring the earth as the inhabited landscape close to man, and at the same time place the closeness of neighborly dwelling under the expanse of the sky."[10] The basic property of man-made places is therefore concentration and enclosure. They are "insides" in a full sense, which means that they "gather" what is known. To fulfill this function they have opening that relate to the outside. (Only an *inside* can in fact have openings). Buildings are furthermore related to their environment by resting on the ground and rising towards the sky. Finally the man-made environments comprise artifacts or "things," which may serve as internal foci, and emphasize the gather function of the settlement. . . .

A first step is taken with a distinction of natural and man-made phenomena, or in concrete terms between "landscape" and "settlement." A second step is represented by categories of earth-sky (horizontal-vertical) and outside-inside.

These categories have spatial implications and "space" is hence re-introduced, not primarily as a mathematical concept, but as an existential dimension.[11] A final and particularly important step is taken with the concept of "character." Character is determined by *how* things are, and gives an investigation a basis in the concrete phenomena of our everyday life-world. Only in this way may we fully grasp the *genius loci*, the "spirit of place" which the ancients recognized as that "opposite" man has come to terms with, to be able to dwell.[12]

8. Ibid., 97, 99.
9. Martin Heidegger, *Hebel der Hausfreund*. (Pfullingen: Neske, 1957), 13.
10. Ibid., 13.
11. Christian Norberg-Schulz, *Existence, Space and Architecture* (London: Studio Vista, 1971), where the concept "existential space" is used.
12. Heidegger points out the relationship between the words *gegen* (against, opposite) and *Gegend* (environment, locality).

THE STRUCTURE OF PLACE

Our preliminary discussion of the phenomena of place led to the conclusion that the structure of place ought to be described in terms of "landscape" and "settlement," and analyzed by means of the categories "space" and "character." Whereas "space" denotes the three-dimensional organization of the elements which make up a place, "character" denotes the general "atmosphere" which is the most comprehensive property of any place. Instead of making a distinction between space and character, it is of course possible to employ one comprehensive concept, such as "lived space."[13] For our purpose, however, it is practical to distinguish between space and character. Similar spatial organizations may possess very different characters according to the concrete treatment of the space-defining elements (the *boundary*). In history the basic spatial forms have been given ever new characterizing interpretations.[14] On the other hand it has to be pointed out that the spatial organization puts certain limits to characterization, and that the two concepts are interdependent.

"Space" is certainly no new term in architectural theory. But space can mean many things. In current literature we may distinguish between two uses: space as three-dimensional geometry, and space as perceptual field.[15] None of these however are satisfactory, being abstractions from the intuitive three-dimensional totality of everyday experience, which we may call "concrete space." Concrete human actions in fact do not take place in an homogeneous isotropic space, but in a space distinguished by qualitative differences, such as "up" and "down." In architectural theory several attempts have been made to define space in concrete, qualitative terms. Giedion, thus uses the distinction between "outside" and "inside" as the basis for a grand view of architectural history.[16] Kevin Lynch penetrates deeper into the structure of concrete space, introducing the concepts of "node" ("landmark"), "path," "edge" and "district," to denote those elements which form the basis for men's orientation in space.[17] Paolo Portoghesi finally defines space as a "system of places," implying that the concept of space has its roots in concrete situations, although spaces may be *described* by means of mathematics.[18] The latter view corresponds to Heidegger's statement that "spaces receive their being from locations and not from 'space.'"[19] The outside–inside relation which is a primary aspect of concrete space, implies that spaces possess a varying degree of *extension* and *enclosure*. Whereas landscapes are distinguished by a varied, but basically continuous extension, settlements are enclosed entities. Settlement and landscape therefore have a *figure-ground* relationship. In general any enclosure becomes manifest as a "figure" in relation to the extended ground of the landscape. A settlement loses its identity if this relationship is corrupted, just as much as the landscape loses its identity as comprehensive extension. In a wider context any enclosure becomes a *centre*, which may function as a "focus" for its surroundings. From the centre space extends with a varying degree of continuity (rhythm) in different directions. Evidently the main directions are horizontal and vertical, that is, the directions of earth and sky. *Centralization, direction* and *rhythm* are therefore other important

13. This has been done by some writers such as K. Graf von Dürckheim, E. Straus and O. F. Bollnow.

14. We may compare with Alberti's distinction between "beauty" and "ornament."

15. Norberg-Schulz, *Existence*, 12.

16. Sigried Giedion, *The Eternal Present: The Beginnings of Architecture* (London: Oxford University Press, 1964).

17. Kevin Lynch, *The Image of the City* (Cambridge: MIT Press, 1960).

18. Paolo Portoghesi, *Le Inibizioni dell'Architettura Moderna* (Bari: Laterza, 1975), 88.

19. Heidegger, *Hebel der Hausfreund*, 154.

properties of concrete space. Finally it has to be mentioned that natural elements (such as hills) and settlements may be clustered or grouped with a varying degree of *proximity*. . . .

Any enclosure is defined by a boundary. Heidegger says: "A boundary is not that at which something stops but, as the Greeks recognized, the boundary is that, from which something begins its presencing."[20] The boundaries of a built space are known as *floor*, *wall* and *ceiling*. The boundaries of a landscape are structurally similar, and consist of ground, horizon, and sky. This simple structural similarity is of basic importance for the relationship between natural and man-made places. The enclosing properties of a boundary are determined by its *openings*, as was poetically intuited by Trakl when using the images of window, door and threshold. In general the boundary, and in particular the wall, makes the spatial structure visible as continuous or discontinuous extension, direction and rhythm.

"Character" is at the same time a more general and a more concrete concept than "space." On the one hand it denotes a general comprehensive atmosphere, and on the other the concrete form and substance of the space-defining elements. Any real *presence* is intimately linked with a character.[21] A phenomenology of character has to comprise a survey of manifest characters as an investigation of their concrete determinants. We have pointed out that different actions demand places with a different character. A dwelling has to be "protective," an office "practical," a ball-room "festive" and a church "solemn." When we visit a foreign city, we are usually struck by its particular character, which becomes an important part of the experience. Landscapes also possess character, some of which are of a particular "natural" kind. Thus we talk about "barren" and "fertile," "smiling" and "threatening" landscapes. In general we have to emphasize that *all places have character*, and that character is the basic mode in which the world is "given." To some extent the character of a place is a function of time; it changes with the seasons, the course of the day and the weather, factors which above all determine different conditions of *light*.

The character is determined by the material and formal constitution of the place. We must therefore ask: *how* is the ground on which we walk, *how* is the sky above our heads, or in general; *how* are the boundaries which define the place. How a boundary is depends upon its formal articulation, which is again related to the way it is "built." Looking at a building from this point of view, we have to consider how it rests on the ground and how it rises towards the sky.

Particular attention has to be given to its lateral boundaries, or walls, which also contribute decisively to determine the character of the *urban* environment. . . .

The structure of place becomes manifest as environmental totalities which comprise the aspects of character and space. Such places are known as "countries," "regions," "landscapes," "settlements" and "buildings." Here we return to the concrete "things" of our everyday life-world, which was our point of departure, and remember Rilke's words: "Are we perhaps *here* to say . . ." When places are classified we should therefore use terms

20. Ibid., "Presence is the old word for being."
21. Otto F. Bollnow, *Das Wesen der Stimmungen* (Frankfurt: Klosermann, 1956).

such as "island," "promontory," "bay," "forest," "grove," or "square," "street," "courtyard," and "floor," "wall," "roof," "ceiling," "window" and "door."

Places are hence designated by *nouns*. This implies that they are considered real "things that exist," which is the original meaning of the word "substantive." Space, instead, as a system of relations, is denoted by *prepositions*. In our daily life we hardly talk about "space," but about things that are "over" or "under," "before" or "behind" each other, or we use prepositions such as "at," "in," "within," "on," "upon," "to," "from," "along," "next." All these prepositions denote topological relations of the kind mentioned before. Character, finally, is denoted by *adjectives*, as was indicated above. A character is a complex totality, and a single adjective evidently cannot cover more than one aspect of this totality. Often, however, a character is so distinct that one word seems sufficient to grasp its essence. We see, thus, that the very structure of everyday language confirms our analysis of place.

Countries, regions, landscapes, settlements, buildings (and their sub-places) form a series with a gradually diminishing scale. The steps in this series may be called "environmental levels."[22] At the "top" of the series we find the more comprehensive natural places which "contain" the man-made places on the "lower" levels. The latter have the "gathering" and "focusing" function mentioned above. In other words, man "receives" the environment and makes it focus in buildings and things. The things thereby "explain" the environment and make its character manifest. Thereby the things themselves become meaningful. That is the basic function of *detail* in our surroundings.[23] This does not imply, however, that the different levels must have the same structure. Architectural history in fact shows that this is rarely the case. Vernacular settlements usually have a topological organization, although the single houses may be strictly geometrical. In larger cities we often find topologically organized neighbourhoods within a general geometrical structure, etc. We shall return to the particular problems of structural correspondence later, but have to say some words about the main "step" in the scale of environmental levels: the relation between natural and man-made places. . . .

THE SPIRIT OF PLACE

Genius loci is a Roman concept. According to ancient Roman belief every "independent" being has its *genius*, its guardian spirit. This spirit gives life to people and places, accompanies them from birth to death, and determines their character or essence. Even the gods had their *genius*, a fact which illustrates the fundamental nature of the concept.[24] The *genius* thus denotes what a this *is*, or what it "wants to be," to use a word of Louis Kahn. It is not necessary in our context to go into the history of the concept of *genius* and its relationship to the *daimon* of the Greeks. It suffices to point out that ancient man experienced his environment as consisting of definite characters. In particular he recognized that it is of great existential importance to come to terms with the *genius* of the locality where his life takes place. In the past survival depended on a "good" relationship to the place in a physical as well as psychic sense. In ancient Egypt, for instance, the country

22. Norberg-Schulz, *Existence*, 27.
23. Ibid., 32.
24. *Paulys Realencyclopedie der Classischen Altertumswissenschaft.* VII, 1, 1155.

was not only cultivated in accordance with the Nile floods, but the very structure of the landscape served as a model for the lay-out of the "public" buildings which should give man a sense of security by symbolizing an eternal environmental order.[25]

During the course of history the *genius loci* has remained a living reality, although it may not have been expressively named as such. Artists and writers have found inspiration in local character and have "explained" the phenomena of everyday life as well as art, referring to landscapes and urban milieus. Thus Goethe says: "It is evident, that the eye is educated by the things it sees from childhood on, and therefore Venetian painters must see everything clearer and with more joy than other people."[26]

Still in 1960 Lawrence Durrell wrote: "As you get to know Europe slowly, tasting the wines, cheeses and characters of the different countries you begin to realize the important determinant of any culture is after all the spirit of place."[27]

Modern tourism proves that the experience of different places is a major human interest, although also this value today tends to get lost. In fact modern man for a long time believed that science and technology had freed him from a direct dependence on places.[28] This belief has proved an illusion; pollution and environmental chaos have suddenly appeared as a frightening *nemesis*, and as a result the problem of place has regained its true importance.

We have used the word "dwelling" to indicate the total man–place relationship. To understand more fully what this word implies, it is useful to return to the distinction between "space" and "character." When man dwells, he is simultaneously located in space and exposed to a certain environmental character. The two psychological functions involved, may be called "orientation" and "identification."[29] To gain an existential foothold man has to be able to *orientate* himself; he has to know *where* he is. But he also has to *identify* himself with the environment, that is, he has to know *how* he is a certain place.

. . .

The *identity* of a person is defined in terms of the schemata developed, because they determine the "world" which is accessible. This fact is confirmed by common linguistic usage. When a person wants to tell who he is, it is in fact usual to say: "I am a New Yorker," or "I am a Roman." This means something much more concrete than to say: "I am an architect," or perhaps: "I am an optimist." We understand that human identity is to a high extent a function of places and things. Thus Heidegger says: "Wir sind die Be-Dingten."[30] It is therefore not only important that our environment has a spatial structure which facilitates orientation, but that it consists of concrete objects of identification. *Human identity presupposes the identity of place.*

Identification and orientation are primary aspects of man's being-in-the-world. Whereas identification is the basis for man's sense of *belonging*, orientation is the function which enables him to be that *homo viator*, which is part of his nature. It is characteristic for modern man that for a long time he gave the role as a wanderer pride of place. He wanted to be "free" and conquer the world. Today we start to realize that true freedom presupposes belonging, and that "dwelling" means belonging to a concrete place.

25. Christian Norberg-Schulz, *Meaning in Western Architecture* (London: Studio Vista, 1975), 10.

26. Johann W. Goethe, *Italienische Reise*, October 8, 1786.

27. L. Durrell, *Spirit of Place* (London: Faber & Faber, 1969), 156.

28. See Melvin M. Webber, *Explorations into Urban Structure* (Philadelphia: University of Pennsylvania Press, 1963), who talks about "non-place urban realm."

29. Norberg-Schulz, *Intentions*, where the concepts "cognitive orientation" and "cathectic orientation" are used.

30. Martin Heidegger, *Poetry, Language, and Thought*, trans. Albert Hofstadter (New York: HarperCollins, 1971), 181. "We are the be-thinged," the conditioned ones.

The word to "dwell" has several connotations which confirm and illuminate our thesis. Firstly it ought to be mentioned that "dwell" is derived from the Old Norse *dvelja*, which meant to linger or remain. Analogously Heidegger related the German "wohnen" to "bleiben" and "sich aufhalten."[31] Furthermore he points out that the Gothic *wunian* meant to "be at peace," "to remain in peace." The German word for Peace, *Friede*, means to be free; that is, protected from harm and danger. This protection is achieved by means of an *Umfriedung* or enclosure. "Friede" is also related to *zufrieden* (content), *Freund* (friend) and the Gothic *frijōn* (love). Heidegger uses these linguistic relationships to show that *dwelling means to be at peace in a protected place*. We should also mention that the German word for dwelling, *Wohnung*, derives from *das Gewohnte*, which means what is known or habitual. "Habit" and "habitat" show an analogous relationship. In other words, man knows what has become accessible to him through dwelling. We here return to the *Übereinstimmung* or correspondence between man and his environment, and arrive at the very root of the problem of "gathering." To gather means that the everyday life-world has become "gewohnt" or "habitual." But gathering is a concrete phenomenon, and thus leads us to the final connotation of "dwelling." Again it is Heidegger who has uncovered a fundamental relationship. Thus he points out that the Old English and High German word for "building," *buan*, meant to dwell, and that it is intimately related to the verb *to be*. "What then does *ich bin* mean? The old word *bauen*, to which the *bin* belongs, answers: *ich bin, du bist*, mean: I dwell, you dwell. The way in which you are and I am, the manner in which we humans *are* on earth, is *buan*, dwelling."[32] We may conclude that dwelling means to gather the world as a concrete building or "thing," and that the archetypal act of building is the *Umfriedung* or enclosure. . . .

Man dwells when he is able to concretize the world in buildings things. As we have mentioned above, "concretization" is the function of the work of art, as opposed to the "abstraction" of science.[33] Works of art concretize what remains "between" the pure objects of science. Our everyday life-world *consists of* such "intermediary" objects, and we understand that the fundamental function of art is to gather the contradictions and complexities of the life-world. Being an *imago mundi*, the work of art helps man to dwell. Hölderlin was right when he said, "Full of merit, yet poetically, man dwells on this earth."

This means: man's merits do not count much if he is unable to dwell *poetically*, that is, to dwell in the true sense of the word. Thus Heidegger says "Poetry does not fly above and surmount the earth in order to escape it and hover over it. Poetry is what first brings man into the earth, making him belong to it, and thus brings him into dwelling."[34] Only poetry in all its forms (also as the "art of living") makes human existence meaningful, and *meaning* is the fundamental human need. Architecture belongs to poetry, and its purpose is to help man to dwell. But architecture is a difficult art. To make practical towns and buildings is not enough. Architecture comes into being when a "total environment is made visible," to quote the definition of Susanne Langer.[35] In general, this means to concretize the *genius loci*. We have seen that this is done by means of buildings which gather the properties of the place and bring them close to man. The basic act of

31. Heidegger, "Building Dwelling Thinking," in *Poetry*, 146.
32. Ibid., 147.
33. Ibid., 168.
34. Ibid., 218.
35. Susanne Langer, *Feeling and Form: A Theory of Art* (New York: Scribner, 1953).

architecture is therefore to understand the "vocation" of the place. In this way we protect the earth and become ourselves part of a comprehensive totality. What is here advocated is not some kind of "environmental determinism." We only recognize the fact that man *is* an integral part of the environment, and that it can only lead to human alienation and environmental disruption if he forgets that. To belong to a place means to have an existential foothold, in a concrete everyday sense. When God said to Adam: "You shall be a fugitive and a wanderer on the Earth;[36] he put man in front of his most basic problem: to cross the threshold and regain the lost place.

36. Genesis 4:12.

Reflective Text

E. RELPH, EXCERPTS FROM *PLACE AND PLACELESSNESS.*

First Published in 1976

PLACE AND THE PHENOMENOLOGICAL BASIS OF GEOGRAPHY

THE CONCEPT OF PLACE

"A knowledge of places," Hugh Prince has written, "is an indispensable link in the chain of knowledge."[37] And in terms of the practical everyday knowledge that we need to organise our experiences of the world there can be little disputing this, for we have to know, differentiate, and respond to the various places where we work, relax, and sleep. But in itself this practical knowing of places, although essential to our existence, is quite superficial and is based mainly on the explicit functions that places have for us. That the significance of place in human experience goes far deeper than this is apparent in the actions of individuals and groups protecting *their* places against outside forces of destruction, or is known to anyone who has experienced homesickness and nostalgia for particular places. To be human is to live in a world that is filled with significant places: to be human is to have and to know *your* place. The philosopher Martin Heidegger declared that "'place' places man in such a way that it reveals the external bonds of his existence and at the same time the depths of his freedom and reality."[38] It is a profound and complex aspect of man's experience of the world.

The apparent importance of place, both functionally and existentially, has not been reflected in examinations of either the concept of place or of the nature of experience of place. Even architects and planners have displayed a distinct lack of interest; yet their task can be well understood as "the possession of place,"[39] as the "creation of place,"[40] or as the development of a system of meaningful places that give form and structure to our experiences of the world.[41] . . .

An analysis of the concept of place as it is used by Lukermann reveals six major components:[42]

37. Hugh C. Prince, "The Geographical Imagination," *Landscape*, 11 (1961): 22.

38. Martin Heidegger, "An Ontological Consideration of Place," in *The Question of Being* (New York: Twayne Publishers, 1958), 19.

39. Charles Moore, Donlyn Lyndon, Patrick Quinn, and Sim van der Ryn, "Towards Making Places," *Landscape,* 12 (1962): 33–34.

40. Sinclair Gauldie, *Architecture: The Appreciation of the Arts I* (London: Oxford University Press, 1969), 173.

41. Christian Norberg-Schulz, "Meaning in architecture" in *Meaning in Architecture,* ed. Charles Jencks (London: The Cresset Press, 1969), 226.

42. Fred Lukermann, "Geography as a Formal Intellectual Discipline and the Way in Which it Contributes to Human Knowledge," *Canadian Geographer,* 8 (1964): 167–172.

1. The idea of location, especially location as it relates to other things and places, is absolutely fundamental. Location can be described in terms of internal characteristics (site) and external connectivity to other locations (situation); thus places have spatial extension and an inside and outside.

2. Place involves an integration of elements of nature and culture; "each place has its own order, its special *ensemble*, which distinguishes it from the next place." This clearly implies that every place is a unique entity.[43]

3. Although every place is unique, they are interconnected by a system of spatial interactions and transfers; they are part of a framework of *circulation*.

4. Places are localised—they are parts of larger areas and are focuses in a system of localisation.

5. Places are emerging or becoming; with historical and cultural change new elements are added and old elements disappear. Thus places have a distinct historical component.

6. Places have meaning: they are characterised by the beliefs of man. "Geographers wish to understand not only why place is a factual event in human consciousness, but what beliefs people hold about place. . . . It is this alone that underlies man's acts which are in turn what give character to a place."[44]

Thus Lukermann understands places as complex integrations of nature and culture that have developed and are developing in particular locations, and which are linked by flows of people and goods to other places. A place is not just the "where" of something; it is the location plus everything that occupies that location seen as an integrated and meaningful phenomenon.

The concept of place is not, however, quite as coherent as this discussion perhaps implies. First of all it must be recognised, as May points out, that Lukermann does not distinguish clearly between the concepts of "place," "region," "area," and "location," and indeed uses these interchangeably.[45] Hence he is preserving much of the confusion that is inherent in these terms and which has never been satisfactorily resolved by geographers, and is in effect bundling together a whole variety of different approaches and ideas. Taking a more analytic approach May points out that the notion "place" has been used in three and perhaps four distinct senses by geographers. First, it has been used to refer to the entire surface of the earth, as for instance in the idea of the earth as the place of man. Second, it has been used to refer to a unit of space such as a city, province, or country, in which sense it cannot be clearly differentiated from "region." Third, it has been used to refer to a particular and specific part of space and to what may occupy that space, "as when we think of our place of residence as being a particular building or talk of a place of worship or a place of amusement." Finally, place has been used to mean "location" in the sense of exact position, although strictly location is more specific than place, for "place is made up of a number of things that can be specifically located." May argues that only in the third of these senses is there something distinctive about the idea of place, for in

43. Ibid., 170.
44. Ibid., 169.
45. J. A. May, *Kant's Concept of Geography* (Toronto: University of Toronto, Department of Geography, Research Publication No.4, 1970), 214.

this meaning place appears to possess some "perceptual unity" that is given to it by our experiences with unique and real places. . . .

SPACE AND PLACE

The space we experience of sky or sea or landscape, or of a city spread out beneath us when viewed from a tall building, the built space of the street, of buildings viewed from the outside or experienced from the inside, the reasoned space of maps, plans, cosmographies, and geometries, interstellar space, the space possessed by objects or claimed by countries or devoted to the gods—this is the range of our experiences and understanding of space. Space is amorphous and intangible and not an entity that can be directly described and analysed. Yet, however we feel or know or explain space, there is nearly always some associated sense or concept of place. In general it seems that space provides the context for places but derives its meaning from particular places.

The nature of space has been the subject of much discussion by philosophers, scientists, and others.[46] These discussions have never been resolved and it is not easy to formulate any framework which embraces the variety of forms of space that have been identified and which is reasonably consistent. It would not be relevant to become involved in these debates, yet it is important to clarify the relations between space and place, and thus to avoid the separation of places from their conceptual and experiential context. This dilemma is sidestepped here somewhat arbitrarily by recognising that the various forms of space lie within a continuum that has direct experience at one extreme and abstract thought at the other extreme. Within this continuum certain types of space can be distinguished, for instance that of unselfconscious and pragmatic experiences, the selfconsciously experienced perceptual space of individuals, the built spaces of architecture, and the abstract space of geometry.[47] Of particular importance is "existential" or "lived" space, for this seems to be especially relevant to a phenomenological understanding of place. Of course, concepts or experiences or created spaces do not always fall neatly into one of these categories, and this classification is really only a heuristic device for clarifying space-place relationships. In this it is useful because it covers such a broad range of ideas, experiences, and activities involving space, and hence introduces some of the diverse meanings of place.

PRAGMATIC OR PRIMITIVE SPACE

Primitive space is the space of instinctive behaviour and unselfconscious action in which we always act and move without reflection. This is an organic space that is rooted in things concrete and substantial and which involves no images or concepts of space and spatial relations. Such space is comparable to, and well characterised in terms of, the "functional circle" of animals—that is, the environment in which animals survive and function but of which so far as we can know, they have not abstract images. Indeed primitive space is perhaps less well developed than functional circles for, as Ernst Cassirer has pointed out, "a child has to learn many skills an animal is born with."[48]

46. Max Jammer, *Concepts of Space* (Cambridge: Harvard University Press, 1969); David Hawkins, *The Language of Nature* (Garden City, NY: Doubleday, 1964).

47. Christian Norberg-Schulz, *Existence, Space and Architecture* (New York: Praeger, 1971), 9–12.

48. Ernst Cassirer, *An Essay on Man* (Toronto: Bantam Books, 1970), 46–48.

Primitive space is structured unselfconsciously by basic individual experiences, beginning in infancy, associated with the movement of the body and with the senses. It is these that provide the fundamental dimensions of left and right, above and below, in front of and behind, within reach and beyond reach, within hearing and beyond hearing, within sight and beyond sight.[49] Since these experiences are common to almost everyone they are intersubjective and must be understood as not merely individual but as part of the basic spatial context of all cultural groups . . .

At this primitive level it is difficult to distinguish space and place. Perhaps space is simply a continuous series of egocentric places where things performing certain functions or meeting needs can be found, but of which no mental picture has formed. Spivak has in fact suggested that there are some thirteen irreducible settings or "archetypal places" required for unimpaired human behaviour.[50] Each of these is identified with a significant whole behaviour, such as sleeping, feeding, excreting, playing, or sheltering. More remarkable is the proposal of Adolf Portmann, based on his careful observations of animals and insects, that these often display an attachment to secure and safe places that is so powerful that these places are best understood as *homes*.[51] If Spivak and Portmann are correct then there is a deep and presymbolic differentiation of and attachment to place that is perhaps a biological rather than a peculiarly human characteristic, and it is only on the cultural and symbolic levels that place experience takes on a distinctively human quality.

PERCEPTUAL SPACE

Man's inferiority to animals in terms of organic, primitive space is more than compensated for by his ability to reflect systematically on space and to experience it and encounter it selfconsciously. There is, of course, no sudden leap from an organic involvement to sophisticated abstraction and selfconsciousness; rather there are several levels of awareness and abstraction. The most immediate form of awareness is that of "perceptual space"—the egocentric space perceived and confronted by each individual. This is a space that has content and meaning, for it cannot be divorced from experiences and intentions.

Perceptual space is a space of action centred on immediate needs and practices, and as such it has a clearly developed structure. This is described by Nitschke: "Perceptual space has a centre, which is perceiving man, and it therefore has an excellent system of directions which change with the movement of the human body; it is limited and in no sense neutral; in other words it is finite, heterogeneous and subjectively defined and perceived; distances and directions are fixed and relative to man."[52] This structure can clearly be in no way understood as objective or measurable—rather distances and directions are experienced as qualities of near or far, this way or that, and even when these are made explicit as paths or trails they are known with their special meaning. Wallace Stegner describes the satisfaction and delight he experienced in wearing paths and tracks on his father's farm in Saskatchewan: "they were ceremonial, an insistence not only that we had a right to be in sight on the prairie but that we owned and controlled a piece of

49. Yi-fu Tuan, *Topophilia* (Englewood Cliffs: Prentice-Hall, 1974), 5–29.

50. Mayer Spivak, "Archetypal Place," in *Environmental Design Research: Proceedings of 4th EDRA Conference*, ed. Wolfgang F. E. Preiser (Stroudsberg, Pa: Dowden, Hutchinson and Ross, 1973), 33–46.

51. Marjorie Grene, *Approaches to a Philosophical Biology* (New York: Basic Books, 1965), 38–39.

52. Norberg-Schulz, *Existence*, 13.

it. . . . Wearing any such path in the earth's rind is an intimate act, an act like love."[53] Although not always with such clear expression as this, in perceptual space each individual groups the world around him as "a field of domination," and he singles out those elements which may serve as a means or an end for his use or enjoyment. Theoretically it might even be possible to draw contour lines of equal significance and relevance for each individual.[54] But these would, of course, change as the individual's intentions and circumstances alter—just as when we move to a new place of residence, the shops and streets that were formerly so significant in our daily life cease to be of any importance.

Perceptual space is also the realm of direct emotional encounters with the spaces of the earth, sea, and sky or with built and created spaces. Matoré writes: "We do not grasp space only by our senses . . . we live in it, we project our personality into it, we are tied to it by emotional bonds; space is not just perceived . . . it is lived."[55] Space is never empty but has content and substance that derive both from human intention and imagination and from the character of the space. Such "substantive space" is "the blue of the sky as a frontier between the visible and the invisible; it is the emptiness of the desert, a space for death; it is the frozen space of an ice bank . . . the depressing space of a heath in a storm."[56] It is also the 'telluric space' that we can experience in the depth and solidity of the earth—"a concrete and immediate experience in which we feel the material intimacy of the crust of the earth, a setting down of roots, a type of foundation for geographical reality."[57] It can be the mysterious, enclosing, intimate space of the forest,[58] or the spaces of water and air with their "shadows, reflections, haze and mist that dance lightly and blend our feelings with the fantasies of the world."[59] And substantive space can also be experienced in any of the infinite variety of man-made spaces of buildings, streets, and landscapes.[60] Such experiences of substantive space may sometimes be overwhelming or intense, as when we round a corner and come abruptly upon some magnificent view. Henry Miller describes such an experience: "My eye suddenly caught a view which took my breath away. From what was virtually an oubliette I was looking down on one of the oldest quarters of Paris. The vista was so sweepingly soft and intoxicating it brought tears to my eyes."[61] More usually our experiences of perceptual space are fleeting and unexceptional, and accepted as part of the natural course of things. They are no less important for that, for it is these personal experiences of space that are the basis for much of the meaning that environments and landscapes have for us.

Through particular encounters and experiences perceptual space is richly differentiated into places, or centres of special personal significance. Paul Shepard suggests that for each individual "the organising of thinking, perception and meaning is intimately related to specific places," and no doubt we all have private places to which we can retreat in order to meditate.[62] For children in particular, places constitute the basis for the discovery of the self, and caves or trees or even a corner of the house may be claimed as "my place."[63] These childhood places frequently take on great significance and are remembered with reverence; thus Albert Camus found that the memory of the ruins of Tipasa which he knew as a child provided an ongoing source of stability and meaning for him.[64] Both

53. Wallace E. Stegner, *Wolf Willow* (New York: The Viking Press, 1962), 271–273.
54. Alfred Schütz, *Collected Papers* (The Hague: Martinus Nijhoff, 1962), vol. II, 93.
55. Georges Matoré, *L'Espace Humain* (Paris: La Columbe, 1962), 22–23.
56. Eric Dardel, *L'Homme et la Terre: Nature de Realité Géographique* (Paris: Presses Universitaires de France, 1952), 10.
57. Ibid., 20.
58. Gaston Bachelard, *The Poetics of Space* (Boston: Beacon Press, 1969), 185–189.
59. Dardel, *L'Homme et la Terre*, 31.
60. Tuan, *Topophilia*, 27–29.
61. Henry Miller, *Remember to Remember* (Norfolk: New Direction Books, 1947), 343.
62. Paul Shepard, *Man in the Landscape* (New York: Ballantine Books, 1967), 32.
63. Edith Cobb, "The Ecology of Imagination in Childhood," in *The Subversive Science*, eds. Paul Shepard and Daniel McKinley (Boston: Houghton Mifflin, 1970).
64. Albert Camus, *The Myth of Sisyphus* (New York: Vintage Books, 1955).

remembered and currently significant places are essentially concentrations of meaning and intention within the broader structure of perceptual space. They are fundamental elements of the lived-geography of the world. Dardel writes: "For man geographical reality is first of all the place he is in, the places of his childhood, the environment which summons him to its presence."[65]

Although they are personal, perceptual spaces and places are not entirely isolated within the individual, for there are common landscapes that are experienced. . . . But perhaps a more common and significant means of release from the isolation of perceptual space is given by the intersubjective linking of culture, experience, and intention. . . . In short, the individual is not merely in his own place at the centre of his own space, but recognises from the start that all other individuals have their perceptual spaces and places. Furthermore he is aware that these constitute just part of the more or less agreed on and consistent lived-space of the entire social or cultural group of which he is a member.

EXISTENTIAL SPACE

Existential or lived-space is the inner structure of space as it appears to us in our concrete experiences of the world as members of a cultural group.[66] It is intersubjective and hence amenable to all members of that group for they have all been socialised according to a common set of experiences, signs, and symbols.[67] The meanings of existential space are therefore those of a culture as experienced by an individual, rather than a summation of the meanings of individual perceptual spaces, though in many cases the two probably coincide. Furthermore existential space is not merely a passive space waiting to be experienced, but is constantly being created and remade by human activities. It is the space in which "human intention inscribes itself on the earth," and in so doing creates unselfconsciously patterns and structures of significance through the building of towns, villages, and houses, and the making of landscapes.[68] . . .

Because . . . existential space is meaningful within one culture group does not mean that it is communicable to members of other cultures, at least not without some considerable effort of understanding on their part. Consider for example Rapoport's account of the way in which aborigines and Europeans see the landscape of north-west Australia:

Many Europeans have spoken of the uniformity and featurelessness of the Australian landscape. The aborigines, however, see the landscape in a totally different way. Every feature of the landscape is known and has meaning—they then perceive differences which the European cannot see. These differences may be in terms of detail or in terms of a magical and invisible landscape, the symbolic landscape being even more varied than the perceived physical space. As one example, every individual feature of Ayer's Rock is linked to a significant myth and the mythological beings who created it. Every tree, every stain, hole and fissure

65. Dardel, *L'Homme et la Terre*, 46.
66. Otto Bollnow, "Lived Space," in *Readings in Existential Phenomenology*, eds. Nathaniel Lawrence and Daniel O'Connor (Englewood Cliffs, N J: Prentice-Hall, 1967); and Schütz, *Collected Papers*, 122–127.
67. Peter L. Berger and Thomas Luckmann, *The Social Construction of Reality* (Garden City, N Y: Doubleday, 1967), 130–131.
68. Dardel, *L'Homme et la Terre*, 40.

has meaning. Thus what to a European is an empty land may be full of noticeable differences to the aborigines and hence rich and complex.[69]

This example is of interest not only because it shows that existential space is culturally defined and hence it is difficult to experience the space of another culture, but also because it indicates some ways in which the space of a "primitive" culture differs from that of Europeans. Thus Rapoport notes that while Europeans—and indeed the members of all modern technological societies—possess space by building and organise it mainly in terms of material objects and functions, for the aborigines it is structured according to places of myth, ceremony, and ritual, and is everywhere peopled by spirit-beings. Space is full with significance, and the landscape, rather than being comprised of physical and geological features, is a record of mythical history in which the rocks and trees for us are experienced as ancestors and spirits by the aborigines. There is in fact a very clear distinction to be drawn between the existential space of a culture like that of the aborigines and most technological and industrial cultures—the former is 'sacred' and symbolic, while the latter are 'geographical' and significant mainly for functional and utilitarian purposes. . . .

GEOGRAPHICAL SPACE

. . . Space is claimed for man by naming it. Jacquetta Hawkes writes: "Place names are among the things that link men most intimately with their territory" and suggests that since Palaeolithic times peopled landscapes have never been without some name to enrich and confirm their personality.[70] The naming of regions and places is indeed part of a fundamental structuring of existential space. Irving Hallowell has stated: "Place naming, star naming, maps, myth and tale, the orientations of building, the spatial implications in dances and ceremonies, all facilitate the construction and maintenance of spatial patterns in which the individual must live and act."[71] Where there are no names the environment is chaotic, lacking in orientation, even fearful, for it has no humanised and familiar points of reference. Thus when the Masai of Kenya were forced to relocate they took with them the names of hills, rivers and plains and fitted them to the new topography; similarly North America is sprinkled with the borrowed place names of Europe, for these once provided familiarity in an otherwise strange land.[72] Indeed one of man's first acts on entering any unexplored or uninhabited region is to give names to at least the most prominent features and thus to humanise the wilderness.

Geographical space is not objective and indifferent but full of significance for people. Dardel suggests that it appears us "essentially qualified in a concrete situation which affects man"—it has colour, depth, density, and solidity, it has associations and symbols, it both offers possibilities for and yet restricts experience.[73] It is not an indifferent space that can be arranged or dismissed, but always has meaning in terms of some human task or lived-experience. Thus a prairie is "vast," a mountain "impassable," a house "spacious" or a street "constricted" only with reference to a particular human intention.

69. Amos Rapoport, "Australian Aborigines and the Definition of Place," in *Environmental Design: Research and Practice: Proceedings of the 3rd EDRA Conference*, ed. W. J. Mitchell (Los Angeles: University of California Press, 1972), 3-3-4.

70. Jacquetta Hawkes, *A Land* (London: The Cresset Press, 1951), 151.

71. Irving Hallowell, *Culture and Experience* (Philadelphia: University of Pennsylvania Press, 1955), 186.

72. Kevin Lynch, *What Time Is This Place?* (Cambridge, Mass: MIT Press, 1972), 41.

73. Dardel, *L'Homme et la Terre*, 12.

But of course such things as prairies or houses are not experienced in some isolated way—intentionality merely gives direction to experience and the actual experiences are composed of whole complexes of visual, auditory and olfactory sensations, present circumstances and purposes, past experiences and associations, the unfolding sequence of vistas and the various cultural and aesthetic criteria by which we judge buildings and landscapes. For a farmer the space of the countryside is primarily the extent of his farm, the view across his fields, the way to the market—all experienced as enduring yet seasonally changing complexes. Such space, such landscape is not something just to be looked at, but is "for the insertion of man into the world, a place of combat for life."[74] For the city-dweller the space of the city is only spread-out and extensive on those rare occasions when he looks down on it from some vantage point. More commonly his experience of cities is that of his home, his place of work, and the space of the street in all its variety of views, sounds and smells: "The town as geographical reality is the street—the street as the centre and realm of everyday life."[75]

The geographical space of countryside and town involves a close association between the experience and the creation of space. Landscape and townscape surround yet express human intention and presence for they are man-made or built. Building, suggests Heidegger, is dwelling;[76] dwelling is the essence of existence, the very manner by which men and women are on the earth, and involves an openness to and acceptance of the earth, the sky, the gods and our mortality.[77] In building which embraces dwelling there is no deliberate or selfconscious attempt to mould space as though it is an object—rather space is moulded, created, and possessed by the very act of building or landscape modification. The result is places which evolve, and have an organic quality, which have what Heidegger calls the character of "sparing"—the tolerance of something for itself without trying to change it or control it—places which are evidence of care and concern for the earth and for other men. Such spaces and places are full with meaning; they have an order and a sense that can be experienced directly, yet which is infinitely variable.

When the fusion of dwelling and building, of the earth and the sky and the gods and mortals, is total, then geographical space is essentially sacred. It is tempting to identify this with the space of nonliterate and vernacular cultures where unselfconscious and traditional design and building procedures exist. . . . But this is too easy, a too simple dismissal of significant experience in industrial cultures and selfconscious space-making. Even the most uniform and "care-lessly" planned spaces of contemporary urban development are named and structured into distinctive centres and districts. And even in deepest suburbia people put down roots and develop a concern for where they live.[78] Such experience is clearly not the same as that of the peasant in his home in the Black Forest described by Heidegger, and it cannot have the equivalent intensity and depth of architectural expression, if only because the houses are built by subcontractors working from designs in pattern books.[79] But at the same time we cannot easily judge it as a lesser experience, for it still involves the intentions, the hopes and fears of men and women. Of experience, as of happiness and despair, we have no measure.[80]

74. Ibid., 44.
75. Ibid., 37; see also Bernard Rudofsky, *Streets for People* (Garden City, N Y: Doubleday, 1969).
76. Vincent Vycinas, *Earth and Gods* (The Hague: Martinus Nijhoff, 1961), 14–15.
77. It is impossible to do justice to Heidegger's thought here, even though his writings are possibly the most relevant and the most significant on ontological foundations of place, space, building, and world. Furthermore any attempt at summary is unnecessary since an excellent introduction to these themes in Heidegger's work is available in Vvcinas, *Earth and Gods*.
78. Nicholas Taylor, *The Village in the City* (London: Temple Smith, 1973).
79. Vycinas, *Earth and Gods*, 16, 261.
80. Ernest van den Haag, "Of Happiness and Despair We Have No Measure," in *Man Alone*, eds Eric Josephson and Mary Josephson (New York: Dell, 1962), 199.

STRUCTURE OF GEOGRAPHICAL SPACE

. . . Norberg-Schulz gives a more formal analysis of the structuring of existential space, and identifies both a vertical and a horizontal structure—basing the latter very much on Lynch's analysis.[81] First he identifies several levels of existential space. The widest and most comprehensive of these is that of "geography"—the level at which meaning is given to nations, continents, and regions beyond our direct experience (it therefore has a cognitive character). The next level is that of landscape, the background to man's actions and a reflection of his interactions with environment on a major scale. Below this is an urban level, differing from that of landscape in that it is almost entirely a built space created through human effort and purpose. The next level is that of the street, the basis of our experience of cities; and below that is the house, or more precisely the home, the central reference point of human existence; "our home is our corner of the world . . . it is our first universe, a real cosmos in every sense of the word."[82] Of all levels of existential space this is perhaps the most fundamental, for, as Bachelard points out, "all really inhabited space bears the essence of the notion of home."[83] Finally there is the level of the object—a material space in which the value of objects is determined by their significance as utensils, or a symbolic space in which the objects or things represent other spaces and experiences.

This structure reflects both a change in scale from the largest to the smallest extent and an increasing humanisation of space. Such a structure is not, of course, explicit in all our experiences, and the levels need not always be of exactly the form presented here. But in general it seems that we do live in terms of a variety of levels though at anyone moment our attention is focused on just one level: in voting our concern is with national space, but in finding the polling booth it is the spaces of the city and street that are important.

At each of these levels there is a more or less clearly identifiable horizontal structure. This comprises three major elements. First there is a set of *districts* or regions of particular significance, defined by the interests and experiences of the groups concerned: "these various realms of relevances are intermingled, showing the most manifold interpenetrations and enclaves," they are not clear-cut, disparate regions.[84] These are organised and opened up by *paths* or routes which reflect the directions and intensities of intentions and experiences, and which serve as the structural axes of existential space. They radiate from and lead towards nodes or centres of special importance and meaning which are distinguished by their quality of insideness. These are *places.* This pattern of places, paths and districts is repeated in some form at all the levels of existential space. Sometimes it corresponds directly to the physical features of the landscape—roads, buildings, vistas; sometimes it corresponds to mythical phenomena, such as paths to heaven and hell or the sites of mythical events; and sometimes it reflects particular intentions or biases, such as an architect's concern with buildings. In short, the structure has no fixed orientation or scale, but reflects the interests and concerns of the cultural group of which it is an expression.

81. Norberg-Schulz, *Existence*, ch. 2.
82. Bachelard, *The Poetics of Space*, 4.
83. Ibid., 5.
84. Schütz, *Collected Papers*, 126.

Places in existential space can therefore be understood as centres of meaning, or focuses of intention and purpose. The types of meanings and functions defining places need not be the same for all cultural groups, nor do the centres have to be clearly demarcated by physical features, but they must have an inside that can be experienced as something differing from an outside. For many religious peoples places are holy and within the context of a powerful symbolic and sacred space. For the contemporary European or North American most places have a much weaker symbolic content than this, and are defined largely by the meanings or significant associations attached to buildings, landforms, or areas in specific locations. But in both cases places constitute significant centres of experience within the context of the lived-space of the everyday social world.

ARCHITECTURAL SPACE AND PLANNING SPACE

Existential space combines an experience of space with a remaking of the spaces of the lived-world, and both these activities are largely without formal conceptualisation. In contrast, architectural space, although founded on and contributing to unselfconscious spatial experiences, involves a deliberate attempt to create spaces.[85] The space of city planning, however, is not based on experiences of space, but is concerned primarily with function in two-dimensional map space.

Siegfried Giedion has identified three major manifestations of architectural space—each corresponding to a phase of architectural development.[86] The first of these is the space created by an interplay between volumes, and this was associated especially with the buildings of the Greek and Egyptian civilisations; thus Greek temples defined space largely in terms of the relationship between them. The second form of space is that of hollowed-out interior space, and this was manifest in a style that dated from the building of the Pantheon to the late 18th century and was apparent not only in temple and church interiors but also in such external features as Renaissance plazas. The third form is the treatment of space from several perspectives simultaneously, involving the free manipulation of the relationships between inside and outside that characterises much contemporary architecture. The implications of this classification for the present discussion have been expressed well by Gauldie.[87] He notes that while architectural space has a variety of expressions, these are all initially concerned with the imaginative experience of space; the ability to create architectural space which encourages such experiences is very dependent on individual genius, but the possibility of achieving them appears to be greatest where abstract ideas of space are most highly developed.

The space of urban planning is well linked to architectural space—indeed in the Renaissance they were essentially the same and there was a resulting continuity between buildings and streets and squares. More recently architectural space has come to be that of individual buildings conceived and constructed in isolation. In comparison to the attention lavished on these individual structures the nature and experience of the spaces between buildings has been left largely to chance, resulting in what Brett has termed SLOIP, an appropriately awful acronym for Space Left Over in Planning.[88] Planning for

85. Norberg-Schulz, *Existence*, 13–16.
86. Sigfried Giedion, *Space, Time and Architecture* (Cambridge: Harvard University Press, 1941).
87. Gauldie, *Architecture*, 78.
88. Lionel Brett, *Parameters and Images* (London: Weidenfeld and Nicolson, 1970), 117.

the *experience* of total urban space has been meagre indeed, and the space of modern urban planning is primarily the two-dimensional, cognitive space of maps and plans. This is obvious in the widespread use of grids and curvilinear street patterns, in the careful separation of function categories of land-use, in the casual laying-down of transportation networks. Space is understood to be empty and undifferentiated and objectively manipulable according to the constraints of functional efficiency, economics, and the whims of planners and developers. Thus Wingo describes space as a resource to meet future growth requirements, and suggests that the main problem it presents is how to structure most efficiently the social and economic activities to be located.[89] In short, planning space does not involve direct or imaginative experience but order on maps and land-use efficiency.

This may be overstressing the differences between planning and architectural space. There is, of course, a functional architectural tradition in which little attention has been paid to the experience of the spaces of buildings in any sense—reflecting perhaps the assertion of Gropius that "architecture is the mastery of space."[90] But that there is nevertheless a significant difference in the attitude of architects and planners is particularly apparent in their discussions and use of the notion of place. The essential task of the architect, Sinclair Gauldie maintains, is "the creation of place in the sense that he has to set about endowing some considerable part of the human environment with a new and special order."[91] Susanne Langer adopts a similar line of thought, suggesting that architects deal with created space and that this is something quite imaginary or conceptual which has been translated into visual and other impressions.[92] Within the context of created spaces she finds the basic abstraction of architecture is the 'ethnic domain,' that is, "a place made visible, tangible, sensible." To illustrate what she means by this she gives the example of a gypsy camp: "Literally we say the camp is *in* a place; culturally it *is* a place," and has its own functional realm and its own symbolic properties; it is in effect both the centre of and a symbol for the whole world. The architect's task is thus to express this cultural and symbolic complex of the ethnic domain, and to achieve selfconsciously and deliberately the creation of significant places within the context of existential space.

There have been selfconscious attempts to capitalise on the idea of place, and Jencks suggests that there is something akin to a 'place' movement in modern architecture, in which a deliberate effort is made to capture 'multi-meaning,' to provide a sense of the identity and reality of place.[93] Of course this is one among many and diverse approaches in contemporary architecture but it is important to recognise that whatever principles or theories or concepts the architect works with the created building will inevitably be experienced in some way by its users or its viewers as a place, as a centre of human associations and significances.

PLACELESSNESS

There is a widespread and familiar sentiment that the localism and variety of the places and landscapes that characterised preindustrial societies and unselfconscious, handicraft cultures are being diminished and perhaps eradicated. In their stead we are creating, in

89. Lowden Wingo, ed., *Cities and Space* (Baltimore: Johns Hopkins University Press, 1963), 7.
90. Brett, *Parameters and Images*, 46.
91. Gauldie, *Architecture*, 173.
92. Langer, *Feeling and Form*, 93–96.
93. Charles Jencks, *Modern Movements in Architecture* (Garden City, N Y: Doubleday, 1973), 302–328.

Norberg-Schulz's terse phrase, "a flatscape," lacking intentional depth and providing possibilities only for commonplace and mediocre experiences.[94] C. W. Moore has written that "the richly varied places of the world . . . are rapidly being obliterated under a meaningless pattern of buildings, monotonous and chaotic";[95] and Gordon Cullen suggests of Britain that "we appear to be forsaking nodal points for a thinly spread coast-to-coast continuity of people, food, power and entertainment; a universal wasteland . . . a chromium-plated chaos."[96] Such comments indicate the possibility of a placeless geography, lacking both diverse landscapes and significant places, and also imply that we are at present subjecting ourselves to the forces of placelessness and are losing our sense of place. . . .

A geography that is based on wholly authentic place-experience and place-making has probably never occurred, but in many cultures less technologically sophisticated than our own a profound sense of place has certainly prevailed. The depth of meaning and diversity of places associated with such authentic experience are, however, greatly weakened in most contemporary cultures. The development and diffusion of the inauthentic attitudes to place of kitsch and *technique*, and the standardised manifestations of these attitudes in the landscape, appear to be widespread and increasing in most of the western world. The trend is towards an environment of few significant places—towards a placeless geography, a flatscape, a meaningless pattern of buildings.

It is now possible to summarise the main components of such a "placeless geography" in which different localities both look and feel alike, and in which distinctive places are experienced only through superficial and stereotyped images, and as "indistinct and unstable" backgrounds to our social and economic roles. The following listing is simply an attempt to summarise and tie together the previous discussion on placelessness and inauthentic attitudes to place, and a classification of the main characteristics of a placeless landscape.

1. Manifestations of placelessness

    A. *Other-directedness in places*

        • Landscape made for tourists
        • Entertainment districts
        • Commercial strips
        • Synthetic or pseudo-places: Disneyfied places, Museumised places, and Futurist places

    B. *Uniformity and standardisation in places*

        • Instant new towns and suburbs
        • Industrial commercial developments

94. Norberg-Schulz, "Meaning in Architecture."
95. Lyndon, et al., "Towards Making Places," 33–34.
96. Gordon Cullen, *The Concise Townscape* (London: The Architectural Press, 1971), 59.

- New roads and airports, etc
- International styles in design and architecture

C. *Formlessness and lack of human scale and order in places*

- Subtopias
- Gigantism (skyscrapers, megalopoli)
- Individual features unrelated to cultural or physical setting

D. *Place destruction (Abbau)*

- Impersonal destruction in war (e.g. Hiroshima, villages in Vietnam)
- Destruction by excavation, burial
- Destruction by expropriation and redevelopment by outsiders (e.g. urban expansion)

E. *Impermanence and instability of places*

- Places undergoing continuous redevelopment (e.g. many central business districts)
- Abandoned places

The characteristics identified in this simple classification are not necessarily all-inclusive, nor are they mutually exclusive—one locality may possess several of the manifestations of placelessness. Furthermore these particular features are merely the superficial expressions of deeper processes and attitudes which encourage placelessness.

2. Media and systems transmitting placelessness

A. Mass communication and modes of diffusion of mass attitudes and fashions of kitsch.

B. Mass culture of dictated and standardised values; maintained by but making possible mass communications.

C. Big business and multi-national corporations: these encourage standardisation of products and needs to ensure economic survival, and they supply the objects of kitsch through the application of *technique*.

D. Central authorities: these encourage uniformity of places in the interests of efficiency and through the exercise of a uniform power.

E. The economic system: the abstract system, dominated by *technique*, which underlies and embraces all of the above.

These media constitute, in effect, the interrelated processes through which placeless landscapes develop. To some extent their influence is direct, as for example in the International Style offices of big business, but they also are channels for the transmission and dissemination of the fundamental attitudes that stand behind placelessness, and for their translation into physical and visual form.

3.   Inauthentic attitude to place

    A.   Attitudes relating to *technique*, in which places are understood to be manipulable in the public interest and are seen only in terms of their functional and technical properties and potentials.

    B.   Attitudes relating to kitsch, in which places are experienced and created only in terms of stereotyped, contrived, superficial and mass values.

These inauthentic attitudes to place are themselves specific forms of an inauthentic mode of existence in which both individuals and societies fail to recognise the realities and responsibilities of existence, and do not experience the world and its places for what they are. Such an inauthentic existence is the very root and essence of placelessness, and the superficial expressions that constitute placeless geographies can only be properly understood in terms of such profound inauthenticity.

Philosophical Text

KATHRYN MOORE, "GENIUS LOCI: HIDDEN TRUTH OR HIDDEN AGENDA?"

First Published in 2003

The "Single agreed law of landscape design," according to Tom Turner, is to "consult the genius of the place."[97] I believe, however, that this notion is based on an outdated philosophical position which Rorty suggests has outlived its usefulness?[98] Relying on the genius loci mystifies the design process—which is not only discouraging for students of design, but also responsible at least in part for a lingering conservatism within the landscape profession, leading inevitably to limited design ambition. It also reinforces suspicion of the visual dimension of design and contributes to the continuing disassociation of practice from theory. In short, it is damaging any attempts to construct places of meaning and significance.

The concept of the genius loci emerges from the philosophical tradition of the "peculiarly metaphysical dualisms" inherited from the Greeks.[99] This "whole nest and brood of dualisms" is endemic, leading to separations and distinctions being made between "reality and appearance, pure radiance and diffuse reflection, intellectual rigour and sensual sloppiness, orderly semiotics and rambling semiosis"[100] as well as those between subject and object, body and mind, absolute and relative, nature and convention. Underlying all these distinctions is a set of beliefs and practices based on the notion that there are different kinds of truth, different types of reasoning, independent logic and determinate facts. This rationalist tradition has been consistently undermined over the last century, but has proved "remarkably resilient and resourceful,"[101] mainly because these distinctions are so deeply embedded in our culture, they have become part of Western common sense.[102] But this alone is a good enough argument for retaining them.

It is now widely recognised that if we remove the assumption that there are different types of truth, it dismantles the idea that there are different types of reasoning, or separate modes of thinking. There is not a particular kind of thinking that is intuitive, compared with one that is more logical, or one that is subjective (usually associated with

97. Tom Turner, *City as Landscape: A Post-postmodern View* of *Design and Planning* (London: E&FN Spon, 1996).

98. Richard Rorty, *Philosophy and Social Hope* (New York: The Penguin Group, 1999); Richard Rorty, "The Pragmatist's Progress," in *Umberto Eco: Interpretation and Over Interpretation*, ed. Stefan Collini (Cambridge: Cambridge University Press, 1992).

99. Rorty, *Philosophy*, 47.

100. Rorty, "The Pragmatist's Progress."

101. Stanley Fish, *Doing What Comes Naturally: Change, Rhetoric and the Practice of Theory in Literary and Legal Studies* (Oxford: Duke University Press, 1989).

102. Rorty, *Philosophy*, xix.

emotion and art) as opposed to objective (usually associated with language and science), divergent or convergent, masculine or feminine. The *way* we think is the same. All thinking, whether in the arts or sciences is shown to be interpretative and metaphorical; none of these disciplines use a special kind of reasoning. Understanding ideas, feelings, emotions or artistic responses uses the one and only kind of reasoning we have to make sense of anything. We interpret, judge, try to understand our feelings and make sense of what we see.

One of the main philosophical traditions exploring this line of inquiry is pragmatism. From a pragmatic perspective, the problem is not *how* we think, but how *we think* we think?[103] Challenging the metaphysical basis of disciplines, pragmatism sets itself apart from, and against, the tradition of analytical philosophy and evolutionary psychology. It does so by questioning the utility of the vocabulary inherited from Plato and Aristotle.[104]

Drawing on the work of the early American pragmatists and more recently the work of Rorty[105] and Putnam,[106] I would argue that if a pragmatic line of inquiry is followed, it is also possible to dispense with the duality between visual and verbal thinking. This dichotomy has particular significance for design education, theory and philosophy. Allegedly fundamental to the debate, it has until recently more or less escaped the anti-dualist focus, so powerful is the belief that only numbers and words can have any logic or intellectual significance. The visual/verbal dichotomy is integral to the concept of the genius loci.

WHAT IS THE GENIUS LOCI?

The qualitative, phenomenological analyses of a sense of place, implying that "a landscape holds hidden spirits or qualities waiting to be discovered"[107] were a welcome relief from the mechanical abstractions dominating design theory in the 60s and early 70s. With seductive descriptions of how and what makes a place tick, they also legitimised the role of intuition and subjectivity in the design process. Loosely defined as the spirit of place, sense of place or genius of place, the genius loci, which is acknowledged as "less tangible than other components or dialectics of place" is thought potentially to "to link and embrace them."[108] The concept may have become less significant in architecture in recent years, however the genius loci remains an important part of landscape architectural theory and practice.[109] It has, for example, recently been cited in government research as one of the key concerns of urban design.[110] Its prevalence is such, that quite often, if a design does not have its quotient of "subjective discourse" with the site, and ideas are brought from "outside" the site to generate form, it is dismissed as artificial or superficial, a meaningless imposition.

A PRAGMATIC PERSPECTIVE

It is the metaphysical nature of the genius loci that causes problems. Adopting a pragmatic approach gives us the opportunity to reconceptualise many issues traditionally thought

103. Louis Menand, ed., *Pragmatism: A Reader* (New York: Vintage Books, 1997).

104. Rorty, *Philosophy*, xvii.

105. Rorty, *Philosophy*; and Rorty "The Pragmatist's Progress."

106. Hilary Putnam, *The Threefold Cord: Mind, Body and World* (New York: Colombia University Press, 1999).

107. Matthew Potteiger and Jamie Purinton, *Landscape Narratives: Design Practices for Telling Stories* (New York: John Wiley & Sons, 1988).

108. Edward Relph, *Place and Placelessness* (London: Pion, 1976).

109. Paul-Alan Johnson, *The Theory of Architecture: Concepts, Themes and Practices* (New York: Van Nostrand Reinhold, 1994).

110. Davies and Mitchell, "Training for Urban Design," Report on a Small Scale Research Project, Department of the Environment, Transport and Regions, 2000.

to be within its domain in a way that facilitates a more straightforward artistic and conceptual discussion about constructing place.

Pragmatism is anti-foundational. Foundational theories attempt "to ground inquiry and communication in something more firm and stable than mere beliefs or unexamined practice. This ground must be invariant across cultures and even contexts; it must stand apart from political, partisan and "subjective" concerns, in relation to which it must act as a constraint, and it must provide a reference point or checkpoint against which claims to knowledge and success can be measured and adjudicated."[111] Various candidates include "God, the material or 'brute act' world, rationality in general, or logic in particular" and "the set of eternal values."[112] Within design, "objective" contenders include universal laws sought by modernists, based on pure reason, or the "objective neutrality" sought by the design methodologists of the 60s and 70s whose ambition was to capture design expertise in a diagram, so that the process was rationalised and would "not be held back ever again by individual opinions or personal creativity."[113] From the subjective perspective, the usual suspects include subconscious responses, essences of place, archetypes, nature and ecology and more recently, the concept of sustainability. Each of these apparently provides some kind of framework which underlies and provides some kind of stability in the complexity of our individual subjective worlds. Each is thought to have the potential to ground practice in something more genuine and important than the everyday.

The desire to identify these kinds of grand theories is the sort of thing Dewey hoped we might cease to feel because from a pragmatic perspective there is nothing down there to refer to, no true reality or "the world as it really is" to be found, no universal truth or framework underlying our culture.[114] Instead, everything is seen as a social construction. "Discursive practices," as Rorty says, "Go all the way down."[115]

IMPLIED MEANING BENEATH THE SURFACE

But the genius loci *is* the idea that there is something beyond our culture to be sensed, intuited, or perceived (verbs that became fashionable in the 1940s to set themselves apart from commonplace verbs such as observe, see or understand).[116] To commune with the genius loci, we are supposed to sense underneath, behind, beyond, below what we have in front of our eyes, to find the true spirit of place.

Derrida calls the sense that there is a "full presence beyond the reach of play" the metaphysics of presence.[117] In "consulting the genius loci" many landscape architects find themselves trying to do just what Rorty satirises scholars as doing: cracking codes, peeling away accidents to reveal essence, stripping away veils of appearance to reveal reality.[118] Robin Evans accuses architectural critics of the same offence. They are not lacking circumspection, he assures us, as they work to "delve, uncover, disclose, reveal, divulge, discover, unfold and show to the reader what lies hidden or unseen, to get to the bottom of things, to plumb the depths, to see beneath the surface, behind the curtain, forced by the conviction that drawings have hidden meanings." What they end up doing, he adds, is to "to fabricate virtual meanings for the drawing to represent in place of what they know

111. Fish, *Doing What Comes Naturally*, 343.
112. Ibid.
113. Geoffrey Broadbent, *Design in Architecture: Architecture and the Human Sciences* Letchworth: David Fulton Publishers, 1988). First published in 1975.
114. Richard Rorty, *Achieving Our Country Leftist Thought in Twentieth Century America* (Cambridge: Harvard University Press, 1999), 38.
115. Ibid., 35.
116. Gilbert Ryle, *The Concept of Mind* (London: Penguin Books, 1949), 202.
117. Rorty, *Philosophy*, xviii.
118. Rorty, "The Pragmatist's Progress," 89.

they cannot find." His admiration is laced with irony when he adds, "and remarkably inventive about it they are."[119] The impetus for this labour, Rorty suggests, is the excitement of finding "deep meanings hidden from the vulgar, meanings which only those lucky enough to have cracked a very difficult code can know."[120]

Educationally, this is dubious and dangerous. The notion that there is "knowledge of something not merely human" needed in order to achieve a design, loads the dice against the student. From a pragmatic perspective it sets up a whole series of impossible tasks which are bewildering and undemocratic.[121]

STEPPING OUTSIDE OUR CULTURE

Take the problem of "sensing" the genius loci. The story goes that, "the more open and honest such experiences are, and the less constrained by theoretical or intellectual preconceptions, the greater the degree of authenticity." The idea is that an authentic attitude to place should not be "mediated and distorted through series of quite arbitrary social and intellectual fashions about how that experience should be, nor following stereotyped conventions."[122] Is it really possible to step outside what we know to understand a place as it really is without the encumbrances of our culture, so as to glimpse things as they really are? Can intelligence and experience cloud the issue? Is it really possible to deliberately forget what we know?

The search for a "residing invisible spirit and an underlying order that must be revealed, searched for, listened to, felt or understood by careful observation" is also a bit strange.[123] It implies that it is necessary to use the senses or emotions to perceive, without contaminating the process by thinking conceptually. The hazy intuitions picked up by this process are supposedly distilled, structured and formalised, before being passed on to serve intelligence. The senses are thought to act as a filter or a censor, sorting out the differences between what is real and what is apparent.

As far as the pragmatic argument is concerned, these propositions make no sense at all. Pragmatism, summed up by the slogan "all awareness is a linguistic affair" is based on the tenet that "we shall never be able to step outside of language never be able to grasp reality unmediated by a linguistic description."[124] There is no sensory language separate from the verbal language, and no way of knowing that is not linguistic. We do not need, as Hilary Putnam has pointed out, to "conceive of our sensory experiences as intermediaries between us and the world."[125]

In terms of understanding the significance of a place, the implications of this paradigmatic shift are deceptively simple. Rather than thinking a place can "speak" to you, reveal what it "wants to be" by imposing on your thoughts in a particular way, a place can be seen as simply "providing some sort of stimuli which you can respond to."[126] It is not a quest for truth, objectivity or underlying essences. There is no need to ask, "Am I describing it as it really is?" The value of what you see is in the sense you make of it. This is an analytical and critical skill that requires an understanding of the problems and possibilities of the site, given a particular brief or potential concept. Inspirational

119. Robin Evans, "In Front of Lines That Leave Nothing Behind," in *Architecture Theory since 1968*, ed. K. Michael Hays, (Cambridge: MIT Press, 2000): 482–489. First published in 1984.
120. Rorty, "The Pragmatist's Progress."
121. Rorty, *Philosophy*, 20.
122. Relph, *Place and Placelessness*, 64.
123. Potteiger and Purinton, *Landscape Narratives*, 143.
124. Rorty, *Philosophy*, 48.
125. Putnam, *The Threefold Cord.*
126. Rorty, "The Pragmatist's Progress," 103.

interpretations of the site will be inventive, imaginative and artistic. They are still utilitarian and purposeful—they give a clue as to how to proceed. Judgement, confidence and expertise are needed to discern whether one way or another of interpreting the site might be the more productive, a richer vein to mine.

Also from this perspective, intuition, rather than being the window to a universal truth or the essence of place, can be understood as a preconception that is culturally formed and shaped. As educationalists, we spend time trying to encourage students *not* to rely on their intuitions, because for novice students of design, these habits of thought are so limited by inexperience or unfamiliarity within a particular discipline. Old habits die hard—as Bryson points out (quoting Kubler): "The cage of routine binds [the individual] so closely that it is almost impossible for him to stumble into an inventive act: he is like a tightrope walker whom vast forces so bind to the cable that he cannot fall, even if he wishes, into the unknown."[127] The problem with the concept of the genius loci is that it seems to give credibility to these preconceptions, rather than challenge or provoke a more imaginative response.

LIMITS DISCOURSE

As mysterious and elusive as any other metaphysical concept, reliance on the genius loci also limits imaginative and intelligent debate. If the genius loci has been consulted, when it speaks to you, is it always right? Must we defer to its authority in order to establish the true essence of the site, or instructions on which to base the form of the design?

If it is presented as self evident and abundantly clear, with no need of further explanation, there is an assumption that you are "in the know"—and who would be brave enough to admit they are not? This is the meaning of peer pressure. To question the genius loci implies ignorance or—worse—a lack of sensitivity or awareness. Even those with the gall to say, "I do not understand this" are hamstrung, because on what basis can there be any disagreement? The concept by its very nature has no substance; it is indefinable. As a consequence, by stealth, this convenient spirit absolves us from taking responsibility for why things look the way they do. The genius loci becomes an integral part of what Johnson describes as the "false consciousness" architects and landscape architects often project, used to "justify the correctness of what they design, mostly without external verification."[128] Fish suggests that "whenever a so-called outside or external or independent constraint is invoked, what is really being invoked is an interested agenda."[129] So when for example we are convinced and excited by a landscape or architecture apparently inspired by the genius loci, what excites and convinces us is a function of our needs and purposes, rather than the recognition that a design accurately captures and expresses the essence of place.[130]

The problem in both landscape and architecture is that this agenda has, over the last few decades and for a number of reasons, been dominated by the desire to return to traditional practices and traditional solutions. Invocation of the genius loci has been therefore primarily used as a way of referring "longingly to spirits of the past animated by legend"[131] or "an old way of seeing."[132]

127. Norman Bryson, *Looking at the Overlooked: Four Essays on Still Life Painting* (London: Reakiton Books, 1990), 139.
128. Johnson, *The Theory of Architecture*.
129. Fish, *Doing What Comes Naturally*, 13.
130. Rorty, "The Pragmatist's Progress," 35.
131. Potteiger and Purinton, *Landscape Narratives*.
132. Jonathan Hale, *The Old Way of Seeing* (Boston: Houghton-Mifflin Company, 1994).

This inherently conservative agenda has also been used to justify creating places which "possess both internal harmony and which fit in their context." In many respects this is a fine ambition, especially when the context is worth fitting in with. But given the backward gaze of many designers, it sets the scene for heritage, restoration and conservation projects, irrespective of the situation and stifles the ambition to create something new, to mix old and new, to find contemporary solutions to old problems.

Responding to the genius loci is also characterised as a kind of "unselfconscious place making," having a "lack of theoretical or aesthetic pretension," as though the designer plays no role in designing, just does as told by the amenable spirit, without thinking too much about it.[133] In this way the genius loci is responsible for the "naturalistic fallacy" Johnson identifies, "of projecting what ought to be from what is."[134] A variation on McHarg's ecological determinism, it has also led, as Thompson has pointed out, to a desire for places that fit in, are unobtrusive, or invisible, merging in, integrating, blending, being "absent."[135] And we wonder why landscape architecture has a low profile!

Typically this low-key approach is seen as being a preferable alternative to designs identified pejoratively as egotistical, airy-fairy, or having pretensions to be works of art. However, rather than falling back on the old philosophical dichotomy between aesthetics and function, art and design, from a pragmatic point of view it is possible to think about the extent to which any design has been artistically conceived and executed. The truly expressive act according to Dewey, requires the "primitive and raw material of experience to be reworked." This transformation is not only of the physical materials, but also of "images, memories, observations and emotions" and the "work is artistic in the degree in which the two functions of transformation are effected by a single operation."[136] The medium of work, he suggests, is relatively unimportant. Discussions about the merits of one design against another can therefore more productively centre on how well this transformation has been achieved, how intelligently and artistically ideas have been investigated and applied within a design, rather than the visibility or invisibility of the product or to what extent a design is egotistical or otherwise.

OVERLOOKING THE VISUAL DIMENSION

The concept of the genius loci fuels the prejudice existing against the visual dimension in design; this prejudice is its oxygen. But there is a growing philosophical, psychological and cultural interest in the visual, in response to the belief that we are living in an increasingly visual world. Broadly, there are two views. On the one hand, there is the realisation that the visual may have been overlooked due to the emphasis on language and numbers. On the other, there is the view that an over-reliance on the "cool and distant realm of vision" may be responsible for the lack of sensuality or experience of "being in the world." In either case, the argument is founded on the assumption that visual understanding, aesthetic perception or creativity is dependent on a visual, sensory mode of thinking. Typically this is characterised as being innate, primitive, subjective and unrelated to intelligence and therefore impossible to teach. This characterisation

133. Relph, *Place and Placelessness*.

134. Johnson, *The Theory of Architecture*, 394.

135. Ian Thompson, *Ecology, Community and Delight: Sources of Values in Landscape Architecture* (London: E & FN Spon, 2000).

136. John Dewey, *Art as Experience* (New York: The Berkley Publishing Group, 1980), 73. First published in 1934.

insinuates itself into the way we think we think about visual phenomena such as pictures, landscape and architecture. Considering the generation of form or the visual appearance of a design is therefore also thought to be devoid of intellectual content, to some indulgent and unnecessary to others, an impossibly subjective task that does not bear close examination,[137] is even suggested that the invisible essence of architecture is so important, that time spent articulating "a building's corporeal presence" might compromise the "allusive poetics of its form" or "diminish architecture's capacity for representational values."[138] Being diverted by the earthy tectonics and the physicality of what we see might sidetrack us into missing the real picture. And so, what a landscape signifies, symbolises or represents is thought to be far more significant than the way it looks; its embodied meaning is there to be sensed, not seen, its invisible essence of more value than its visible presence. As an eminent design historian declared defiantly at a recent conference, "We are not interested in what the landscape looks like but what it means." This is the problem. The visual, physical form of the landscape is systematically overlooked in the quest for embodied (invisible) meaning.

It has become very chic to use various philosophical and cultural theories to embellish the rhetoric of design criticism and practice, in the hope that making design more "theoretical" will improve its quality and status as a discipline. But without investigating or making explicit the visual, spatial implications of these ideas, the continuing disassociation between practice and theory are simply exacerbated. The gap between what is said and what it is supposed to look like becomes ever wider. To resolve this disjunction, we need to make distinctions, as Dewey suggests, "Not between practice (craft based, sensory, earthy) and theory (conceptual, representation and symbolic) but between those modes of practice that are not intelligent, not inherent and immediately enjoyable and those which are full of enjoyed meanings."[139] How well informed are the designs that we see? Why do things specifically look the way they do? What do they make us feel and why?

THE VALUE OF LOOKING GOOD

Redefining the relationship between the senses and intelligence makes it clear that meaning is not embodied in the landscape, but is entirely dependent on the sense *we make* of what *we see* in front of us. There is no need to try and commune with residing spirits or sense essences of place lurking beneath the surface to fathom out what we are looking at. Waiting expectantly to have "three or four dimensional pure 'perceptions'" is rather like waiting for Godot.[140] To understand what we see in the landscape is more straightforward. It requires a strong feeling for our culture and traditions. It requires critical, analytical skill and knowledge of the visual and conceptual medium of our practice—an intellectual understanding and appreciation of why things look like they do, given the time, place and context. This kind of understanding is not something just reserved for the critic. It is what we need in order to design places of meaning and significance. Dispensing with the concept of the genius loci gives us the opportunity to clarify many

137. Thomas A. Dutton, "Introduction: Architectural Education, Post Modernism, and Critical Pedagogy," in *Voices in Architectural Education: Cultural Politics and Pedagogy* (New York: Bergin & Garvey, 1991).

138. Harry F. Mallgrave, "Foreword," *Studies in Tectonic Culture: The Poetics of Construction in Nineteenth and Twentieth Century Architecture*, Kenneth Frampton and John Cava (Cambridge: MIT Press, 1995).

139. John Dewey, "Experience, Nature and Art," in *Experience and Nature: Pragmatism: A Reader*, ed. Louis Menand (New York: Vintage Books, 1925), 236.

140. Stephen Holl, Juhani Pallasmaa, and Alberto Perez-Gomez, "Questions of Perception," *Architecture and Urbanism, Special Issue* (July 1994), 46.

aspects of the design process in a sensible, intelligent way. The significance of why things look like they do can be made explicit. The manner in which ideas have been followed through from the inspiration, concept and principles to design detail can be explained in pictures *and* in words, spatially *and* conceptually. The process can be systematic, methodical and have a clear educational rationale without losing the poetry or artistry of good design.

There is also an important political and social dimension to the argument. From this perspective, the value of good looking environments can be clearly articulated, freed of the idea that it is simply a matter of taste, too subjective to be of significance or self evident because the genius loci has worked its arcane magic. This puts an onus on us as landscape architects. If we value the landscape, we need to be far more rigorous in the way we describe it and the uses we identify for it. The language we use needs to be more precise and differentiated. And we need to be far more ambitious in our aspirations for the landscape, its construction and care.

It is a political issue. We need to know, clearly and unambiguously, what the landscape has to offer, be it urban, urban fringe, rural, post-industrial, coastal, or whatever. We need to know how to recognise its potential and how it can be transformed. It is crucial that we create places that have a unique visual identity, which will not only promote and develop culture and tradition but also instill a sense of pride and optimism. This is a vital component of sustainable economic growth.

The concept of the genius loci is part of a philosophical paradigm that prevents us from having informed discussions about the value and significance of the way things look or even beginning to understand how this might contribute to the social and economic viability of a place. This is no longer sustainable. We need to drop the dualist vocabulary and begin to imaginatively "re-describe the familiar in unfamiliar terms."[141] We need to make clear the political value of the public realm and the social benefit of good quality places.

The genius loci, bless it, is like any old hat. No matter how much you cherish it, there comes a time to put it on one side and buy another. For the future of landscape architecture, for the sake of our profession, it is time to move on.

141. Rorty, *Philosophy*, 87.

Writing and Discussion Questions

ANALYSIS

1. What was Norburg-Shulz arguing for and against? What excerpt/quotation best represents this?
2. What was Relph arguing for and against? What excerpt/quotation best represents this?
3. What was Moore arguing for and against? What excerpt/quotation best represents this?

SYNTHESIS

1. Regarding concepts of nature, discuss one major difference regarding Norburg-Shulz's, Relph's, and Moore's texts.
2. Regarding concepts of nature, discuss one primary commonality regarding Norburg-Shulz's, Relph's, and Moore's texts.

SELF-REFLECTION

1. For each of the texts, discuss a major issue with which you most agree and most disagree; reflect upon why you hold these views.
2. Select a recent design project, or a current project on which you are working. Discuss the characteristics of the project in regards to nature, in light of the discussion and texts introduced in this chapter. What attitudes regarding nature does your work illustrate?

PROSPECTION

1. Select one of the texts listed in the bibliography for this chapter; locate and read it. To what degree is that text and the attitudes it represents still relevant to architecture today and in the near future?

2. What is the role of nature in architecture today? Have concepts of nature increased in importance, decreased in importance, or remained the same in architecture over the past century? In other words, if a fourth text were added to this chapter, what would the argument be?

Other Readings on Natural and Constructed

Bidwell, Nicola J., and David Browning. "Pursuing Genius Loci: Interaction Design and Natural Places," *Personal and Ubiquitous Computing,* 14 (2010): 15–30.

Canizaro, Vincent, ed. *Architectural Regionalism: Collected Writings on Place, Identity, Modernity, and Tradition* (New York: Princeton Architectural Press, 2007).

Forster, Kurt, and Mildred Friedman, eds. *Site: The Meaning of Place in Art and Architecture: Design Quarterly 122* (Cambridge: MIT Press, 1983).

Frampton, Kenneth. "Prospects for a Critical Regionalism," *Perspecta,* 20 (1983): 147–162.

Hayden, Delores. *The Power of Place: Urban Landscapes as Public History* (Cambridge: MIT Press, 1995).

Heidegger, Martin. "Building, Dwelling, Thinking," in *Poetry, Language, and Thought,* trans. Albert Hofstadter (New York: HarperCollins, 1971).

Holl, Stephen, Juhani Pallasmaa, and Alberto Perez-Gomez. "Questions of Perception," *Architecture and Urbanism, Special Issue* (July 1994).

Jackson, John B. *A Sense of Place, A Sense of Time* (New Haven: Yale University Press, 1994).

Kunze, Donald. *Thought and Place: The Architecture of Eternal Place in the Philosophy of Giambattista Vico* (New York: Peter Lang Publishing, 1987).

Lefaivre, Liane, and Alexander Tzonis. *Critical Regionalism* (New York: St. Martin's Press, 1995).

Tuan, Yi-Fu. *Space and Place: The Perspective of Experience* (Minneapolis: University of Minnesota Press, 1977).

Appendix 1

GUIDE TO READING COMPREHENSION

Architectural theory includes a diverse array of topics—structural engineering, aesthetics, human behavior, etc.—and takes on many forms—critiques or "juries," written texts, built works, etc. In college courses, architecture students often engage the world of architectural theory through reading and writing. Students read texts by Vitruvius, Alberti, or Le Corbusier, and attempt to decipher what is being said. Students then do one of two things: (1) as a group, they gather with the professor to discuss the content of the readings or, (2) alone, they develop a written summary, response paper, or other commentary about the assigned readings. Some students enjoy this; some hate it. Some enjoy writing; some prefer discussions. Some simply find pleasure and interest in reading; some find it frustrating.

In any case, without a thorough understanding of the readings, group discussion and solo writing are untenable. In my experience, the primary cause of student frustrations in reading, writing, and discussion is difficulty in understanding the primary and secondary messages of the reading—reading comprehension. Through my experiences as both a student and a teacher, with the help of many former students, and through other sources, I have identified several strategies for improving reading comprehension in architectural theory. It includes three important pieces of advice: find the "right time" to read, find the "right place" to read, and find the "right way" to read. Keep in mind, however, there is more than one "right" time, place, and way. It is about identifying what works best for you.

RIGHT TIME

What time of day are you most productive—morning, mid-day, evening? It seems obvious, whatever the time of day that you are most focused and clear-minded is the time you want to devote to reading. For many people the morning is the best time. Your mind and body are well rested, and focused attention comes easier. Another productive time, as research has shown, is shortly after vigorous exercise. Exercise stimulates blood flow to the body and the brain, and reduces stress, thereby freeing the brain to focus on reading.

Identify the best time for you and make reading habitual. Read at the same time daily as part of a routine, rather than reading at different times of day. Likewise, for longer readings, break your reading into smaller blocks of time over several days, rather than trying to read everything in one sitting on one day. The more frequently and regularly you are exposed to a text, the more deeply it will become part of your long-term memory. Reading at the right time will lead to greater clarity and interest in what you read.

RIGHT PLACE

Where do you work most productively and where do you most like to read—sitting at a desk, lounging in a comfy chair, or lying in bed; at the library, on the bus, or in the kitchen; in the sun or under a lamp; with background noise or with silence? Some people like to read alone, with soft light and no distractions. Others like to read amongst bustling surroundings. Roland Barthes wrote:

> To be with the one I love and to think of something else: this is how I have my best ideas, how I best invent what is necessary to my work. Likewise for the text: it produces, in me, the best pleasure if it manages to make itself heard indirectly; if, reading it, I am led to look up often, to listen to something else.[1]

As students of architecture, we know that the built environment affects us physically, psychologically, and emotionally. We should not be surprised that our surroundings would affect our ability to process information, such as reading. Like finding the right time, the right place, once identified, needs to be part of the reading routine. The right *physical* place will help to put and keep you in the right *mental* place.

RIGHT WAY

Like times and places, there are many *ways* to read. In working with students, however, I have found that the choices are less expansive. There is a three-phase process that students have found very helpful, which I call "Skim, Reflect, Remember." Phase 1—Skim— involves skimming, simply looking at any pictures and reading the captions, reading the headings and any bold or italicized words and phrases, and reading the first and last sentences of each paragraph. This gives you the "big picture" of the text. Phase 2— Reflect—involves a full reading of the text and writing down your thoughts about what you read. This is a process of both highlighting the major points of the text and jotting down your own thoughts. There are several ways to do this. Some students prefer to take notes and write their thoughts on the reading itself (in digital or printed form). Others like to have a separate notebook or "journal." In either case, it is helpful to develop a system for efficient note taking. For example, I use different symbols that I write directly on a printed copy of the reading, e.g., a squiggly vertical line means I disagree with the author's statement. You can develop your own shorthand, which allows you to take notes faster, to record your thoughts quickly, and to easily go back to your notes after you have

1. Roland Barthes, *The Pleasure of the Text*, Richard Miller, trans. (New York: Farrar, Straus, and Giroux, 1975), 24.

finished reading. During Phase 2, your goals are to (1) identify the author's main points and (2) reflect on your own thoughts about these main points. Connect the text to your previous knowledge or experiences, and consider the extent to which you agree or disagree with the ideas. Phase 3—Remember—is a simple re-reading of the text from beginning to end. The purpose is to gain clarity and long-term memory of the main points and phrases in the text.

Phase 1 is intended to be very brief. Phase 2 is intended to be the lengthiest. Phase 3 simply moves at the speed you read. Ideally, there is a day or two between each phase of reading. Some instructors suggest reversing Phase 2 and Phase 3, first reading for comprehension, then reading/writing to reflect. However, I have found that the first full reading of a text is the best time to reflect. For me, at least, it is difficult to suppress my own thoughts as I read. Students have said the same. Incorporating your own thoughts as you read, rather than curbing them, is the best way to build reading comprehension.

TIPS FOR READING THIS BOOK

There is no single time, place, or way to read. Find what works best for you. There are two more helpful tips specific to the texts in this book. First, make sure to read both the introductory and concluding questions of each chapter carefully. Do this before, during, and after reading the texts. Make note of your answers to the questions each time, and consider how your answers have changed. Again, making your thoughts central to the reading process will build stronger comprehension and, ultimately, will help you to formulate your views of architecture. Second, find time outside of class, preferably in a relaxed setting, to chat about readings with classmates. Hearing others talk about the readings, and sharing your own views, will improve your comprehension and memory, as oftentimes you or someone else will say something in a way that is clear and concise and resonates with your thinking. Sometimes you will come up with a phrase that is better than what the author used. This will boost your confidence and increase your success for future readings.

USEFUL RESOURCES

Behrens, Laurence, and Leonard J. Rosen. *Writing and Reading Across the Curriculum, 4th Ed.* (New York: HarperCollins Publishers, 1991).

Daiek, Deborah, and Nancy Anter. *Critical Reading for College and Beyond* (New York: McGraw-Hill, 2004).

Elder, Janet. *Exercise Your College Reading Skills: Developing More Powerful Comprehension* (New York: McGraw-Hill, 2004).

Mayfield, Marlys. *Thinking for Yourself: Developing Critical Thinking Skills through Reading and Writing, 8th Ed.* (Belmont, CA: Wadsworth, 2009).

Spears, Deanne. *Developing Critical Reading Skills, 8th Ed.* (New York: McGraw-Hill, 2008).

Spears, Deanne. *Improving Reading Skills: Contemporary Readings for College Students, 6th Ed.* (New York: McGraw-Hill, 2009).

Appendix 2

GUIDE TO DESCRIPTIVE, ANALYTICAL, AND
DISPUTATIONAL WRITING

Although architecture is predominantly a discipline of visual communication, effective written and verbal communication are critical skills. In fact, Smit and Hoag reported that architecture graduates with strong written communication skills who are contributing to the written materials of their architectural firm have a starting salary up to $5,000 (£3,050) more than their peers.[1] Nevertheless, the goal here is not to provide exhaustive recommendations regarding grammar, syntax, and other aspects of writing. There are many wonderful resources on writing, which you may want to consult, in addition to seeking the writing support center at your college or university. My goal, instead, is to give a few simple tips and explain the different types of architectural writing. There are many forms, or "genres," of writing—poetry, letters, personal journals, research, short stories, etc.—and writing can be either formal or informal. In architecture, the three most common genres of writing are: description, analysis/critique, and persuasion/disputation. The genre depends on the topic, purpose, and audience of the writing.

DESCRIPTIVE WRITING

Descriptive writing is common among both students and professionals, especially in regards to "describing" their architectural works. The goal of descriptive writing in architecture is to portray a complete, detailed, vivid image. The reader needs to feel as if she/he could draw or build the project from the written text. Descriptive writing might include information about any/all of the following:

- the purpose, reasoning, or justification of the project
- the context of the work, including description of: the historical or cultural context or time period; the climate, the region, and/or the natural landscape; the immediate physical situation or geography; the economic, demographic, and/or political context; the client or end-user; etc.

1. David Smit and Richard Hoag, "Genre and Transfer in the Writing of Designers," National Conference on the Beginning Design Student, March 19, 2010, University of North Carolina—Charlotte.

401

- the programmatic or spatial organization of the project
- the structural system or tectonic language of the project
- the intended experience of the occupant/user in regards to: lighting, acoustics, views, temperature, tactility, movement and repose, gathering and solitude, etc.
- the interrelationships among the aforementioned.

In my experience, students often use language that is too vague or generalized. Other common mistakes include: relying on cliché phrases, overuse of the first-person (I, me, my, etc.), overuse of the forms of the verb "be" (is, are, was, were, etc.), run-on or overly lengthy or complicated sentences, and a lack of variety in punctuation and sentence structure.

The primary challenge in descriptive writing is providing specificity. It is not sufficient to state that a project "deals with light." You need to *describe* exactly what the lighting phenomenon, principle, or strategy is (e.g., "indirect clerestory day lighting"), the effects or why it was utilized (e.g., "to gain even, ambient light in a group work space"), how it was done (e.g., "utilizing an angled ceiling plane and continuous, north-facing glazing along the roof line"). As you write and edit a descriptive essay, ask three questions of each sentence and each paragraph:

- Does the sentence/paragraph give *detail about what* was done?
- Does the sentence/paragraph give *detail about how* it was done?
- Does the sentence/paragraph give *detail about why* it was done?

Apply these questions to all aspects of the writing, from describing the physical context, to describing the structural system, to describing the way a building is experienced.

CRITICISM AND ANALYTICAL WRITING

Criticism and analytical writing in architecture focus on the implications of an architecture work (or works, architect, or architects). Criticism and analysis necessarily build upon descriptive writing. According to Edmund Burke Feldman, description is the starting point of critique.[2] Like descriptive writing, analytical writing in architecture requires a detailed understanding of the architectural "parts" being discussed—space, structure, use, materials, lighting, etc. Nevertheless, criticism/analysis advances beyond descriptive writing. Ultimately, critical/analytical writing seeks to answer the following question: what are the effects, results, or consequences of the work? In criticism/analysis, the voice of the author becomes more apparent. This may come in the form of the author's opinions, but not always. The structure and organization of the writing becomes more significant, as the author seeks to illustrate the connections—similarities, differences, or cause–effect relationships—between "parts," or the hidden consequences of one or more aspects of the architectural work. In descriptive writing, the author seeks to articulate what is most apparent; in analytical writing, the author describes what is apparent and builds toward revealing otherwise hidden concepts, relationships, or consequences. Students typically

2. Edmund Burke Feldman, *Becoming Human through Art: Aesthetic Experience in the School* (Englewood Cliffs, NJ: Prentice-Hall, 1970).

have difficulty in one of two respects: (1) remaining descriptive and never transitioning into an analytical voice or (2) relying too heavily on personal opinion without building upon a descriptive foundation. A balance between description and analysis needs to be maintained. In order to do this, the author usually does not describe all aspects of the architectural work, but focuses on a few key aspects. As you write and edit a critical/analytical essay, ask the three questions listed above in the descriptive section. Additionally, ask the following of your writing:

- On what aspects of the architectural work are you focusing?
- What hidden relationships or implications are you drawing out or explaining?
- Are these relationships/implications supported by descriptive text?
- How are the parts of the writing organized to clarify these relationships/implications?

PERSUASION AND DISPUTATION

Nearly all genres of writing have a "persuasive" aspect to them, in the sense that—whether a fiction writer, a philosopher, or a scientist—you want to be convincing. At the same time, persuasive and disputational writing involve aspects of both descriptive and analytical writing. Persuasion/disputation, as such, is more difficult to define. Nevertheless, disputation has a long history and it is essential to architectural theory. Disputation advances the importance of the author's control over the organization and flow of the writing previously described. Advancing this concept, disputation relies heavily on the author's "assembling" of the text in often creative or unexpected ways without compromising clarity or logic. Disputation is not simply about picking one side of an argument. Disputation, much like the organization of the chapters in this book, moves back and forth between competing arguments, concepts, or theories, and often concludes in the emergence of a new concept or theory. This new concept/theory, however, arises from the logic of the preceding text, not as a surprise to the reader. Disputation is challenging because it requires a mixing of creativity and rigorous logic, objective analysis and passionate prose. Students, therefore, struggle to find the appropriate voice in the writing. Students sometimes sound either too passionate (sometimes harsh) or too logical (either dogmatic or boring). In addition to the questions above, ask the following of your writing:

- Is there an equal balance and voice given to all sides of the argument?
- Are the similarities and differences among all sides of the argument made clear?
- Are the implications of each side of the argument made clear?
- Does a new or hidden facet to the argument emerge, which builds upon the descriptive and analytical writing that precedes it?

CONCLUSION

Keep in mind the subject matter of the writing. Architecture cuts across many areas: geography, art, engineering and physics, history and the humanities, sociology and psychology, etc. Each subject and audience has particular conventions of writing. Know what they are and how they differ.[3]

Most importantly, as I often tell my students, "Writing is not about writing; writing is about editing." Like all things, writing well takes practice. Some people have more natural aptitude as writers, but everyone's writing can improve with diligence and practice, from the most gifted writers to those that find writing challenging. Understanding your own writing tendencies is central. Some people tend to write lengthy, run-on sentences. Some people overuse transitional phrases. Some people tend to be vague and lack specificity in writing. Some people overuse clichés or colloquialisms. Some people use too much or too little variety in punctuation or sentence structure. Identify your tendencies and keep them in mind as you write and edit. Your instructor, an editor, or the writing center at your college or university—even your roommate or peers—can help in this process.

USEFUL RESOURCES

Barnet, Sylvan. *Short Guide to Writing about Art, 6th Ed.* (New York: Longman, 2000).

Bullock, Richard. *The Norton Field Guide to Writing* (London: W. W. Norton & Co., 2006).

Engels, Norbert, and John Engels. *Writing Techniques with Illustrative Readings* (New York: David McKay Co., 1962).

Mabbett, I. W. *Writing History Essays: A Student's Guide* (New York: Palgrave Macmillan, 2007).

Northey, Margot, and Joan McKibbin. *Making Sense: A Student's Guide to Research and Writing* (New York: Oxford University Press, 2010).

Northey, Margot, and Judi Jewinski. *Making Sense in Engineering and the Technical Sciences: A Student's Guide to Research and Writing* (New York: Oxford University Press, 2011).

Northey, Margot, David Knight, and Dianne Draper. *Making Sense in Geography and Environmental Sciences: A Student's Guide to Research and Writing* (New York: Oxford University Press, 2010).

Northey, Margot, and Patrick von Aderkas. *Making Sense in the Life Sciences: A Student's Guide to Research and Writing* (New York: Oxford University Press, 2011).

Northey, Margot, Lorne Tepperman, and Patrizia Albanese. *Making Sense in the Social Sciences: A Student's Guide to Research and Writing* (New York: Oxford University Press, 2010).

Rozakis, Laurie. *Schaum's Quick Guide to Writing Great Research Papers, 2nd Ed.* (New York: McGraw-Hill, 2007).

Storey, William. *Writing History: A Guide for Students* (New York: Oxford University Press, 2009).

3. Oxford University Press has a series of books co-authored by Margot Northey on research and writing in a variety of disciplines. These books are listed under "Useful Resources" in this appendix.

Appendix 3

GUIDE TO CITATION STYLES

Part of almost any research project—from composing a short paper for a college class, to publishing a scholarly journal article, to writing a large science or history book—involves citing appropriate references. In essence, it is simply an overview and classification of prior research, theories, and knowledge. The process of finding, reading, and reorganizing these references, however, is often one of the least enjoyable tasks, among both students and scholars. Nevertheless, it is a process necessary to architectural theory, and, with a little knowledge, citing essential references can be made much more efficient.

WHY CITATIONS ARE NECESSARY

Many books and teachers talk about citations from the standpoint of academic integrity or plagiarism. For me, this is secondary and sends a negative, rather than positive, message regarding the importance of citations. Citations are important for a number of reasons. First, finding and organizing the references and resources is central to the author's task of understanding the breadth, depth, and diversity of issues associated with the topic. It helps the author to organize her own thoughts and develop a strategy for organizing the book. It also helps the author to see multiple viewpoints—where there is agreement and where there is disagreement—and to find her own opinions and voice. It is through this process that the *author* becomes an *authority*.

Second, citations and references provide background, context, and richness to the work. Direct quotations can provide specificity, clarity, and punch. Primary sources—such as, interviews, diaries, and artifacts—can add validity, depth, and interest. Secondary sources—such as, magazine articles, history books, and textbooks—can offer an overview or synthesis of multiple concepts or theories.

Lastly, citations carry different values and uses for different readers. Imagine a new book is published entitled *A History of London's Aldwych Tube Station*. The author provides an overview of how the London subway system and Aldwych, in particular, came to be. She gives descriptions of the neighborhoods—people, architecture, etc.—surrounding

Aldwych, and how Aldwych station was used as a shelter during the German "blitz" of WWII. She also describes the variety of films that were shot at Aldwych, as well as the political and economic reasons that Adlwych was eventually closed. Now ask, who would be interested in this book; who would buy it? Historians of London's transportation systems? People who live or lived near Aldwych? People who enjoy reading history books about lesser-known places and how they are connected to larger world events? Maybe a student doing a research paper on the architecture of London's subway stops, or on the effects of public policy on London's Tube System, or on the portrayal of public spaces in film? The author of this hypothetical book had these people in mind as she was writing. She likely worked to make the book interesting and enjoyable, as well as specific and grounded, for each of them. Likewise, the citations were an integral part of this book. Furthermore, each of the aforementioned readers has different interests and needs regarding the citations.

Some readers, say the person who lives near Aldwych and saw the book at a local bookstore or the casual reader of history books, may not even bother reading the citations except for when curiosity prods. Other readers, possibly the fellow historian, might flip to the citations first, to ensure that the work is thorough, before purchasing it. Yet other readers—students of architecture, public policy, or film, for instance—might find the citations most applicable to the research he is doing as a way of identifying other resources.

CITATION STYLES: THE MAIN THREE

There are three main citation styles: (1) parenthetical references, (2) footnotes, and (3) endnotes. Each comes with a set of strengths and weaknesses; not all are appropriate in all cases (see Table 1). Parenthetical references take place within the text, footnotes take place at the bottom of each page, and endnotes take place at the end of the work. Parenthetical references usually appear in parentheses, though not always, where the last name(s) of the author(s) and the year of publication are shown. For example, the parenthetical reference for this book would show up like this: (Smith, 2012). This is accompanied by a list of "references" at the end of the work. Footnotes and endnotes are both noted in the text by numbers or symbols, which correspond to full citation at the bottom of the page (footnote) or at the end of the work (endnote). Generally, footnotes and endnotes take on the same format as one another; it is simply their location that differs.

Parenthetical references are often used in scientific writing, while footnotes and endnotes are often used in historical writing, though there are plenty of exceptions. Parenthetical references provide the reader with the citation/reference information as they read. This allows the reader to see who is being cited and how frequently as they read. Parenthetical references, however, can compromise the flow of reading, especially in a text with many references. Footnotes and endnotes, on the other hand, separate the citation information from the text, which provides increased readability. In the case of endnotes, however, the convenience of locating referenced sources is compromised, as the reader must flip to the back of the work and find the citation number that corresponds

TABLE A3.1 Location, Strengths, and Weaknesses of Citation Styles

Citation Style	Location	Strengths and Weaknesses		
		Convenience	Readability/ Flow	Compatibility with Graphics
Parenthetical	In the body text with a corresponding reference section at the back of the work.	Strength	Weakness	Strength*
Footnotes	At the bottom of each page with a corresponding number or symbol in the body text.	Strength	Strength†	Weakness‡
Endnotes	At the end of the work with a corresponding number in the body text.	Weakness	Strength	Strength

* This can be a weakness if there are a large number of parenthetical references that become visually distracting.
† This can be a weakness if the footnotes are lengthy, e.g., longer than the body text.
‡ This can be a strength if the notes are brief and can easily be located in the side margins.

to the text. This inconvenience is alleviated a bit in footnotes, as the citation takes place on the same page as the text. Footnotes do, however, have a graphical drawback, as bringing together the text and footnotes with images can pose layout challenges. As such, architectural texts with many images often utilize endnotes. A variation on footnotes is sometimes used, where the notes take place to the sides (in the margin) rather than at the bottom.

Once you understand the differences among the three types, it becomes easy to decide which citation style to use. Consider the following questions as part of your decision-making process:

- What is the subject matter of the work and who is the audience?
- What is more important, for the reader to know the references as they read, or the flow of the text?
- Will there be graphic content, e.g., photographs, charts, etc.?

If readability and flow were important, then parenthetical references would likely not be used. If convenience of finding the references was important, then endnotes would likely not be used. If graphic content was important, then footnotes would likely not be used, unless they could be accommodated in the side margins.

DEALING WITH THE TEDIUM, EFFICIENTLY

It is best to keep a running log of your citations/references as you go, rather than trying to compile them at the end. Recording the citations/references as you go will diminish the tedium and will lessen the likelihood that you inadvertently miss a key source or make citation errors. There are many software programs now available that can speed this process. Ask your librarian or professor for assistance.

USEFUL RESOURCES

Columbia Law Review, Harvard Law Review, University of Pennsylvania Law Review, and Yale Law Journal. *The Bluebook: A Uniform System of Citation, 19th Ed.* (Cambridge: Harvard Law Review Association, 2010).

The Chicago Manual of Style, 15th Ed. (Chicago: University of Chicago Press, 2003).

MLA Handbook for Writers of Research Papers, 7th Ed. (New York: Modern Language Association of America, 2009).

Publication Manual of the American Psychological Association, 6th Ed. (Washington, DC: American Psychological Association, 2009).

Appendix 4

GUIDE TO LIBRARY-BASED RESEARCH

A part of nearly all scholarship is doing library-based research. Finding relevant books, journal articles, dissertations and theses, newspaper and magazine articles, and other sources is necessary in everything from short papers to dissertations. This part of the scholarly process—what is often called a "literature review"—can be confusing and tedious. Conducting a literature review is both art and science. Like soccer or chess, the first time you do it can be very confusing, but the process becomes clearer and you get a little better each time. Building upon Appendix 3, a few strategies can help to increase your efficacy in library-based research.

A CYCLIC PROCESS

Identifying and specifying the topic of your research is the greatest but most important challenge. It is from a specific topic that you can set boundaries—what to include and what to exclude—regarding your library-based research. From here, you are able to identify the right search processes and sources. This is not a linear process, however. It is a cyclic process. The mistake of many books and book chapters on conducting literature reviews is that they imply a linear process. Instead, think of literature reviews as akin to the design process. Your curiosities and interests provoke a topic of inquiry. You narrow and specify this topic as you think about it, write about it, and discuss it with peers or professors. The topic transforms as you find and read sources that are similar to your interests. One source leads to another, and the topic may shift. You keep thinking, writing, and talking about the topic, and it transforms and narrows yet again. Then you keep searching for more helpful sources.

FINDING SOURCES

There are three main ways to identify useful sources. First, current or former professors are an excellent resource. Professors who are interested in and knowledgeable about your topic are often willing to help out. They might have a readily available bibliography and/or a personal library of useful sources, in addition to the knowledge they have accumulated and can share. Seeking out professors for help can be a good starting point as you are beginning to formulate the topic. Equally, professors can be helpful later in the process, as your topic has become more refined.

Second, utilizing library databases will be essential. There are many types of databases available, from Internet search engines (e.g., Google) to subject-specific data-bases (e.g., Avery Index to Architectural Periodicals). The Internet can be a good resource at the beginning, but can also be very time consuming with few quality results. Scholarly databases, on the other hand, are far more precise and efficient. You first need to identify if you are looking for books or journal/magazine articles, as they require the use of two different databases. It is likely that you will use both. I find it helpful to start broadly by searching terms or phrasing you have been using in talking or writing about your research project. Sometimes the words you are using are the same as the terms used by experts and scholars. Oftentimes they are different. As you begin the search and start to find articles or books that are close to your topic of interest, note the terms and phrases that other authors are using. Use those terms to continue your search. Also note the difference between "keywords," which are supplied by each individual author, and "subject terms," which are defined by an entire discipline or library system. Jot down these subject terms, as they will be the most useful in finding good sources quickly. Then, as you use the subject terms, read the titles of the works you find. If the title seems relevant, go on to reading the abstract, or summary, of the work. If the abstract is clearly related to your topic, save the information and keep searching. After you have collected a significant number of sources, then you can start reading them and modifying your topic as needed.

Third, make use of the sources you have found to be the most relevant. Using the first two strategies, you will come across a number of sources that you find both helpful and interesting. Most of these sources will have references, notes, and/or a bibliography. Read through the references, notes, or bibliography to identify more sources.

Like design, you could keep searching forever. Time constraints and other factors, invariably, require that you make a decision to stop. It is difficult to know when the literature review is sufficient. Again, use all three strategies of searching, and use them cyclically. You will come to a point when you start seeing the same references or names over and over. When the sources seem interwoven and start to reference one another, and you recognize the names or sources being cited, you are close to a complete literature review. Your professors can help you in this process. Also utilize the lists of "Useful Resources" seen at the end of Appendices 1–3.

Index

Page numbers in **bold** are for illustrations.

cast iron 72, 82
cathetus (perpendicular line) 233
Cato 110, 118
CBS building, New York City 302
Center Monumental 297
central authorities 385
centrality 243
centralization 367
centuriation 347
Chandigarh, Palace of the Assembly 266, 267
character 167, 170, 366, 367, 368, 369, 370, 380
Chicago: Lake Shore Drive 349–50; World's Columbian Exposition (1893) 145, 296
Chinese architecture 55
Choisy, Auguste 49
Church of the Autostrada, Florence 30
"Cinema Style" 59, 60
circulation 243, 251–2, 374
Cité Industrielle 171
City Beautiful movement 296–7
city planning and design 9, 275–330, 382–3
city walls 315–16
clarity 18, 23–4, 25, 33
Classical architecture 8, 29, 55, 71, 91–2, 93, 232; *see also* Greek architecture; Roman architecture
clay 112–13
cleared site 334, 347–9, 350–1, 355
climate 123–4, 313–14, 316, 362
Coleridge, Samuel Taylor 166–7
collage 301
Collins, Peter, *Changing Ideals in Modern Architecture* 173
colonization, European 40–1n2
colored glass 98
colored light 98
columns 217–18, 333, 336–40
complexity and simplicity 16–36
"composite" architecture 72n
composition 252–3
concepts 198
concrete: poured-in-place 100, 101; reinforced 57, 98, 100
concrete space 367–8
concretization 371
conflict and reciprocity 156–9

constructed site 334, 349–51, 355
construction 115–24; authenticity of 128
Constructivists 59
context 274–330, 342, 343, 352
contextualism 9, 298–305, 312, 325, 326
continuity 182, 184–7
contradiction 18, 27
contrast 26
convenance (fitness) 169–70
convention 55
Copernicus, Nicolaus 5
Copper, Wayne 301, 304
Corinthian Order 232
Cornell University 304–5, 325, 326
cornerstones 119
cornices 117, 120–1
Cortona, Pietro da, Santi Luca e Martina, Rome **39**
Cousins, Mark 135
Croney, John 230n34
Crystal Palace, London 157
Cubists 130, 304
cultural development 42, 44
cultural resonance 5
culture 59–60, 362, 374; mass 385; nature and 334; space and 378–9
Cuvier, Georges 165

Dadaists 52
Damisch, Hubert 234
Dardel, Eric 378, 379
Darwin, Charles 175
dashed lines (*linee occulte*) 233–5
de l'Orme, Philibert 338
De Stijl movement 59, 300
debate 6, 9–11
Decentrists 293–4, 295
deception and honesty 71–104
"decorated sheds" 61, 62, 63
Denis, Maurice 57
der Sturm 52
Dermée, Paul 52
Derrida, Jacques 389; *Chora L Works* 137
Descartes, René 72, 86, 87, 88, 92, 235
design 5; usefulness and 195, 207
destruction 363, 385
Deutscher Werkbund 157
Dewey, John 389, 392, 393